IN FLIGHT FROM CO
VIOLENCE

The impact of violence and conflict on refugee status determination and international protection is a key developing field. Given the contemporary dynamics of armed conflict, how to interpret and apply the refugee definitions at regional and global levels is increasingly relevant to governmental policy-makers, decision-makers, legal practitioners, academics and students. This book provides a comprehensive analysis of the global and regional refugee instruments as they apply to claimants in flight from situations of armed conflict and violence, exploring their inter-relationship and how they are interpreted and applied (or should be applied). As part of a broader UNHCR project to develop guidelines on the interpretation and application of international refugee law instruments to claimants fleeing armed conflict and other situations of violence, it includes contributions from leading scholars and practitioners in this field as well as emerging authors with specific expertise.

VOLKER TÜRK is UNHCR's Assistant High Commissioner for Protection.

ALICE EDWARDS is Head of the Secretariat of the Convention against Torture Initiative.

CORNELIS WOUTERS is the Senior Refugee Law Advisor in the Division · of International Protection of UNHCR in Geneva.

IN FLIGHT FROM CONFLICT AND VIOLENCE

UNHCR's Consultations on Refugee Status and Other
Forms of International Protection

Edited by

VOLKER TÜRK

ALICE EDWARDS

CORNELIS WOUTERS

CAMBRIDGE
UNIVERSITY PRESS

CAMBRIDGE
UNIVERSITY PRESS

University Printing House, Cambridge CB2 8BS, United Kingdom

One Liberty Plaza, 20th Floor, New York, NY 10006, USA

477 Williamstown Road, Port Melbourne, VIC 3207, Australia

4843/24, 2nd Floor, Ansari Road, Daryaganj, Delhi – 110002, India

79 Anson Road, #06–04/06, Singapore 079906

Cambridge University Press is part of the University of Cambridge.

It furthers the University's mission by disseminating knowledge in the pursuit of education, learning and research at the highest international levels of excellence.

www.cambridge.org
Information on this title: www.cambridge.org/9781107171992
10.1017/9781316771143

First published 2017

Printed in the United Kingdom by Clays, St Ives plc

A catalogue record for this publication is available from the British Library.

Library of Congress Cataloging-in-Publication Data
Names: Türk, Volker. | Edwards, Alice. | Wouters, C. W. (Cornelis Wolfram)
Title: In flight from conflict and violence : UNHCR's consultations on refugee status and other forms of international protection / edited by Volker Turk, Alice Edwards, Cornelis Wouters.
Description: Cambridge [UK] ; New York : Cambridge University Press, 2017.
Identifiers: LCCN 2016046823 | ISBN 9781107171992 (hardback)
Subjects: LCSH: Refugees – Legal status, laws, etc. | Refugees – Protection – International cooperation. | Office of the United Nations High Commissioner for Refugees. | War victims – Legal status, laws, etc.
Classification: LCC KZ6530 .I54 2017 | DDC 341.4/86–dc23
LC record available at https://lccn.loc.gov/2016046823

ISBN 978-1-107-17199-2 Hardback
ISBN 978-1-316-62309-1 Paperback

CONTENTS

NOTES ON CONTRIBUTORS AND EDITORS

MARGARET BRETT holds an LL.M in International Human Rights Law from the National University of Ireland (First Class Honours) and has a BA (Hons) *Literae Humaniores* from St. Hilda's College, University of Oxford. She has previously worked for the International Committee of the Red Cross, the Centre for Civil and Political Rights and the NGO Group for the Convention on the Rights of the Child.

RACHEL BRETT holds an LL.M in International Human Rights Law from the University of Essex (Distinction). She taught law and international human rights law at the University of Essex and developed a project for their Human Rights Centre on the Organization on Security and Cooperation in Europe. From 1993 to 2015 she worked on human rights and refugees issues for the Quaker United Nations Office in Geneva. Brett is author of numerous books and publications about child soldiers, conscientious objection to military service and other human rights and refugee issues and on the United Nations Human Rights system and the role of human rights non-governmental organizations at the United Nations.

ALICE EDWARDS was the United Nations High Commissioner for Refugees' Senior Legal Coordinator and Chief of Protection Policy and Legal Advice, based in Geneva from 2010 to 2015, where she was responsible for shaping international refugee law standards and positions. She has been the focal point for the legal aspects of both the fiftieth and sixtieth anniversaries of the 1951 Refugee Convention in 2001–2002 and 2010–2011 respectively. Her other assignments with UNHCR have been in Bosnia and Herzegovina, Rwanda, Morocco and Geneva. Alice has also held academic appointments in law at the universities of Oxford and Nottingham, worked for Amnesty International in London and is widely published. Her publications include *Violence against Women under International Human Rights Law* (Cambridge University Press, 2011; paperback, 2013) and two co-edited collections, *Human Security and*

Non-Citizens: Law, Policy and International Affairs (Cambridge University Press, 2010) and *Nationality and Statelessness under International Law* (Cambridge University Press, 2014). She is on the editorial boards of the *Journal of International Humanitarian Legal Studies*, the *Refugee Law Reader* and the *Migration Studies Journal.* She holds degrees in law and political science from the University of Tasmania, an LL.M in Public International Law from the University of Nottingham (Distinction) and a PhD from the Australian National University. She is presently Head of the Secretariat of the Convention against Torture Initiative (www.cti2024.org), a global initiative being spearheaded by the governments of Chile, Denmark, Ghana, Indonesia and Morocco to achieve universal ratification and implementation of the Convention against Torture by 2024.

THEO FARRELL is a professor of war in the modern world and head of the Department of War Studies at King's College London. He has advised the UK government and the International Security Assistance Force (ISAF) command on the counterinsurgency campaign in Afghanistan. He served on strategic assessment teams for two Commanders of ISAF (General McChrystal in 2010 and General Dunford in 2013) and undertook the first command assessment for the Commander of ISAF Joint Command in 2010. Professor Farrell has authored or edited ten books and over forty-five research papers on military affairs and security studies. His latest books are (as co-editor) *Military Adaptation in Afghanistan* (2013) and (as co-author) *Transforming Military Power Since the Cold War* (Cambridge University Press, 2013). His current projects are a history of Britain's war in Afghanistan, 2001–2014, and a history of the Taliban's war in Afghanistan; both projects are funded by the UK Economic and Social Research Council.

MADELINE GARLICK is Chief of the Protection Policy and Legal Advice Section in the Division of International Protection at the Office of the United Nations High Commissioner for Refugees (UNHCR) in Geneva. She is a Guest Researcher at the Centre for Migration Law at Radboud University and teaches on an occasional basis at Sciences Po and at the College of Europe. She was previously responsible for UNHCR's liaison to the EU institutions from 2004 to 2013. She has worked for the Migration Policy Institute, for the United Nations in Cyprus and in Bosnia and Herzegovina on legal issues related to the rights of displaced people. She is qualified as a barrister and solicitor in Victoria, Australia.

VANESSA HOLZER is Head of Research Coordination at the Hector Research Institute of Education Sciences and Psychology at the University of Tübingen. Previously, she was British Red Cross Senior Research Fellow at the University of Cambridge, where she led a research team for the project on customary international humanitarian law of the British Red Cross and the ICRC. She has also worked as a research fellow at the Max Planck Institute of Comparative Public Law and International Law and was a visiting fellow at the Refugee Studies Centre in Oxford. Vanessa holds a doctorate in law from Goethe University and an LL.M in International Law from the London School of Economics and Political Science, where she was awarded the Blackstone Chambers Prize.

MICHAEL REED-HURTADO is a faculty fellow and senior lecturer at Yale University, associated with the MacMillan Center. Current teaching and research interests include prosecution of complex crimes, transitional justice, dynamics of violence in armed conflict and state crime. He is a Colombian/US lawyer and journalist with twenty years of experience in the human rights field. He has conducted research and engaged in activism in the following areas: criminal due process, effective criminal prosecution of system crimes, prison conditions and reform, military criminal jurisdiction, enforced disappearances and forced displacement, amongst others. He has also worked in the humanitarian field with UNHCR, particularly in internal displacement settings. He has worked mainly in Latin America, with sporadic work in Asia and Africa. He holds BA and Bachelor of Journalism degrees from the University of Texas and a *Juris Doctor* degree from the University of Minnesota. He is an active columnist and commentator in various Colombian news media (print); he is a regular columnist in the daily newspaper *El Colombiano*. He has written and edited several books and articles. He is also a founding member and associate of *Punto de Vista* (www.cpvista.org), an interdisciplinary human rights organization that produces specialized knowledge, provides advisory services and conducts monitoring and evaluation studies.

VALERIE OOSTERVELD is an associate professor with tenure at the University of Western Ontario Faculty of Law. She teaches international criminal law, international human rights law, international organizations and public international law. Her research and writing focus on gender issues within international criminal justice mechanisms. Before joining Western Law in July 2005, she served in the Legal Affairs Bureau of

Canada's Department of Foreign Affairs and International Trade. In this role, she provided legal advice on international criminal accountability for genocide, crimes against humanity and war crimes, especially with respect to the International Criminal Court, the International Criminal Tribunals for the Former Yugoslavia and Rwanda, the Sierra Leone Special Court and other transitional justice mechanisms such as truth and reconciliation commissions. She was a member of the Canadian delegation to the International Criminal Court negotiations, the subsequent Assembly of States Parties and the 2010 Review Conference of the Rome Statute of the International Criminal Court. She holds degrees from Columbia Law School (JSD and LL.M), the University of Toronto Faculty of Law (LL.B) and the University of Ottawa (B.Soc.Sc.).

HAIFA RASHED is a research associate with the University of London's Human Rights Consortium and holds an MA in Understanding and Securing Human Rights from the Institute of Commonwealth Studies (Distinction). Her research interests include women's rights, genocide, decolonization and the Israeli–Palestinian conflict. Her work has been published in the *International Journal of Human Rights* and *Holy Land Studies*. She is a research assistant at the London School of Economics (LSE) Gender Institute on the Politics section of the 2015 LSE Commission on Gender Inequality and Power. She has previously worked for a variety of non-governmental organizations in the United Kingdom, Spain and Switzerland, including the Quaker United Nations Office in Geneva.

PROFESSOR BONAVENTURE RUTINWA holds an LL.M from the Queens University at Kingston, Canada, a certificate in Refugee and Humanitarian Studies from the University of Oxford and a Doctorate of Philosophy from the University of Oxford. Since 2007, he has been working as the Coordinator of the International Migration Management Programme at the University of Dar es Salaam and currently holds the position of Dean of the School of Law, University of Dar es Salaam. His publications cover various aspects of the legal situation of refugees in Africa. His experience on refugee issues acquired through teaching, practice and research on refugee law is extensive.

OLIVIER SCHMITT is an associate professor of international relations at the University of Southern Denmark, where he is a member of the Centre for War Studies. He is also the Secretary-General of the *Association pour les*

Études sur la Guerre et la Stratégie (Association for War and Strategic Studies). A reserve officer in the French Navy, he has work experiences at the policy-planning staff of the French MoD, NATO and several think tanks. His research interests include comparative defence policies in Europe, multinational military operations and the changing character of contemporary warfare. He holds a PhD from the Department of War Studies at King's College London and has won research fellowships at Sciences Po, the University of Montréal Centre for International Studies (CÉRIUM) and the NATO Defence College.

MARINA SHARPE is a Steinberg Post-Doctoral Research Fellow in International Migration Law and Policy at the Faculty of Law, McGill University. She was called to the bar of England and Wales in 2010 and to the New York bar in 2006 and spent several years in private practice at Cravath, Swaine & Moore, LLP, in New York and then London. Prior to this, she worked as a legal advisor with the Refugee Law Project in Kampala and later returned to Uganda as legal officer of the International Refugee Rights Initiative. She has also worked with AMERA-Egypt and the refugee programme of Fahamu and regularly undertakes consultancy work for organizations including Amnesty International, the European Bank for Reconstruction and Development and UNHCR. She has guest lectured at the Universities of Oxford and Tripoli, at Georgetown University's Center for Transnational Legal Studies and at Yale University and has taught courses at the Universities of London and Sherbrooke. She co-founded and served as Director of the US NGO Asylum Access. She holds a doctorate in law from the University of Oxford, where she studied as a Trudeau Scholar, degrees in civil and common law from McGill University, an MSc in Development Management from the LSE and a BA in Economics and International Development Studies from McGill. Her work has been published in edited collections and journals, including the *African Journal of International and Comparative Law*, the *International Journal of Refugee Law*, the *Journal of Refugee Studies* and the *McGill Law Journal*.

VOLKER TÜRK is UNHCR's Assistant High Commissioner for Protection, having previously served as the Director of the Division of International Protection from September 2009 to February 2015. From April 2008 to September 2009 he was Director for Organizational Development and Management in Geneva, leading UNHCR's structural and management change process. From 2004 to March 2008, he occupied various positions in many parts of the world, including in Malaysia; Kosovo

(S/RES/1244 (1999)1), Bosnia and Herzegovina; the Democratic Republic of the Congo and Kuwait. From 2000 to 2004, he was Chief of the Protection Policy and Legal Advice Section at UNHCR Headquarters in Geneva, which had particular responsibilities for the global consultations process. Prior to his time with UNHCR, he worked as a University Assistant at the Institute of International Law at the University of Vienna, where he finished his doctoral thesis on UNHCR and its mandate (published in 1992). From 1985 to 1988, he was a Research Assistant at the Institute of Criminal Law at the University of Linz. He has published widely on international refugee and human rights law.

CORNELIS WOUTERS is the Senior Refugee Law Advisor in the Division of International Protection of UNHCR, responsible for monitoring international refugee law developments and the adoption of national laws ensuring application of the 1951 Refugee Convention, providing advice on refugee law matters both internally and to partners and, between 2009 and 2015, steering UNHCR's global judicial engagement strategy. In the past he has worked as a researcher and lecturer at the Institute of Immigration Law at Leiden University, where in 2009 he obtained a doctoral (PhD) degree with a thesis on International Legal Standards for the Protection from *Refoulement*. He has worked for various non-governmental organizations in the Netherlands, such as Amnesty International and the Dutch Council for Refugees, and was a member of the Sub-Committee on Asylum and Refugee Law of the Permanent Committee of Experts on International Immigration, Refugee and Criminal Law (Meijers Committee). He has also worked in Asia as a staff member and lecturer at the Office of Human Rights Studies and Social Development of Mahidol University in Thailand (2000–2004) and as a lawyer for the Centre on Housing Rights and Evictions (2005–2009). In 2005 he joined COHRE, where he was responsible for setting up and managing the national office of COHRE in Sri Lanka. In 2007 and 2008 he worked as a consultant and legal officer for COHRE's Asia and Pacific Programme and was involved in various projects concerning housing, land and property restitution for refugees and displaced persons. He has published widely, in particular, on matters concerning international refugee law.

FOREWORD

The world today is witnessing many protracted conflicts, violent crises and human rights violations causing enormous human suffering. Several contemporary conflicts have become so complex and widespread that in some places, no one is safe. More than 60 million people have been forcibly displaced from their homes worldwide, including some 20 million who have sought refuge outside their own countries.

The 1951 Convention Relating to the Status of Refugees and its 1967 Protocol are the central legal instruments for the protection of refugees today. Drawn up in the aftermath of the Second World War, they continue to provide a strong legal and ethical basis for the protection of people at risk of persecution, especially those fleeing the devastating effects of armed conflict and violence. As a response to today's mass movements, we have seen both the generous welcoming spirit that binds us as a human family and ever more attempts to prevent refugees from seeking safety. In addition, the increasing reach of non-state actors – armed groups, smugglers and traffickers or organized criminal gangs – has made the world a very dangerous place for refugees.

Against this background, the 1951 Convention has come under scrutiny both as to its legal parameters and as to how it may offer practical responses to people on the move. Too often its application to those in need of international protection has been wrongly questioned. At other times the 1951 Convention has become the scapegoat for a lack of political will to help people in need. These are extraordinarily difficult times for the institution of asylum.

However, the problem of determining the status of people fleeing armed conflict and violence does not generally lie with the legal framework or with the refugee definition. One of the key challenges is how to strengthen the processes in place at the national level to ensure the interpretation and application of the 1951 Convention in a more harmonized and inclusive manner across countries, such as to enable asylum claims from persons fleeing similar circumstances to be processed quickly. States need to introduce measures both individually and collectively to reduce the (perceived) arbitrariness in decision-making and accompanying uncertainty for applicants while minimizing the need for onward movements in search of sanctuary. Many other practical and financial solutions are also needed to help states hosting large numbers of refugees and to support the international community's collective search for solutions.

As part of a project of UNHCR's Division of International Protection focused on persons fleeing armed conflict and violence, this edited collection represents state-of-the-art scholarship on the legal aspects of the 1951 Convention. Even though it is acknowledged that many practical responses are required to deal with the mass movements of today, the legal framework and the rule of law remain fundamental aspects of every functioning system of governance. UNHCR was established first and foremost as a legal protection agency, with a mandate to supervise the implementation by states of the 1951 Convention and with a broad mandate for international protection and solutions. The contributions to this book will assist UNHCR to exercise this mandate for refugees and will in particular feed into new *Guidelines on International Protection*, complementary to the *Handbook on Criteria and Procedures for Determining Refugee Status*, aimed at supporting governments, practitioners, judges and decision-makers with the proper interpretation and application of global and regional refugee instruments to people fleeing situations of armed conflict and violence.

I thank the authors sincerely for their thoughtful contributions to this book. The theme of this new publication could not be timelier.

Filippo Grandi
United Nations High Commissioner for Refugees

ABBREVIATIONS

1951 Convention	Convention Relating to the Status of Refugees
1967 Protocol	Protocol Relating to the Status of Refugees
AILA	American Immigration Lawyers Association
AIT	Asylum and Immigration Tribunal (UK)
AMISOM	African Union Mission in Somalia
ANSF	Afghan National Security Forces
ANSO	Afghan NGO Safety Office
AU	African Union
AUC	Autodefensas Unidas de Colombia
BVerwG	Bundesverwaltungsgericht (Germany)
Cartagena Declaration	Cartagena Declaration on Refugees
CEAS	Common European Asylum System
CEDAW	Convention on the Elimination of All Forms of Discrimination Against Women
CIREFCA	International Conference on Central American Refugees (Guatemala City, 1989)
CJEU	Court of Justice of the European Union
CNDA	Cour Nationale du Droit d'Asile (French National Asylum Court)
CNDH	Comisión Nacional de los Derechos Humanos
CODER	Comisión para la Determinación de la Condición de Personas Refugiadas
COMAR	Mexican Commission for the Assistance of Refugees
CONARE	Comitê Nacional para os Refugiados (Brazilian Refugee Committee)
COW	Correlates of War Project
CRC	Convention on the Rights of the Child
CRC-OPAC	Optional Protocol to the Convention on the Rights of the Child
DIP	Division of International Protection (UNHCR)
DRC	Democratic Republic of the Congo
EASO	European Asylum Support Office

ECHR	European Convention on Human Rights and Fundamental Freedoms
ECOSOC	Economic and Social Council
ECtHR	European Court of Human Rights
EU	European Union
ExCom	Executive Committee of the High Commissioner's Programme
FARC	Fuerzas Armadas Revolucionarias de Colombia
HRW	Human Rights Watch
IAC	internal armed conflict
IACommHR	Inter-American Commission on Human Rights
IACourtHR	Inter-American Court of Human Rights
ICRC	International Committee of the Red Cross
ICTY	International Criminal Tribunal for the Former Yugoslavia
ICU	Islamic Courts Union
IDP	internally displaced person
IED	improvised explosive device
IFA	internal flight or relocation alternative
IHL	international humanitarian law
IIDH	Instituto Interamericano de Derechos Humanos
ILO	International Labour Organization
IMI	International Migration Initiative
IRB	Immigration and Refugee Board (Canada)
IRO	International Refugee Organization
ISAF	International Security Assistance Force
LTTE	Liberation Tigers of Tamil Eelam
MPSG	membership of a particular social group
NGO	non-governmental organization
OAS	Organization of American States
OAU Convention	Convention Governing Specific Aspects of Refugee Problems in Africa
OAU	Organization of African Unity
Rome Statute	Rome Statute of the International Criminal Court
RPG	rocket-propelled grenade
RSAA	Refugee Status Appeals Authority (New Zealand)
RSD	refugee status determination
TFEU	Treaty on the Functioning of the European Union
TFG	Transitional Federated Government (Somalia)
UCDP	Uppsala Conflict Data Programme
UN	United Nations
UNHCR	United Nations High Commissioner for Refugees

UNITA	National Union for the Total Independence of Angola
UNSC	United Nations Security Council
UNTS	United Nations Treaty Series
US	United States of America
USCENTCOM	US Central Command

~

Introduction

VOLKER TÜRK, ALICE EDWARDS AND CORNELIS WOUTERS[*]

The dangers inherent in armed conflict and violence are the major causes of refugee movements in the twenty-first century. New conflicts have broken out or been reignited, while few of the old ones have found a proper solution. These conflicts have spread in unpredictable ways, and their conduct has become increasingly complex.

At the time of finalizing the entries in this edited collection, there were over four and a half million Syrian refugees in the immediate region and over 810,000 asylum applications submitted in European countries since 2011.[1] Syria is now the greatest refugee producing country in the world, the conflict straining the hospitality of neighbouring countries and prompting more and more Syrians to move out of the immediate region. The situation in Iraq continues to force people to flee, with more than 100,000 Iraqi refugees in the region and over 3 million displaced internally. Many more countries can be added to the list of places experiencing conflict where violence is prevalent and producing refugees, including Afghanistan, Burundi, the Central African Republic, Colombia, the Democratic Republic of Congo, Libya, Mali, Nigeria, Somalia, South Sudan, Sudan, Myanmar, the Northern Triangle countries of Central America, Ukraine and Yemen.[2]

Armed conflict and violence invariably cause human suffering, most directly threatening the lives and physical and mental integrity of affected civilian populations. The indirect consequences can destroy state and social infrastructure, disrupt economies and cause crises in health care and food security. Forms of sexual and gender-based violence are

[*] The authors thank Charlotte Luelf for her assistance in the preparation of this Introduction.
[1] UNHCR, 'Syria Regional Refugee Response', available at: http://data.unhcr.org/syrianrefugees/regional.php.
[2] UNHCR, 'Note on International Protection', 8 June 2015, EC/66/SC/CRP.10, available at: www.refworld.org/docid/55c1dacf4.html.

1

prevalent, and children are also targets, for example, for forced recruitment. Internal and external displacements can be key indicators of the extent of the violence and human suffering. In 2014, the number of refugees had risen to 19.5 million and 1.8 million asylum applicants.[3] Nearly 11 million other persons were newly displaced within their own countries by conflict and persecution in the same year.[4]

In response, over the past sixty-five years, the 1951 Convention Relating to the Status of Refugees and its 1967 Protocol (hereafter the 1951 Convention) have afforded refugee protection to people fleeing a wide array of threats in their countries of origin. In fact, these global refugee instruments are more than just legal texts. They have served to crystallize and catalyse a grand humanitarian and ethical tradition that has helped millions of vulnerable people at risk.

The 1951 Convention and 1967 Protocol equally reflect the recognition that refugee issues are of international concern, involve international responsibilities and make international cooperation a necessity. The framework of the 1951 Convention sets out a broad yet minimalist set of state responsibilities. Its fundaments are unchallengeable and as essential today as they were in 1951. No one can contest that people should not be returned to danger, that they should not be discriminated against and that they should enjoy a minimum standard of treatment, such as freedom of movement, basic health, social and economic rights and recognition of identity and legal status, the latter being particularly important in a world that is so reliant on legal identity.

Yet, when it comes to people fleeing armed conflict and violence, different practices are discernible, including in relation to the 1951 Convention. The discrepancies between refugees recognized under the 1951 Convention, on the one hand, and the broader group of persons in need of international protection, on the other, arise in part from the way in which the definition of 'refugee' in the 1951 Convention has been interpreted and applied by some states and in part from limitations inherent in the instrument itself. Over time, these discrepancies have been reduced through, *inter alia*, the subsequent adoption of the 1967 Protocol to the 1951 Convention and regional refugee instruments and the evolution in the elaboration and application of certain non-return obligations under international human rights law, as well as state practice and jurisprudence.

---

[3] UNHCR, 'World at War: Global Trends. Forced Displacement in 2014', June 2015, 2.
[4] *Ibid.*

Specifically, observing the various recognition rates of national status-determination procedures for claimants fleeing situations of armed conflict and violence,[5] in some sense rendering national asylum systems into asylum lotteries,[6] this book attempts to address some of the main misconceptions and ambiguities in the interpretation and application of the 1951 Convention to such claims. These inconsistencies fragment the overall objective of the global refugee protection system to provide a single, universal standard of access to and quality of international protection that is applied to all refugees.

This book also looks at the regional refugee definitions, in particular, those developed in Africa and Latin America, and their relationship with the 1951 Convention definition. The existence of these 'extended' regional definitions, grounded in responses to humanitarian situations, has raised questions about their inter-operability and relationship. This book also examines the European Union's subsidiary protection system under the EU Asylum Acquis.

This edited collection represents a response by UNHCR, in collaboration with leading experts in the field, to how international refugee law applies in times of conflict and violence. It has been produced as part of a consultation process towards the elaboration of guidelines on international protection.[7] This consultation process has included several expert roundtables, namely:

> 2011: *Summary Conclusions on the Relevance of International Criminal Law and International Human Rights Law Jurisprudence to the Interpretation of the 1951 Convention*, from an expert meeting jointly organized by UNHCR and the International Criminal Tribunal for Rwanda, with the participation of the International Criminal Tribunal for the former Yugoslavia, the International Criminal Court and the International Committee of the Red Cross ('Arusha Summary Conclusions').[8]

---

[5] See e.g. UNHCR, 'Safe at Last? Law and Practice in Selected EU Member States with Respect to Asylum-Seekers Fleeing Indiscriminate Violence', 27 July 2011, available at: www.refworld.org/docid/4e2ee0022.html.

[6] The term 'refugee roulette' was coined by J. Ramji-Nogales, A. I. Schoenholtz and P. G. Schrag in *Refugee Roulette: Disparities in Asylum Adjudication and Proposals for Reform* (New York University Press, 2011).

[7] The *Guidelines on International Protection* complement UNHCR, *Handbook on Criteria and Procedures for Determining Refugee Status* (Geneva, 1979), re-issued together in 2011, available at: www.unhcr.org/refworld/docid/4f33c8d92.html.

[8] UNHCR and ICTR, 'Expert Meeting on Complementarities between International Refugee Law, International Criminal Law and International Human Rights Law: Summary Conclusions', July 2011, available at: www.refworld.org/docid/4e1729d52.html.

2012: *Summary Conclusions on International Protection for Persons Fleeing Conflict and Other Situations of Violence*, from an expert meeting held in Cape Town ('Cape Town Summary Conclusions').[9] In preparation for the meeting in Cape Town, UNHCR commissioned five background studies, which have been refined and updated for this publication.[10]

2013: *Summary Conclusions on the Interpretation of the Extended Refugee Definition in the 1984 Cartagena Declaration*, from an expert meeting on the Cartagena Declaration on Refugees held in Montevideo, Uruguay ('Montevideo Summary Conclusions').[11]

It is hoped that this edited collection will contribute to a more consistent application of the existing instruments in all national jurisdictions and provide legal certainty for claimants for refugee status.

For the purposes of this book, the phrase 'situations of armed conflict and violence' is used to refer to situations marked by a certain level or spread of violence or other forms of serious public disorder that affect civilian populations.

The Changing Character of Conflict and Its Effects on Refugee Status Determination

The character of conflict has changed over time. Most significantly, civilians are playing an increasingly important role both as participants in armed conflicts and as victims of their impact. The transformation in the nature of violence is also linked to a number of factors, not least the relationship between state fragility and violence. Shifts in power in fragile states are evident – for example, from state to de facto authorities who exercise control over territory and people and who have at least some sense of responsibility towards them to a myriad of private actors with no such sense of responsibility. The demobilization of paramilitary or guerrilla forces in different countries in Latin America, Asia and Africa, for

---

[9] UNHCR, 'Summary Conclusions on International Protection of Persons Fleeing Armed Conflict and Other Situations of Violence; Roundtable 13 and 14 September 2012, Cape Town, South Africa', 20 December 2012, available at: www.refworld.org/docid/50d32e5e2.html.

[10] All documents from the Roundtable on International Protection of Persons Fleeing Armed Conflict and Other Situations of Violence, Cape Town, South Africa, 13–14 September 2012, hosted by the Refugee Rights Project of the University of Cape Town, are available at: www.unhcr.org/3e5f78bc4.html.

[11] UNHCR, 'Summary Conclusions on the Interpretation of the Extended Refugee Definition in the 1984 Cartagena Declaration, Expert Roundtable, 15 and 16 October 2013', Montevideo, Uruguay, 7 July 2014, available at: www.refworld.org/docid/53c52e7d4.html.

example, has often led to the emergence of an array of violent criminal organizations that are not only involved in trafficking drugs, arms and people but also in the control of land for economic exploitation. They may in some instances be linked to parts of the elite and are likely to act in collusion with local authorities. Their activities are often more concentrated in border zones or areas where civilian state presence is weak or where the state's ability to provide protection is limited. However, there is also a spill-over effect into the urban environment with intra-urban violence on the rise, resulting in further displacement.

Chapter 1 by Theo Farrell and Oliver Schmitt, using both quantitative and qualitative data from six country studies, explains these changes and sets the scene for the remainder of this book. As they note, we have seen not only an increase in the number of armed conflicts, but they have become more complex in regards to actors, objectives and military tactics and weapons deployed. Today's conflicts are also more likely to be internal or internationalized, marked by the involvement of one or more non-state armed groups and their fight against a state counterpart or one another – and often with the involvement of and support from other states.[12]

Farrell and Schmitt note a decline in the overall lethality of conflicts since the Second World War. In 2014, however, there were forty-two active conflicts, less than in the preceding ten years, but with much higher fatalities.[13] The targeting of civilians through other means, including displacement, is also increasing, alongside the long-term indirect effects of prolonged violence. Hostilities are often taking place in crowded urban spaces.

The drivers of armed conflict and violence remain primarily those of race/ethnicity, religion, political opinion and social group. Not much has changed in this regard since the Second World War. These drivers are often intertwined with other motivations such as economics, the pursuit of profit and organized crime. The complexity of motivations has complicated the choice of the appropriate 1951 Convention grounds in refugee status-determination procedures yet also reinforces the fact that those grounds remain applicable to today's situations. On the causes of contemporary armed conflict and other situations of violence, there is

---

[12] For a chart on the development of intra- and inter-state conflicts, see Chapter 1 of this book, and for charts since 1945, see Institute for International Conflict Research Heidelberg, *Conflict Barometer 2014*, 17.

[13] International Institute for Strategic Studies, Armed Conflict Database Monitoring Conflicts Worldwide, available at: https://acd.iiss.org/en/acdindex.

usually no singular explanation for a particular conflict. In fact, there are often multiple and overlapping causes, which may change over time. Different or similar causes may lead to the perpetuation of conflict or may reignite it.[14]

The rise in non-state actors has become part of the landscape of contemporary conflicts. The issue of non-state agents of persecution and the 1951 Convention refugee definition has now thankfully been resolved. In situations of armed conflict and violence, states have proven unable and, at times, unwilling to implement their international obligations vis-à-vis civilian victims. In UNHCR's understanding, persecution can emanate from non-state groups or sections of the population or even private individuals if their persecutory actions are knowingly tolerated by the authorities or if the authorities refuse, or prove unable, to offer protection. UNHCR's view is now reflected in the EU Qualification Directive[15] and in most national jurisdictions. In particular, this interpretation has allowed the claims of women to be more easily included in the 1951 Convention refugee definition.[16]

An additional change in contemporary conflicts is the blurred distinction between civilians as victims of hostilities and as active participants in the conflict. This blurring can cause challenges for adjudicators, for instance, in regard to exclusion from refugee status.[17]

The adverse effects on the civilian population and the increased general level of violence in many countries often prevent internal flight alternatives. A seemingly perpetual cycle of violence in many countries has been part of the daily reality of people and communities over extended periods. Many conflicts are not only protracted but also intractable in the absence of broad-based, determined political resolve to end

---

[14] UNHCR, 'Cape Town Summary Conclusions', para. 4.

[15] European Union: Council of the European Union, *Directive 2011/95/EU of the European Parliament and of the Council of 13 December 2011 on Standards for the Qualification of Third-Country Nationals or Stateless Persons as Beneficiaries of International Protection, for a Uniform Status for Refugees or for Persons Eligible for Subsidiary Protection, and for the Content of the Protection Granted (recast)*, 20 December 2011, OJL 337/9–337/26; 20.12.2011, 2011/95/EU.

[16] See, UNHCR, 'Guidelines on International Protection No. 1: Gender-Related Persecution within the Context of Article 1A(2) of the 1951 Convention and/or its 1967 Protocol Relating to the Status of Refugees', 7 May 2002, HCR/GIP/02/01, available at: www .refworld.org/docid/3d36f1c64.html.

[17] See UNCHR, 'Guidelines on International Protection No. 5: Application of the Exclusion Clause: Article 1F of the 1951 Convention Relating to the Status of Refugees', 4 September 2003, HCR/GIP/03/05, available at: www.refworld.org/docid/3f5857684 .html.

them. The reality is sadly not always reflected in the protection provided to those fleeing such situations.

The interpretation and application of international protection instruments in today's world requires, firstly, the need to understand fully the particular situation of violence and conflict and its effects on civilians. Secondly, many of today's situations are similar and yet at times also distinct from those in the minds of the drafters of the 1951 Convention or the regional instruments. This does not mean, however, that these instruments are not applicable to current realities. Considered a living instrument, the 1951 Convention and the whole field of international refugee law need to be read and interpreted in light of changing realities and the tenets of international treaty law.[18]

The Applicability of the 1951 Convention Definition in Times of Armed Conflict and Violence

The scale and character of contemporary situations of violence and conflict have led to some major misconceptions regarding the applicability of the 1951 Convention refugee definition, which this book seeks to address. Yet, as agreed by the participants in UNHCR's Cape Town expert roundtable on this subject, reflecting the general threads of a discussion with an esteemed group of experts,

> Nothing in the text, context or object and purpose of the 1951 Convention hinders its application to armed conflict or other situations of violence. In fact, the 1951 Convention makes no distinction between refugees fleeing peacetime or wartime situations. Drafted in the aftermath of World War II, the drafters understood that individuals fleeing from armed conflict and other situations of violence may have a well-founded fear of being persecuted for one or more Convention grounds.[19]

So, why is its application challenged today? Situations of widespread violence have sometimes been misinterpreted to mean that such violence is indiscriminate rather than persecutory for one or more 1951 Convention grounds. While violence may often seem on the surface to be general in nature – general in the sense of being widespread, large-scale and indiscriminate – a deeper excavation of the socio-economic–political context

---

[18] 'It would be an error to construe the definition so as to ignore the changing circumstances of the world in which the Convention now operates.' A and Another v. Minister for Immigration and Ethnic Affairs and Another. (1997) Australia: High Court, 190 CLR 225, per Kirby J, para. 227.

[19] UNHCR, 'Cape Town Summary Conclusions', para. 6.

may show that the situation in fact involves many incidences of specific targeting of individuals, groups or whole communities. Persons are often targeted on racial, ethnic, religious, political or social lines, or because they are perceived as opposing the groups in control, or simply for being an obstacle or hindrance to their goals by mere presence. Violence is not undertaken for its own sake but has a deeper underlying motivation or purpose.[20] The characterization of such violence as 'generalized' is frequently misleading. UNHCR has on numerous occasions underlined that it is based on a wrongful understanding of contemporary conflicts, in particular, with regard to the character of contemporary warfare and its discriminate character.[21]

In a few jurisdictions, courts have even held that claimants fleeing conflict situations need to show a fear of persecution 'over and above the risk to life and liberty inherent in the civil war'.[22] This has been referred to as a 'differentiated' risk criterion. Other courts have held, for example, that '[t]he harm suffered must be particularized to the individual. Harm arising from general conditions such as anarchy, civil war, or mob violence will not ordinarily support a claim of persecution.'[23]

In response, Chapter 2 by Vanessa Holzer on the application of the 1951 Convention to such situations provides an overview of a number of problematic trends in the case law and questions their basis in the 1951 Convention. She rightly argues that these restrictive views find no explanation in the 1951 Convention. Article 1A(2) requires that applicants establish only that they have a well-founded fear of being persecuted for a 1951 Convention reason, 'nothing more, nothing less'.[24] There is no

---

[20] See Presentation by V. Türk, 'Protection Gaps in Europe? Persons Fleeing the Indiscriminate Effects of Generalized Violence', Brussels, 18 January 2011, pp. 4–5, available at: www.refworld.org/docid/4d37d8402.html.

[21] See e.g. UNHCR, 'Note on Interpreting Article 1 of the 1951 Convention Relating to the Status of Refugees', April 2001, para. 20, available at: www.unhcr.org/refworld/pdfid/3b20a3914.pdf. See also B. Tax, 'Refuge by Association', Forced Migration Review 47 (2014), available at: www.fmreview.org/syria/tax.

[22] See e.g. Adan v. Secretary of State for the Home Department, [1998] 2 WLR 702, per Lord Slynn of Hadley (case concerned Somalia).

[23] Mohamed v. Ashcroft, 396 F.3d 999, 1006 (8th Cir. 2005), para. II.A (case concerned Somalia).

[24] See presentations by A. Edwards, 'Using the 1951 Convention Relating to the Status of Refugees to Protect People Fleeing Armed Conflict and Other Situations of Violence: Key Legal Challenges', Luxembourg, 20 October 2014, available at: www.refworld.org/pdfid/545b43884.pdf; and A. Edwards, 'Coping with Contemporary Conflicts: "Conflict Refugees" and the 1951 Convention Protection Regime', 70th Course on International Refugee Law International Institute of Humanitarian Law San Remo, Italy, 23 April 2013, available at: www.refworld.org/docid/5178d7c44.html.

justification for asserting a higher risk threshold during wartime – when persons are generally in fear – than in peacetime. In fact, to do so would be absurd. The better and proper approach is well expressed by Justice McHugh in the Australian High Court case of *Haji Ibrahim*, in which he stated

> I see no basis in the text of the Convention or otherwise for holding that, in conditions of civil war or unrest, a person can prove persecution only when he or she can establish a risk of harm over and above that of others caught up in those conditions ... It is not the degree or differentiation of risk that determines whether a person caught in a civil war is a refugee under the Convention definition. It is a complex of factors that is determinative – the motivation of the oppressor; the degree and repetition of harm to the rights, interests or dignity of the individual; the justification, if any, for the infliction of that harm and the proportionality of the means used to achieve the justification.[25]

A 2008 Canadian Federal Court Case likewise noted that 'while accepting the need for a personalised risk, it was acknowledged that an individual's personalised risk may be shared by many other individuals.'[26] This view is also supported by the New Zealand Refugee Status Appeals Authority.[27]

The Cape Town Summary Conclusions restated these views, by noting the fact that many or all members of a particular community may be equally at risk and that this does not undermine the validity of any particular claim. The test is rather whether an individual's fear of being persecuted is well founded. In fact, at times, the impact of a conflict on an entire community increases, rather than weakens, the risk to any particular individual.[28] Further, there is nothing in the text of the 1951 Convention to suggest that a refugee has to be singled out for persecution either generally or over and above other persons at risk of being persecuted.[29]

In some conflict situations, the fighting and its effects may look at first glance as generalized and/or random in the sense of having no obvious targets, or at least not having targets such as civilian populations of particular ethnic or religious groups. Many conflicts today, however,

---

[25] *Minister for Immigration and Multicultural Affairs* v. *Haji Ibrahim*, [2000] HCA 55, para. 70 (case concerned Somalia).

[26] *Prophète* v. *Canada (Minister of Citizenship and Immigration)* 2008 FC 331, para. 18 (case concerned Haiti).

[27] *Refugee Appeal No 76551*, [2010] NZRSAA 103 (21 September 2010), para. 66 (case concerned Somalia), available at: www.refworld.org/pdfid/4cbf0ea62.pdf.

[28] UNHCR, 'Cape Town Summary Conclusions', para 8.   [29] *Ibid.*, para 9.

are deeply rooted in political, ethnic, religious or social divisions such that civilians are at risk because of their real or perceived political opinion, race/nationality, religion or membership in particular groups. They may be direct targets or they may be deprived of protection because of their link to a 1951 Convention ground. Ethnic cleansing, sexual and gender-based violence and forced displacement are often part of political or military strategies and are each closely associated with one or more of the 1951 Convention grounds. The consequence of bombing particular areas may also lead to impoverishment or lack of means of survival for particular communities. Furthermore, many ordinary civilians may be at risk of harm from shelling, suicide attacks or improvised explosive devices. These methods of violence may be used in areas where civilians of specific ethnic or political profiles reside or gather. All of this would mean that civilians on both sides (or multiple sides) of a conflict could be entitled to refugee protection under the 1951 Convention.

What each of these misperceptions reinforces is the importance of gathering up-to-date and comprehensive information and documentation on such situations. Obtaining such information in a timely manner is not, however, always feasible owing to the very context of the violence and conflict, nor is the reliability of such information ensured when situations are fluid and rapidly changing. The 'information gap' is one of the real challenges facing decision-makers.

Age and Gender Dimensions in Situations of Armed Conflict and Violence

Building on the work of UNHCR since the Global Consultations on International Protection in 2001–2 and the elaboration of UNHCR's first Guidelines on International Protection on Gender-Related Persecution within the context of Article 1A(2) of the 1951 Convention in 2002, the experiences of violence and conflict on the basis of age and gender form an important contribution to this book. In a detailed and broad jurisprudential analysis, Valerie Oosterveld examines in Chapter 6 how decision-makers have dealt with gender-specific experiences of women and girls in contexts of armed conflict and violence. Case law from Australia, Canada, New Zealand, the United Kingdom and the United States from 2004 to 2012 illustrates that a gender-sensitive interpretation of the 1951 Convention definition is often missing.

There are two particularly interesting findings from Valerie Oosterveld's research: the first is that during conflict, gender norms often take on even greater socio-political significance than during peacetime. For example, 'the role of women in the biological and social reproduction of group identity places them in a position of particular vulnerability.'[30] In this way, gender-related acts in conflict take on deeper meanings or have a wider impact (for families, for communities), thereby creating gendered experiences. According to the research, such impacts are rarely recognized in asylum adjudication processes. There continue to be cases, for example, that incorrectly characterize rape or other forms of sexual violence committed in conflict as 'private' or 'criminal' conduct and therefore not persecutory.

A second, more entrenched problem is that decision-makers often classify gender-related violence as part of the general indiscriminate consequences of conflict and therefore not persecutory in the sense of the refugee definition. This appears to be done without necessarily considering the potential gender-related reasons for that violence (e.g. the various ways in which rape is used as a weapon or strategy of war) or the broader political and other dimensions of conflict.[31]

Low-level warfare often aims at disrupting social and cultural relations, thus affecting civilians.[32] As noted by A. T. Nathan, '[w]omen are the bearers of culture not just in the clichéd senses that they socialize children ... but in the more fundamental sense that groups of people define their identities – what makes them different – in large part through the statuses and roles that they ascribe to women.'[33] Being allocated such a role and the responsibility which attaches to that role, military/political tactics aimed at disrupting the social, political and cultural foundations of a particular society are often perpetrated through and on women's bodies. Such acts can rarely be characterized as indiscriminate but rather as deeply embedded in politics, ethnicity, religion, social processes *and* gender – and should as such be recognized as legitimate grounds for refugee status.[34]

A third consideration in claims to refugee status relating to sexual and gender-based violence is to note that such acts are perpetrated also

---

[30] H. Crawley, *Refugees and Gender: Law and Process* (Bristol, UK: Jordan Publishing, 2001), 88, as referred to in Chapter 6 in this book.

[31] See Chapter 6.   [32] See Chapter 6.

[33] A. T. Nathan, 'Universalism: A Particularistic Account', in L. S. Bell, A. J. Nathan and I. Peleg (eds.), *Negotiating Culture and Human Rights* (New York: Columbia University Press, 2001), 249, at 356.

[34] See A. Edwards, 'Judging Gender: Asylum Adjudication and Issues of Gender, Gender Identity and Sexual Orientation', Geneva, 26 October 2012, available at: www.refworld .org/docid/509cc8252.html.

against men and boys, owing to understandings of gender in society, either alone or in combination with other factors, and can thus be persecutory.[35] The Cape Town expert meeting concluded that in assessing the credibility of a claim for refugee status based on gender-related persecution, decision-makers need to ensure that they do not succumb to stereotyped assessments of how women or girls – or men or boys – respond (or are expected to respond) to such violence.[36] Particular considerations may also arise in relation to claims to refugee status related to sexual orientation and/or gender identity, for which further study may be needed.

The phenomenon of recruitment of child soldiers was highlighted at the Cape Town expert meeting as a pervasive characteristic of contemporary conflicts, including the challenges their cases present for refugee status decision-makers and adjudicators. One particular issue that arises is how to assess voluntariness.[37] While children may appear to make rational decisions to join armed groups or the armed forces, this decision cannot be determined to be voluntary in circumstances where the decision is based on fear or for the purposes of ensuring their own economic survival or safety. A determinative consideration in refugee status determination is the illegality of child recruitment. Rachel Brett, Margret Brett and Haifa Rashed in Chapter 7 draw attention to children fleeing armed conflict against the background of international refugee and human rights law. A child-sensitive interpretation of the 1951 Convention is needed to assess comprehensively their claims for international protection. While child-specific forms of persecution or child-related manifestations of persecution linked to age, maturity and vulnerability must be considered, equally important is the question whether the nexus to the 1951 Convention grounds needs special attention in the context of child refugee claims.

Chapter 7 goes beyond merely considering children as 'collateral damage' but encompasses a detailed, substantive analysis of children as victims of persecution. It also considers an analysis of the actions of children within the context of Article 1F of the 1951 Convention. For its part, UNHCR's guidelines on child asylum claims and, more recently, guidelines on claims relating to military service clarify that

> Despite the different age limits set by international law, it is UNHCR's view that forced recruitment and/or direct participation in hostilities of

---

[35] UNHCR, 'Cape Town Summary Conclusions', para. 20.   [36] *Ibid.*, para. 22.
[37] *Ibid.*, para. 5.

a child below the age of 18 years in the armed forces of the State or by a non-State armed group would amount to persecution.[38]

The Regional Frameworks for Refugee Protection

Developed against a background of violence and conflicts in the 1960s in Africa and in the 1980s in Latin America, two regional refugee instruments have been elaborated. Although the 1951 Convention remains the universal and primary legal instrument for refugees, as acknowledged in both those regional instruments,[39] the existence of regional definitions has nonetheless raised questions regarding the relevance and applicability of the 1951 Convention definition to individual cases or particular factual situations. The coherent interpretation and implementation of the regional instruments in Africa and Latin America require guidance.

The 1969 OAU Convention Governing the Specific Aspects of Refugee problems in Africa and its relation to the 1951 Convention is clarified in two chapters. Bonaventure Rutinwa in Chapter 4 provides an historical account of the drafting and negotiation of the African treaty, one that he conclusively frames as complementary. Emphasizing the political and legal context of the drafting and entry into force of the 1969 OAU Convention and the influence of the 1951 Convention on that process, Rutinwa discusses two schools of thought regarding how to understand

---

[38] UNHCR, 'Guidelines on International Protection No. 8: Child Asylum Claims under Articles 1(A)2 and 1(F) of the 1951 Convention and/or 1967 Protocol Relating to the Status of Refugees', 22 December 2009, HCR/GIP/09/08, paras. 19–23, available at: www .refworld.org/docid/4b2f4f6d2.html; UNHCR, 'Guidelines on International Protection No. 10: Claims to Refugee Status Related to Military Service within the context of Article 1A(2) of the 1951 Convention and/or the 1967 Protocol Relating to the Status of Refugees', 3 December 2013, HCR/GIP/13/10/Corr. 1, para. 12, available at: www .refworld.org/docid/529ee33b4.html. Both documents refer to Convention on the Rights of the Child, 20 November 1989 (entered into force 2 September 1990), 1577 UNTS 3 (CRC), Art. 38; Optional Protocol to the Convention on the Rights of the Child on the Involvement of Children in Armed Conflict, 25 May 2000 (entered into force 12 February 2002), 2173 UNTS 222, Arts. 2 and 3; Rome Statute of the International Criminal Court, 17 July 1998 (entered into force 1 July 2002), 2187 UNTS 90 (ICC Statute), Arts. 8(2)(b)(xxvi) and 8(2)(e)(vii).

[39] See Organization of African Unity Convention Governing the Specific Aspects of Refugee Problems in Africa (entered into force 20 June 1974), 1001 UNTS 45 (OAU Convention), ninth preamble paragraph; *Cartagena Declaration on Refugees, Colloquium on the International Protection of Refugees in Central America, Mexico and Panama*, 22 November 1984, Conclusions III(1), (2), (3) and (8), available at: www .refworld.org/docid/3ae6b36ec.html. See also, 'EXCOM Conclusion No. 87(L) 1999', para. (f); 'EXCOM Conclusion No. 89 (LI) 2000'.

the global and regional definitions. The first suggests that the concept of persecution in the 1951 Convention was not considered sufficiently wide to cover the refugee situations in Africa in the 1960s (the so-called distinctness school of thought). The second school of thought noted through archival research that once the 1967 Protocol was agreed to, the two definitions cannot be considered entirely separately and that there is 'overlap' between them. Rutinwa concludes that the most apt way to describe the 1969 OAU Convention's definition is in terms that it more easily facilitated recognition to specific situations, an approach that in UNHCR's view rightly favours the second school of thought.

In Chapter 5 by Marina Sharpe on the application of the 1969 OAU Convention in the context of individual refugee status-determination procedures, the specifics of this regional instrument are critically observed in their practical application. Data drawn from a questionnaire for state decision-making bodies distributed to UNHCR country offices in 2013 highlight the application of the regional definition as well as the 1951 Convention definition. In particular, Sharpe notes that some states adopt a sequential assessment such that status is first determined under the 1951 Convention before moving to the 1969 OAU Convention definition; in other states, she observes that, depending on the situation at hand, the 1969 OAU Convention may be prioritized (what she calls the 'nature of flight approach'), and finally, she notes that an approach may be adopted to apply the 1969 OAU Convention for pragmatic and efficiency reasons, without considering the 1951 Convention. While legal certainty might suggest that the sequential approach is the most appropriate, UNHCR is cognisant that the situation-based 1969 OAU Convention definition allows for its rapid application in particular settings and that this may be appropriate. The fact that persons recognized under either instrument obtain refugee status and the rights set out in both instruments serves to minimize concerns regarding the latter approaches. This is also the view taken by participants at the Cape Town expert roundtable.[40]

The Cartagena Declaration on Refugees, adopted in 1984 as a non-binding instrument for Latin American states, equally enshrines protection for people fleeing generalized situations of violence. As such, it builds a second regional framework explicitly addressing conflict-induced external displacement. Through its widespread incorporation into national legislation in Latin American countries, the legal force of the extended definition has been strengthened. Most recently, the

[40] UNHCR, 'Cape Town Summary Conclusions', para. 32.

adoption in December 2014 of the Brazil Declaration and Plan of Action has reaffirmed the commitment of Latin American and Caribbean states to upholding the highest protection standards.[41]

As a follow-up to the Cape Town expert roundtable and as a contribution to the anniversary events, UNHCR organized a further consultation specifically on the Cartagena Declaration in Montevideo, Uruguay.[42] That roundtable noted that the situation-based focus of the Cartagena Declaration lends itself to its application in situations characterized by indiscriminate, unpredictable or collective risks affecting individuals, groups of persons or even the population at large. As with any refugee claim, the Cartagena definition requires an assessment of the situation in the country of origin as well as the particular circumstances of the individual or group of persons who seek protection as refugees. The focus of the assessment is, however, on the exposure of the individual or group of persons to the risks inherent in the five situations contained in the definition. For example, civilians whose lives, security or freedoms are at risk from confrontations between armed groups fighting for control over territory, and which endangers the lives and security of anyone living in the area, would fall within the Cartagena definition of a refugee. They are not required to show an individual risk over and above others similarly situated. The Montevideo expert meeting noted that the risk can even be established from being 'in the wrong place at the wrong time'. The Cartagena Declaration also covers indirect effects arising from the five situations – including, for example, poverty, economic decline, inflation, violence, disease, food insecurity and malnourishment and displacement.[43]

In Chapter 6, Michael Reed-Hurtado also reconfirms the protection-driven process to agree to the Cartagena Declaration and explains the situations that were taking place in Central and South America at the time. In looking at state practice, he notes: 'Paradoxically, the Cartagena Declaration has been seldom applied in practice, guidance on its interpretation is undeveloped and national authorities rarely consult its provisions when providing international refugee protection.' Painting a negative picture of its actual application, Reed-Hurtado's analysis emphasizes the under development of the regional refugee definition and some procedural challenges for decision-making authorities to

---

[41] *Brazil Declaration and Plan of Action*, 3 December 2014, available at: www.refworld.org /docid/5487065b4.html.
[42] UNHCR, 'Montevideo Summary Conclusions'.   [43] *Ibid.*, 3.

apply the Cartagena definition coherently and consistently. As part of its forthcoming Guidelines on International Protection, UNHCR hopes to provide greater support to states in applying the Cartagena Declaration definition.

Moreover, in Asia, in the context of the Asian-African Legal Consultative Organization, the adoption of a revised consolidated text of the Bangkok Principles on the Status and Treatment of Refugees in New Delhi, India, on 24 June 2001, was an important step forward in reaching a common understanding of refugee protection in some parts of the world where accession to the 1951 Convention by important host countries has not yet occurred.[44]

European Union and Subsidiary Protection

The last part of the collection is dedicated to the European subsidiary protection regime initially established in 2004 by the EU Qualification Directive EC/2004/83[45] and amended in 2011 by recast 2011/95/EU.[46] Like its African and Latin American counterparts, the European Union also decided that a regional common framework for asylum based on the 1951 Convention was important in the harmonization of national approaches in the European Union. This particular complementary protection mechanism provides for a status for persons not eligible for refugee protection but, according to Article 15(c), at risk of 'serious and individual threat to a civilian's life or person by reason of indiscriminate violence in situations of international or internal armed conflict'. Unlike the 'complementary' regimes in Africa and Latin America, the EU Qualification Directive sets up a 'subsidiary' protection framework.

The codification of the Qualification Directive and its subsequent transposition in national laws are at first glance positive and promising developments, although in practice they have raised numerous questions.

---

[44] Asian-African Legal Consultative Organization (AALCO), 'Bangkok Principles on the Status and Treatment of Refugees' ('Bangkok Principles'), 31 December 1966, available at: www.refworld.org/docid/3de5f2d52.html. The final text of the AALCO's 1966 'Bangkok Principles on Status and Treatment of Refugees' were adopted on 24 June 2001, at the AALCO's 40th Session, New Delhi, India.

[45] European Union: Council of the European Union, *Council Directive 2004/83/EC of 29 April 2004 on Minimum Standards for the Qualification and Status of Third Country Nationals or Stateless Persons as Refugees or as Persons Who Otherwise Need International Protection and the Content of the Protection Granted,* 30 September 2004, OJL 304/ 12–304/23; 30.9.2004, 2004/83/EC.

[46] European Union: Council of the European Union, *Qualification Directive (recast).*

According to the Preamble as well as Article 78 of the Treaty on the Functioning of the European Union, its subordinated status in relation to the 1951 Convention seems to be straightforward. However, the strongly deviating recognition rates of people fleeing the same country of origin, oscillating between the different statuses, query this positive assessment.

UNHCR's own research has found considerable variation in recognition rates of refugees from three countries, Afghanistan, Iraq and Somalia, in a 2011 report, *Safe at Last?*.[47] Such variation in recognition rates creates severe legal uncertainties in access to asylum as refugees. One particular problem is that single procedures are not in place in all countries, allowing for sequential status determination to ensure that subsidiary protection complements and does not undermine refugee status under the 1951 Convention.

Against relevant jurisprudence by the European Court of Human Rights and the Court of Justice of the European Union, Madeline Garlick evaluates the subsidiary protection scheme at its current state in Chapter 8. She notes that the European Commission's original goal was to fill a gap in the European protection framework, namely, for people fleeing indiscriminate violence in conflict, who may not for various reasons fulfil the criteria for refugee status. At the same time, she notes that the desire of some Member States to expand the scope of their protection obligations was limited and led to lengthy debates around the wording of the subsidiary provisions. The trouble remains in the variable application of important legal concepts by different Member States and a tendency to grant through accelerated procedures subsidiary protection to persons who would otherwise qualify for refugee status. Although there has been considerable alignment between the rights for refugees and those attributable to holders of subsidiary protection during the recast exercise in Europe, unlike Africa and Latin America, there remain some distinctions notably with regard to family reunification, making it particularly important that the 1951 Convention is applied first and properly.

International Humanitarian Law and Refugee Status

One final aspect that is of particular interest in relation to refugee status determination related to armed conflict and violence, and which is touched on in several chapters in this book, is the extent of the relevance

[47] See UNHCR, 'Safe at Last'.

of international humanitarian law (IHL) to refugee status determination. In 2011, as part of the anniversary events, UNHCR co-hosted an event with the International Criminal Tribunal for Rwanda, in Arusha, Tanzania, in which the question of the inter-relationship between international refugee law, on the one hand, and IHL and international criminal law (ICL), on the other, was explored.[48]

Given their shared foundational principles of protection, participants at the Arusha roundtable considered whether these areas of law should influence developments in another, to strengthen and consolidate the international normative order. However, they concluded that this is not necessarily the case. While these different international legal regimes may rely on similar concepts and terms in relevant treaties and international instruments, they were developed with distinct purposes and have a separate legal existence, which, in turn, influences the manner in which these terms are interpreted and applied.[49] Notably, the roundtable found that the crime of persecution in ICL should not be used to inform the use in the refugee definition, while the relevance of IHL and ICL to Article 1F is well understood, albeit not to be accepted wholesale, owing to the explicit reference in Article 1F. International humanitarian law is also critically important in two other areas of refugee status determination, alongside relevant developments in international human rights law: in relation to the claims of refugee children and child soldiers (see Chapter 7),[50] as well as claims to refugee status related to military service, such as draft evaders or deserters or conscientious objectors.[51]

As Koskenniemi has pointed out in his seminal study: '[T]he point of the emergence of something like "international criminal law" or "international human rights law" (or any other special law) is precisely to institutionalize the new priorities carried within such fields.'[52] To require uniformity would potentially undermine the purpose of the particular regime at issue. Therefore, harmonization of various bodies of

---

[48] UNHCR, 'Arusha Summary Conclusions'.   [49] Ibid., para. 2.

[50] See UNHCR, 'Guidelines on International Protection No. 8: Child Asylum Claims; UNHCR, 'Guidelines on International Protection No. 10: Claims to Refugee Status Related to Military Service', para. 12.

[51] UNHCR, 'Guidelines on International Protection No. 10: Claims to Refugee Status Related to Military Service'.

[52] Marrti Koskenniemi, 'The Fate of Public International Law: Between Technique and Politics', Modern Law Review 70(1) (2007), 5. See International Law Commission, Fragmentation of International Law: Difficulties Arising from the Diversification and Expansion of International Law, Report of the Study Group of the International Law Commission, UN Doc. A/CN.4/L.682, 30 April 2006, finalized by Martti Koskenniemi.

law 'is not an objective in and of itself; the overriding concern should be clarity on the ordinary meaning of the provisions at hand guided by the object and purpose of each regime or instrument, or the particular norm in question.'[53] With regard to refugee protection, the impetus that shapes legal developments is the underlying premise to provide the most comprehensive level of protection possible.

It is also UNHCR's view that while in some circumstances armed conflict and violence situations may be categorized as an international (IAC) or a non-international armed conflict (NIAC) within the meaning of IHL, for the purpose of refugee status determination, such categorization is not required.[54] 'Armed conflicts' may not necessarily be classified as such for IHL purposes, such designations also often relying on extraneous considerations, yet the means employed and their consequences may be just as violent or persecutory.[55] Other labels – such as a situation of generalized violence – have also been used by decision-makers to describe a particular context. Regardless of such characterizations, the method of assessing the claim to refugee status is unchanged – a full and inclusive application of the refugee definition in the 1915 Convention to the situation at hand is required.

This position on the limited relevance of IHL to applications for international protection is also mirrored in the Court of Justice of the European Union's case of *Aboubacar Diakité* v. *Commissaire général aux réfugiés et aux apatrides*, in which the Court held that 'while [IHL] is designed, *inter alia*, to provide protection for civilian populations in a conflict zone by restricting the effects of wars on persons and property, it does not ... provide for international protection to be granted to certain civilians who are outside both the conflict zone and the territory of the conflicting parties.' The Court concluded

> On a proper construction of Article 15(c) of Council Directive 2004/83/ EC of 29 April 2004 on minimum standards for the qualification and status of third country nationals or stateless persons as refugees or as persons who otherwise need international protection and the content of the protection granted, it must be acknowledged that an internal armed conflict exists, for the purposes of applying that provision, if a State's

---

[53] UNHCR, 'Arusha Summary Conclusions', para. 4.

[54] By analogy, this is the position taken by the CJEU in *Aboubacar Diakité* v. *Commissaire général aux réfugiés et aux apatrides*, C-285/12, European Union: Court of Justice of the European Union, 30 January 2014, para. 23, available at: www.refworld.org/docid/ 52ea51f54.html.

[55] UNHCR, 'Cape Town Summary Conclusions', para. 12.

armed forces confront one or more armed groups or if two or more armed groups confront each other. It is not necessary for that conflict to be categorised as 'armed conflict not of an international character' under international humanitarian law; nor is it necessary to carry out, in addition to an appraisal of the level of violence present in the territory concerned, a separate assessment of the intensity of the armed confrontations, the level of organization of the armed forces involved or the duration of the conflict.[56]

As for the relevance to the regional refugee instruments, an exception can be carved out in relation to the Cartagena refugee definition. The term 'internal conflicts' in the Cartagena definition has traditionally been accepted by Latin American countries as referring to non-international armed conflicts (NIACs) within the meaning of IHL.[57] Accepting that internal conflicts so deemed would be covered by the Cartagena definition, IHL is nonetheless considered only to be informative, though not determinative, as to whether an internal conflict actually exists, not least owing to the different prevailing understandings of NIACs and the lack of a single declaratory body to make such pronouncements.[58] For situations short of a NIAC, for purposes of the Cartagena definition, they may be better captured under the ground of 'generalized violence'.

Conclusion

As the chapters in this book illustrate, the 1951 Convention and 1967 Protocol continue to provide a solid legal basis for the protection of those fleeing the turmoil of armed conflict and violence. It is clear from the object and purpose of the 1951 Convention, the drafting records and the historical context that the 1951 Convention's provisions were intended to

---

[56] *Ibid.*, para. 36.
[57] See 'Principles and Criteria for the Protection and Assistance of Central American Refugees, Returnees and Internally Displaced in Latin America' (CIREFCA, 89/9), April 1989, available at: www.refworld.org/docid/4370ca8b4.html. See Article 1 of 'Protocol Additional to the Geneva Conventions of 12 August 1949, and Relating to the Protection of Victims of Non-International Armed Conflicts' ('Protocol II'), 8 June 1977, 1125 UNTS 609, available at: www.refworld.org/docid/3ae6b37f40.html; and *Prosecutor v. Dusko Tadic aka 'Dule' (Decision on the Defence Motion for Interlocutory Appeal on Jurisdiction)*, IT-94-1, International Criminal Tribunal for the former Yugoslavia (ICTY), 2 October 1995, para. 70, available at: www.refworld.org/docid/47fdfb520.html.
[58] For example, while UN Security Council designation of a situation as a non-international armed conflict would be sufficient for the purposes of the Cartagena refugee definition, such a qualification cannot be a requirement. See also UNHCR, 'Arusha Summary Conclusions'.

be given an interpretation consistent with the generous spirit in which they were conceived. For UNHCR, it has always been understood that the refugee definition was meant to have an inclusive meaning, in accordance with its fundamental objective of providing international protection to all who need it.

The problem does therefore not lie in the text or the scope of the 1951 Convention but rather in the machinery and processes in place to implement it, or their absence. The challenge is therefore how to strengthen its application in an inclusive manner. Clarifying existing obligations must be the starting point. Perceived limitations of the 1951 Convention and the 1967 Protocol to cope with the character, size and scale of contemporary conflicts and other violent situations have been expressed by some. Several regional and complementary instruments have entered into force explicitly covering situations of armed conflict and violence, and these remain relevant, while recognizing the primacy of the 1951 Convention.

Conflict studies have identified multiple and often overlapping causes of such violence on political, ethnic or religious grounds or tensions against particular social groups, thus reinforcing the primacy and relevance of the 1951 Convention. In situations of purely indiscriminate violence without a link to one of the 1951 Convention grounds, regional refugee law instruments or complementary and subsidiary forms of protection anchored in human rights law can provide important sources of protection for people affected by such violence.

International law is not calcified but comes to life in its interaction with reality. In the forced-displacement context, the aim must be to sustain a predictable multilateral response to people at risk and in need of international protection.

PART I

Causes, Character and Effects

PART I

Culture, Character and Effects

The Causes, Character and Conduct of Internal Armed Conflict and the Effects on Civilian Populations, 1990–2010

THEO FARRELL AND OLIVIER SCHMITT

Introduction

It is clear that the end of the cold war did not usher in a period of peace in the world. Quite the opposite: Asia, Africa, the Middle East, Latin America and even Europe have all endured armed conflicts since 1990. The vast bulk of these have been internal wars. Of the ninety-six armed conflicts that occurred between 1989 and 1996, only five were between states.[1] This trend became even more pronounced in the 2000s. As one major survey notes, '[w]hat stands out in the 21st century is the lack of large-scale interstate conflict.' Thus, of fourteen armed conflicts recorded in 2014, only one was between states; the rest occurred within states.[2] This chapter explores causes, character and conduct of internal armed conflicts since 1990 and the effects on civilian populations.

The first part of this chapter critically reviews the scholarship on the causes, changing character and conduct of internal armed conflicts. The rise of civil wars is contrasted with the decline of inter-state wars. Ethnic hatreds are seen to replace 'reason of state' as a driver of conflict. Violence directed against civilians is identified as a particular character-istic of these so-called new wars.[3] We also review quantitative analysis of armed conflicts since 1990, especially with regard to conflict frequency

---

[1] S. R. David, 'Internal Wars: Causes and Cures', *World Politics* 49 (1997, 552–76.

[2] T. Pettersson and P. Wallensteen, 'Armed Conflicts, 1946–2014', *Journal of Peace Research* 52 (2015), 537.

[3] M. van Creveld, *The Transformation of War* (New York: Free Press, 1991); M. Kaldor, *New and Old Wars* (Cambridge, UK: Polity, 1999); M. Munkler, *The New Wars* (Cambridge, UK: Polity, 2005). For critical literature reviews, see S. N. Kalyvas, 'New and Old Civil Wars: A Valid Distinction?', *World Politics* 54 (2001), 99–118; E. Newman, 'The "New Wars" Debate: A Historical Perspective is Needed', *Security Dialogue* 35 (2004), 173–89;

and impact on civilian populations. In broad terms, contrary to the 'new wars' literature, the quantitative data suggest that armed conflicts since 1990 have become *less* lethal for civilians. However, qualitative analysis of armed conflicts points to severe effects that are not captured in the major quantitative data sets on war. We outline two effects. Firstly, conflict directly causes major civilian suffering below the threshold of death. Secondly, internal armed conflicts indirectly kill large numbers of civilians by causing or greatly exacerbating food insecurity, population displacement and disease.

To explore these themes and trends, in the second part of this chapter we employ qualitative analysis of six case studies of armed conflict that exhibit variation in the cause, character, conduct and effects on civilians: Afghanistan, Colombia, Democratic Republic of Congo (DRC), Mexico, Somalia and Sri Lanka. These cases also have been selected to provide regional variation. The purpose of our comparative case-study analysis is not to 'test' some theory of conflict but rather to demonstrate that the categories commonly employed in social science theory and international law (e.g. inter- versus intra-state conflict, new versus old wars, combatant versus civilian) fail to capture the complex reality of armed conflict in the global system.

Internal Armed Conflict, 1990–2010: Causes and Character

Terms such as 'civil wars' and 'ethnic conflict' quickly came into use in the 1990s as shorthand descriptors for the armed conflicts in Africa, Asia and Europe. Such terms reinforced the common view that these were mainly intra-state affairs that were triggered and fuelled by virulent ethno-nationalism. However, in most cases, these conflicts involved regional actors and trans-border activities and were driven by a mix of factors and not simply ethnic difference. In this chapter, we adopt the generic term 'internal armed conflict' (IAC). At the same time, we recognize (and discuss later) the international, regional and cross-border dimensions of IACs. Thus, we do consider cases of internationalized wars, such as the war in the DRC (1994–2003) and the Afghanistan wars (1979–89, 2001–present). We do not look specifically at international wars such as the Eritrean–Ethiopian war (1998–2003), the Iraq war (2003) or the Libyan war (2011), given that they are so few in number

and M. Berdal, 'The "New Wars" Thesis Revisited', in H. Strachan and S. Scheipers, eds., *The Changing Character of War* (Oxford University Press, 2011), 109–33.

since 1990. Moreover, this chapter is not a legal analysis and hence does not categorize the conflicts studied according to international humanitarian law, but rather takes a more general approach.

In broad terms, the growing Western focus on the humanitarian and security challenges associated with IACs reflected their growing prevalence. The most thorough data sets on armed conflict are provided by the Uppsala Conflict Data Programme (UCDP).[4] Quantitative analysis by the UCDP clearly shows IACs growing both in absolute terms and in relation to inter-state conflicts over the post–World War II period. A recent survey of UCDP data set shows a succession of step-changes in the growth of IACs each decade from the 1960s to 1980s, with the major step-change in the late 1970s.[5] This suggests that the main change in the 1990s was in international awareness rather than prevalence of IACs. That said, the number of IACs did peak in the mid-1990s, and this in-decade increase probably fed growing international attention to the problem.

The Causes of Armed Conflict

There are two main schools of thought on the causes of IAC; one emphasizes the role of ethnic and religious identity, and the other focuses on the political economy of conflict. This is often called the 'greed versus grievance debate', and it is useful for clarifying the various potential drivers of IACs.[6] But to adopt the position that IAC is primarily driven by ethnic difference or economic conditions seems unnecessarily limiting to us. For instance, in its 'World Development Report 2011', the World Bank observes that 'cost-benefit motives' may not sufficiently account for armed conflict. Instead, economic conditions may operate in conjunction with social identity dynamics to

---

[4] The UCDP draws upon a range of sources including the Factiva database of 10,000 news media and various other IGO, NGO and academic reports. A case must have twenty-five or more battle-related deaths (military and/or civilian) per year to be coded as an 'armed conflict'. Another major collection of quantitative data sets on armed conflict is that provided by the Correlates of War (COW) Project. COW is a more established programme than UCDP and has been more extensively used by US social scientists. Like the UCDP, COW has data sets on inter-, intra- and non-state armed wars. However, under COW, a case must have 1,000 or more battle-related deaths per year to be coded as a 'war'. All URLs last checked on 1 March 2012.

[5] Pettersson and Wallensteen, 'Armed Conflicts', 539, fig. 1.

[6] M. Berdal and D. M. Malone, eds., Greed and Grievance in Civil Wars (Boulder, CO: Lynne Rienner, 2000).

generate conflict.[7] Thus, we examine evidence of a mix of conflict drivers in our case studies.

The Character and Conduct of Armed Conflict

The traditional lines in inter-state conflict – between war and peace, combatant and civilian, state and non-state – often are blurred in IACs. Even though the state practice of formally declaring war has gone out of fashion, inter-state war still is delineated by the onset and cessation of armed hostilities. In contrast, IACs usually just rumble on. Periods of less violence are often just interludes between periods of greater intensification of armed violence. In general, states that experience an IAC are very likely to relapse into further armed conflict. Of the eighty-one IACs that occurred in the 1990s, 67 per cent broke out in a country that had already experienced an IAC. In the 2000s, this figure rose to 90 per cent (although the total number dropped to thirty-nine IACs).[8] IACs are characterized by a diversity of irregular military actors including paramilitary groups, militias, insurgents, warring tribes, bandits, feral gangs, terrorists and private security companies.[9] The 'commercialization of military force' in contemporary conflict reinforces the point that whatever the causes of a particular IAC, it is sustained by economic interests that are antithetical to peace.[10] This also underlines the relationship between IACs and organized crime. It is too simplistic to argue that IACs are driven solely by organized crime, but criminal enterprise is often a key feature of IACs.[11] This, in turn, should direct our attention to the impact on civilian populations of violent organized crime. Traditional state-based security forces – military and police – also play a significant role in IACs. Sometimes this role is to protect civilian populations as well as the state. But where security forces are highly corrupt or serve factional interests, they may prey on the population and feed off the state.

A particular feature of IACs is the extensive use of child soldiers. Until fairly recently, there was no outright ban on child soldiers under international law. The Additional Protocol I (1977) of the Geneva

---

[7] The World Bank, 'World Development Report (WDR) 2011', 11 April 2011, 79.

[8] B. F. Walter, 'Conflict Relapse and the Sustainability of Post-Conflict Peace', WDR 2011 Background Paper, World Bank, 13 September 2010, 1–2.

[9] J. Mackinlay, *The Insurgent Archipelago* (London: Hurst, 2009), 73.

[10] Munkler, The New Wars, 16.

[11] J. Mueller, *The Remnants of War* (Ithaca, NY: Cornell University Press, 2004).

Conventions and the Convention on the Rights of the Child both prohibited states from recruiting soldiers under the age of fifteen, but there was no prohibition against children choosing to fight in conflicts. This situation changed from 2000 on. The use of child soldiers was so extensive in the conflict in Sierra Leone (more than 10,000), and with such barbaric results, that the United Nations authorized a special tribunal to prosecute those with the 'greater responsibility' for violations of international humanitarian law, including the use of child soldiers. Moreover, the Rome Statute of the International Criminal Court, which entered into force in July 2002, specifies that the military recruitment or use in hostilities of children under the age of fifteen constitutes a war crime. Notwithstanding a firming up of the law on this, extensive use continues to be made of child soldiers in armed conflicts.[12] This is hardly surprising as children are a cheap and ready source of military labour. Children are also easy to coerce into military service and easy to control. In addition, some children and young people voluntarily join armed groups as a way to escape desperate poverty or because of the promise of social status and economic advancement. Either way, through brutalization, intoxication or empowerment through the gun, children and young people produce some of the worst excesses of violence in IACs.[13]

The 'new wars' literature of the early 2000s draws a distinction between the modes of violence in the 'old' inter-state wars and the 'new' IACs. Where inter-state wars involved extensive use of heavy weapons (artillery, armoured vehicles and warplanes), IACs involve extensive use of light weapons (machetes, automatic weapons, landmines and rocket-propelled grenades). Violence in 'old wars' is mostly high tech and directed at capturing territory and destroying enemy forces. Violence in 'new wars' is mostly low tech and directed towards plunder and dominating the population.[14] A decade on, it is now understood that IACs often encompass many modes of violence. The reality of IACs as characterized by multiple,

---

[12] Protocol Additional to the Geneva Conventions of 12 August 1949, and Relating to the Protection of Victims of International Armed Conflicts ('Protocol I') (entered into force 7 December 1979), 1125 UNTS 3; Convention on the Rights of the Child (entered into force 2 September 1990), 1577 UNTS 3; Rome Statute of the International Criminal Court (entered into force 1 July 2002), 2187 UNTS 90; G. S. Goodwin-Gill, 'The Challenge of the Child Soldier', in H. Strachan and S. Scheipers (eds.), *The Changing Character of War* (Oxford University Press, 2011), 410–41.

[13] Munkler, *The New Wars*, 76–9.

[14] Kaldor, *New and Old Wars*, 7–8; Munkler, *The New Wars*, 74–6; Van Creveld, *The Transformation of War*.

inter-linked modes of violence is captured in the concept of 'hybrid warfare', which has gained wide currency among Western militaries. Hybrid warfare recognizes that in contemporary and future conflicts, Western forces face opponents who may use and blend multiple forces of violence – regular, irregular and criminal – in order to achieve their objectives.[15]

The Effects of IAC on Civilian Populations

War's true toll is difficult to know. Civilians are killed directly by conflict and indirectly by the effects of conflict on population displacement, food insecurity and ill-health. These direct and indirect casualties are 'excess deaths'; i.e. deaths that would not have occurred in the absence of armed conflict. Given the challenges of gathering reliable data and the controversies over methodology, there is considerable debate over the number of excess deaths in particular conflicts. For example, two reputable studies produced wildly differing numbers for excess civilian deaths in the Iraq war: 100,000 between March 2003 and March 2004 versus 12,000 from January 2003 to January 2004.[16]

The 'new wars' literature argues that IACs are especially deadly for civilians. Kaldor claims that in the wars of the early twentieth century the ratio of combatant to civilian casualties was 8:1 but that in the IACs of the 1990s this ratio was reversed, with 80 per cent of casualties being civilian.[17] Kaldor's 1:8 ratio has been widely cited. However, recent analysis of quantitative data from the UCDP suggests that she is wrong on this point. Wars from the late twentieth century onwards have proven to be less lethal in general, killing fewer combatants and civilians. Moreover, a comparison of battle deaths and war-related deaths over time reveals that the ratio of civilian to combatant death has actually *fallen*. IACs during the cold war killed far more combatants and civilians than post–cold war IACs.[18] Within this overall downward trend, the

---

[15] F. G. Hoffman, *Conflict in the 21st Century: The Rise of Hybrid Wars* (Arlington, VA: Potomac Institute for Policy Studies, 2007); US Government Accountability Office, 'Hybrid Warfare', briefing to House Armed Services Committee, US Congress, 10 September 2010, GAO-10-1036R.

[16] The higher figure was from L. Roberts et al., 'Mortality Before and After the 2003 Invasion of Iraq: Cluster Sample Survey', *Lancet*, published online 29 October 2004. The lower figure is from the Iraq Body Count interactive data set.

[17] Kaldor, *New and Old Wars*, 8, 100.

[18] E. Melander, M. Oberg and J. Hall, 'Are "New Wars" More Atrocious? Battle Severity, Civilians Killed and Forced Displacement Before and After the Cold War', *European Journal of International Relations* 15 (2009), 505–36; B. Lacina, N. P. Gledistch and

UCDP data set shows that the lethality of IACs has fluctuated since 1989, with a major peak in the early 1990s and a smaller peak in the early 2000s (see Tables 1 and 2).

However, statistics reveal little about the broader effects of armed violence on civilians. Here we highlight three broader effects. First are the *direct* causal effects on civilian disabilities; that is, the use of armed violence to dominate and abuse civilian populations which results in widespread physical and psychological harm. Second are the *indirect* effects of armed conflict in causing excess civilian deaths and disabilities, and third is the impact on population displacement.

Conflict Violence and Civilian Harm

Combatants find many ways and reasons to victimize civilians in IACs, resulting in serious and widespread harm. Civilian populations may be threatened with, or subjected to, violence in order to extract resources or labour. We see this with the Fuerzas Armadas Revolucionarias de Colombia (FARC) in Colombia, the Lord's Resistance Army in Central Africa and the Taliban in Afghanistan. Extreme violence may be used to exterminate a rival ethnic or political group, as happened in the Rwandan genocide of 1994, or to displace civilian populations and claim territory, as in Bosnia in 1992–5 and Kosovo in 1999. Sometimes IACs involve orgies of indiscriminate raping, maiming and killing of civilians which serve no apparent strategic purpose, as occurred when rebels seized the Sierra Leone capital, Freetown, in 1999. Civilians trapped in the middle of an IAC may face violence from rebel and state forces. Some 290,000 civilians took flight from Brazzaville, the capital of Congo, when civil war broke out in December 1998. A survey of families returning a year later found that 65 per cent had been attacked by rebels when they fled and attacked again by government forces as they attempted to return.[19]

Serious gender-based violence is common in IACs. Of the 300,000 child soldiers, some 120,000 are female. In the IACs in Uganda, Sierra Leone, Liberia and the DRC, girls are abducted or conscripted by rebel forces to be sexually exploited by male combatants. Rape on non-conscripted women and girls is also widespread. Of 109 women admitted

B. Russett, 'The Declining Risk of Death in Battle', *International Studies Quarterly* 50 (2006), 673–80.

[19] H. Slim, *Killing Civilians: Method, Madness and Morality in War* (London: Hurst, 2007), 37–8.

for rape injuries into a NGO hospital in the DRC in 2000, 47 per cent were under eighteen and 60 per cent had been gang raped.[20] There is also growing evidence of sexual forms of violence being perpetrated against enemy men and boys.[21] For example, one survey of 998 households in eastern DRC in 2010 found that 39.7 per cent of females and 23.6 per cent of males had been victims of sexual violence.[22]

A final challenge related to armed conflict is that of generalized violence, recently highlighted by UNHCR as violence that is 'widespread, large-scale and indiscriminate'.[23] Violence on this scale may occur in non-conflict settings. For example, 1,000 people were killed and 350,000 displaced by violence that broke out in Kenya in 2008 over disputed elections of the year before.[24] At the same time, it is easy to see how generalized violence may accompany IACs, either as a precursor to the outbreak of general armed conflict (as in Libya in 2011) or as an inter-linked element of the overall pattern of violence within an IAC (as in Iraq from 2004 to 2009). Furthermore, the conditions that accompany IACs (discussed later) – state failure, population displacement and food insecurity – provide fertile ground for generalized violence.

The concept of generalized violence is not unproblematic. It implies a level of violence that is so intense as to warrant international protection for those fleeing the effects. This, in turn, raises the question of threshold, especially when applied to states that normally experience very high levels of violence. One obvious way to assess this is by the number of civilians killed each year. There are two ways of measuring this – the absolute number and the homicide rate (i.e. death per 100,000 population). By themselves, both numbers may be misleading. For example, 15,241 civilians were murdered in the United States in 2009, but with a homicide rate of 5.0, nobody could seriously suggest that a situation of generalized violence existed in the United States that year. Equally, the Bahamas had a homicide rate of 28.0 in 2010, but given a population of around 350,000, this only amounted only to ninety-six murders. Some

---

[20] *Ibid.*, 68.
[21] S. Sivakumaran, 'Sexual Violence Against Men in Armed Conflict', *EJIL* 18 (2007), 253–76.
[22] K. Johnson et al., 'Association of Sexual Violence and Human Rights Violations with Physical and Mental Health in Territories of the Eastern Democratic Republic of the Congo', *Journal of the American Medical Association* 304 (2010), 553–62.
[23] UNHCR, 'Protection Gaps in Europe? Persons Fleeing the Indiscriminate Effects of Generalized Violence', V. Turk, Director of International Protection, 18 January 2011.
[24] Geneva Declaration Secretariat, *Global Burden of Armed Violence 2011* (Cambridge University Press, 2011), 21.

cases present a large absolute number and high homicide rate, such as South Africa, which had 16,800 homicides and a rate of 33.8 in 2009. However, with representative and stable government, security forces not targeting the population, no major inter-tribal/ethnic conflict and a strong tourist trade, it seems counter-intuitive to declare South Africa to be experiencing generalized violence (although it may be appropriate to apply this concept to discrete areas of South Africa).[25] These three examples underline the importance of situating statistical data in qualitative analysis of case studies. This is the approach taken in this chapter.

Armed Conflict and Indirect Civilian Deaths

Far more civilians die as an indirect consequence of armed conflict than directly in armed conflict itself. War causes famine, disease, poverty and population displacement. Indeed, there is a strong correlation between armed conflict, underdevelopment and state failure. The causal links are difficult to untangle, but the data are clear: most states that experience IACs also happen to be underdeveloped and have failing public institutions and therefore are less able to provide the protection of fundamental human rights.[26]

War makes people and states much poorer. Personal assets may be depleted through theft or war-induced economic inflation. Combatants may seize or destroy agricultural produce or otherwise prevent agricultural activity. People's livelihoods may be threatened by the effects of war on economic growth or by forced displacement. Armed conflict is especially damaging to trade and foreign investment. Trade can fall by up to 40 per cent due to IACs, and it takes, on average, twenty years for trade to return to pre-war levels.[27] The typical IACs last seven years and reduce annual economic growth by 2.3 per cent per year, thus leaving a country 15 per cent poorer at the end.[28] Not surprisingly, armed conflict is a major cause of food insecurity. By one estimate, conflict in Africa cost the continent up to $120 billion worth of agricultural

---

[25] Homicide figures and rates from United Nations Office on Drugs and Crime, 'Global Study on Homicide 2011', table 8.1.

[26] S. Gates et al., 'Consequences of Civil War', WDR 2011 Background Paper, World Bank, 26 October 2010; R. Rotberg, *When States Fail: Causes and Consequences* (Princeton, NJ: Princeton University Press, 2004); R. Bates, 'State Failure', *Annual Review of Political Science* 11 (2008), 1–11.

[27] Gates et al., 'Consequences of Civil War', 64.

[28] P. Collier, *The Bottom Billion* (Oxford University Press, 2007), 27.

production between 1960 and 2006. Analysis of cross-national quantitative data reveals that the median armed conflict between 1990 and 2004 will have increased the number of undernourished in the general population by 3.3 per cent, or 300,000 persons.[29] Sub-Saharan countries are especially at risk, as conflict further undermines the resilience of states and communities to deal with drought.[30]

Armed conflict greatly increases the risk of disease and reduces the capacities of individuals and states to deal with health problems. One study on mortality in the Darfur conflict found that over 80 per cent of almost 300,000 excess deaths from 2004 to 2008 occurred not as a direct result of armed violence but from diseases such as diarrhoea.[31] Population displacement caused by conflict and food insecurity also exacerbates the problems of disease because '[e]pidemic diseases – tuberculosis, measles, pneumonia, cholera, typhoid, and dysentery – are likely to emerge from crowding, bad weather and poor sanitation in camps, while malnutrition and stress compromise people's immune systems.'[32] Armed conflict causes vaccination programmes to breakdown, and this puts children in crowded refugee camps especially at risk. Families and states have fewer resources to tackle disease as a consequence of the economic hardships caused by conflict. Moreover, armed violence may directly undermine health services through the destruction of infrastructure and loss of medical professionals. According to the International Committee of the Red Cross, some 20,000 doctors have fled Iraq, and 2,500 doctors and nurses were killed between 2003 and 2008.[33]

Armed Conflict and Population Displacement

Conflict forces people to flee their homes to escape the direct effects (bodily harm) and the indirect effects (poverty, famine and disease) of armed violence. Since the early 1990s, the United Nations Security Council (UNSC) has recognized the causal link between armed conflict and forced displacement. In resolutions on Iraq in 1991 (UNSC Res. 688),

---

[29] Gates et al., 'Consequences of Civil War', 29–30, 34.

[30] D. Guha-Sapir and O. D'Aoust, 'Demographic and Health Consequences of Civil Conflict', WDR 2011 Background Paper, World Bank, October 2010, 22–3.

[31] O. Degomme and D. Guha-Sapir, 'Patterns of Mortality Rates in the Darfur Conflict', *Lancet* 373 (2010), 297.

[32] H. A. Ghobarah, P. K. Huth and B. M. Russett, 'Civil Wars Kill and Main People – Long after the Shooting Stops', *American Political Science Review* 97 (2003), 192.

[33] Guha-Sapir and D'Aoust, 'Demographic and Health Consequences of Civil Conflict', 16.

Bosnia in 1993 (UNSC Res. 819), Haiti in 1993 (UNSC Res. 841), Kosovo in 1998 (UNSC Res. 1199) and East Timor in 1999 (UNSC Res. 1239), the Security Council expressed deep concern at the mass displacement of civilians by these armed conflicts.[34] The UNHCR estimated that in 2010 the number of people displaced from their homes by armed violence and human rights violations stood at around 25 million; of these, 10.5 million were refugees and 14.5 million were internally displaced persons.[35]

In this respect, it is ironic that the 1951 Convention Relating to the Status of Refugees (1951 Convention) does not explicitly provide international protection to civilians fleeing armed violence, given that it was a response to the mass displacement of civilians caused by the social, economic and political upheavals in Europe during the two world wars. Interpreters of the 1951 Convention have maintained a fiction that persecution of civilians is an activity that exists apart from war when, as we have argued, often it is integral to the modes of economic and social mobilization in, and the conduct of, armed conflict. Moreover, this relationship between the violent persecution of civilians and war is not peculiar to the post–cold war IACs. Indeed, it was integral to how Germany waged the Second World War, especially on the Eastern Front.[36] The violence, persecution and mass displacement of civilians were also a feature of the wars of decolonization and ideological armed conflicts that raged in Latin America, Africa and Asia during the cold war.[37] It is commendable that African and Latin American regional instruments on protection – the African Convention on Refugees (OAU Convention) and 1984 Cartagena Declaration on Refugees (Cartagena Declaration) – are more specific than the 1951 Convention in explicitly recognizing as refugees persons who must flee their homes as a consequence of foreign aggression, internal conflict, generalized violence or serious disturbances to public order.[38]

---

[34] G. S. Goodwin-Gill and J. McAdam, *The Refugee in International Law*, 3rd edn. (Oxford University Press, 2007), 5–6.

[35] UNHCR, 'Global Report 2010', 172–3.

[36] Convention Relating to the Status of Refugees (adopted 28 July 1951, entered into force 22 April 1954), 189 UNTS 137 ('1951 Convention'); O. Bartov, *Germany's War and the Holocaust* (Ithaca, NY: Cornell University Press, 2003).

[37] A. E. Zolberg, A. Suhrke and S. Aguayo, *Escape from Violence: Conflict and the Refugee Crisis in the Developing World* (Oxford University Press, 1989); G. Loescher, *Beyond Charity: International Cooperation and the Global Refugee Crisis* (Oxford University Press, 1993).

[38] Organization of African Unity Convention Governing the Specific Aspects of Refugee Problems in Africa (entered into force 20 June 1974), 1001 UNTS 45 (OAU Convention);

Displaced populations, especially cross-border refugee flows, can further exacerbate the risk and intensity of conflict. Indeed, in UNSC Res. 688 on Iraq and UNSC Res. 841 on Haiti, the UNSC recognized that mass displacement was a threat to international peace and security. The mass arrival of refugees and displaced persons can heighten the *perception* of insecurity in three ways. Firstly, they may ferment or support opposition to the existing political authorities. Secondly, they may be seen as a burden on domestic resources, especially in developing states that already struggle to provide for their own citizens. Thirdly, they may be seen as a threat to social, cultural or ethnic balance.[39] Political, economic and social security is often fragile in states that are or have recently experienced IAC, and it is in this context that the heightened perception of insecurity may result in renewal or intensification of conflict.

Displaced persons usually end up in camps, often in neighbouring states. Some camps are makeshift with few facilities. Even those with state and/or international support often fail to provide access to adequate food, sanitation, clean water and medical care. Moreover, armed groups frequently take sanctuary in and operate from refugee camps (as happened in Pakistan in the 1980s and Zaire and Tanzania in the 1990s), further threatening civilian security.[40]

Armed Conflict: Comparative Case-Study Analysis

We turn now from general analysis of armed conflicts to look at six specific case studies. The purpose is to demonstrate the complexity of

1984 Cartagena Declaration on Refugees (adopted 22 November 1984) (Cartagena Declaration); Article 15(c) of the 2004 EC Qualification Directive provides subsidiary protection for persons fleeing armed conflict provided they are able to demonstrate a 'serious and individual threat'. The Qualification Directive is intended to harmonize national protection practices across the European Union. However, English and French courts have interpreted Article 15(c) in different but both restrictive ways, and thus, its full potential has not been realized in terms of extending the scope of subsidiary protection. The Court of Justice of the European Union has also adopted a very high threshold. See *Elgafaji* v. *Staatssecretaris van Justitie*, C-465/07, Court of Justice of the European Union, 17 February 2009, [2009] ECR, I-00921; H. Lambert and T. Farrell, 'The Changing Character of Armed Conflict and the Implications for Refugee Protection Jurisprudence', *IJRL* 22 (2010), 237–73.

[39] M. Weiner, 'Security, Stability and International Migration', *International Security* 17 (1992–3), 103–17. Examples from Loescher, *Beyond Charity*, 25–6.

[40] S. K. Lischer, *Dangerous Sanctuaries: Refugee Camps, Civil War and the Dilemmas of Humanitarian Aid* (Ithaca, NY: Cornell University Press, 2005).

contemporary IACs. Afghanistan is the largest producer of refugees in the world, with around 2 million from 2006 to 2009 rising to well over 3 million in 2010. Colombia has the largest internally displaced population from conflict in the world, with around 3 million from 2006 to 2010. Accordingly, we examine these two cases. The DRC conflict is Africa's largest war, drawing in all neighbouring states. Somalia's armed conflict has involved a tapestry of military actors, including clan militia, criminal gangs, Islamic insurgents and terrorists, pirates, neighbouring armies, UN peacekeepers and international forces. DRC and Somalia also have very large internally displaced populations, well in excess of 1 million each for 2006–10. Hence, we consider these two cases. Sri Lanka and Mexico give us glimpses into the future of armed conflict. Sri Lanka is examined as a classic case of hybrid warfare. The Tamil anti-government forces used a mix of guerrilla tactics, suicide terrorist attacks and conventional capabilities. Government forces engaged in increasingly brutal tactics in an ultimately successful drive to eliminate the rebel organization. Mexico is not an armed conflict in the traditional sense. The state does not face an organized armed opposition to its government. However, Mexico is a battleground for rival criminal organizations that are waging a drug war against each other and the security forces. Mexico has experienced levels of armed violence that are normally associated with armed conflict. Indeed, far more civilians have died violently each year in Mexico than in Afghanistan or Somalia. Thus, Sri Lanka and Mexico complete our set of case studies. We examine the cases in alphabetical order.

Afghanistan

Afghanistan has endured almost continuous armed conflict since 1978. Before then, the country had enjoyed four decades of peace and stability. 1978–1979 saw a popular rural uprising against the social and land reforms of a new Marxist government. The Soviet Union invaded in 1979 to install a more reliable regime, triggering a decade-long conflict against a vigorous Islamic insurgency. After the withdrawal of Soviet forces, Kabul continued to receive Soviet aid up to December 1991, at which point the Soviet Union collapsed, followed shortly thereafter by its Afghan client regime. A vicious civil war followed in 1992, as the uneasy Mujahideen alliance broke down and rival Pashtun, Tajik, Uzbeck and Hazara warlords fought each other for land and power. The Taliban, a radical Islamic and mostly Pashtun movement, emerged in 1994 in response to the chaos, corruption and brutality of the Mujahideen civil war. Starting from Kandahar province in the South, the Taliban defeated the major warlords in quick succession, taking the western city of Herat, eastern city of Jalalabad, and finally Kabul in 1996, followed by the northern city of Mazar-i-Sharif in 1997. By 1998, the Taliban had established control over most of Afghanistan. The Taliban war rumbled on against a loose Northern Alliance of Tajik, Hazara and rival Pashtun militias who were held up in the mountains of north and north-eastern Afghanistan.[41]

The US-led invasion in October 2001 led to the rapid defeat of the Taliban and the appointment of a new interim government composed of Northern Alliance and former Mujahideen warlords. Between 2002 and 2005, there was a brief interlude in the Afghanistan conflict. The rump Taliban had retreated to Pakistan, and the international presence ensured that the jostling for power between rival warlords did not break out into open conflict. In 2003, the North Atlantic Treaty Organization took charge of the International Security Assistance Force (ISAF) and began to expand the ISAF beyond Kabul into the relatively permissive north and west of Afghanistan. The conflict reignited in 2005–6 as the ISAF expanded in the southern and eastern provinces. In 2009, the United States redoubled its commitment to the Afghanistan war under newly elected President Barak Obama, resulting in a surge of US forces and funding. A new commander of the ISAF and US forces, General Stanley McChrystal, also brought renewed drive and direction to the military campaign. 2009–2011 saw an intensification of military operations, with major ISAF offensives in the south and east (leading to some displacement of Taliban activity into the more stable north and west), a ramping up of special forces raids to kill and capture Taliban leaders and an accelerated effort to develop the Afghan security forces.[42] With increased international funding and activity has come a massive growth in private security contractors, with over 110,000 in country by 2013.[43]

---

[41] T. Barfield, *Afghanistan: A Cultural and Political History* (Princeton, NJ: Princeton University Press, 2010), 225–61; B. R. Rubin, *The Fragmentation of Afghanistan*, 2nd edn. (New Haven, CT: Yale University Press, 2002); A. Rashid, *Taliban* (London: Pan Books, 2000).

[42] R. Chaudhuri and T. Farrell, 'Campaign Disconnect: Operational Progress and Strategic Obstacles in Afghanistan, 2009-2011', *International Affairs* 87 (2011), 271–96.

[43] US Central Command estimates for first quarter of 2013 reported by professional overseas contractors, 'Contractor Support of US Operations in the USCENTCOM Area of Responsibility to Include Iraq and Afghanistan', 2013.

The IAC in Afghanistan has had multiple causes. Much like the jihad against Soviet forces from 1979 to 1989, the conflict since 2001 is an Islamic insurgency against an 'infidel invader', currently led by Taliban in alliance with the other two major insurgent groups in the East (the Haqqani network and Hekmatyar's Hizb-i-Islami Gulbuddin (HIG)). The current conflict is also a civil war. Some view it as a war between Ghilzai Pashtuns (who form the core of the Taliban) and the victorious Northern Alliance (Durrani Pashtuns, Tajiks, Uzbecks and Hazaras). However, the Taliban appear to draw support from all Afghan ethnic groups.[44] At the local level, competition between kinship groups frames a violent competition for resources (land, water, control of routes and narcotics revenue). For example, the conflict in northern Helmand is primarily a struggle between three Pashtun tribal groups – the Alizai, Alikozai and Ishaqzai. The situation in central Helmand is less defined along tribal lines due to the complex tapestry of kinship groups, but still much of the insurgency is defined by various groups resisting abuse by the Afghan police who are locally dominated by the Noorzai tribe.[45] This illustrates the larger point that because Afghan politics is based on patrimonialism, the natural order is for government positions to be used to sustain one kinship group at the expense of others.[46] This, in turn, further challenges the simple view of the conflict as an Islamic insurgency against an elected government. Finally, the conflict also has a significant trans-border dimension. The Taliban developed in the 1990s with the support of the Pakistani intelligence service (ISI) in the two unruly provinces that border Afghanistan – Baluchistan and the North-West Frontier. The Taliban retreated across the border to Pakistan in 2002 and continue to generate forces and direct attacks against the Afghan government and the ISAF from these two provinces with the support of the ISI.[47]

Between 600,000 and 2.5 million civilians were killed in the Soviet war. The Mujahideen civil war also saw widespread indiscriminate violence against civilians; for example, around 10,000 were killed in the struggle for Kabul in 1993.[48] In contrast, civilian fatalities since 2006

---

[44] A. Giustozzi, *Koran, Kalashnikov, and Laptop: The Neo-Taliban Insurgency* (London: Hurst, 2007); A. Giustozzi, *Decoding the New Taliban* (London: Hurst, 2009).

[45] M. Martin, *An Intimate War* (London: Hurst 2014).

[46] A. Giustozzi, *The Art of Coercion* (London: Hurst, 2011).

[47] C. J. Chivers, 'Tensions Flare as GIs Take Fire Out of Pakistan', *New York Times*, 16 October 2011.

[48] R. Johnson, *The Afghan Way of War* (London: Hurst, 2011), 249, 251.

have been relatively modest. Starting from under 1,000 in 2006, direct civilian deaths from the conflict have risen by approximately 500 each year to over 2,700 in 2010. Civilian casualties caused by the ISAF attract much media attention and Afghan government criticism, but most civilians are killed by insurgent action (ranging from a low of 55 per cent in 2008 to highs of 72 per cent in 2006 and 75 per cent in 2010).[49]

Between 2006 and 2009, around 2 million Afghans were refugees (out of an estimated Afghan population of 30 million).[50] While many of these are legacy refugees from the 1980s and 1990s, the large numbers are also indicative of the general lack of security, especially in the southern and eastern provinces. In rural communities, civilians face daily threats of violence from corrupt security forces, insurgents, organized crime and other armed groups. Afghan police commonly prey on the civilian communities they are supposed to protect (though this problem has improved since 2010).[51] While the Taliban tries to win local consent, it uses violence and intimidation when it is unable to subvert tribal clans through subtle means.[52]

The overall trend in the current IAC in Afghanistan is one of steady intensification in attacks by anti-government forces since 2006. The insurgency is most active in the summer months, when the poppy crop has been harvested and before the winter begins. The Afghan NGO Safety Office (ANSO) records attacks by anti-government forces peaking at 335 in July 2006, 405 in July 2007, 634 in August 2008, 1,093 in August 2009 and 1,541 in August 2010. The armed conflict has been most intense in the south and east of Afghanistan. Insurgent attacks exceed 100 per quarter (in most cases, many times so) in the southern provinces of Helmand and Kandahar and the eastern provinces of Ghazni, Nangarhar, Paktya, Khost and Kunar. In recent years, security appears to have grown worse in the west and north of the country. A major offensive by the ISAF and the Afghan Army in the south in

---

[49] I. S. Livingston and M. O'Hanlon, 'Afghanistan Index', Brookings Institution, 30 November 2011, figures 1.31 and 1.32.

[50] See Table 1. The Afghan refugee population dramatically rises by a million in 2010. This may be due to the major ISAF and ANSF offensives in the southern provinces of Helmand and Kandahar in 2010, which may have caused local nationals to flee into Pakistan.

[51] Royal United Services Institute and Foreign Policy Research Institute, 'Reforming the Afghan National Police', Joint Report, November 2009, 8–14; T. Hardy, 'Afghan Police Corruption in Fuelling Insurgency', *Daily Telegraph*, 3 June 2010.

[52] Johnson, *The Art of Coercion*, 272–75; R. Rivera, S. Fiullah and E. Schmitt, 'Militants Turn to Death Squads in Afghanistan', *New York Times*, 28 November 2011.

2010 resulted in displacement of insurgent activity to the west, especially Farah province. From 2010, there was evidence of increased insurgent presence and activity in the north, especially along the major northern logistical route for the ISAF, which runs through Kunduz and Baghlan provinces.[53] In December 2014, the ISAF mission came to an end, but the war has not. The withdrawal of Western combat forces has given a new lease on life to the insurgency. The Taliban have come close to overrunning a number of district centres in the south and east, and by mid-2015, the Taliban had captured the suburbs of Kunduz City.[54] Understandably, throughout Afghanistan, the public perception of insecurity remains high. In the largest survey of Afghan public opinion in 2014, 34 per cent of respondents identified insecurity as the greatest problem.[55]

Colombia

The conflict in Colombia can be traced back to 'la Violencia', a ten-year undeclared civil war that emerged in 1948. After the liberal military coup d'état of 1953, the new leader, Gustavo Rojas Pinilla, appealed to all armed groups to lay down their arms. Nonetheless, over the years and fuelled by the increased repression and censorship of the Pinilla regime, left-wing groups retained their weapons and sought refuge in the mountainous regions of the country. A number of Soviet-style communists, Maoists or Castrists groups emerged in the 1960s, the most significant for the ongoing conflict being FARC. These various groups engaged in some coordinated actions against the government, particularly after the establishment of the Simon Bolivar Guerrilla Coordinating Committee in 1987. The guerrillas, particularly the FARC, generate revenue through business dealings with the Colombian narcotics industry, although they claim that this does not compromise their ideological agenda.[56]

[53] Data from the Afghanistan NGO Safety Office, 'ANSO Quarterly Report, Q1 2011', 1 January–31 March 2011, 7–10; Farrell interviews with command staff at ISAF Regional Commands (RC), RC-North (Mazar-i-Sharif), RC-West (Herat), RC-Southwest (Camp Bastion), RC-South (KAF), and RC-East (BAF), Afghanistan, October 2010; A. Giustozzi and C. Reuter, 'The Northern Front: The Afghan Insurgency Spreading beyond the Pashtuns', Briefing Paper 3, Afghan Analysts Network, 2010.

[54] J. Goldstein and T. Shah, 'Taliban Strike Crucial District in Afghanistan', New York Times, 18 June 2015; 'Season of Bloodshed', The Economist, 30 May 2015.

[55] 'Afghanistan in 2014: A Survey of the Afghan People', Asia Foundation, 2014, 24. Survey of almost 9,300 people in all thirty-four provinces.

[56] G. Leech, The FARC: The Longest Insurgency (London: Zed Books, 2011).

The emergence of guerrilla movements has been matched by the creation of self-defence paramilitary groups under an umbrella organization, the Autodefensas Unidas de Colombia (AUC), which massacred civilians suspected of being guerrilla sympathizers. The AUC was officially demobilized in December 2005, but some elements continue to pursue criminal activities, in particular, drug trafficking, and to challenge the authority of the government and the armed forces.

President Uribe's election in 2002 and subsequent re-election in 2006 showed an escalation in the government's offensive against the armed groups, a policy followed by his successor in 2010, Juan Manuel Santos, and supported by the United States. From 2000 to 2007, Colombia received more than US$5 billion in US assistance for the military and the police.[57] The human cost of this policy is reflected in the high number of deaths caused directly by the conflict, although figures show a relative decline due to the increasing success of the government's campaign against the FARC and other armed groups, falling from 3,633 in 2004 to 1,463 in 2009. Overall, the conflict is believed to have caused over 73,000 fatalities since 1963.[58] It has also produced a very large forced displacement, mostly within Colombia. In 2010, there were over 110,000 refugees and 3.5 million internally displaced persons (see Table 1). The conflict defies neat characterization. It is an insurgency, a civil war, a war against civilians and generalized violence.[59]

Tactics used by government forces, in particular, the use of antipersonnel landmines, have caused widespread civilian harm and suffering. Human Rights Watch notes that landmines leave 'hundreds of civilians maimed, blind, deaf or dead every year. Many of the survivors are among Colombia's poorest and most vulnerable citizens: peasants or others who live in impoverished rural regions, far from state authorities and hospitals, and who are often caught in the middle of the conflict.'[60] Hostage taking is common, either to deter operations by security forces ('political' hostages) or to finance the insurgency through ransoms ('economic' hostages). In 2008, the FARC alone

---

[57] 'US Aid to Colombia: 2000–2007', *Just the Facts, A Civilian's Guide to US Defense and Security Assistance to Latin America*. The level of military aid declines after 2007 but remains important.

[58] International Institute for Strategic Studies, the Armed Conflicts Database.

[59] E. P. Carbó, 'Guerra Civil? El Lenguaje Del Conflicto En Colombia', Fundación Ideas para la Paz, Bogota, 2001.

[60] Human Rights Watch, 'Maiming the People: Guerrilla Use of Antipersonnel Landmines and Other Indiscriminate Weapons in Colombia', July 2007, 1.

was believed to have held forty political hostages and about seven hundred economic hostages.[61] Use of child soldiers is also a particular problem. Guerrilla propaganda encourages some children to join insurgent forces. Insurgents also abduct around twenty-eight children per month. In total, between 11,000 and 14,000 child soldiers are currently enrolled in guerrilla groups, accounting for 30 per cent of the FARC fighting force.[62]

Guerrilla violence is matched by that of the AUC successor groups, who regularly commit massacres, killings, rape and extortion.[63] Government forces have also been accused of serious violations of human rights.[64] The overall level of violence in this conflict-afflicted country is reflected in the number of homicides, 20,000 in 2004, falling to around 16,000 in 2009. Gender-based violence is extensive, with 85 per cent of rape victims being underage. Compounding the problem is government failure to prosecute those responsible for gender violence.[65]

Although one might assume that Colombia's complex geography (mountains, rivers and hills divide the country in different regions with distinct identities) would lead to a geographical distribution of violence affecting more remote areas, the opposite can be observed. About half of the country's population lives in the triangle between and including the three cities of Bogota, Medellin and Cali. Most of the armed violence is concentrated in this area, especially the most populated cities. The more remote areas of the country are affected by armed violence primarily when the security forces undertake operations in such areas. The high rate of homicides in Bogota, Medellin and Cali can largely be attributed to wars between rival gangs over the control of drug production and trafficking routes, emphasizing the conflict's complex and multi faceted nature.

Democratic Republic of the Congo

The conflict in the DRC, a country as large as two-thirds the size of Western Europe and rich in natural resources (diamonds, oil, uranium,

---

[61] V. M. Bouvier, 'Colombia's Crossroads: The FARC and the Future of the Hostages', United States Institute of Peace Briefing, June 2008.

[62] L. S. Pagan, 'Colombia's War on Child Soldiers', *Media Global News*, 4 October 2011.

[63] Human Rights Watch, 'Paramilitaries' Heirs: The New Face of Violence in Colombia', February 2010.

[64] Amnesty International, 'Annual Report 2011: Colombia', 2011.

[65] Amnesty International, '"This Is What We Demand. Justice": Impunity for Sexual Violence against Women in Colombia's Armed Conflict', September 2011.

gold, copper, coltan and cobalt), is the widest inter-state war in African history. There are no less than three different conflicts fought simultaneously. The first is an ethnic conflict between the Hutu and the Tutsi. The victory of the Tutsi-led Rwandan Patriotic Front in 1994 caused more than a million Hutu refugees to flee Rwanda for the DRC. The refugee camps effectively became bases for the Hutu militia that carried out the Rwandan genocide, with violent and destabilizing effects on local Congolese Hutus and Tutsis. The second is an insurgency by several rebel groups. The third is a series of proxy wars involving neighbouring countries: Burundi, Rwanda and Uganda supporting the rebels, with Chad, Namibia and Zimbabwe supporting the government, each country wanting to secure its access to the DRC's natural resources.[66]

The Congolese war formally ended in January 2003 but without a political settlement. The government controls only small parts of its territory, as the regions of North and South Kivu, Ituri and Northern Katanga are mainly run by rebel movements financed by the exploitation of the DRC's natural resources. The presidential elections of 28 November 2011, contested by four of President Kabila's main opponents, illustrate once again the failures of the peace-building strategy established by the international community. The discursive frame elaborated by international actors precluded action on violence at the local level, although it is believed by scholars to be the main driver of the conflict at the national and regional levels.[67]

The human cost of the conflict is tremendous. The widely cited figure of 5.4 million deaths between 1998 and 2007 has been challenged on methodological grounds, but the numbers remain staggering. More conservative estimates claim a death toll of 3.3 million deaths in this timeframe.[68] Refugees are estimated at close to 500,000 with another 1.7 million internally displaced persons. Most of those displaced within the country are fleeing the provinces of North and South Kivu bordering Rwanda, where civilians have been the targets of deliberate attacks perpetrated by government forces and non-government armed groups:

---

[66] J. Stearns, *Dancing in the Glory of Monsters: The Collapse of the Congo and the Great War of Africa* (New York: Public Affairs Press, 2011); G. Prunier, *Africa's World War: Congo, the Rwandan Genocide, and the Making of a Continental Catastrophe* (Oxford University Press, 2011).

[67] S. Autesserre, *The Trouble with the Congo: Local Violence and the Failure of International Peacebuilding* (Cambridge University Press, 2010).

[68] T. Gambino, 'Democratic Republic of the Congo', WDR Report 2011 Background Case Study, World Bank, 2 March 2011.

the number of IDPs fleeing North and South Kivu alone adds up to more than a million. Most violent assaults are committed in North and South Kivu, as well as the Ituri and North Katanga regions. Unsurprisingly, these areas are border regions, remote from the control of the central power (the distance between Kinshasa and South Kivu is approximately 1,000 km) and subject to the influence of neighbours having a vested interest in keeping these regions destabilized. The emerging picture is one of an unsettled and violent periphery (the northern and eastern parts of the country) in which the government cannot hold control.

Armed groups engage in many forms of violence to exert social control, including homicide, robbery, forced labour, torture and rape.[69] Sexual violence is particularly widespread. Two in five women and one in four men report they have been victims of sexual violence in the eastern region of the country.[70] Rape is used by government forces and rebel groups as a tool of war in order to subdue foes and civilians.[71] In addition, a recent study has found that rapes carried out by civilians increased seventeen-fold between 2004 and 2008, suggesting a gradual brutalization of the conflict.[72] The United Nations estimates that 200,000 women and girls have been assaulted between 1997 and 2009, with more than 18,000 cases reported between January and September 2008 alone.[73]

The issue of re-integration of child soldiers is proving especially challenging in the DRC. Around 30,000 children, one-third of them girls, have been turned into soldiers by the different armed groups and the army. The DRC has a demobilization programme, but it is difficult for a brainwashed and traumatized generation to return to a life without violence. A disturbing 75 per cent of the children socialized into military service during the war continue to associate it with positive emotions (thrill, bloodlust and power) and hence are at risk of re-enrolment.[74] The brutalization of Congolese young people, and society in general, is

---

[69] Human Rights Watch, 'Always on the Run: The Vicious Cycle of Displacement in Eastern Congo', 14 September 2010.

[70] L. Melhado, 'Rates of Sexual Violence Are High in Democratic Republic of the Congo', *International Perspectives on Sexual and Reproductive Health* 36 (2010), 210.

[71] Human Rights Watch, 'Soldiers who Rape, Commanders who Condone', July 2009.

[72] Harvard Humanitarian Initiative with support from Oxfam America, '"Now, The World Is without Me": An Investigation of Sexual Violence in Eastern Democratic Republic of Congo', April 2010.

[73] United Nations Population Fund, 'Secretary-General Calls Attention to Scourge of Sexual Violence in DRC', 1 March 2009.

[74] K. Palitza, 'Rehabilitating Former Child Soldiers Who "Liked Killing"', IPS News Service, 2 November 2011.

almost certainly a major contributing factor to the very high number of homicides; between 2004 and 2009, over 100,000 people were murdered in non-conflict violence in the DRC (see Table 2). Thus, the homicide and rape figures suggest that the risk to civilians from violence remains exceptionally high even after the formal end of the war in 2003.

Mexico

For over a decade, Mexico has experienced a level of armed violence that is normally associated with IAC. In this case, however, the conflict is driven purely by profit, as rival criminal organizations fight to control the trade in drugs and people across the border into the United States. During the 1980s and 1990s, the demise of the Colombian drug cartels created space for an expansion and diversification of organized crime in Mexico. The conflict between criminal groups remained in the 1990s, but armed violence grew to alarming levels in the 2000s.

With the election of President Vicente Fox in 2000, Mexico adopted a more vigorous approach to tackling organized crime. In fact, 1,500 soldiers and federal police were deployed in 2005 into seven of Mexico's thirty-one states – Baja California, Chihuahua, Nuevo León, Tamaulipas, Quintana Roo, Sinaloa and Veracruz – and into the Federal District. However, in the same year, the Gulf and Sinaloa cartels violently clashed over control of the city of Nuevo Laredo in Tamaulipas, causing an estimated 110 fatalities over the January–August 2005 period alone.[75] Fox was criticized for underestimating the security threat posed by the cartels. His successor, Felipe Calderón, initiated an even more aggressive approach upon his election as president in December 2006. Calderón handed the job over to the military, and 40,000 soldiers were deployed in five states: Baja California, Sinoloa, Tamaulipas and Nuevo León, as before, and Michoacán. In February 2007, Calderón increased the salaries of rank-and-file soldiers by 46 per cent and undertook a number of other measures to tackle corruption in the security forces and improve co-operation with the United States. Civilians have borne the brunt of this more aggressive approach, with the number of violent deaths rising from over 10,000 in 2007 to around 13,500 in 2008 and a new high of 16,500 in 2009 (see Table 2).[76]

[75] C. Marshall, 'Gang Wars Plague Mexican Drugs Hub', *BBC News*, 14 August 2005.
[76] For an historical overview of the conflict and the evolution of Mexican cartels, see J. Langton, *Gangland: The Rise of the Mexican Drug Cartels from El Paso to Vancouver* (London: Wiley, 2011).

The conflict has been called a 'mosaic cartel war'. As Kan explains, 'there are several conflicts occurring at once that blend into each other. There is the conflict of cartels among each other, the conflict within cartels, cartels against the Mexican state, cartels and gangs against the Mexican people and gangs versus gangs.'[77] This is a key aspect of the conflict: although the cartels furnish some social services in the areas they control, their ultimate objective is not to seize power, despite claims by the government to the contrary.[78] As they do not advance any political agenda, the cartels do not attract popular support; polls constantly show a strong popular support for the government's violent anti-drug policy.[79] The other defining aspect is the quality and strength of the military equipment the cartels use. According to one reputable estimate, the cartels have 100,000 foot soldiers facing a 130,000 strong Mexican army.[80] Cartel mercenaries deploy advanced equipment (assault rifles, Kevlar helmets, body armour, grenade launchers, etc.) and demonstrate a mastery of advanced infantry tactics (gun battles, raids, ambush, blockades, etc.). Recently, they deployed light armoured vehicles, dubbed as 'narco-tanks' (in fact, trucks enhanced with armour plating and gun ports), giving them a tactical advantage over dismounted forces such as state and federal police.[81] Finally, the cartels have also been able to engage in 'shaping' operations, notably by assuring a presence on social media such as Twitter and Facebook.[82]

Civilians have been caught in the middle of this armed violence and suffered terribly for it. The cartels use extreme violence to impose their will, broadcasting executions on YouTube,[83] targeting citizens to undermine the government's authority (including attacks on nightclubs or crowded places, kidnapping and death threats) and torturing and killing persons on their way from Latin America or Mexico to the United States who refused to join their organizations.[84] The militarization of the counter-narcotics operations is also problematic. Intended

---

[77] P. R. Kan, 'Mexico: A Mosaic Cartel War', *Small Wars Journal*, 12 June 2011.

[78] 'Mexican Cartels Move Beyond Drugs, Seek Domination', *MSNBC News*, 4 August 2010.

[79] R. Wike, 'Mexicans Continue Support for Drug War', Pew Research Center, 12 August 2010.

[80] International Institute for Strategic Studies, Armed Conflict Database.

[81] J. P. Sullivan and A. Elkus, 'Narco-Armor in Mexico', *Small Wars Journal*, 14 July 2011.

[82] J. D. Goodman, 'In Mexico, Social Media Become a Battleground in the Drug War', *New York Times*, 15 September 2011.

[83] M. Roig-Franzia, 'Mexican Drug Cartels Leave a Bloody Trail on YouTube', *Washington Post*, 9 April 2007.

[84] 'Crossing Continents, Murder, Migration and Mexico', *BBC Radio 4*, 11 August 2011.

as a response to the violence waged by the cartels, the 'war' initiated by Calderón has been undermined by accusations of massive human rights violations including torture, enforced disappearances and extra-judicial killings. There have been 4,803 complaints reported between 2007 and 2010, compared to the 691 cases registered between 2003 and 2006.[85]

The violence has not been evenly distributed across Mexico. From 2004 to 2009, Mexico had an average annual homicide rate of 11.5 per 100,000, which is three times lower than that of South Africa. However, some of Mexico's states have experienced extremely high levels of violence. The average homicide rate is worst in Chihuahua, at 108 per 100,000. Generally, the violence is concentrated in the half dozen or so states – including Chihuahua, Sonora and Baja California on the US border and Sinaloa and Guerrero on the coast – where the cartels are based. Gender-based violence is also concentrated in these states. The national femicide rate in 2009 was 3.5 per 100,000. But the rate was many times higher in Chihuahua (13.1), Baja California (10.1) and Guerrero (10.1). Violence can and does spread, however. States not affected by violence one year can experience high levels the next. For example, 1,209 civilians were killed by armed violence in Tamaulipas in 2010, whereas only ninety were killed the year before.[86] In late 2011 and early 2012, the violence spread into cities that were previously considered safe – Guadalajara, Veracruz and Mexico City itself.[87] The level of violence, especially in northwest Mexico, produces modest levels of 'narco-refugees'.[88] But the general concentration of violence that leaves many parts of the country largely free from armed violence, combined with measures by US authorities to prevent illegal entry into the United States, has meant that most of those forcibly displaced by armed violence have relocated within Mexico. Estimates of the number of internally displaced persons range between 120,000 and 750,000.[89]

---

[85] Human Rights Watch, 'Neither Rights nor Security: Killings, Torture and Disappearances in Mexico's "War on Drugs"', November 2011.

[86] Geneva Declaration Secretariat, Global Burden of Armed Violence 2011, 30–1, 121.

[87] R. C. Archibold, 'Mexico's Drug War Bloodies Areas Thought Safe', New York Times, 18 January 2012.

[88] P. R. Kan, Mexico's 'Narco-Refugees': The Looming Challenge for US National Security (Carisle, PA: Strategic Studies Institute, US Army War College, 2011).

[89] Lower estimate from the Internal Displacement Monitoring Centre. Higher estimate from the International Institute for Strategic Studies, Armed Conflict Database.

Somalia

The current period of conflict in Somalia began with armed opposition to the brutal regime of Siad Barre in 1986, escalating to full-scale civil war following Barre's fall from power in 1991. Over the past two decades, the conflict has involved inter-clan warfare, territorial separatism (Somaliland and Puntland), failed military interventions by US- and UN-led missions (1992–1995), political and military involvement of regional actors (Ethiopia and Kenya), fears of gradual Islamist radicalization and links with terrorist networks such as Al-Qaeda, famines and the spread of piracy in the Gulf of Aden.[90]

The conflict has been characterized by multiple forms of armed violence, ranging from intimate to large-scale military operations, and has involved a wide range of military actors including criminal gangs, Islamic terrorists, tribal militias, the armed forces of regional powers and international military forces. Tribal militias display a range of military capabilities, using light weapons (assault rifles, rocket-propelled grenades and mortars) and infantry tactics, 'technicals' (heavy machine guns on pickup trucks), as well as insurgent tactics and IEDs. The conflict since 2004 has centred on a struggle between a secular tribal grouping, the Transitional Federated Government (TFG) and various Islamic groups. The rise of the Islamic Courts Union (ICU), an extreme Islamic grouping which captured the Somali capital, Mogadishu, in June 2006, led to Ethiopian military intervention to back the TFG. The United States also conducted airstrikes against ICU strongholds in 2007. Ethiopian forces withdrew in December 2008, following military defeat of the ICU. Islamic groups, especially the al-Shabaab militia, continued to wage a guerrilla war against the TFG. Since 2009, TFG forces have been supported by the African Union Mission in Somalia (AMISOM) mostly comprising troops from Uganda and Burundi with some armoured vehicles and helicopters. Regional actors continue to intervene militarily in the Somali conflict. In October 2011, Kenya sent forces into Somalia in pursuit of al-Shabaab rebels. While this intervention was not opposed by the TFG, there may have been territorial ambition behind Kenya's military deployment into Somalia.[91] There are also reports that Ethiopia sent its army back into Somalia in November 2011.[92]

---

[90] Space constraints prevent a fuller treatment of this complex conflict. For an introduction, see A. A. Elmi, *Understanding the Somalia Conflagration: Identity, Political Islam and Peacebuilding* (London: Pluto Press, 2010).

[91] J.-P. Rémy, 'La Somalie, Théâtre des Ambitions Kenyanes', *Le Monde*, 3 November 2011.

[92] J. Gettleman, 'Ethiopian Troops Said to Enter Somalia, Opening New Front Against Militants', *New York Times*, 20 November 2011.

For the most part, the armed conflict has been concentrated in central and southern Somalia, especially around Mogadishu and the other two main population centres, the town of Baidoa in central Somali and the southern port of Kismayu. The Islamic al-Shabaab militia presence in southern Somalia has limited humanitarian access because of the suspicion of the militias towards Western aid.[93] This has devastating implications in a country where half the population, around 3 million people, depend on aid for survival. Both sides, the TFG and the Islamic militias, have engaged in disproportionate indiscriminate use of armed force with regard for civilian populations. Al-Shabaab have also been responsible for large-scale human rights violations in their enforcement of strict *sharia* law, including amputations, executions and torture.[94] In contrast, northern Somalia is relatively peaceful. The secessionist state of Somaliland in north-west Somalia and the non-secessionist autonomous state of Puntland in north-east Somalia both have functioning governments that are able to collect taxes, provide basic services and maintain good public security.[95]

A more recent problem has been rising Somali piracy in the Gulf of Aden. The International Maritime Bureau reports 213 attacks by Somali pirates in 2010, which has quadrupled since 2007. Somali pirates are responsible for almost half (48 per cent) of all attempted attacks against shipping worldwide and for 25 per cent of all successful attacks.[96] In 2010, Somalia pirates seized 1,181 hostages.[97] This level of violence is not directly generated by the power struggles in Mogadishu but seems to be more economically driven. Intelligence reports seem to suggest that the pirates are now being subsidized by foreign-based criminal groups to conduct their illicit activities, showing evidence of 'business-type' integrated structures.[98]

---

[93] M. Tran, 'Relief Groups Fear for Aid Efforts in Somalia as Military Tension Rises', *The Guardian*, 27 October 2007.

[94] Human Rights Watch, 'Harsh War, Harsh Peace, Abuses by al-Shabaab, the Transitional Federal Government, and AMISOM in Somalia', April 2010.

[95] K. Menkhaus, 'Governance without Government in Somalia: Spoilers, State-Building and the Politics of Coping', *International Security* 31 (2006–7), 83, 91–3.

[96] Geneva Declaration Secretariat, *Global Burden of Armed Violence 2011*, 16.

[97] 'Pirates Seized Record 1,181 Hostages in 2010 – Report', *BBC News Africa*, 18 January 2011.

[98] Major-General Buster Howes, OBE, Operation Commander EU NAVFOR, 'Making Counter-Piracy Operations Effective', speech to the International Institute for Strategic Studies, 5 July 2011.

The effects on civilian populations of armed conflict are tremendous. All parties have been accused of war crimes during the conflict, including indiscriminate attacks on civilians, unlawful killings and recruitment of child soldiers.[99] The conflict is believed to have caused over 391,000 casualties since 1991.[100] It produced over 750,000 refugees in 2010 and displaced almost 1.5 million within the country. Refugees flee to Kenya en masse, mostly to end up in a camp at Dadaab, the world's largest refugee camp, with 460,000 people, where they are vulnerable to human rights abuses at the hands of Kenyan security forces.[101] The situation for internally displaced people is no better as the conflict hinders aid organizations from providing humanitarian relief.[102]

Sri Lanka

Once a British colony, Sri Lanka acquired independence in 1948 and adopted a democratic political system. The population is split between a predominantly Buddhist Sinhalese majority (around 74 per cent) and a Hindu Tamil minority (around 8 per cent comprising native and Indian-origin Tamils), with smaller Moors (predominantly Muslim) communities.[103] After the declaration of Sinhalese as the country's official language in 1956, the Tamil minority feared that the state would abuse their communal rights, and driven by ethnic violence and institutionalized anti-Tamil bias in government and education, Tamil political leaders began to favour separatism by the mid-1970s. The Liberation Tigers of Tamil Eelam (LTTE) emerged as the main Tamil militant group and started to engage armed actions against the government in 1983. Despite several attempts by external parties (including India and Norway) to broker peace agreements, the conflict raged until the government's military victory in 2009. While this might appear as an endgame to the conflict, critics notice that the Tamil's

---

[99] Human Rights Watch, "'You Don't Know Who to Blame", War Crimes in Somalia', August 2011.

[100] International Institute for Strategic Studies, Armed Conflict Database.

[101] Human Rights Watch, "'Welcome to Kenya", Police Abuses of Somali Refugees', 17 June 2010.

[102] L. Ford, 'Somalia Famine Eases but Situation Is Still "Fragile"', *The Guardian*, 18 November 2011.

[103] 'Sri Lanka', *CIA World Factbook*, based on data from November 2011.

grievances have not been addressed, and hence, the potential exists for the conflict to re-ignite.[104]

The conflict was primarily characterized by LTTE using a mix of guerrilla and regular warfare to defend territory in northern and eastern parts of Sri Lanka and suicide terrorism to threaten the capital, Colombo, and other population centres controlled by the government. One significant terrorist attack happened every year in Colombo between 1996 and 2002.[105] The LTTE also launched occasional spectacular actions, including an air attack on Colombo in February 2009.[106] The LTTE was well known for employing women[107] and child soldiers.[108] Sri Lanka is an almost textbook example of the 'hybrid warfare' concept, with a politically motivated opponent of the central government using a combination of regular and irregular military means.

Both sides were ruthless in this war. The LTTE targeted moderate Tamils who would not agree with its strategy of no-holds-barred military action against the government.[109] Equally, the government has repeatedly been accused of human rights violations during its military actions against the LTTE, notably of enforced disappearances, torture, arbitrary arrests and extra-judicial executions.[110] The number of direct-conflict deaths rose sharply in the closing years, rising from 4,500 in 2007 to 11,144 in 2008 and 15,565 in 2009, as government forces pursued a military solution. During the very last phase of the conflict, the government was accused of intentionally shelling civilians and hospitals.[111] In total, the conflict is estimated to have caused over 90,000 combatant and civilian fatalities since 1983.[112]

---

[104] For an overview of the conflict that also involves Sinhalese Maoist groups, see A. Bandarage, *The Separatist Conflict in Sri Lanka: Terrorism, Ethnicity, Political Economy* (Oxon, UK: Routledge, 2009).

[105] Col. R. Hariharan (retd.), 'Sri Lanka, How Strong Are the Tigers?', South Asia Analysis Group, n. 297, 28 February 2006.

[106] A. Jones, 'Tamil Tigers Attack Colombo with Aircrafts', *The Guardian*, 21 February 2009.

[107] A. S. O'Connor, 'Lions, Tigers, and Freedom Birds: How and Why the Liberation Tigers of Tamil Eelam Employs Women', *Terrorism and Political Violence* 17 (2007), 43–63.

[108] Human Rights Watch, 'Living in Fear: Child Soldiers and the Tamil Tigers in Sri Lanka', November 2004.

[109] M. R. N. Swamy, *The Tiger Vanquished: LTTE's Story* (London: Sage, 2010).

[110] Human Rights Watch, 'Return to War: Human Rights under Siege', 5 August 2007.

[111] International Crisis Group, 'War Crimes in Sri Lanka, Asia Report no. 191', 17 May 2010.

[112] International Institute for Strategic Studies, Armed Conflict Database.

The intensity of the conflict is reflected in the number of refugees or internally displaced persons, which numbered, respectively, 140,000 and over 270,000 in 2010 (see Table 1). The 1.5 million landmines distributed in the country are proving to be a major obstacle to 'resettlement, livelihoods, food security and recovery'.[113] Another legacy of the war is increased gender inequality. The militarization of Sinhalese society led to a large increase in sex workers to service the Sri Lankan armed forces, yet sex workers continue to be classified as criminals in Sri Lanka. The LTTE encouraged paternalistic behaviours and sexual surveillance in the Tamil community, both as an operational security measure and as a way to promote its perceived national culture. The cumulative impact of these measures has been most detrimental to the empowerment of Sri Lankan women.[114] The war also had a disruptive effect on the economy, as shown by the average 0.9 per cent annual growth over the 2000–9 period, and mostly affected the populations of the north and east, as it 'interrupted productive activities there, pervasively damaged the economic and social infrastructure, deterred private sector investment, discouraged tourism and contributed to an exodus of qualified professionals'.[115]

Conclusions

The quantitative data on armed conflict since 1990 suggest that conflict occurrence is decreasing, as are the effects of conflict on civilians. Similarly, some scholars argue that war is on an historical trajectory of decline.[116] In this chapter we have presented a different picture. The character of armed conflict has evolved to encompass a broader range of violent actors and activity. The traditional view of war as an activity undertaken by organized armed groups for political purposes no longer captures the complex reality of armed conflict. Armed violence is

---

[113] United Nations Office for the Coordination of Humanitarian Affairs, 'Sri Lanka', based on data from 2011.

[114] Y. Tambiah, 'Turncoat Bodies: Sexuality and Sex Work under Militarization in Sri Lanka', *Gender and Society* 19 (2005), 243–61.

[115] UNDP, 'Sri Lanka Country Assessment: The Asia-Pacific Rights and Justice Initiative', 25 August 2010, 9–10.

[116] S. Pinker, *The Better Angels of Our Nature: The Decline of Violence in History and Its Causes* (London: Allen Lane, 2011); M. Mandlebaum, 'Is Major War Obsolete?', *Survival* 40 (1998–9), 20–6; J. Mueller, *Retreat from Doomsday: The Obsolence of Major War* (New York: Basic Books, 1989); Mueller, The Remnants of War.

used for political, economic and personal gain. Alongside the more traditional armed actors such as state-based security forces and organized insurgents are criminal gangs, trans-national terrorists, pirates, various militia and private security contractors. Finally, contemporary conflict combines political, criminal and interpersonal violence. As noted in the Introduction, these factors have implications for understanding displacement and in the determination of who should receive international protection.

The case studies illustrate that IAC has many causes. In two cases, we can see a dominant conflict driver – Tamil grievance in the case of Sri Lanka and criminal greed in the case of Mexico. The others all display a mix of political and economic conflict drivers. Afghanistan, Colombia, the DRC and Somalia all demonstrate typical war economies, where the conflict is fuelled by the exploitation of natural resources, vulnerable populations and the ready availability of small arms. While the FARC and the Taliban leadership have clear political agendas, groups within each organization use the armed cause to advance economic interests. Somalia combines politically, religiously and economically motivated armed violence.

All six case studies illustrate the problem of IACs that just rumble on. The Colombia IAC started over sixty years ago. The IACs in Somalia and Sri Lanka both started in the mid-1980s. Defeat of the major rebel alliance in Somalia in late 2008 (the ICU) did little to end the conflict. In contrast, defeat of the LTTE in Sri Lanka does appear to have temporarily ended the conflict. But without a political resolution of Tamil grievances, the chances of the conflict re-starting must be high. In many cases, countries have endured a series of IACs that have blurred into one another. The Congolese war comprised an ethnic conflict between Hutus and Tutsis from neighbouring Rwanda that spilled into the DRC, insurgency by a number of rebel groups and a regional war that drew in six neighbouring states. Afghanistan has experienced a series of conflicts – including the Soviet war, the Mujahideen civil war and the current war against the Taliban – with only a few brief interludes of relative peace over the past thirty years.

The case studies also reveal the many modes of violence in contemporary IAC. The conflicts in Afghanistan, the DRC, Somalia and Sri Lanka have all involved major combat operations by state militaries, guerrilla warfare by insurgent groups, terrorist attacks and armed violence by criminal groups. Colombia and Mexico both have involved the use of the army to suppress organized violent crime. All cases have involved extensive use of children by armed groups.[117]

We have argued that a narrow focus on conflict deaths fails to capture the real effects of IAC on civilian populations. Certainly, the number of directly caused civilian deaths in Afghanistan, the DRC and Somalia indicates a general downward trend. The conflicts in each country annually killed civilians in the tens of thousands in the 1990s. Direct-conflict deaths in each country are in the low thousands for 2004–9. However, when the wider effects of armed conflict in producing violence in society are examined, the picture becomes more alarming.[118]

Violent deaths in conflict and generalized violence present the tip of the iceberg in terms of the effects of conflict on civilian populations. We noted in our literature survey that violence is used against civilians for political, economic and criminal purposes, producing physical and psychological harm below the threshold of death. Reports indicate extensive and serious human rights abuses by all sides in the conflicts in Colombia, the DRC, Somalia and Sri Lanka and by insurgents in Afghanistan and organized crime in Mexico. Gender-based violence has also been endemic in Colombia, the DRC, Sri Lanka and some parts of Mexico. The situation has been especially chronic in the DRC.

Excess deaths are caused indirectly by the conflict through poverty, famine, population displacement and disease, yet the causal links – especially direction of causation – are difficult to untangle. Armed conflict additionally hinders economic development, negatively affects personal income and community health care and worsens population displacement's effects on disease. But given the iterative cycle of conflict and chronic underdevelopment, it is extremely difficult to demonstrate conclusively in any case that conflict was the primary cause of deaths through famine and disease.[119]

---

[117] E. Dickinson, 'Child Soldiers in the Mexican Drug War', UN dispatch, 20 June 2011.

[118] IAC also increases the risk of homicide as a consequence of conflict trauma, greater societal tolerance of violence and the wide availability of guns. Geneva Declaration Secretariat, Global Burden of Armed Violence 2011, 70.

[119] This problem was noted by the UK Asylum and Immigration Tribunal (AIT) in the GS (Afghanistan) case in 2009. For discussion on this and the flaw in the AIT reasoning, see Lambert and Farrell, 'The Changing Character of Armed Conflict'.

Given space constraints, we have not been able to process trace causation between conflict, development and excess civilian deaths in our case studies. However, the quantitative data do suggest that in countries where state fragility is high (due to social and economic pressures and government corruption) and where poverty is high, armed conflict is likely to generate more excess deaths through famine and disease (especially among young children) than in countries that are stable and have less poverty (see Table 3). In failing states, there is less social resilience by the state and by communities to the disruption caused by armed conflict. Underdeveloped and fragile states are also far more likely to experience a repetitive cycle of conflict. This underlines the imperative to tackle economic and state under development in order to enable the vulnerable civilian populations of such states to escape the 'conflict trap'.[120]

Table 1 *Population Displacement, 2006–2010 (per 1,000 population)*

Country		2006	2007	2008	2009	2010
Afghanistan	Refugees	2,107	1,910	1,818	1,906	3,055
	IDPs	129	154	231	297	352
Colombia	Refugees	73	70	77	104	113
	IDPs	3,000	3,000	3,000	3,303	3,672
DRC	Refugees	401	370	368	455	476
	IDPs	1,075	1,318	1,460	2,053	1,721
Mexico	Refugees	3	5	6	6	7
	IDPs	No data	No data	No data	No data	120–750[a]
Somalia	Refugees	464	455	559	678	770
	IDPs	400	1,000	1,277	1,551	1,465
Sri Lanka	Refugees	117	135	138	146	141
	IDPs	469	459	505	435	274

[a] See note 81.

Source: UNHCR Statistical Population Database, available at: www.unhcr.org /pages/49c3646c4d6.html.

[120] Collier, The Bottom Billion, 17–37.

Table 2 *Annual Violence Deaths, 2004–2009*

Country	Category	2004	2005	2006	2007	2008	2009
Afghanistan	Homicide	813	813	813	707	707	707
	Direct-conflict deaths	917	1,000	4,000	7,109	6,312	6,938
	Total violent deaths	1,730	1,813	4,813	7,816	7,019	7,645
Colombia	Homicide	20,210	18,111	17,479	17,198	16,140	15,817
	Direct-conflict deaths	3,633	3,358	2,168	3,271	1,670	1,463
	Total violent deaths	23,843	21,469	19,647	20,469	17,810	17,280
DRC	Homicide	20,061	20,061	20,061	13,558	13,558	13,558
	Direct-conflict deaths	3,500	3,750	746	1,351	1,500	2,828
	Total violent deaths	23,561	23,811	20,807	14,909	15,058	16,386
Mexico	Homicide	11,799	11,405	11,948	10,417	13,425	16,426
	Direct-conflict deaths	38	180	65	0	0	0
	Total violent deaths	11,837	11,585	12,013	10,417	13,425	16,426
Somalia	Homicide	265	265	265	138	138	138
	Direct-conflict deaths	760	285	879	6,500	3,000	1,000
	Total violent deaths	1,025	550	1,144	6,638	3,138	1,138
Sri Lanka	Homicide	1,377	1,221	2,045	1,663	1,488	958
	Direct-conflict deaths	109	330	4,126	4,500	11,144	15,565
	Total violent deaths	1,486	1,551	6,171	6,163	12,632	16,523

Note: 'Direct-conflict deaths' include combatants and civilians.
Source: The Global Burden of Armed Violence Project Team.

Table 3 *Socio-Economic Data on Case Studies*

Case study	Failed-states index	Population millions	GNI per capita, US$	Child malnutrition, per cent of under age 5	Under age 5 deaths per 1,000
Afghanistan	7	34.5	290	32.9	199
Colombia	44	46.2	5,510	5.1	19
Congo, DR	4	65.9	180	28.2	199
Mexico	94	113.4	8,930	3.4	85
Somalia	1	9.3	150	32.8	180
Sri Lanka	29	20.8	2,240	21.1	15

Sources: World Bank, *World Development Report 2011*, tables 1, 2, and 3, 344–9; World Bank Country Profiles, available at http://data.worldbank.org/country.

PART II

Refugee Status under Global and Regional
Instruments

2

The 1951 Refugee Convention and the Protection of People Fleeing Armed Conflict and Other Situations of Violence

VANESSA HOLZER[*]

Introduction

Armed conflicts and other situations of violence have long been major reasons for forced displacements across borders. Often fought for ethnic, political or religious reasons,[1] conflicts have shaped the development of international refugee law in the early and mid-twentieth century. Many recent conflicts have seen mass exoduses triggered by widespread violence and by a variety of political, psychological and economic measures aimed at intimidating certain groups. Often, violence is deliberately directed against civilians,[2] and more specifically, sexual violence has frequently been employed as a weapon of warfare.[3] There is nothing in the wording of the refugee definition contained in Article 1A(2) of the 1951 Convention Relating to the Status of Refugees ('1951 refugee definition'),[4] or in the remainder of the 1951 Convention itself, that

---

[*] I thank Jessica Anderson, Michael Barutciski, Kathleen Claussen, Tim Howe, Ian Kysel, Tim McLellan, Mark von Sternberg and Hugo Storey for their advice and support. Many thanks are also due to Alice Edwards, Cornelis Wouters and various other members of the UNHCR staff who provided invaluable assistance. Any errors are my own.

[1] See M. Kaldor, *New and Old Wars*, 2nd edn. (Cambridge, UK: Polity Press, 2006), 7. For a comprehensive analysis that scrutinizes Kaldor's and other arguments, see T. Farrell and O. Schmitt, 'The Causes, Character and Conduct of Armed Conflict, and the Effects of on Civilian Populations, 1990–2010', *Legal and Protection Policy Research Series*, 2012. All URLs last accessed on 25 February 2013.

[2] See UN Secretary General, 'Report of the Secretary General to the Security Council on the Protection of Civilians in Armed Conflict', 8 September 1999, UN Doc. S/1999/957, para. 12.

[3] See UNHCR ExCom, 'Conclusion No. 73 (XLIV)', 1993, UN Doc. A/47/12/Add.1, first preamble recital.

[4] Convention Relating to the Status of Refugees (adopted 28 July 1951, entered into force 22 April 1954), 189 UNTS 137 ('1951 Convention'). Throughout this chapter, references to

would hinder its application to armed conflict and other situations of violence.[5]

Nonetheless, armed conflicts and other situations of violence pose a challenge for the interpretation and application of the 1951 Convention and its 1967 Protocol. This chapter explores the meaning and scope of the 1951 refugee definition in regards to refugee protection claims of individuals who have fled armed conflict and other situations of violence and identifies conflicting trends in international refugee law and practice concerning such claims. On the one hand, it has been generally accepted by a number of states,[6] UNHCR[7] and scholars[8] that people fleeing armed

the 1951 Convention relate to this convention as modified by its Protocol Relating to the Status of Refugees (entered into force 4 October 1967), 606 UNTS 267 ('1967 Protocol') or to only the 1967 Protocol with respect to states that ratified the 1967 Protocol but not the 1951 Convention. Article 1A(2) of the 1951 Convention defines a 'refugee' as a person who 'owing to well-founded fear of being persecuted for reasons of race, religion, nationality, membership of a particular social group or political opinion, is outside the country of his [or her] nationality and is unable or, owing to such fear, is unwilling to avail himself [or herself] of the protection of that country; or who, not having a nationality and being outside the country of his [or her] former habitual residence as a result of such events, is unable or, owing to such fear, is unwilling to return to it.'

[5] See UNHCR, 'Information Note on Article 1 of the 1951 Convention', 1995. For a comprehensive analysis, see also V. Holzer, *Refugees from Armed Conflict: The 1951 Refugee Convention and International Humanitarian Law* (Cambridge, UK: Intersentia, 2015).

[6] See e.g. Immigration and Refugee Board of Canada, 'Civilian Non-Combatants Fearing Persecution in Civil War Situations: Guidelines Issued by the Chairperson Pursuant to Section s65(3) of the Immigration Act', 1996; UK Border Agency, 'Considering the Protection (Asylum) Claim and Assessing Credibility', 2011, 25; *Minister for Immigration and Multicultural Affairs* v. *Haji Ibrahim*, [2000] HCA 55 (Australia), para. 141, per Gummow J; Federal Administrative Court (*Bundesverwaltungsgericht*), BVerwG 1 C 21.04 (1 November 2005) (Germany), para. 24; Council of the European Union, 'Joint Position Defined by the Council on the Basis of Article K.3 of the Treaty on European Union on the Harmonized Application of the Definition of the Term "Refugee" in Article 1 of the Geneva Convention of 28 July 1951 Relating to the Status of Refugees (Annex 1)', 1996, para. 6; *Refugee Appeal No 76551*, [2010] NZRSAA 103 (21 September 2010) (New Zealand), para. 66; *Refugee Appeal No. 75653*, [2006] NZRSAA 59 (23 March 2006) (New Zealand), para. 77; *Mohamed* v. *Ashcroft*, 396 F.3d 999, 1006 (8th Cir. 2005) (US).

[7] See UNHCR, 'Note on International Protection', 1 September 1995, UN Doc. A/AC.96/850, para. 11; UNHCR, 'Interpreting Article 1 of the 1951 Convention Relating to the Status of Refugees', 2001. Various UNHCR eligibility guidelines confirm this view. Suffice it to point as an example to UNHCR, 'Eligibility Guidelines for Assessing the International Protection Needs of Asylum-Seekers from Afghanistan', 2009, 12–13.

[8] There are various refugee law scholars expressing this view, including W. Kälin, 'Refugees and Civil Wars: Only a Matter of Interpretation?', *IJRL* 3(3) (1991), 435–51; H. Storey and R. Wallace, 'War and Peace in Refugee Law Jurisprudence', *AJIL* 95 (2001), 349–63; M. R. von Sternberg, *The Grounds of Refugee Protection in the Context of International Human Rights and Humanitarian Law: Canadian and United States Case Law Compared*

conflict and other situations of violence may qualify as 1951 Convention refugees, though the mere fact of having fled from conflict and violence does not per se suffice.

On the other hand, an armed conflict and other situations of violence in the country of origin often prompt national decision-makers to apply a more restrictive interpretation of the 1951 refugee definition.[9] Some decision-makers have even understood such a situation as precluding the finding of a well-founded fear of being persecuted for any of the five 1951 Convention grounds.[10] The stark variations in refugee recognition rates at first instance for Afghan, Somali and Iraqi claimants in various European states indicate significant divergences in the interpretation of the refugee definition with regard to refugee claims based on armed conflict and other situations of violence.[11]

This chapter argues that the 1951 Convention is a relevant tool for the protection of people who have fled armed conflict and other situations of violence in their countries of origin. While having fled from such situations does not in and of itself substantiate a claim to refugee status under the 1951 Convention, the wording of the 1951 refugee definition, the object and purpose of the 1951 Convention and its historical background warrant an inclusive interpretation regarding refugee protection claims arising out of armed conflict and other situations of violence.

This chapter proceeds in three steps. It scrutinizes the historical evolution of international refugee law in light of forced displacement caused by armed conflict and other situations of violence. Next, the interpretation of the refugee definition in the context of armed conflict

(The Hague: Martinus Nijhoff, 2002), 5; and N. Markard, *Kriegsflüchtlinge. Gewalt gegen Zivilpersonen in bewaffneten Konflikten als Herausforderung für das Flüchtlingsrecht und den subsidiären Schutz* (Tübingen: Mohr Siebeck, 2012).

[9] See e.g. *Adan* v. *Secretary of State for the Home Department*, [1998] 2 WLR 702 (UK), per Lord Slynn of Hadley.

[10] See G. S. Goodwin-Gill and J. McAdam, *The Refugee in International Law*, 3rd edn. (Oxford University Press, 2007), 126. See also UNHCR and ICTR, 'Summary Conclusions, Expert Meeting on Complementarities between International Refugee Law, International Criminal Law and International Human Rights Law', Arusha, Tanzania, 11–13 April 2011, para. 25; UNHCR, 'Note on International Protection', 7 September 1994, UN Doc. A/AC.96/830, para. 22.

[11] See UNHCR, 'Safe at Last? Law and Practice in Selected Member States with Respect to Asylum-Seekers Fleeing Indiscriminate Violence', 2011, 17.

and other situations of violence is examined through its constituent elements. Finally, the chapter ends with concluding observations.

Methodology and Scope

This chapter examines the interpretation of the 1951 refugee definition by looking at the practices of a limited number of states which are parties to the 1951 Convention and/or its 1967 Protocol and the views of UNHCR and scholars. Rather than comprehensively analyzing all aspects of the 1951 refugee definition, the chapter focuses on the elements that are most contentious with regard to refugee protection claims based on armed conflict and other situations of violence. The chapter draws on practice from the following receiving countries: the United States, Canada, Australia, New Zealand, Belgium, France, the Netherlands, Germany, Sweden and the United Kingdom.[12]

The chapter does not draw on practice from Africa and Latin America because of the application of regional refugee law instruments, with the exception of Costa Rica and Venezuela, which exclusively employed the 1951 refugee definition.[13] The examined jurisprudence primarily concerns refugee claimants from the following countries of origin: Afghanistan, the Democratic Republic of Congo (DRC), Somalia, Iraq, Sri Lanka, Mexico and Colombia. Between 2001 and 2011, these states experienced armed conflict or other situations of violence.[14] Since 2001, they have also been amongst the main countries of origin of asylum-seekers in the examined receiving states.[15]

Although this chapter focuses on practice after 11 September 2001, given the caesura that this event marks for asylum law and for the policies of many states, prior significant legal developments are also considered. The chapter analyses the 1951 Convention's inclusion clause of Article 1A(2). It does not examine exclusion from or cessation of refugee status, temporary or complementary protection or the broader refugee definitions at the regional level.

---

[12] The chapter does not purport to show how each of the examined states interprets each of the elements of the refugee definition. Rather, it concentrates on selected elements of the definition and examines the most insightful state practice in this respect.

[13] The analysis of practice in Costa Rica and Venezuela is exclusively based on information provided by UNHCR. The practice of Asian states is not considered.

[14] Where significant legal developments relate to other countries of origin, they were nonetheless considered. This chapter does not focus on gang-related violence.

[15] Based on the UNHCR, 'Asylum Trends and Levels in Industrialized Countries between 2000 and 2010'.

Terminology and Concepts

This chapter examines refugee protection claims that arise in the context of armed conflicts or other situations of violence. It draws on the definition of non-international armed conflicts by the Appeals Chamber of the International Criminal Tribunal for the former Yugoslavia (ICTY), which states, '[A]n armed conflict exists whenever there is a resort to armed force between states or protracted armed violence between government authorities and organized armed groups or between such groups within a state.'[16] Key criteria are that the armed violence reaches a minimum level of intensity and that the parties to the conflict exhibit a minimum of organization.[17] Other situations of violence fall below the threshold of armed conflict either regarding the minimum level of intensity of the armed violence, the minimum degree of organization of the parties, or both.

When determining refugee status in the context of armed conflict and other situations of violence, national decision-makers have used various terms to frame the situation in the country of origin, including 'fighting between clans engaged in civil war',[18] 'civil unrest in the form of an armed conflict',[19] 'internal armed conflict',[20] 'a tragic situation of war or armed conflict',[21] 'a very high level of widespread violence'[22] and 'civil war'.[23] The terms used to describe the factual circumstances in a country of origin are crucial because they convey an understanding of the situation and its consequences for the affected persons and may determine whether to use the 1951 refugee definition, broader refugee

---

[16] *The Prosecutor* v. *Dusko Tadić*, Decision on the Defence Motion for Interlocutory Appeal on Jurisdiction, IT-94-1-A, 2 October 1995, para. 70. Similarly, UNHCR and ICTR, 'Summary Conclusions', para. 22.

[17] See ICRC, 'How Is the Term "Armed Conflict" Defined in International Humanitarian Law? Opinion Chapter', 17 March 2008.

[18] *Adan* v. *Secretary of State for the Home Department*, per Lord Lloyd of Berwick regarding Somalia.

[19] *In re S-P-*, 21 I. & N. Doc. 486, Interim Decision 3287, 1996 WL 422990 (BIA) (US), 493, regarding Sri Lanka.

[20] *Refugee Appeal No. 76289*, (8 May 2009) (New Zealand), para. 36, regarding Colombia.

[21] *Sheriff* v. *Canada (Minister of Citizenship and Immigration)*, 2002 FCT 8 (Canada), regarding Sierra Leone.

[22] *X (Re)*, 2002 Can. LII 52651, (IRB) (Canada), regarding Colombia.

[23] Immigration and Refugee Board of Canada, 'Civilian Non-Combatants Fearing Persecution in Civil War Situations' (this reference is not country-specific); *Assy Diouf* v. *Holder*, 388 F. Appx. 525 (6th Cir. 2010) (United States) (regarding the DRC), 1; *Refugee Appeal No. 76551*, para. 62 (regarding Somalia).

definitions or complementary protection.[24] In the case of *Haji Ibrahim* before the High Court of Australia, Judge Gummow found that the 'widespread disorder' in Somalia cannot be considered a civil war without 'a risk that there will be a blurring of the distinction between the persecutory acts which the asylum-seeker must show and the broader circumstances to those acts'.[25] Judge Gummow further observed that '[t]he notions of "civil war" ... and "object" or "motivation" of that "civil war" are distractions from applying the text of the Convention definition.'[26] Indeed, individuals fleeing from generalized violence are often not considered to be 1951 Convention refugees.[27] Thus, the way in which a situation in a country of origin is framed may affect the interpretation of the 1951 refugee definition and may even mislead decision-makers.

A general classification of a situation in a country of origin might distort the interpretation and application of the 1951 refugee definition by incorrectly insinuating a certain level, type, impact or scope of the conflict or violence. Such a classification ought not to be relevant for the interpretation of the 1951 refugee definition. For the purpose of applying the 1951 refugee definition, it is important to describe the situation in the country of origin in clear and objective terms and to understand it in its proper context.

Historical Evolution of International Refugee Law in Light of Armed Conflict and Other Situations of Violence

Armed conflict and other situations of violence underpin much of the development of international refugee law. During the inter-war period and after the Second World War, international refugee law evolved against the backdrop of armed conflict and other situations of violence, as well as other contextual factors such as economic depression and political oppression.

The first group of refugees addressed by the League of Nations consisted of Russians fleeing the civil war, the Bolshevik Revolution and the

---

[24] See *Haji Ibrahim*, para. 12, per Gummow J.   [25] *Ibid.*, para. 145.   [26] *Ibid.*, para. 147.
[27] According to UNHCR, Costa Rica used to deny 1951 Convention refugee protection to Central American asylum-seekers because they were considered to flee generalized violence. In *SZNQI* v. *Minister for Immigration & Anor*, [2009] FMCA 918 (17 September 2009) (Australia), the court affirmed that 'the risk for the applicant was of being caught up in random generalised violence, and not that he [or she] would be targeted for any Convention reason' (para. 54).

famine.[28] The loss of protection from their country of origin prompted their need for international protection,[29] with the League of Nations regularizing their status in 1922.[30] The fact of having fled from armed conflict or other situations of violence was irrelevant for refugee status under this arrangement as well as under the 1924 extension to Armenian refugees.[31] Subsequent arrangements included two definitional criteria such that refugees must lack protection from the state of origin and be of a specific ethnic or territorial origin.[32] While having fled from an armed conflict or other situation of violence was not a legally relevant criterion for refugee status, it did not rule out a finding of refugee status either.

In 1926, the League of Nations Council discussed the expansion of existing arrangements for the protection of refugees in analogous situations.[33] Three criteria were used in identifying additional refugee groups: (1) de jure lack of protection by the country of origin, (2) flight from events connected to the First World War, and (3) territorial or ethnic origin.[34] The extension of refugee protection thus was meant to include people who fled from armed conflict and other situations of violence in

---

[28] See J. H. Simpson, *The Refugee Problem: Report of a Survey* (Oxford University Press, 1939), 62–3; L. W. Holborn, *The International Refugee Organization: A Specialized Agency of the United Nations – Its History and Work 1946–1952* (Oxford University Press, 1956), 3.

[29] See J. C. Hathaway, 'The Evolution of Refugee Status in International Law: 1920–1950', *ICLQ* 33 (1984), 348, 351. Similarly, see C. M. Skran, 'Historical Development of International Refugee Law', in A. Zimmermann et al. (eds.), *The 1951 Convention Relating to the Status of Refugees and Its 1967 Protocol* (Oxford University Press, 2011), 7, nn. 4 and 5.

[30] Arrangement with Regard to the Issue of Certificates of Identity to Russian Refugees of 5 July 1922, 355 LNTS 238. See also Hathaway, 'The Evolution of Refugee Status in International Law', 350–2; W. von Glahn, *Der Kompetenzwandel Internationaler Flüchtlingsorganisationen – vom Völkerbund bis zu den Vereinten Nationen* (Baden-Baden: Nomos, 1992), 16–17.

[31] See 'Plan for the Issue of a Certificate of Identity to Armenian Refugees', *League of Nations Official Journal* 31 (May 1924), 7–10, 969–70.

[32] See Arrangement Relating to the Issue of Identity Certificates to Russian and Armenian Refugees of 12 May 1926, 89 LNTS 47; and Arrangement Relating to the Legal Status of Russian and Armenian Refugees of 30 June 1928, 89 LNTS 53. Further, see Hathaway, 'The Evolution of Refugee Status in International Law', 360.

[33] See *League of Nations Official Journal* 2 (1927), 155; and *League of Nations Official Journal* 10 (1927), 1336. Further, see I. C. Jackson, *The Refugee Concept in Group Situations* (The Hague: Martinus Nijhoff, 1999), 15–18; J. C. Hathaway, *The Rights of Refugees under International Law* (Cambridge University Press, 2005), 86–8.

[34] See *League of Nations Official Journal* 10 (1927), 1138; and Arrangement Concerning the Extension to Other Categories of Refugees of Certain Measures Taken in Favour of Russian and Armenian Refugees of 30 June 1928, 2006 LNTS 64. Further, see Hathaway, 'The Evolution of Refugee Status in International Law', 360–1.

the context of the First World War when protection by the country of origin was absent. Other refugee instruments adopted during this time do not shed any further light on the definition of who is a refugee in the context of armed conflict and other situations of violence.

The forced displacement of at least 40 million people as a result of the Second World War, together with subsequent further displacement, provided the impetus for the establishment of the International Refugee Organization (IRO) in 1946. The IRO's constitution alludes to the Second World War in defining several, but not all, categories of refugees and displaced persons.[35] There were certain conditions under which distinct individuals would become of concern to the IRO.[36] 'Persecution, or fear, based on reasonable grounds of persecution because of race, religion, nationality or political opinions'[37] was such a condition. Thus, an armed conflict or other situation of violence in the country of origin was not a decisive criterion for opposing return.[38] Yet, such a situation did not preclude a person from coming within the personal scope of the IRO mandate either.

After the IRO's dissolution,[39] UNHCR was established in 1950 as a temporary organization 'with the sole responsibility of addressing the needs of refugees in Europe who had been displaced by the Second World War'.[40] Paragraph 6 lit. (ii) of the UNHCR Statute confers competence on UNHCR with regard to persons who have been considered refugees under several inter-war refugee instruments as well as persons with a well-founded fear of persecution on account of several proscribed grounds.[41] UNHCR's competence *ratione personae* has since evolved to

---

[35] Part I, sec. AI(1)(b)–(c) and (3) of Annex 1 and Part I, sec. B of Annex 1 to the Constitution of the International Refugee Organization (adopted 15 December 1946, entered into force 20 August 1948), 18 UNTS 3. See also the reference to 'war orphans' in Part I, sec. A(4) of Annex 1 to the IRO Constitution. See further the individualized definition in Part I, sec. A (2) of Annex 1 to the IRO Constitution.

[36] See Part I, sec. C of Annex 1 to the IRO Constitution.

[37] Part I, sec. C(1)(a)(i) of Annex 1 to the IRO Constitution.

[38] Similarly, see T. Einarsen, 'Drafting History of the 1951 Convention and the 1967 Protocol', in A. Zimmermann et al. (eds.), *The 1951 Convention Relating to the Status of Refugees and Its 1967 Protocol* (Oxford University Press, 2011), 56, n. 33.

[39] See V. Türk, *Das Flüchtlingshochkommissariat der Vereinten Nationen (UNHCR)* (Berlin: Duncker & Humblot, 1992), 20; and Hathaway, 'The Evolution of Refugee Status in International Law', 91.

[40] G. Loescher et al., *The United Nations High Commissioner for Refugees (UNHCR): The Politics and Practice of Refugee Protection into the Twenty-First Century* (London: Routledge, 2008), 1.

[41] See para. 6A(i) and (ii) of the UNHCR Statute.

cover people fleeing from 'serious (including indiscriminate) threats to life, physical integrity or freedom resulting from generalized violence or events seriously disturbing public order'.[42]

The preparatory works of the 1951 Convention illustrate the drafters' view that armed conflicts or other situations of violence may give rise to a well-founded fear of being persecuted for a 1951 Convention ground. The drafters of the 1951 Convention generally understood the substance of the refugee definition to be broad and applicable to almost all known categories or groups of refugees.[43] They developed the refugee definition against the backdrop of thirty years of experience with refugees.[44]

Originally, the 1951 refugee definition was temporarily and geographically limited because the negotiating states hesitated to commit to protecting an unforeseeable population of future refugees, with the US representative arguing, for example, that '[t]oo vague a definition, which would amount ... to a blank cheque, would not be sufficient'.[45] The drafters were thus concerned with limiting the personal scope of the 1951 Convention. The Israeli representative observed that the refugee definition

> obviously did not refer to refugees from natural disasters, for it was difficult to imagine that fires, floods, earthquakes or volcanic eruptions, for instance, differentiated between their victims on the grounds of race, religion, or political opinion. Nor did the text cover all man-made events. There was no provision, for example, for refugees fleeing from hostilities unless they were otherwise covered by article 1 of the Convention.[46]

The key element of this statement is the differentiation required for victims of hostilities to be considered refugees, acknowledging that if armed conflicts or other situations of violence in some way differentiate between victims, the victims may fall within the 1951 refugee definition.

---

[42] UNHCR, 'UNHCR Statement on Subsidiary Protection under the EC Qualification Directive for People Threatened by Indiscriminate Violence', 2008, 2.

[43] See Einarsen, 'Drafting History of the 1951 Convention and the 1967 Protocol', 66, n. 64.

[44] Ibid., 67, n. 64.

[45] UN ECOSOC, Ad Hoc Committee on Statelessness and Related Problems, 'Summary Record of the Third Meeting, 26 January 1950', UN Doc. E/AC.32/SR.3, para. 37. See also P. Weis, 'Legal Aspects of the Convention of 21 July 1951 Relating to the Status of Refugees', BYBIL 30 (1953), 478, 479.

[46] UNGA, 'Conference of the Plenipotentiaries on the Status of Refugees and Stateless Persons: Summary Record of the Twenty-Second Meeting', 26 November 1951, UN Doc. A/CONF.2/SR.22, 6.

This statement demonstrates the understanding that persons who flee from armed conflict and other situations of violence could fall within the scope of Article 1A(2) of the 1951 Convention if they fulfilled the criteria therein. The drafters knew that persecution during armed conflict had created large numbers of bona fide refugees in the past.[47]

The statement of the Israeli delegate also indicates that the drafters of the 1951 Convention's definition did not intend for its scope *ratione personae* to cover persons who 'merely' fled from general dangers arising from events such as armed conflicts. The drafters' rejection of a proposal by the International Committee of the Red Cross (ICRC) reaffirms this position. The ICRC had suggested that '[e]very person forced by grave events to seek refuge outside his [or her] country of ordinary residence is entitled to be received.'[48] Armed conflicts or other situations of violence surely would have constituted such grave events.

Interpretation of the 1951 Refugee Definition in the Context of Armed Conflict and Other Situations of Violence

While certain states and the UNHCR have reaffirmed the relevance of the 1951 Convention for the protection of people fleeing from armed conflict and other situations of violence, restrictive interpretative trends in other state practice threaten to undermine this relevance.

Reaffirmed Relevance of the 1951 Convention

The evolution of some state practice as well as the views and refugee status determination (RSD) practice of the UNHCR reiterate the relevance of the 1951 Convention for the protection of people fleeing armed conflict and other situations of violence in their countries of origin. The French Council of State (*Conseil d'État*) found in 1997 that the existence of an armed conflict could give rise to a well-founded fear of persecution in the sense of the 1951 Convention.[49] This decision put an

---

[47] See Einarsen, 'Drafting History of the 1951 Convention and the 1967 Protocol', 67, n. 65. See also A. Edwards and A. Hurwitz, 'Introductory Note to the Arusha Summary Conclusions on Complementarities between International Refugee Law, International Criminal Law, and International Human Rights Law', *IJRL* 23 (2011), 856, 858.

[48] 'Aide Memoire on the Refugee Question, Statement Submitted by the International Committee on the Red Cross', 4 July 1951, UN Doc. A/CONF./NGO.2, 1.

[49] See Council of State (*Conseil d'État*), No. 154321, Mlle STRBO, 12 May 1997 (France). In 2009, the Council of State held that as soon as a persecution ground exists and the other conditions for qualifying for refugee status are fulfilled, refugee protection must be

end to the jurisprudence of the Refugee Appeals Board (*Commission des recours des réfugiés*) according to which the dangers arising from a situation of conflict did not pose a risk of persecution within the meaning of the 1951 Convention.[50] Nonetheless, the Refugee Appeals Board still seems to frequently deny refugee status because the general situation in the country of origin does not give rise to a clearly individualized risk of persecution.[51] Pre-2001 jurisprudence in the United States and Canada also exhibits a more restrictive approach to refugee claimants fleeing armed conflict and other situations of violence than more current jurisprudence.[52] Costa Rica has recently begun to recognize persons from Central America who have escaped situations of violence as 1951 Convention refugees, having previously denied them refugee status because they were considered to have merely escaped from generalized violence.[53] Venezuela has also been gradually adopting an interpretation of the 1951 refugee definition that accommodates people having fled situations of violence.[54]

UNHCR's position on protecting people fleeing armed conflict and other situations of violence has also evolved. The pivot of UNHCR's views on extending refugee protection to such individuals can be found in the UNHCR *Handbook*: 'Persons compelled to leave their country of origin as a result of international or national armed conflicts are not normally considered refugees under the 1951 Convention or

---

granted rather than subsidiary protection, including in a context of generalized violence. Conseil d'État, *No. 292564, Mlle K*, 15 May 2009 (France).

[50] See e.g. Commission des recours des réfugiés, *Zein El Abiddine*, 13 June 1985 (France); *Taha*, 30 October 1989 (France).

[51] See V. Chetail, 'The Implementation of the Qualification Directive in France: One Step Forward and Two Steps Backwards', in K. Zwaan (ed.), *The Qualification Directive: Central Themes, Problem Issues, and Implementation in Selected Member States* (Nijmegen: Wolf, 2007), 94.

[52] As argued by Markard, *Kriegsflüchtlinge. Gewalt gegen Zivilpersonen in bewaffneten Konflikten als Herausforderung für das Flüchtlingsrecht und den subsidiären Schutz*, 130, referring to *Salibian* v. *Canada (Minister of Employment and Immigration)*, 1990 3 FC 250 (Canada), 258, and *Zavala Bonilla* v. *I.N.S.*, 730 F.2d 562 (9th Cir. 1984) (United States). Both judgements ended the previously more restrictive approaches that required particularized evidence (Canada) or being singled out for persecution (United States). With *In re H-*, 21 I. & N. Doc. 337, Interim Decision 3276, 1996 WL 291910 (BIA), the jurisprudence in the United States began to reject the view that persons having fled from clan warfare or civil strife cannot qualify as refugees under the 1967 Protocol. See Sternberg, *The Grounds of Refugee Protection in the Context of International Human Rights and Humanitarian Law.*

[53] Based on information provided by UNHCR.

[54] Based on information provided by UNHCR.

Protocol.'[55] This statement suggests that people fleeing from armed conflict are only refugees in exceptional circumstances.[56] UNHCR has since clarified that in many situations, persons fleeing armed conflict and other situations of violence may have a well-founded fear of persecution for a 1951 Convention ground.[57]

While conducting individual RSD, UNHCR's experiences indicate, with regard to people currently fleeing countries experiencing armed conflict and other situations of violence, that most successful claimants are now found to be refugees under the 1951 refugee definition rather than under broader refugee definitions contained in regional refugee law instruments. This focus on the 1951 Convention, as opposed to the broader refugee definitions regarding people fleeing armed conflict and other situations of violence in UNHCR's mandate-led RSD operations, stems from the nature of internal armed conflicts, which are increasingly rooted in religious, ethnic and/or political disputes and where groups with specific profiles are targeted.[58]

Well-Founded Fear

To qualify for refugee status under the 1951 Convention, a person needs to demonstrate a well-founded fear of being persecuted, with the notion of 'fear' indicating a 'forward-looking expectation of risk'.[59] A claimant's risk of being persecuted must be assessed in the context of the situation in the country of origin as well as the individual's profile, experiences and activities.[60] To establish a well-founded fear of persecution, a claimant would need to show a relationship between the general circumstances in the country of origin, on the one hand, and individualized facts, on the other.[61] In respect of the degree of individualization and the level of

---

[55] UNHCR, *Handbook and Guidelines on Procedures and Criteria for Determining Refugee Status under the 1951 Convention and the 1967 Protocol Relating to the Status of Refugees*, December 2011, HCR/1P/4/Eng./Rev.3, paras 164–5 (footnotes omitted).

[56] See Storey and Wallace, 'War and Peace in Refugee Law Jurisprudence', 350.

[57] See UNHCR, 'Note on International Protection', para. 11.

[58] Based on information provided by UNHCR.

[59] A. Zimmermann and C. Mahler, 'Article 1A, Paragraph 2' in A. Zimmermann et al. (eds.), *The 1951 Convention Relating to the Status of Refugees and its 1967 Protocol: A Commentary* (Oxford University Press, 2011), 341, n. 199.

[60] See e.g. UNHCR, 'Eligibility Guidelines for Assessing the International Protection Needs of Asylum-Seekers from Sri Lanka', 2009, 29.

[61] See M. R. von Sternberg, 'Outline of United States Asylum Law: Substantive Criteria and Procedural Concerns', in Practising Law Institute, *Practice Skills Course Handbook Series: Defending Immigration Removal Proceedings* (New York, 2011), 33.

risk recognized, state practice can be broadly divided into a restrictive approach (also known as 'differential risk analysis')[62] and a liberal approach.

The judgement of the UK House of Lords in *Adan* epitomizes the restrictive position. Lord Slynn of Hadley considered the situation in Somalia at a time when 'law and order have broken down and where . . . every group seems to be fighting some other group or groups in an endeavour to gain power.' In such a context, he found that the claimant 'must be able to show fear of persecution for Convention grounds over and above the risk to life and liberty inherent in the civil war'.[63] The high level of violence in Somalia in the late 1990s and its group-based and widespread nature affected the risk assessment, thus leading their Lordships to require a higher level of risk than that which is required in times of peace. In this view, an individualized risk of persecution results when a higher risk of persecution, compared with the rest of the population or other members of the group, is present.[64]

The US Eighth Circuit Court of Appeals also adopted a restrictive approach. The court held: '[T]he harm suffered must be particularized to the individual . . . Harm arising from general conditions such as anarchy, civil war, or mob violence will not ordinarily support a claim of persecution.'[65] This position requires a high level of individualization of the threat irrespective of the characteristics of the underlying conflict and fails to acknowledge that the general situation in the country of origin forms part of the risk assessment. It appears to also conflate the risk element with the causal link to a 1951 Convention ground.[66]

The judgement in *Prophète* v. *Canada* opposes the differential risk requirement, stressing that there can be situations in which 'an individual who may have a personalized risk, but one that is shared by many other individuals'.[67] The experiences of similarly situated persons can support

---

[62] See e.g. H. Storey, 'Armed Conflict in Asylum Law: The "War Flaw"', *RSQ* 31 (2012), 2, 11.

[63] *Adan* v. *Secretary of State for the Home Department*, per Lord Slynn of Hadley. The UKIAT subsequently applied the requirement of a higher risk in *NM and Others (Lone Women – Ashraf) Somalia* v. *Secretary of State for the Home Department CG*, [2005] UKIAT 00076 (UK), paras 118 and 135.

[64] See Markard, *Kriegsflüchtlinge. Gewalt gegen Zivilpersonen in bewaffneten Konflikten als Herausforderung für das Flüchtlingsrecht und den subsidiären Schutz*, 133.

[65] *Mohamed* v. *Ashcroft*, 1006.

[66] The problem of such conflation is addressed by *Refugee Appeal No. 71462*, [1999] NZRSAA (27 September 1999) (New Zealand), para. 52.

[67] *Prophète* v. *Canada (Minister of Citizenship and Immigration)*, 2008 FC 331 (Canada), para 18. See also *Gonzales-Neyra* v. *I.N.S.*, 122 F.3d 1293, 1295 (9th Cir. 1997) (United

a claim of being at risk of persecution. The jurisprudence in Australia and New Zealand,[68] as well as UNHCR,[69] also rejects the 'differential risk' or 'singled out' requirement. For example, the Refugee Status Appeals Authority (RSAA) of New Zealand held that 'the claimant must only establish the "ordinary" real chance of being persecuted and not some increased level of risk or that he/she has been singled out for persecution.'[70] UNHCR stressed, 'Whole communities may risk or suffer persecution for Convention reasons. The fact that all members of the community are equally affected does not in any way undermine the legitimacy of any particular individual claim.'[71]

The underlying rationale of requiring a higher level of risk may well be found in the political realm rather than in the legal sphere. Concerns have been voiced that unless a higher level of risk is required, individuals on either side of a conflict could qualify for refugee protection,[72] thus potentially leading to large numbers of refugee claimants.[73] There is nothing in the wording of the 1951 refugee definition to suggest that a refugee has to be singled out for persecution, either generally or over and above other persecuted persons. Requiring otherwise ignores the potentially evidentiary value of the experiences of similarly situated people and goes against the object and purpose of the 1951 Convention.

States), as amended on denial of rehearing, 133 F.3d 726 (9th Cir, 1998), acknowledging that the group of persons facing the same risk as the applicant is not limited in size.

[68] See *Haji Ibrahim*, para. 70 (also at para. 147), per Gummow J; *Refugee Appeal No. 71462*, para. 77; *Minister for Immigration and Multicultural Affairs* v. *Abdi*, [1999] FCA 299 (Australia), per O'Connor, Tamberlin and Mansfield JJ. See further M. Kagan and W. P. Johnson, 'Persecution in the Fog of War: The House of Lords' Decision in *Adan*', *Michigan Journal of International Law* 23 (2001–2), 247–64; Kälin, 'Refugees and Civil Wars'; Storey and Wallace, 'War and Peace in Refugee Law Jurisprudence'.

[69] See UNHCR, 'Eligibility Guidelines for Assessing the International Protection Needs of Iraqi Asylum-Seekers', August 2007, 129.

[70] *Refugee Appeal No. 76551*, para. 66.

[71] UNHCR, 'Eligibility Guidelines for Assessing the International Protection Needs of Iraqi Asylum-Seekers', August 2007, 129.

[72] See *Isa* v. *Canada (Secretary of State)*, [1995] FCJ No. 354 (Canada), 72. As noted by Storey and Wallace, 'War and Peace in Refugee Law Jurisprudence', 351.

[73] In *Adan* v. *Secretary of State for the Home Department*, Lord Lloyd of Berwick guarded against an interpretation of the 1951 refugee definition that would result in 'participants on both sides of the civil war . . . [being] entitled to protection under the Convention'. Durieux identifies a 'contamination of qualitative criteria by quantitative factors' in J.-F. Durieux, 'Of War, Flows, Laws and Flaws: A Reply to Hugo Storey', *RSQ* 31(3) (2012), 161, 164.

Persecution

Whether or not conduct constitutes persecution must be determined in light of all the circumstances, taking into consideration the individual's profile, experiences, activities, age and gender.[74] An act can constitute persecution irrespective of whether it occurs during peacetime, armed conflict and other situations of violence.[75] Contrastingly, the US Eleventh Circuit Court of Appeals indicated that when serious violence is widespread, a higher level of severity is necessary for an act to constitute persecution.[76] It considered death threats by a guerrilla group in Colombia, in a 'place where the awful is ordinary',[77] of insufficient severity to constitute persecution.[78] Yet, the threshold of severity for persecution must be assessed irrespective of the number of people affected. UNHCR exemplifies this by considering 'indiscriminate forms of violence such as suicide attacks and improvised explosive devices' as persecution.[79] The cumulative effect of harmful acts must be taken into account, as UNHCR notes: 'Regular exposure to measures such as security checks, raids, interrogation, personal and property searches, and restrictions on freedom of movement may ... cumulatively amount to persecution.'[80]

---

[74] See UNHCR, *Handbook and Guidelines*, para. 52; UNHCR, 'Eligibility Guidelines for Assessing the International Protection Needs of Asylum-Seekers from Afghanistan', 2009, 17.

[75] See *Haji Ibrahim*, para. 18 per Gaudron J. See also *In re H-*, 21 I. & N. Dec. 337, Interim Decision 3276, 1996 WL 291910 (BIA) (United States), 343: 'While inter-clan violence may arise during the course of civil strife, such circumstances do not preclude the possibility that harm inflicted during the course of such strife may constitute persecution ... and, persecution may occur irrespective of whether or not a national government exists.' *Matter of Villalta*, 20 I&N Dec. 142 (BIA 1990) (United States) (finding that persecution can and often does occur in the context of civil war).

[76] As noted in the dissenting opinion by Carnes J. in *Silva* v. *US Attorney General*, 448 F.3d 1299 (11th Cir. 2006) (United States), 1248. German courts have considered death threats experienced by claimants from Iraq and Afghanistan to substantiate a well-founded fear of persecution: VG Aachen 17 January 2011, 4 K 1344/09.A; VG Trier 13 September 2011, 1 K 1314/10.TR.

[77] *Silva* v. *US Attorney General*, 1242.

[78] See *Sepulveda* v. *US Attorney General*, 401 F.3d 1226 (11th Cir. 2004) (United States), 1231; *Silva* v. *US Attorney General*, 1233. Swedish authorities generally require a level of severity for persecutory acts that has been criticized as too high. See UNHCR, 'Quality in the Swedish Asylum Procedure: A Study of the Swedish Migration Board's Examination of and Decision on Applications for International Protection', 2011, 6–7 (on file with author).

[79] See UNHCR, 'Eligibility Guidelines for Assessing the International Protection Needs of Afghan Asylum-Seekers', 2007, para. 63.

[80] *Ibid.*, 17. But see *Gomez Zuluaga* v. *US Attorney General*, 527 F.3d 330 (3rd Cir. 2008) (United States), 24, in which the court failed to consider the cumulative effect of relatively short periods of detention.

Within armed conflict or situations of violence, measures taken to restore or maintain law and order can raise questions of determining whether or not they are persecutory. The two specific issues at play are, firstly, whether the measures were undertaken for a legitimate purpose and, secondly, whether the measures were proportionate to the pursuit of that objective. The unification of a country[81] and the suppression of terrorist activities[82] have been considered as legitimate objectives in the jurisprudence. References to potential justifications for conduct do not necessarily remove such conduct from the scope of persecution. State measures are not legitimate attempts to maintain law and order if they are disproportionate or affect persons who do not or no longer take part in the violence.[83]

International humanitarian law (IHL) may be relevant for the interpretation of persecution in the context of armed conflict. A few states have drawn on IHL for the interpretation of persecution in the context of armed conflict.[84] However, there is also more sceptical jurisprudence on this matter. Discussing in *Adan* what 'distinguishes persecution from the ordinary incidents of civil war', Lord Lloyd rejected the proposition that

---

[81] See *Haji Ibrahim*, para. 67 per McHugh J. According to Bem, the Dutch Council of State held in the case *ARRvS*, 24 February 1988, RV 1988, nr. 4, that measures to ensure a country's unity cannot be persecution but subsequently departed from this doctrine in the case *ARRvS*, 14 September 1988, RV 1988, nr. 6. See K. K. Bem, *Defining the Refugee: American and Dutch Asylum Case-Law 1975–2005*, Academisch Proefschrift (Amsterdam: Vrije Universiteit Amsterdam, 2007), 145.

[82] See Federal Constitutional Court (*Bundesverfassungsgericht*), BVerfG 2 BvR 752/97 (15 February 2000); Federal Administrative Court (*Bundesverwaltungsgericht*), BVerwG 9 C 33/85 (3 December 1986) (both Germany), as pointed out by Markard, *Kriegsflüchtlinge. Gewalt gegen Zivilpersonen in bewaffneten Konflikten als Herausforderung für das Flüchtlingsrecht und den subsidiären Schutz*, 167–8. Similarly, see Kälin, 'Refugees and Civil Wars', 441.

[83] See *Haji Ibrahim*, para. 67 per McHugh J; Federal Constitutional Court (*Bundesverfassungsgericht*), BVerfG, 2 BvR 752/97 (15 February 2000) (Germany); Federal Administrative Court (*Bundesverwaltungsgericht*), BVerwG 9 C 33/85 (3 December 1986) (Germany), as pointed out by Markard, *Kriegsflüchtlinge. Gewalt gegen Zivilpersonen in bewaffneten Konflikten als Herausforderung für das Flüchtlingsrecht und den subsidiären Schutz*, 167–8. Similarly, see Kälin, 'Refugees and Civil Wars', 441.

[84] See e.g. US Immigration and Naturalization Service, *The Basic Law Manual: US Law and INS Refugee/Asylum Adjudications* (1995), 22, cited by von Sternberg, *The Grounds of Refugee Protection in the Context of International Human Rights and Humanitarian Law*, 37. Further, see *Montecino* v. *Immigration and Naturalization Service*, 915 F.2d 518 (9th Cir. 1990) (United States), 520; *In re S-P-*, 493–4; Immigration and Refugee Board of Canada, 'Civilian Non-Combatants Fearing Persecution in Civil War Situations', although the references to IHL in these guidelines have rarely been used in recent Canadian jurisprudence, as illustrated by *Sheriff* v. *Canada (Minister of Citizenship and Immigration)*.

a reference to IHL would be helpful.[85] Yet, in 2008, the UK Asylum and Immigration Tribunal (AIT) found that subsequent legal developments warranted a renewed look at the guidance in *Adan*, suggesting that 'serious violations of peremptory norms of IHL and human rights' do indeed constitute persecution.[86] The 1996 Joint Position of the Council of the European Union noted, '[T]he use of the armed forces does not constitute persecution where it is in accordance with international rules of war.'[87]

IHL complements international refugee law in that breaches of IHL may inform the interpretation of persecution.[88] However, the notion of persecution in armed conflict should not be strictly tied to violations of IHL.[89] Use of force may be lawful under IHL but may, for other reasons, constitute persecution, for example, because the overall purpose of the conflict is to expel or destroy a certain group.

The Nexus to the 1951 Convention Grounds

A refugee must have a well-founded fear of persecution *for reasons of* race, religion, nationality, membership of a particular social group or political opinion. This nexus (or 'causal link') requirement refers to the claimant's predicament rather than the persecutor's mind set.[90] It is one of the main issues that courts grapple with in the context of armed conflict and other situations of violence. A refugee's predicament may be affected by the causes, character and impact of the armed conflict and

---

[85] See *Adan* v. *Secretary of State for the Home Department*, per Lord Lloyd of Berwick.

[86] *AM & AM* v. *Secretary of State for the Home Department* (armed conflict: risk categories), *Somalia CG*, [2008] UKAIT 00091 (United Kingdom), para. 76.

[87] Council of the European Union, 'Joint Position Defined by the Council', para. 6.

[88] See UNHCR, 'Note on International Protection', 2 July 2003, UN Doc. A/AC.96/975, para. 53. See also UNHCR ExCom, 'Conclusion No. 73 (XLIV)', first preamble recital; UNHCR, *Handbook and Guidelines*, para. 164; UNHCR ExCom, 'Conclusion No. 89 (LI) on International Protection', December 2009, para. 32. Several scholars advocate drawing on IHL in the interpretation of persecution, including e.g. von Sternberg, *The Grounds of Refugee Protection in the Context of International Human Rights and Humanitarian Law*; and Storey and Wallace, 'War and Peace in Refugee Law Jurisprudence'. But see Durieux, 'Of War, Flows, Laws and Flaws'.

[89] Similarly, a UNHCR expert roundtable noted that although international refugee law and international criminal law consider many of the same acts as amounting to persecution, differences remain between the respective concepts. See UNHCR and ICTR, 'Summary Conclusions', para 13.

[90] See UNHCR, 'Guidance Note on Refugee Claims Relating to Sexual Orientation and Gender Identity', 21 November 2008, para. 28.

other situations of violence in the country of origin, making these elements relevant for interpretation of the nexus requirement.

The argument that violence is 'indiscriminate' in nature is often used against finding a nexus to a 1951 Convention ground. However, it is important to consider the context of such violence. Violence can be widespread *and* targeted,[91] for example, because means of violence with indiscriminate effects are used intentionally in areas where civilians with specific ethnic or political profiles predominantly reside or gather.[92]

Some jurisprudence shows awareness of the different ways in which an armed conflict or a situation of violence may reveal a nexus between the refugee claimant's predicament and a 1951 Convention ground. For instance, the Australian Refugee Review Tribunal noted regarding Afghanistan that 'the violence continues to manifest itself ... on ethnic, political and/or religious lines; and thus comes well within the grounds provided for by the Refugee Convention.'[93] But there are also less 'conflict-sensitive' approaches to the nexus requirement. For example, the Australian High Court rejected the proposition that a decision-maker would be required to determine whether the objective of a war is directed against persons because of a 1951 Convention ground.[94]

Some causes of conflict, such as economic gains, are unrelated to a 1951 Convention ground.[95] The presence of economic motivations ought not

---

[91] See V. Türk, 'Protection Gaps in Europe? Persons Fleeing the Indiscriminate Effects of Generalized Violence', UNHCR, 18 January 2011, 4–5.

[92] See UNHCR, 'Eligibility Guidelines for Assessing the International Protection Needs of Asylum-Seekers from Sri Lanka', 32. Further: UNHCR ExCom, 'Conclusion No. 85 (XLIX)', para. c.

[93] *Case No. 071329032*, [2007] RRTA 82 (23 April 2007) (Australia). Similarly, see *NA (Risk Categories – Hema) Democratic Republic of Congo v. Secretary of State for the Home Department CG*, [2008] UKAIT 00071 (United Kingdom), para. 37; Immigration and Refugee Board of Canada, 'Civilian Non-Combatants Fearing Persecution in Civil War Situations'. On Germany, see Markard, *Kriegsflüchtlinge. Gewalt gegen Zivilpersonen in bewaffneten Konflikten als Herausforderung für das Flüchtlingsrecht und den subsidiären Schutz*, 2, who notes the Federal Constitutional Court (*Bundesverfassungsgericht*), BVerfGE 80, 315 (10 July 1989), at 319–20; BVerfG-K- 2 BvR 752/97 (15 February 2000), para. 30.

[94] See *Haji Ibrahim*, para. 102, per McHugh J, para. 146 per Gummow J, Gleeson CJ and Hayne J agreeing. The UK House of Lords found that a nexus to a 1951 Convention ground in the context of clan-based warfare cannot be established by looking at the overall context of the conflict alone: *Adan, Adan v. Secretary of State for the Home Department*, per Lord Lloyd of Berwick. Dutch jurisprudence generally does not examine the nexus requirement in any detail. See Bem, *Defining the Refugee*, 175, 184.

[95] See Markard, *Kriegsflüchtlinge. Gewalt gegen Zivilpersonen in bewaffneten Konflikten als Herausforderung für das Flüchtlingsrecht und den subsidiären Schutz*, 271.

to preclude further investigation into whether other causes, or the conflict's impact or characteristics, reveal a nexus between the claimant's predicament and a 1951 Convention ground. Economic gain is rarely the only factor underlying a particular conflict.[96] A 1951 Convention ground need not be the sole or even the dominant cause of the refugee's predicament but merely a contributing factor.[97] Moreover, 'if the war or conflict are non-specific in impact', a refugee claimant's fear may be based on 'specific forms of disenfranchisement within the society of origin'.[98]

In the United States, the phrase 'singled out' continues to be used as a shorthand for the nexus requirement,[99] even though *Matter of H* already established in 1996 that the refugee claimant need not show individualized persecution but merely a causal link to a refugee ground.[100] The US Court of Appeals for the Sixth Circuit held that the petitioner 'must establish that he [or she] is at particular risk as a Christian and that his [or her] predicament is appreciably different from the dangers faced by other non-Christian Iraqis'.[101] The court compared the petitioner's predicament to that of non-Christian Iraqis, introducing an additional requirement that he or she be more at risk of serious harm than others. However, the fact that the petitioner's predicament is linked to his or her religion ought to suffice. The predicament of other groups in Iraq is irrelevant for the interpretation of the nexus

---

[96] See Farrell and Schmitt, 'The Causes, Character and Conduct of Armed Conflict', 28.

[97] See UNHCR, 'Guidance Note on Refugee Claims Relating to Sexual Orientation and Gender Identity', para. 28. But see section 91R(1)(c) of the Migration Act 1958 (Australia), which states that the 1951 Convention reason must be 'the essential and significant reason ... for the persecution'; and National Asylum Court (*Cour nationale du droit d'asile*, CNDA), 2 November 2010, *No. 08008523, M.S.* (France). In this case, the CNDA denied refugee status to a Tamil asylum-seeker, *inter alia*, because Tamils are not targeted for persecution by the governmental authorities solely for the reason of their ethnic origin.

[98] J. Hathaway, *The Law of Refugee Status* (Toronto: Butterworths, 1991), 188. See also Kagan and Johnson, 'Persecution in the Fog of War', 259–60 and Kälin, 'Refugees and Civil Wars', 642–3.

[99] See e.g. *Jabba and others* v. *US Attorney General*, 195 F. Appx. 883 (11th Cir. 2006) (United States), 7; *Sepulveda* v. *US Attorney General*, 401 F.3d 1226 (11th Cir. 2004) (United States), 1231.

[100] See *In re H-*, 21 I. & N. Dec. 337, Interim Decision 3276, 1996 WL 291910 (BIA) (United States), 345–6. The 'singled out' doctrine is also prevalent in Dutch jurisprudence. See Bem, *Defining the Refugee*, 170.

[101] *Elias* v. *Gonzales*, 212 F. Appx 441, 448 (6th Cir. 2007). See also *Hanona* v. *Gonzales*, 243 F. Appx. 158, 163 (6th Cir. 2007); *Shasha* v. *Gonzales*, 227 F. Appx. 436, 440 (6th Cir. 2007); *Aoraha* v. *Gonzales*, 209 F. Appx. 473, 476 (6th Cir. 2006); *Toma* v. *Gonzales*, 179 F. Appx. 320, 324 (6th Cir. 2006) (all United States).

requirement.[102] The nexus requirement, in the context of armed conflict and other situations of violence, is often conflated with the risk assessment which forms part of the notion of a 'well-founded fear'. This can result in an incorrect requirement to establish a double-differential risk, as the RSAA of New Zealand noted, '[A] person at real risk of serious harm for reason of his or her religion will be required to establish that he or she is *more* at risk of serious harm for reason of his or her religion than others who are equally at real risk of serious harm for reason of their religion.'[103]

An understanding that there is no nexus to a 1951 Convention ground where a large number of people face persecution would go against the object and purpose of the 1951 Convention.[104] The requirement of individually experienced persecution does not mean that a person be persecuted because of his or her individual activities as opposed to his or her membership in a persecuted group. Being part of a persecuted group should be individual enough.[105] Being personally at risk of persecution should merely mean that the person is purposefully, rather than accidentally, at risk of being harmed.[106] For a finding of a nexus to a 1951 Convention ground, it is not necessary that the asylum-seeker be known to, and sought or targeted personally, by the persecutor(s).[107] Therefore, the non-comparative approach to the nexus requirement, enunciated by the Canadian Federal Court of Appeal, is preferable in a context of armed conflict and other situations of violence:

> [A] situation of civil war in a given country is not an obstacle to a claim provided the fear felt is not that felt indiscriminately by all citizens as

---

[102] Similarly, see Second Colloquium on Challenges to International Refugee Law, 'The Michigan Guidelines on Nexus to a Convention Ground', *Michigan Journal of International Law* 23 (2001–2), 211, 218 (para. 17). US regulations acknowledge that a claimant need not show that he or she would be singled out for persecution if a nexus to a 1951 Convention ground can be established through a pattern or practice in the country of origin that shows that a group to which the applicant belongs is being persecuted for a 1951 Convention ground: 8 CFR § 208.13(b)(2)(iii).

[103] *Refugee Appeal No. 71462*, para. 52 (emphasis in original).

[104] See Storey and Wallace, 'War and Peace in Refugee Law Jurisprudence', 353.

[105] See C. W. Wouters, *International Legal Standards for the Protection from Refoulement* (Antwerp: Intersentia, 2009), 87. See also Kälin, 'Refugees and Civil Wars', 437–8; and S. Jaquemet, 'The Cross-Fertilization of International Humanitarian Law and International Refugee Law', *International Review of the Red Cross* 83(843) (2001), 651, 668.

[106] See Kälin, 'Refugees and Civil Wars', 437–8.

[107] See UNHCR, 'Eligibility Guidelines for Assessing the International Protection Needs of Asylum-Seekers from Sri Lanka', 31–2.

a consequence of the civil war, but that felt by the applicant himself, by a group with which he is associated, or, even, by all citizens on account of a risk of persecution based on one of the reasons stated in the definition.[108]

The 1951 Convention Grounds

Armed conflicts and other situations of violence are often rooted in political, ethnic or religious differences, with different groups facing heightened risks of harm,[109] thus suggesting the applicability of the 1951 Convention grounds. The 1951 Convention grounds are not mutually exclusive; they may overlap.[110] Refugee claimants often have a well-founded fear of being persecuted because of more than one ground.[111] For example, UNHCR found that '[i]n Iraq, journalists, academics, judges, [and] lawyers ... have been targeted by armed groups for complex reasons, including their (imputed) political opinion, religious identity, ethnicity and membership of a particular social group as well as for criminal purposes.'[112]

1. Race, Religion, Nationality

The 1951 Convention grounds of race, religion and nationality are particularly relevant in contemporary armed conflicts and other situations of violence. The 1951 Convention grounds of race and nationality

---

[108] *Salibian* v. *Canada (Minister of Employment and Immigration)*, 259.
[109] See e.g. UNHCR, 'Eligibility Guidelines for Assessing the International Protection Needs of Asylum-Seekers from Sri Lanka', 31–2 (noting that individuals may be at risk on various grounds because the armed conflict is rooted in ethnic and political differences). Farrell and Schmitt emphasize that in most cases, conflicts are driven by a mix of factors and not only ethnic difference. Farrell and Schmitt, 'The Causes, Character and Conduct of Armed Conflict' 2.
[110] See UNHCR, *Handbook and Guidelines*, para. 67.
[111] See e.g. *Refugee Appeal No. 76006*, NZRSAA (16 July 2007) (New Zealand) (Sri Lanka; ethnicity and imputed political opinion); *Refugee Appeal No. 74686*, NZRSAA (New Zealand) (29 November 2004) (Iraq; religion and imputed political opinion); *Refugee Appeal No. 76457*, NZRSAA (15 March 2010) (New Zealand) (Iraq; religion and membership of a particular social group (women)). In France, the CNDA seems to consider in cases concerning refugee claimants from Afghanistan that an ethnic background of such claims alone is insufficient for establishing a 1951 Convention ground; often refugee status is granted for reasons of ethnicity and political opinion. See e.g. CNDA, *Decision No. 08000815, M. Husseini*, 25 June 2010; CNDA *Decision No. 0915005, M. Yusefi*, 1 September 2010; CNDA, *Decision No. 09012012, M. Hussaini*, 2 November 2010; CNDA, *Decision No. 08010018, M. Yaguby*, 2 November 2010.
[112] UNHCR, 'Eligibility Guidelines for Assessing the International Protection Needs of Iraqi Asylum-Seekers', 20.

are closely intertwined; they both encompass ethnicity. Race is to be understood broadly so as to include ethnic groups and persons of common descent usually constituting a minority within a given population.[113] Nationality must also be interpreted broadly and includes membership of a group determined by cultural, ethnic or linguistic identity.[114] Examples of cases that concern persecution for the only reason of ethnicity relate to the Hazara in Afghanistan[115] and the Tamils in Sri Lanka.[116]

However, refugee claims concerning solely the 1951 Convention ground of race are rare partly because many racial or ethnic claims to refugee status are framed and decided on other grounds such as particular social group or political opinion. Ethnic groups are often associated with political movements seeking power, equality or independence, and thus refugee claims of members of such groups are also considered under the ground of political opinion.[117] For example, in the context of the armed conflict in Sri Lanka, a number of claims by Tamil asylum-seekers have been found to have a well-founded fear of persecution for reasons of their ethnicity and their imputed political opinion.[118] During armed conflict and other situations of violence, refugee claimants may be at risk of being persecuted for reasons of their ethnicity, although they

---

[113] See UNHCR, *Handbook and Guidelines*, para. 68. See also Article 10(1)(a) Qualification Directive.

[114] See UNHCR, *Handbook and Guidelines*, para. 74. See also Article 10(1)(c) Qualification Directive.

[115] See *Refugee Appeal Nos. 76294 and 76295*, NZRSAA (30 June 2009) (New Zealand). The UKAIT considered that members of their Hema tribe may be at risk because of their ethnicity, though membership in this tribe alone is insufficient. See *NA (Risk Categories – Hema) Democratic Republic of Congo* v. *Secretary of State for the Home Department CG*.

[116] See *Refugee Appeal Nos. 76294 and 76295*, NZRSAA (30 June 2009) (New Zealand). Another example relates to the Reer Hama Clan in Somalia. See Commission des recours des réfugiés, SR, 29 July 2005, *Mlle A., No. 487336* (France).

[117] See D. Anker, *Law of Asylum in the United States* (Eagan, MN: Thomson West, 2011), sec. 5:83–6. Affirmed by UK Border Agency, 'Considering the Protection (Asylum) Claim and Assessing Credibility', 27; and US Citizenship and Immigration Services, Asylum Officer Basic Training Course, 'Asylum Eligibility Part III: Nexus and the Five Protected Characteristics', 21 March 2009, 17. Similarly: UNHCR, *Handbook and Guidelines*, para. 75.

[118] See *Refugee Appeal No. 76006*, NZRSAA (16 July 2007) (New Zealand); *Refugee Appeal No. 76199*, NZRSAA (11 November 2008) (New Zealand). In France, recognition of refugee status for Afghans is usually not based on ethnicity alone but also on the ground of political opinion. See e.g. CNDA, *Decision No. 08000815, M. Husseini*, 25 June 2010; CNDA *Decision No. 09015005, M. Yusefi*, 1 September 2010; CND *Decision No. 09012012, M. Hussaini*, 2 November 2010; *CNDA Decision No. 08010018, M. Yagbuby*, 2 November 2010.

themselves are not directly involved in the conflict. Based on their ethnicity, the agent of persecution may identify them with a group involved in the conflict.[119] Affiliation or perceived affiliation with a state that is supporting an armed group may also give rise to a fear of persecution based on nationality. For example, the UK AIT found that individuals perceived to have Rwandan connections or to be of Rwandan origin constituted a risk category within the DRC.[120]

The 1951 Convention ground of religion is also relevant, as many conflicts are fought along sectarian lines. Race and nationality also often overlap with the ground of religion. Broadly construed, 'religion' refers to a belief or non-belief, an identity and/or a way of life.[121] For example, Christian claimants from Iraq have often been found to have a well-founded fear of being persecuted for reasons of religion.[122] In armed conflicts and other situations of violence involving groups with different religious identities, such groups usually pursue a political agenda, and the corresponding political opinions may be imputed to members of such groups.[123] In Iraq, violence against Christians in some cases has been informed by their perceived association with the occupying forces, thus giving rise to a well-founded fear of persecution for reasons of religion and imputed political opinion.[124]

2. Membership of a Particular Social Group

Apart from the widely acknowledged political, ethnic and religious dimensions of many modern conflicts, a specific area that is

---

[119] See US Citizenship and Immigration Services, 'Asylum Eligibility Part III', 17. In *Zubeda v. Ashcroft*, 333F.3d 462 (3rd Cir. 2003) (United States), para. 102, the court indicated that a member of the Bemba tribe feared persecution on account of her tribal identity, noting that members of this tribe have been targeted by armed groups supporting the government.

[120] See *AB and DM (Risk categories reviewed, Tutsis added), Democratic Republic of Congo CG*, [2005] UKIAT 00118 (United Kingdom), para. 51.

[121] See UNHCR, 'Guidelines on International Protection No. 6: Religion-Based Refugee Claims under Article 1A(2) of the 1951 Convention and/or the 1967 Protocol Relating to the Status of Refugees', 28 April 2004, paras. 4–5. See also Article 10(1)(b) Qualification Directive.

[122] See e.g. *Refugee Appeal No. 76457*, NZRSAA (15 March 2010) (New Zealand); *Refugee Appeal No. 75879*, NZRSAA (12 February 2007) (New Zealand). There are few cases in Dutch jurisprudence that acknowledge refugee status based on religious persecution. See Bem, *Defining the Refugee*, 172.

[123] See e.g. *Youkhana v. Gonzalez*, 460 F.3d 927 (7th Cir. 2006) (United States), remanding the case of an Assyrian Christian from Iraq who claimed persecution by the ruling Ba'ath Party on account of political opinions imputed to his ethno-religious group. See also Anker, *Law of Asylum in the United States*, § 5:79.

[124] See *Refugee Appeal No. 74686*, [2004] NZRSAA (29 November 2004) (New Zealand), paras. 38 and 41.

under-explored is the application of the ground of membership of a particular social group, in particular, as regards civilians and groups pursuing a certain profession. For the purpose of the refugee definition, it is generally agreed that a group does not have to be homogeneous or internally coherent to constitute a particular social group[125]; the size of the group is also irrelevant.[126] For the existence of a particular social group, it is also not necessary to establish that all members of that group are at risk.[127] The group should not be exclusively defined by a shared fear of persecution.[128]

According to the 'protected characteristics approach', membership of a particular social group means that 'an individual who is a member of a group of persons all of whom share a common, immutable characteristic'.[129] This immutable characteristic may be innate or unalterable for other reasons. The Supreme Court of Canada clarified that 'what is excluded by this definition are groups defined by a characteristic which is changeable or from which disassociation is possible, so long as neither option requires renunciation of basic human rights.'[130] However, the 'social perception approach' provides that '[a] particular social group ... is a collection of persons who share a certain characteristic or element which unites them and enables them to be set apart from society at large.'[131] UNHCR's definition of 'particular social group' reconciles both approaches in a non-cumulative way.[132]

In the context of armed conflicts in which civilians are often directly targeted and bear the brunt of hostilities, the question arises whether civilians can constitute a 'particular social group'. No state practice has

---

[125] See *Minister for Immigration and Cultural Affairs* v. *Khawar*, [2002] HCA 14 (Australia) per Gleeson CJ.

[126] See *Applicant A and Anor* v. *Minister for Immigration and Cultural Affairs*, (1997) 190 CLR 225 (Australia), per Dawson J.

[127] See *Minister for Immigration and Cultural Affairs* v. *Khawar*. See also UNHCR, 'Guidelines on International Protection No. 1: Gender-Related Persecution within the Context of Article 1A(2) of the 1951 Refugee Convention and/or its 1967 Protocol Relating to the Status of Refugees', 2002, UN Doc. HRC/GIP/02/02, 18.

[128] See *Applicant A and Anor* v. *Minister for Immigration and Cultural Affairs*, 242, per Dawson J.

[129] *In re Acosta*, (1985) 191 I. & N. Dec. 211 (United States), para. 10.

[130] *Canada (Attorney General)* v. *Ward*, [1993] 2 SCR 689 (Canada), 737.

[131] *Applicant A and Anor* v. *Minister for Immigration and Cultural Affairs*, per Dawson J. See also UNHCR, 'Guidelines on International Protection No. 2: Membership of a Particular Social Group within the Context of Article 1A(2) of the 1951 Refugee Convention and/or its 1967 Protocol Relating to the Status of Refugees', 2002, HRC/GIP/02/02, para. 14.

[132] See *Ibid.*

been identified that discusses this matter. A 'civilian' is a person who is not a member of the armed forces,[133] a characteristic that could change. Some individuals who object to recruitment into the armed forces or individuals who desert might fall into a narrower social group than 'civilians', and the notion of 'civilian' would not necessarily be relevant for the group's definition. Under the protected characteristics approach, civilians would therefore not constitute a 'particular social group'.

In Belgium, the armed forces have been considered to constitute a particular social group clearly distinguished from the rest of society.[134] It seems difficult to establish that 'the rest of society', i.e. civilians, would conversely constitute a different particular social group, given that a social group must be distinguished from the relevant society at large. For civilians to be perceived as a social group, the society in question would have to be highly militarized, with a fairly prevalent membership in the armed forces so as to make the lack of such membership objectively cognizable.[135] It is conceivable that civilians in a particular context could constitute a particular social group pursuant to the social perceptions approach. That said, civilians may have a well-founded fear of being persecuted on other 1951 Convention grounds, in particular, political opinion. In many conflicts, civilians are obliged to become involved in the conflict.[136]

Groups of persons pursuing certain professions may particularly be at risk in armed conflict and other situations of violence partly because of their status or role within their community. In Iraq, for example, armed groups seem to endeavour to rid the country of its intellectual elite in order to subvert efforts to establish a functioning democratic society and to erode the country's institutions.[137] While several examined judgements do not consider that certain professional associations constitute

---

[133] See J.-M. Henckaerts and L. Doswald-Beck (eds.), Customary International Humanitarian Law, Vol. I: *Rules* (Cambridge University Press, 2005), 17.

[134] See e.g. Permanent Refugee Appeal Commission (*Commission Permanente de Recours des Réfugiés* (CPRR)), *Decision No. 01-1019/F1369/cd (Russe)*, 5 March 2002 (Belgium), recognizing Russian conscripts as a particular social group.

[135] On the requirement that a group be objectively cognizable, see *Applicant S*, (2004) 217 CLR 387 (Australia), 410–11 (69), per McHugh J. Further: M. Foster, 'The "Ground with the Least Clarity": A Comparative Study of Jurisprudential Developments relating to "Membership of a Particular Social Group"', *Legal and Protection Policy Research Series* 25 (2012), 9.

[136] See e.g. UNHCR, 'International Protection Considerations Regarding Colombian Asylum-Seekers and Refugees', 2005, para. 89.

[137] See UNHCR, 'Eligibility Guidelines for Assessing the International Protection Needs of Iraqi Asylum-Seekers', 111.

particular social groups,[138] others have identified particular social groups based on professions.[139] For UNHCR, '[a] particular social group based on the applicant's occupation may . . . be recognized where disassociation from the profession is not possible or this would entail a renunciation of basic human rights.'[140]

3. Political Opinion

Many, if not all, armed conflicts or situations of violence have a political dimension, with some non-state actors pursuing political goals. The application of the 1951 Convention ground of political opinion in such contexts must therefore be examined, in particular, as regards two matters: (1) the meaning of political opinion where the persecutor is a non-state actor and (2) the potential bases for imputing political opinion.

The notion of political opinion is context specific; it must 'reflect the reality of the geographical, historical, political, legal, judicial and socio-cultural context of the country of origin'.[141] In UNHCR's view, 'political opinion' includes 'any opinion on any matter in which the machinery of the State, government, society, or policy may be engaged'.[142] Cases concerning refusals to join or support a party to a conflict or to take sides

---

[138] See *MIG 2009/36*, 22 December 2009 (Sweden) (finding that a profession is not an innate characteristic); Migration Court of Appeal, 21 December 2009, UM 1664-09 (Sweden) (finding that academics are not a particular social group); *Montoya* v. *Secretary of State for the Home Department*, [2002] EWCA Civ. 620 (United States), para. 8 (finding that rich landowners do not share an immutable characteristic); *Lozano Navarro* v. *Canada (Citizenship and Immigration)*, 2011 FC 768 (Canada), para. 35 (holding that business-men and -women are not a particular social group).

[139] See *Orejuela* v. *Gonzalez (Attorney General)*, 423 F.3d 666, (7th Cir. 2005) (United States), 13; *Escobar* v. *Holder*, (2011) U.S. App. LEXIS 18538 (7th Cir. 2011) (United States); Administrative Court (*Verwaltungsgericht*), VG Frankfurt 7 K 1517/00 (2 March 2004) (Germany). Cited by Foster, 'The "Ground with the Least Clarity"', 71.

[140] UNHCR, 'Guidance Note on Refugee Claims Relating to Victims of Organized Gangs', 2010, para. 39. Similarly: Foster, 'The "Ground with the Least Clarity"', 72.

[141] UNHCR, 'Guidance Note on Refugee Claims Relating to Victims of Organized Gangs', 46. See also *Starred Gomez (Non-State Actors: Acero-Garces Disapproved) (Colombia)*, [2000] UKIAT 00007 (UK), paras. 40–1; *Jerez-Spring* v. *Canada*, [1981] 2 F.C. 527 [FCA] (Canada).

[142] UNHCR, 'Guidance Note on Refugee Claims Relating to Victims of Organized Gangs', 32. See also Goodwin-Gill and McAdam, *The Refugee in International Law*, 87. But see *Starred Gomez (Non-State Actors: Acero-Garces Disapproved) (Colombia)*, para. 73(VII), in which the UK AIT noted that '[t]o qualify as political the opinion in question must relate to the major power transactions taking place in that particular society'.

may relate to expressions of political neutrality, which has been considered a political opinion in certain circumstances.[143]

A person with a well-founded fear of being persecuted for reasons of political opinion need not expressly articulate such opinion. Political opinion may be attributed to the victim by the persecutor; it is irrelevant whether this opinion actually corresponds to the victim's views.[144] In such cases, it is the persecutor's perception of the victim's political opinion that matters rather than the victim's own political opinions.[145] Non-state actors may also impute political opinions to their victims.[146]

Political opinion is to be interpreted broadly,[147] but not so broadly that it encompasses any opinion which a non-state agent of persecution may impute on its victim.[148] The challenge is to take into account the political dimension of a conflict and its impact on the individual refugee claimant. The general objectives of the persecutor, or of the party to the conflict to which the persecutor belongs, do not as such suffice to demonstrate imputed political opinion.[149] It may be difficult to ascertain whether

---

[143] In *Sangha v. I.N.S.*, 103 F.3d 1482, 1488 (9th Cir. 1997), the US Court of Appeals for the Ninth Circuit held that 'an applicant can establish a "political opinion" ... [by] show[ing] political neutrality in an environment in which political neutrality is fraught with hazard, from governmental or uncontrolled anti-governmental forces'. See also *Elias-Zacarias* v. *I.N.S.*, 112 S.Ct. 812 (1992) (United States); *Rivera-Moreno* v. *I.N.S.*, No. 98-71463 (9th Cir. 2000) (United States); *Maldonado-Cruz* v. *I.N.S.*, 883 F.2d 788, 791 (9th Cir. 1989) (United States); and Sternberg, *The Grounds of Refugee Protection*, 82–122. UK jurisprudence seems to adopt a broader approach. In *Noune* v. *Secretary of State for the Home Department*, before the Court of Appeal (Civil Division) [2000 WL 1791543, 6 December 2000] (United Kingdom), Schiemann LJ stated, at para. 8, that 'in order to show persecution on account of political opinion it is not necessary to show political action or activity by the victim: in some circumstances, mere inactivity and unwillingness to co-operate can be taken as an expression of political opinion.' See also *Secretary of State for the Home Department (Appellant)* v. *RT (Zimbabwe), SM (Zimbabwe) and AM (Zimbabwe) (Respondents) and the United Nations High Commissioner for Refugees (Intervener)*, Case for the Intervener, 25 May 2012, 2011/0011, para. 10.

[144] See e.g. *Noune* v. *Secretary of State for the Home Department*, para. 8.

[145] See also *Starred Gomez (Non-State Actors: Acero-Garces Disapproved) (Colombia)*, para. 37; *Sangha* v. *I.N.S.*, 1488.

[146] See M. Symes and P. Jorro, *Asylum Law and Practice*, and edn. (Haywards Heath, UK: Bloomsbury Professional, 2010), 222.

[147] See UNHCR, 'Guidelines on International Protection No. 1', 32. See also Goodwin-Gill and McAdam, *The Refugee in International Law*, 87.

[148] See *Starred Gomez (Non-State Actors: Acero-Garces Disapproved) (Colombia)*, 73(VI).

[149] *Ibid.*, para. 73(VI); see also para. 67 regarding the FARC in Colombia. Further, see UK Border Agency, 'Considering the Protection (Asylum) Claim and Assessing Credibility', 31.

a non-state party to a conflict seeks to achieve its political goals without regard to the political views of those harmed or whether it attributes a political opinion to them.[150] Economic or criminal motives may also be involved, but such multiple motives do not negate a finding of a nexus to the 1951 Convention ground of political opinion.[151] Thus, in cases concerning non-state actors, the assessment of whether the opinion attributed to the refugee claimant is a political one requires a careful analysis of the characteristics of the non-state actor, its political objectives, if any, the broader context of the conflict and the individual circumstances of the claimant.[152]

In Colombia, for example, the highly polarized situation[153] and the powerful guerrilla groups which at times carry out state-like functions[154] have been relevant factors in ascertaining that an opinion attributed to a victim by a non-state actor is a political one. The Canadian Immigration and Refugee Board (IRB) found a Colombian refugee claimant to fear persecution for reasons of his pro-government/anti-guerrilla political opinion,[155] noting in a different case that the political nature of this guerrilla group is well established in documentary evidence.[156] The jurisprudence and UNHCR provide some guidance regarding the bases on which a political opinion may be attributed to an individual in contexts of armed conflict and other situations of violence, namely, a person's

---

[150] See Anker, *Law of Asylum in the United States*, sec. 5:55.

[151] Schiemann LJ held: 'The motives of the persecutor may be mixed and they can include non-Convention reasons: it is not necessary to show that they are purely political.' *Noune* v. *Secretary of State for the Home Department*, para. 8. In *Dalit Sing* v. *Minister for Immigration and Multicultural Affairs*, [1999] FCA 1599 (Australia), para. 35, Mansfield J. noted that '[r]evenge may be personal or it may be political.' The US Court of Appeal for the Second Circuit held that 'the conclusion that a cause of persecution is economic does not necessarily imply that there cannot exist other causes of the persecution.' *Osorio* v. *I.N.S.*, 18 F.3d 1017, 1028 (2nd Cir. 1994) (United States). See also *Starred Gomez (Non-State Actors: Acero-Garces Disapproved) (Colombia)*, para. 42.

[152] See *X (Re) 2004 CanLII 56786*, (IRB) (Canada); *Refugee Appeal No. 76289*, para. 43.

[153] See UNHCR, 'International Protection Considerations Regarding Colombian Asylum-Seekers and Refugees', 1 September 2002, para. 22.

[154] See *Starred Gomez (Non-State Actors: Acero-Garces Disapproved) (Colombia)*, para. 21.

[155] *X (Re), 2004 CanLII 56786*, (IRB) (Canada).

[156] *Ibid.* Similarly, regarding FARC: *Refugee Appeal No. 76289*, para. 43. The UKAIT held: 'It is difficult to see how a political opinion can be imputed by a non-State actor who (or which) is not itself a political entity.' *Starred Gomez (Non-State Actors: Acero-Garces Disapproved) (Colombia)*, para. 73(VII).

ethnicity, religion, age or gender,[157] place of residence[158] and profession,[159] as well as affiliation with the government,[160] a hostile state[161] or the international community.[162]

Internal Flight or Relocation Alternative

Although a refugee claimant need not show that he or she has a well-founded fear of being persecuted in the entire country of origin,[163] cases where the fear of being persecuted is confined to a specific part of the

[157] See UNCHR, 'Eligibility Guidelines for Assessing the International Protection Needs of Asylum-Seekers from Sri Lanka', 31.

[158] See *Garcia-Martinez* v. *Ashcroft*, 371 F.3d 1066, 1069–70 (9th Circuit, 2004), concerning a village perceived as supporting an armed group. Further, see Anker, *Law of Asylum in the United States*, sec. 5:31. But see CNDA, *Decision No. 09016633, M. Haroun Abbakar Mohammed*, 1 September 2010 (France); and *Cediel and others* v. *US Attorney General*, 170 Fed. Appx. 89 (11th Cir. 2006) (United States), which failed to consider that a village was perceived as opposing or supporting the government, respectively.

[159] See VGH BWA 2 S 229/07, NVwZ 2008, 447 (8 August 2007); BVerwG, Judgement of 24 June 2008, 10 C 43/07, NVwZ 2008, 1241 (1245), quoted by Markard, *Kriegsflüchtlinge. Gewalt gegen Zivilpersonen in bewaffneten Konflikten als Herausforderung für das Flüchtlingsrecht und den subsidiären Schutz*, 268. Further, see VG Frankfurt, 7 K 3373/09 F.A. (16 September 2010) (concerning, *inter alia*, a female teacher in a girls school); UK Border Agency, 'Considering the Protection (Asylum) Claim and Assessing Credibility', 30.

[160] See *X (Re), 2004 CanLII 56786*, (IRB) (Canada) (Colombian government employee being attributed a pro-government/anti-ELN opinion). But see Conseil d'État, 14 June 2010, No. 323669, OFPRA c/ M.A., in which the court found that involvement in a state's regular police force does not constitute, in itself, the expression of political opinions or the membership of a particular social group. But see *Tamara-Gomez* v. *Gonzalez*, 447 F.3d 343, 15 (5th Cir. 2006) (United States), in which the claimant was targeted because the guerrilla viewed him as a member of the Colombian police. The court considered such targeting a risk inherent in the job of a policeman and therefore unrelated to political opinion, ignoring that the claimant was in fact not a policeman but a civilian mechanic. The UK AIT cautioned 'that those on the side of law and order and justice who face persecution from non-State actors . . . [such as] guerrilla organisations . . . will [necessarily] have a political opinion imputed on them'. *Starred Gomez (Non-State Actors: Acero-Garces Disapproved) (Colombia)*, para. 47.

[161] See *Al-Harbi* v. *I.N.S.*, 242 F.3d 882 (9th Cir. 2001) (United States) (concerning Iraqis airlifted by the United States).

[162] See Bavarian Administrative Court (*Bayrisches Verwaltungsgericht*), M 23 K 09.50296 (19 January 2011)(Germany) (concerning Afghans perceived as affiliated with the international community); UNHCR, 'Eligibility Guidelines for Assessing the International Protection Needs of Afghan Asylum-Seekers', 64.

[163] See Goodwin-Gill and McAdam, *The Refugee in International Law*, 123; and UNHCR, 'Guidelines on International Protection No. 4: Internal Flight or Relocation Alternative within the Context of Article 1A(2) of the 1951 Convention and/or 1967 Protocol Relating to the Status of Refugees', 2003, UN Doc. HRC/GIP/03/04, para. 6.

country, for instance, because the armed conflict or situation of violence is geographically limited,[164] may give rise to the question of whether the refugee claimant has an internal flight or relocation alternative (IFA) within the country of origin. This is normally only required where the persecutor is a non-state agent, as it is presumed that in state persecution cases the state has control throughout the territory.[165] An armed conflict and other situation of violence affect all aspects of the IFA analysis.

A proposed area of relocation must be practically, safely and legally accessible.[166] Security threats arising from armed conflict and other situations of violence in the country of origin, such as mine fields, shifting war fronts and banditry, preclude such accessibility.[167] An IFA may remain inaccessible after the end of an armed conflict or a situation of violence because of e.g. destroyed infrastructure or explosive remnants of war.

The availability of state protection in the proposed area of relocation forms part of the analysis of whether this area is relevant. The UNHCR *Handbook* notes that 'a state of war, civil war or other grave disturbance' may prevent a country from granting protection or may render such protection ineffective.[168] An indicator of whether an IFA exists is the displacement of large groups of people across the border.[169] The intensity of a conflict and the volume of threats to citizens may indicate a state's inability to provide protection to the claimant.[170] In several states,[171] territorial control is considered a crucial factor in assessing the ability of

---

[164] See UNHCR, *Handbook and Guidelines*, para. 91.   [165] *Ibid.*, para. 13.
[166] *Ibid.*, para. 7(i)(a).
[167] See *Thirunavukkarasu v. Canada (Minister of Employment and Immigration*, [1994] 1 FC 589 (C.A.) (Canada); UK Border Agency, 'Considering the Protection (Asylum) Claim and Assessing Credibility', para. 2.12.; UNHCR, *Handbook and Guidelines*, para. 10.
[168] See UNHCR, *Handbook and Guidelines*, para. 98; UNHCR, 'Eligibility Guidelines for Assessing the International Protection Needs of Iraqi Asylum-Seekers', 9; UNHCR, 'Eligibility Guidelines for Assessing the International Protection Needs of Asylum-Seekers from Somalia', 2010, 31.
[169] See Aliens Council (*Conseil du Contentieux des Étrangers*), No. *53151*, (15 December 2010) (Belgium) (concerning the Kivu region, DRC).
[170] See *X (Re) 2004 CanLII 56786* (Canada).
[171] See Federal Administrative Court (*Bundesverwaltungsgericht*), BVerwG 10 C 43.07 – VGH 13 a B 05.30833 (24 June 2008) (Germany), 25; *Lara Deheza v. Canada (Citizenship and Immigration*), 2010 FC 521, para. 36 (Canada); *X (Re) 2004 CanLII 56786*, (IRB) (Canada); *X (Re) 2009 CanLII 90052*, (IRB) (Canada); *X (Re) 2003 CanLII 55250*, (IRB) (Canada). The US Asylum Office notes, 'A government in the midst of a civil war, or one that is unable to exercise its authority over portions of the country (e.g. Colombia, Indonesia, Somalia) will be unable to control the persecutor in areas of the country where

the country of origin to provide protection. Although UNHCR under-stands territorial control as a prerequisite for effective state protection,[172] it also notes that during armed conflict and other situations of violence, state protection may be ineffective despite the state's territorial control over an area.[173] Territorial control is thus a necessary but not sufficient factor in determining the availability of state protection in a proposed area of relocation.

Canadian jurisprudence presumes state protection except in situations of complete breakdown of the state apparatus.[174] Although armed con-flict and other situations of violence may lead to such a breakdown, this view might be too narrow. Even if the state is no longer in a position to provide meaningful protection, a state's armed forces may still be func-tioning, and thus the state apparatus could be considered as not having completely broken down. A better approach could be to presume a lack of state protection if the armed conflict or situation of violence fulfils certain criteria, such as a high level of intensity and frequency of violence or a vast geographical scope of the violence employed, thus shifting the burden of proof from the refugee claimant to the authorities of the receiving state.

Other relevant factors in assessing whether a proposed area of reloca-tion is relevant concern the reach of non-state agents of persecution and the extent to which they exercise territorial control over an area.[175] Yet, lack of territorial control by the non-state agent of persecution over the proposed area of relocation does not suffice to establish that the refugee claimant would be safe from harm emanating from this agent. For example, the Canadian IRB found that although a guerrilla group was not physically present throughout all of Colombia, it was capable of locating targeted individuals anywhere in the country.[176]

---

its influence does not extend.' AOTBC, Asylum Eligibility Part I, cited by Anker, *Law of Asylum in the United States*, para. 2:14, n. 23.

[172] See UNHCR, 'Eligibility Guidelines for Assessing the International Protection Needs of Asylum-Seekers from Sri Lanka', 9.

[173] *Ibid.*, 9. The extent to which actors other than the state can provide effective protection for the purposes of the refugee definition is beyond this chapter's scope.

[174] See *Canada (Attorney General)* v. *Ward*, 724°5; see also *Balasingam* v. *Canada (Minister for Employment and Immigration)*, 2004 FC 1465 (Canada), paras. 30 and 33.

[175] See *AM & AM* v. *Secretary of State for the Home Department*, para. 190.

[176] See *X (Re) 2004 CanLII 56786*, (IRB) (Canada). See also *Rodriguez Gutierrez* v. *Canada (Minister of Citizenship and Immigration)*, 2010 FC 1010, (Canada) paras. 22 and 26. Similarly, see UK Border Agency, 'Considering the Protection (Asylum) Claim and Assessing Credibility', para. 2.13.

A proposed area of relocation would need to be reasonable in all the circumstances, taking into account the volatility of the fighting. [177] The lack of adequate security is a primary reason why France's National Court of Asylum (*Cour Nationale du Droit d'Asile*) has often rejected the existence of an IFA.[178] The existence of an armed conflict and other situation of violence in the country of origin should not mean that the viability of a proposed IFA is solely assessed as regards safety risk. Other factors must also be considered such as 'the destruction of socio-economic infrastructure',[179] the 'inadequacy of essential services'[180] and 'continued economic and security restrictions . . . which prevent civilians from accessing locations used for agriculture, fishing and cattle grazing and other livelihood activities'.[181]

Conclusions

The relevance of the 1951 Convention for the protection of people who flee armed conflict and other situations of violence in their country of origin is widely accepted, yet there remain discrepancies in state practice. This chapter has documented both non-restrictive and restrictive interpretations. The restrictive tendencies evident in several states undermine the relevance of the 1951 Convention for the protection of people in these circumstances.

The question of how individualized a threat of persecution must be underpins many of these restrictive approaches. The notion of individualization is apparent in the interpretation of several elements of the refugee definition. In some states, it results in a higher standard of proof of persecution for people who have fled armed conflict and other situations of violence, while in others such situations require a differentiated risk. The individualization requirement is also apparent in the narrow interpretation of the nexus requirement evident in the jurisprudence of some states. According to this view, the plight of similarly situated people

---

[177] See UNHCR, *Handbook and Guidelines*, para. 27.
[178] See CNDA, *Decision No. 574495, Mlle N.*, 2 April 2008; Commission des recours des réfugiés, *No. 585846, Mlle S.*, 15 March 2007; Commission des recours des réfugiés, SR, *No. 573815, T.*, 16 February 2007 (all France). See also 8 CFR § 208 31(3)(b) (United States). Similarly, see Federal Administrative Court (*Bundesverwaltungsgericht*), BVerwG, 27 June 2008, 10 C 43.07 – VGH 13a B 05.20822 25 (Germany).
[179] *X (Re) 2004 CanLII 56786* (IRB).
[180] UNHCR, 'Eligibility Guidelines for Assessing the International Protection Needs of Asylum-Seekers from Sri Lanka', 10.
[181] *Ibid.*

in the country of origin who fear harm for ethnic, political, religious or other reasons does not substantiate the finding of a nexus to a 1951 Convention ground. The assessment of whether a well-founded fear of being persecuted is *for reasons of* a 1951 Convention ground is probably the most crucial and the least clear aspect of refugee status determination in contexts of armed conflict and other situations of violence.

These restrictive tendencies stand in stark contrast to the historical evolution of refugee law, which was to a large extent triggered by waves of conflict-induced forced displacement. The refugee definitions in the predecessors to the 1951 Convention and the 1951 Convention itself were adopted against the backdrop of armed conflict and other situations of violence, and granting refugee status to such people was understood not to be an exceptional process. The wording of the 1951 refugee definition also does not support an interpretation that is more restrictive in armed conflict and other situations of violence than in peacetime. The 1951 Convention's object and purpose warrant an inclusive and dynamic interpretation that provides protection to people fleeing armed conflict and other situations of violence without confronting them with higher hurdles. Given the various inconsistencies in jurisprudence, the need for clear, authoritative guidance on the interpretation of the 1951 refugee definition in the context of armed conflict and other situations of violence has been demonstrated.

3

Relationship between the 1951 Refugee Convention and the 1969 OAU Convention on Refugees

A Historical Perspective

BONAVENTURE RUTINWA

Introduction

In 1964, the Organization of African Unity (OAU) decided to embark on drafting a refugee instrument that would govern all aspects of the refugee problems in Africa. This decision was influenced by the need to address the political and legal problems that had arisen due to the mass influx of refugees from conflicts related to the decolonization process and civil wars that ensued in some African countries immediately following independence in the early 1960s.

Sometime during the process of drafting that instrument, the OAU strategically decided to abandon the enterprise and instead to develop a convention that would only address the regionally specific aspects of refugee problems in Africa. It would become an effective complement to the UN Convention Relating to the Status of Refugees (1951 Convention).[1] This decision was influenced to a large extent by the efforts then under way to make the 1951 Convention applicable universally by removing the temporal and geographical limitations, a measure that was achieved with adoption of the Protocol Relating to the Status of Refugees (1967 Protocol).[2] The drafting process, as completed in 1969, resulted in what is today known as the OAU (now African Union) Convention

---

[1] Convention Relating to the Status of Refugees (adopted 28 July 1951, entered into force 22 April 1954), 189 UNTS 137 ('1951 Convention').

[2] Protocol Relating to the Status of Refugees (entered into force 4 October 1967), 606 UNTS 267 ('1967 Protocol').

Governing the Specific Aspects of Refugee Problems in Africa (OAU Convention).[3]

Since then, a debate has ensued over the relationship between the OAU Convention and its UN counterpart of 1951. Three relational issues have been at the core of this debate. Firstly, what was the motive for the OAU to develop its own refugee instrument when the 1951 Convention already existed? Specifically, was this due to dissatisfaction with the existing instrument? Secondly, what are the differences between the definition of a refugee under the 1951 Convention and the 'extended' definition of a refugee under the OAU Convention? Are these distinct or overlapping definitions? Thirdly, whether and to what extent are refugees recognized under the OAU Convention entitled to rights of refugees under the 1951 Convention?

These questions are not academic in that they lie at the heart of the recent tendency to treat refugees in or from Africa, particularly those fleeing from situations of conflict and generalized violence, as a distinct genre of refugees who do not fall under, nor are entitled to the benefits of, the 1951 Convention. Taking a historical perspective, this chapter seeks to address these questions in connection with the development of the OAU Convention and its relationship to the 1951 Convention.

The following conclusions can be drawn. Firstly, although the drafting of the OAU Convention started at a time when the 1951 Convention had geographical and temporal limitations which restricted its applicability to most of the African refugees, those limitations were not the impetus for its development. The main motive was to address problems that Africa would still have encountered with or without the limitations in the 1951 Convention. Thus, the OAU Convention was not intended to be an alternative but rather a complement to the 1951 Convention.

Secondly, the 'extended' definition of a refugee under the OAU Convention was not intended to cover only those who fell outside the scope of the definition of the 1951 Convention. The two definitions are not mutually exclusive, and persons falling under the 'extended' definition can, and often are, also refugees within the meaning of the term under the 1951 Convention. In particular, there is nothing in the text, context or object and purpose of the 1951 Convention that hinders its application to refugees fleeing armed conflict and other situations of generalized violence.

Thirdly, the juridical status of refugees recognized under any of the limbs of the refugee definition of the OAU Convention is the same as that

---

[3] Organization of African Unity Convention Governing the Specific Aspects of Refugee Problems in Africa (entered into force 20 June 1974), 1001 UNTS 45 ('OAU Convention').

of refugees recognized under the 1951 Convention, and former refugees are entitled to the enjoyment of all the rights of refugees under the latter instrument.

The sum total of these findings is that the 1951 Convention remains a relevant instrument for addressing refugee problems in Africa, the existence of the OAU Convention notwithstanding. However, guidelines are needed on the interplay between the provisions of the two instruments and on the application of certain provisions of the former instruments in situations of armed conflict and other forms of violence that characterize the refugee landscape in Africa.

The Political and Legal Contexts of the Creation of the OAU Convention

In comparison with the 1951 Convention, there is very little by way of record on the manner and context in which the OAU Convention was created. In the first place, no systematic *travaux préparatoires* on this instrument were ever published.[4] To compound the problem, the state of refugee research in Africa up to the early 1980s was, as Kibreab once pointed out, lamentably poor.[5] This, as Okoth-Obbo rightly notes, is the most serious handicap that any writer on this instrument faces.[6] That said, the historical and political-legal contexts in which the OAU Convention was created can be accounted with reasonable certainty.

The Political Context

The single most important factor in the decision to develop the OAU Convention was the wars that characterized the political scene in Africa in the period leading up to and immediately after independence. Three

---

[4] G. Okoth-Obbo, 'Thirty Years On: A Legal Review of the 1969 OAU Convention Governing the Specific Aspects of Refugee Problem in Africa', *RSQ* 20 (2001), 85. This fine piece of work was one of the three 'core papers' for the Special OAU/UNHCR Meeting of Government and Non-Government Technical Experts on the 30th Anniversary of the 1969 OAU Refugee Convention, held in Conakry, Guinea, 27–29 March 2000. It provides a detailed review of the development of the OAU Convention, albeit focusing on the legal aspects, more or less the same task that this chapter seeks to achieve while focusing on historical, rather than the legal, aspects. Due to the similarities of the objectives, the reliance of this chapter on that paper will soon become evident.

[5] G. Kibreab, 'The State of the Art Review of Refugee Studies in Africa', (1991) *Uppsala Papers in Economic History*, Research Report No. 26, 6.

[6] Okoth-Obbo, 'Thirty Years On', 7.

major reasons caused these refugee flows. The first was the reconfiguration of some colonial boundaries in the period leading to independence. For example, in 1956, the British organized a plebiscite by which Western Togo was united to Ghana. Ghana became independent in 1958, becoming the first African country to break from colonial yoke. In the early 1960s, a group of persons opposed to this unification revolted and were forced to flee from Ghana to Togo, making Ghana the first refugee-producing country in post-independence Africa.

The second reason was that the violent decolonization campaigns, particularly in southern African countries such as Angola, Mozambique, South Africa, Southern Rhodesia and South West Africa, led to massive flight into territories that had already become independent. Major host countries for these refugees included Malawi, Tanzania and Zambia.

The third reason was prolonged civil wars which engulfed a number of central African countries after attaining independence, especially Burundi, the Democratic Republic of the Congo and Rwanda. These civil wars appear to have been the immediate trigger for the efforts to develop an OAU Convention.

The legislative history of the OAU Convention can be traced back to CM/Res. 19(II) on the Problem of Refugees[7] made at the Council's Second Ordinary Session held in Lagos, Nigeria, from 24 to 29 February 1964. The Council made the Resolution after considering the statements concerning the refugee problem in Africa, with particular reference to the refugees from Rwanda, and having noted that these refugees were a very heavy charge on the countries adjacent to Rwanda, where such refugees sought asylum. The reference to 'refugees from Rwanda' suggests that events in Rwanda and their consequences in neighbouring countries provide some historical and political context for the drafting of the OAU Convention.

As stated by Sellstrom, most observers agree that the single most important developments in Rwanda at the time were the ethnic division and conflict that followed the revolutionary transition from the Tutsi-dominated monarchy to the Hutu-led republic, which took place between November 1959 and September 1961, culminating in the proclamation of independence on 1 July 1962.[8] One of the consequences of these conflicts was the mass flight of populations, particularly from the Tutsi community, into neighbouring countries, namely, Uganda and the

---

[7] Organization of African Unity (Council of Ministers), Resolution on the Problem of Refugees in Africa (OAU, Lagos, 24–29 February 1964), CM/Res 19(II).

[8] T. Sellstrom et al., 'Historical Perspective: Some Explanatory Factors', *Study I of the Joint Evaluation of the Emergency Assistance to Rwanda* (1996), 29.

then Tanganyika. It is thus not surprising that in CM/Res. 36(III), Resolution on the Commission on the Problem of Refugees in Africa, the second refugee-specific resolution of the Council of Ministers, it is noted that invitations had been extended to the Commission by the governments of Uganda, the United Republic of Tanganyika and Zanzibar and Burundi to visit their countries on a fact-finding mission.[9]

Over time, the refugee problem spread throughout Africa. In the period between the beginning of the drafting process in 1964 and adoption of the OAU Convention in 1969, Jackson documents at least twelve refugee situations that had spread throughout the continent from the Great Lakes Region to the greater eastern, western and southern Africa.[10]

A review of the decisions adopted by the Assembly of Heads of State and Government and the resolutions of the Council of Ministers between 1964 and 1969 on refugee matters shows that the drafting of the OAU Convention was motivated by the need to deal with the various challenges faced by the countries hosting refugees. As summed up in CM/Res. 104(IX), Resolution on the Problem of Refugees in Africa of September 1976, these challenges included '*the considerable socio-economic, financial, cultural and security problems* which can and do arise for neighbouring countries when large number of refugees stream towards their borders'.[11]

It was in this context that through CM/Res. 19(II) the Council appointed a Commission consisting of Rwanda, Burundi, Congo (Leopoldville), Uganda, Tanganyika, Sudan, Senegal, Nigeria, Ghana and Cameroon to examine the refugee problem in Africa and make recommendations to the Council of Ministers on how it could be resolved and ways and means of maintaining refugees in countries of asylum.[12]

The Legal Context

When the newly independent countries of Africa began experiencing refugee problems in the 1960s, the legal framework for addressing

---

[9] Organization of African Unity (Council of Ministers), Resolution on the Commission on the Problem of Refugees in Africa (OAU, Cairo, 13–17 July 1964), CM/Res 36(III).

[10] I. Jackson, *The Refugee Concept in Group Situations* (The Hague: Martinus Nijhoff, 1999), 143–76. The details of these situations are given later.

[11] Organization of African Unity (Council of Ministers), Resolution on the Problem of Refugees in Africa (OAU, September 1976), CM/Res. 104(IX) (emphasis added).

[12] Jackson, *The Refugee Concept.*

refugee issues was based on the 1951 Convention. This instrument had two limitations in relation to refugee problems in Africa. Firstly, as originally drafted, the 1951 Convention's applicability was restricted to refugees who fled 'as a result of the events in Europe' and 'which occurred before January 1951'. These geographical and temporal limitations essentially restricted the applicability of the 1951 Convention to refugee situations occurring on the African Continent from the 1960s onwards. Secondly, as its name connotes, the 1951 Convention's focus was on the *status of refugees*. It did not address the socio-economic, financial, cultural and security problems associated with the *refugee problem*, which, as noted earlier, was the main concern of the newly independent African states.

It was against this political and legal context that at its third meeting held from 13 to 17 July 1964 in Cairo, the Council of Ministers, having considered the reports submitted by the Commission on the Problem of Refugees in Africa, made several recommendations and invited the Commission 'to draw up a draft Convention covering *all aspects* of the problem of refugees in Africa' and requested the Administrative Secretary-General to circulate the draft convention to member states of the OAU for their comments and observations (emphasis added). Apparently this was pursuant to a similarly worded invitation by the Assembly of Heads of State and Government, made at its First Ordinary Session in Cairo, in July 1964.[13]

Influence of the 1951 Convention on the Drafting of the 1969 OAU Convention on Refugees

The first draft of the OAU Convention was developed rather quickly and submitted to the Fourth Ordinary Meeting of the Council of Ministers held in Nairobi from 26 February to 9 March 1965. Having studied the draft and the accompanying report, the Council of Ministers established a Committee of Legal Experts to examine the draft convention and prepare the final draft for submission to the Fifth Ordinary Session of the Council of Ministers.[14]

According to Jackson, the Committee of Legal Experts met in Leopoldville and developed and adopted a draft which was essentially

[13] *Ibid.*, 180.
[14] Organization of African Unity (Council of Ministers), Resolution on the Problem of Refugees (OAU, Kenya, 26 February–March 1965), CM/Res. 52(IV), para. 3.

a replica of the 1951 Convention. The only substantive differences were the inclusion of provisions prohibiting subversive activities by refugees and the removal of the 1951 dateline.[15] At this juncture, UNHCR had become interested in the draft convention and was keen to ensure that the adoption of an Africa-specific instrument on refugees would not undermine the universality of the 1951 Convention nor dilute its standards. UNHCR briefed the OAU Secretariat on the ongoing initiatives to make the 1951 Convention applicable universally and thus suggested that the OAU Secretariat should prepare an alternative text which would regulate only the regional aspects of refugee problems.[16]

At its Seventh Ordinary Session held in Addis Ababa, Ethiopia, from 31 October to 4 November 1966, the OAU Council of Ministers adopted CM/Res. 88(VII), on the Adoption of a Draft Convention on the Status of Refugees in Africa, in which the Council, *inter alia*, appreciated 'the efforts of the United Nations High Commissioner for Refugees to ensure the United Nations Convention's universality and adaptation to the present realities of the refugee problem, especially in Africa' and expressed the desire 'that the African instrument should govern the specifically African aspects of the refugee problem and that it should come to be the effective regional complement of the 1951 United Nations Convention on the Status of Refugees'.[17] The idea of having a convention on all aspects of the refugee problem was officially abandoned at the Ninth Ordinary Session of the Council of Ministers held in Kinshasa, Congo, from 4 to 10 September 1967, at which the Council passed a resolution recommending, *inter alia*, 'That the OAU Commission on Refugees be instructed to adopt an instrument governing the specific aspects of the problem of African refugees, and that the adoption of that instrument by Member States be recommended'.[18]

The draft convention was next considered and adopted by the OAU Commission on Refugees at its meeting held in Addis Ababa from 17 to 23 June 1968. At its Eleventh Ordinary Session held in Algiers in September 1968, the Council of Ministers, *inter alia*, requested 'Member States which had not yet done so, to communicate to the General Secretariat, before 15th December 1968, their comments on the draft Convention on the Problem of Refugees, which Convention

---

[15] Jackson, *The Refugee Concept*, 180–1.   [16] *Ibid.*, 181–2.

[17] Organization of African Unity (Council of Ministers), Resolution on the Adoption of a Draft Convention on the Status of Refugees in Africa (OAU, Addis Baba, 31 October–4 November 1966), CM/Res. 88(VII), preambles 2 and 4.

[18] CM/Res. 104, para. 2.

(was) actually in their possession'.[19] The OAU Convention Governing the Specific Aspects of the Refugee Problem in Africa was adopted by the Assembly of Heads of State and Government at its Sixth Ordinary Session in Addis Ababa on 10 September 1969.

What is clear from the preceding is that the drafters of the OAU Convention did not have misgivings about the substantive provisions of the 1951 Convention. Their only problem was the geographical and temporal limitations in it. This is why, when they became aware that these limitations would soon go, they decided to focus on the peculiar problems of refugee flows in Africa, which were not covered by the 1951 Convention.

That African states did not have an abiding dissatisfaction with the 1951 Convention is also evidenced by the constant call on African states to ratify the instrument in virtually every session in which they discussed the draft OAU Convention. Thus, in the same Resolution 26(II), on the Problem of Refugees in Africa of 1965, by which the Assembly of Heads of State and Government asked members of the Refugee Commission to provide legal experts at the highest level possible to re-examine the draft OAU Convention in light of the views they had expressed in that session, they also requested 'Member States of the Organisation of African Unity, if they have not already done so, to ratify the United Nations Convention relating to the Status of Refugees and to apply meanwhile the provisions of the said Convention of refugees in Africa'.[20] This request is significant in two ways. Firstly, it clearly indicates that the Heads of States and Government of the OAU did not see the developing African convention as an alternative to the 1951 Convention. Secondly, they also believed that if African states so wished, they could apply the 1951 Convention to African refugees, the temporal and geographical limitations notwithstanding.

The two penultimate Council resolutions on the development of the OAU Convention, namely, Resolution CM/Res. 104(IX), on the Problem of Refugees in Africa of September 1967, and Resolution CM/Res. 141(X), on the Problem of Refugees in Africa of February 1968, reiterated the request to Member States to accede to the 1951 Convention and to the 1967 Protocol if they had not already done so.[21]

---

[19] Quoted in Jackson, *The Refugee Concept*, 190.

[20] Organization of African Unity (Assembly of Heads of State and Government), Resolution on the Problem of Refugees in Africa (OAU, 1965), AHG/Res. 26(II), para. 7.

[21] See CM/Res. 104, para. 1; and Organization of African Unity (Council of Ministers) (OAU, 1968), CM/Res. 141(X), para. 3.

From the preceding it is clear that the OAU Convention was not developed to serve as an alternative to the 1951 Convention. As clarified through Resolution 88(VII), on the Adoption of a Draft Convention on the Status of Refugees in Africa, noted earlier, the intended relationship between the UN Convention and the OAU Convention on refugees was that 'the African instrument should govern the specifically African aspects of the refugee problem and that it should come to be the effective regional complement of the 1951 UN Convention on the Status of Refugees.'[22]

The 'Extended' Definition of the OAU Convention

One of the innovative aspects of the OAU Convention related to the definition of the beneficiaries of international protection. Having re-enacted under its Article I(1) the definition of a refugee under Article 1A of the 1951 Convention, the OAU Convention proceeded, under its Article I(2), to provide that '[t]he term "refugee" shall also apply to every person who, owing to external aggression, occupation, foreign domination or events seriously disturbing public order in either part or the whole of his country of origin or nationality, is compelled to leave his place of habitual residence in order to seek refuge in another country place outside his country of origin or nationality.' This provision is what has come to be known as the 'extended' definition of a refugee.

Since then, a debate has ensued regarding the preceding definition, including its motivation and the respects in which it related to the definition of a refugee under the 1951 Convention. Some commentators maintain that the 'extended' definition was adopted because the definition of a refugee under the 1951 Convention did not, *ex definitione*, cover African refugees, with or without the temporal and geographical limitations. Others disagree, maintaining that the differences and distinctness of the definition of a refugee under the OAU Convention and under the 1951 Convention are exaggerated.

The 'Distinctness' School of Thought

One renowned refugee scholar who maintained the 'distinctness' opinion is the late Paul Weiss, who stated that the concept of persecution 'was not considered sufficiently wide to cover the refugee situations in Africa' and that the extended definition 'was based on objective criteria,

---

[22] CM/Res. 88, preamble para. 6.

i.e. the conditions in the country of origin. Most of the refugee movements in Africa have been mass movements and in such cases it would be difficult to apply the subjective test requiring individual screening.'[23] The proponents of this view have included some of the persons who were directly involved in the development of the OAU Convention. Thus, for example, Joseph Sinde Warioba, former Attorney General of Tanzania, who represented the country in the drafting of the OAU Convention, stated that the test set out in the 1951 Convention was very stringent and could only be satisfied by what are known as political refugees and that this mischief was not cured by adoption of the 1967 Protocol.[24]

The 'definition gap' argument has continued to be expressed in more recent times by policy-makers and academic writers alike. Thus, Salim Ahmed Salim, a former Secretary General of the OAU, has described the OAU Convention as 'one of the most progressive treaty regimes in the world' because 'the convention goes beyond the usual protection given to refugees, in that it extends protection to those who have fled "civil strife or other events that seriously disturb public order."'[25] On his part, H.E. Ambassador Mahamat Habib Doutum, former Assistant Secretary General of the ESCAS Department, hailed the OAU Convention as 'a dynamic document that broke new ground in several key areas, importantly, with the definition of a refugee which included whole groups of people fleeing circumstances beyond their control such as external aggression, occupation, foreign domination or events seriously disturbing public order in either part or whole of his country of origin or nationality'.[26] Implicit in these statements is the assertion that the groups referred to here were not covered by the 1951 Convention.

In the Preface to their extensive research on refugee issues in Africa in the 1990s, the Lawyers Committee for Human Rights praised the OAU

---

[23] P. Weis, 'The Convention of the Organisation of African Unity Governing the Specific Aspects of Refugee problems in Africa', *Revue des droits de l'homme* 3 (1970), 3–70, quoted in Jackson, *The Refugee Concept*, 177.

[24] J. S. Warioba, 'Rights and Obligations of Refugees in African Countries', 1979 Arusha Pan-African Conference on Refugees, quoted in Jackson, *The Refugee Concept*, 177–8.

[25] S. A. Salim, 'Preface', in C. Mulei et al., *Legal Status of Refugee and Internally Displaced Women in Africa* (New York: UNIFEM/AFWC, 1996), v.

[26] See 'Opening Statement at the OAU/UNHCR Meeting of Government and Non-Government Technical Experts on the Thirtieth Anniversary of the 1969 OAU Convention Governing the Specific Aspects of the Refugee Problems in Africa', held in Conakry, Guinea, 27–29 March 2000, by H. E. Ambassador Mahamat Habib Doutum, CONF.P/OAU 30th/Report Annex IV, 48.

Convention as 'the most progressive treaty regime in the world' in that 'in addition to providing protection for refugees in the sense the term is defined internationally, the OAU Convention also extends protection to those who have fled civil strife and other events that seriously disturb public order.'[27] In the same vein, one Tanzanian academic, while commenting on the rationale of the adoption of the extended definition, asserted, 'This was done in the continent's efforts to "find ways and means" of alleviating the refugees' misery and suffering, more so because those covered by the expanded definition were not recognized by the 1951 Refugee Convention and its 1967 Protocol as refugees.'[28]

The 'Overlap' School of Thought

On the other side of the debate are those who maintain the argument that the 'extended' definition of the OAU was adopted because African refugees at the time fell outside the ambit of the definition of a refugee under the 1951 Convention is historically inaccurate. The leading proponent of this view is Ivor Jackson, whose position is based on the archival study of no less than twelve refugee situations in Africa in the period between the early 1960s when development of the OAU Convention began and 1969 when it was finally adopted.

Jackson notes that in dealing with these refugee situations, UNHCR took two broad approaches to characterizing the influxes. Initially, the agency resorted to its 'good offices' to seek appropriate solutions to the problems arising from these influxes. Later, the agency actually treated the refugees arriving in mass influxes as prima facie mandate refugees under its Statute and/or the 1951 Convention.[29]

The first group of refugees to be dealt with on the basis of the 'good offices' of the High Commissioner for Refugees were those who fled from Angola from 1961 onwards into Congo and later into Zambia and Botswana, among other countries. Having noted that the refugees who fled into Congo in 1961 did so to escape severe pacification measures

[27] Lawyers Committee for Human Rights, 'African Exodus: Refugee Crisis, Human Rights and the 1969 OAU Convention', 1995, i.

[28] S. E. Mchome, 'Refugee Policy and Management in Tanzania', unpublished research manual, Council of International Exchange of Scholars and Madeline and Kevin R. Divine Charitable Trust and Centre for International Cooperation, New York, 2003, 37.

[29] UN General Assembly, Statute of the Office of the High Commissioner for Refugees, 14 December 1950, UN Doc. A/RES/428(V); Convention Relating to the Status of Refugees.

imposed on the population by the Portuguese authorities and unrest-rained reprisals of armed Portuguese settlers, Jackson concludes, '[I]t would have probably been possible to address the problems of this group on the basis of a *prima facie* determination of group refugee character according to the statutory definition.'[30] Likewise, the author quotes a senior UNHCR staff member who had examined the facts regarding the reasons for flight for those refugees who went into Zambia and Botswana and reached a conclusion that these influxes similarly could have justified explicit prima facie determination of group character, according to the statutory definition.[31]

The second group of African refugees studied by Jackson was the 6,000 Ghanaians who fled to Togo in the early 1960s. These refugees are said to have fallen into two categories: 'firstly, those who had refused to accept the results of the 1956 plebiscite by which Western Togo had been united to Ghana; they had attempted to revolt and were obliged to flee to Togo in order to evade the measures taken against them by the Ghanaian govern-ment; secondly, there were many smugglers with whom the Ghana Government had dealt with severely in order to protect its revenues.'[32] Jackson concludes that even though UNHCR had dealt with the first category on 'good offices' basis, 'there is little doubt the group could have been characterised *prima facie* as a refugee group under the statutory definition.'[33] Indeed, he goes on to cite passages from a statement of a senior UNHCR official who dealt with this population who said that 'the reason for the departure of most of the refugees in this group *was persecution or fear of persecution for political motives.*'[34]

The third group dealt with by UNHCR on a 'good offices' basis were the Rwandese who fled to neighbouring countries between 1959 and 1963. Jackson quotes a report by the National Catholic Conference which notes the atrocities that led to the mass flight of these persons as including targeted '[m]urder, rape, robbery, cruel extermination by beat-ing, beheading, or burning, destruction of houses, slaughter of children, violence on the rampage'.[35] He goes on to conclude that 'there can be no doubt, that the situation of the Rwandese refugees could well have been assessed explicitly according to the refugee definition in the UNHCR Statute.'[36] This conclusion is supported by a previous study by Stellstrom which, referring to an episode in 1963 in which between 5,000 and 8,000 Tutsis in Bugeseara, which constituted between 10 and 20 per cent of the

---

[30] Jackson, *The Refugee Concept*, 145. [31] *Ibid.*, 147. [32] *Ibid.*, 148. [33] *Ibid.*, 150.
[34] *Ibid.* [35] *Ibid.*, 152. [36] *Ibid.*

entire Tutsi population in the *prefecture*, were exterminated, rightly characterized these killings as 'genocidal'.[37] No one can question the qualification of genocidal killings as persecution within the meaning of the 1950–1951 definitions because genocide by its very nature is a persecutory conduct which at one and the same time targets an entire group of the same gene as well as each and every individual within that group.

Thus, although dealt with on a 'good offices' basis, the refugees from Angola, Ghana and Rwanda noted earlier could have qualified as refugees under the definition of that term under the Statute of UNHCR of 1950. There are two reasons why these groups were dealt with on a 'good offices' basis. In the case of Angolans, the High Commissioner had determined that initially the influx did not pose any protection problems, and the most important need was material assistance, which could best be mobilized by taking a humanitarian approach to the situation.[38] As for the Ghanaian refugees, the 'good offices' approach was seen as the most appropriate given the political sensitivities involved.[39] It would appear that a combination of these two reasons also influenced UNHCR's approach to the Rwandese refugees during this period.

Over time, the UNHCR dealt with the refugees fleeing similar circumstances as refugees within the meaning of its Statute of 1950. One example was the refugees from Portuguese Guinea, who fled into Senegal from 1964 onwards. These refugees were victims of the colonial war waged between the nationalist movements and the Portuguese colonial power. As Jackson notes, '[t]he High Commissioner, with the approval of the international community, had no difficulty in categorising this situation against the background of the refugee definitions in the UNHCR Statute.'[40]

Indeed, in an inter-office/branch office memorandum regarding cessation of refugee status of Guineans (Bissau) after independence issued on 1 December 1975, it was noted that Guineans (Bisau) who had left their country before April 1974 were considered refugees under not only the 1950 UNHCR Statute but also the 1951 Convention and 1967 Protocol, and therefore, the cessation clauses under the 1950 UNHCR Statute and the 1951 Convention were applicable to them.[41] This was notwithstanding the fact that the entire situation in Guinea was, as in the case of

---

[37] Stellstrom et al., 'Historical Perspective', 11, para. (8), 31.
[38] UN General Assembly, Statute of UNHCR; Jackson, *The Refugee Concept*, 145.
[39] Jackson, *The Refugee Concept*, 148.   [40] *Ibid.*, 154.   [41] *Ibid.*

Ghanaian refugees in Togo, 'highly politicised'.[42] The difference would appear to be that the Ghanaian refugee question involved two independent African countries, while that of the Guinean refugees involved a country under colonial domination and an independent country, which raised different types of political sensitivities.

Likewise, the various groups of Mozambicans who fled their country from the mid-1960s onwards were readily considered refugees of concern to the international community. According to Jackson, 'It was assumed that persons obliged to flee due to the civil/liberation war situation, as it existed in Mozambique at the time, were to be considered as refugees, for whom the Office could legitimately act.'[43] Consequently, when Mozambique won its independence in 1975, the cessation clauses under the UNHCR Statute and the 1951 Convention were invoked to end the status of refugees of those who had fled the country during the trouble years.[44]

As time went by, UNHCR increasingly made direct reference to the language or provisions of its Statute or the 1951 Convention to describe refugee influxes in Africa. A case in point is the large number of refugees from the Democratic Republic of Congo (later Zaire) who, in a memorandum dated 16 September 1964, the UNHCR representative in Uganda stated, could reasonably be assumed to have left their country for political reasons, i.e. for a well-founded fear of being persecuted.[45] Similarly, in a report to the High Commissioner dated 8 July 1966 on Burundians who had fled into Rwanda from 1966 onwards, a representative of UNHCR in Rwanda noted that 'the refugees' description of their reasons for leaving the country leave me in no doubt that they did so because they were in fear of persecution because they are of Hutu stock.'[46]

The last major influx of refugees in Africa with which UNHCR was involved before adoption of the OAU Convention was the Ethiopian refugees who fled into Sudan in 1967. At the request by the government of Sudan to UNHCR for assistance to these refugees, the UNHCR Executive Committee, at its Seventeenth Session in May 1967, decided that pending the study of appropriate further measures, if required for submission to the Committee, it should be left to the High Commissioner to deal with the problems of Ethiopian refugees within the limits of his competence as defined in 'the Statute and other relevant resolutions of the General Assembly and within his discretion to draw on the

[42] Ibid., 153.   [43] Ibid., 155.   [44] Ibid., 157–8.   [45] Ibid., 161.   [46] Ibid., 165.

Emergency Funds'.[47] Jackson surmises that the latter phrase can probably be taken as referring to General Assembly resolutions relating to the High Commissioner's competence not *ratione personae* but *ratione materiae* because Ethiopian refugees as a group were considered to fall prima facie within the statutory definition.[48]

On the basis of the preceding review, Jackson reaches the conclusion that

> the 'extended' definition in paragraph 2 of Article 1 should not be regarded as entirely separate from, and unrelated to the 1950/1951 definitions, as reflected in paragraph 1 of the same Article. On the contrary, the 'extended' definition should be seen precisely as overlapping with or as complementary to the 1950/1951 definitions. This complementarity could, for example, also be relevant to the manner in which the 1950/1951 definitions are to be applied in specific refugee situations arising in Africa.[49]

It is clear that just as the development of the OAU Convention was not induced by the irrelevance of the 1951 Convention, neither was the 'extended' definition of a refugee in the former Convention motivated by the inapplicability of the definition of the same term in the latter instrument. Therefore, the distinction which is often drawn between 'political refugees' who fall under the 1951 Convention and 'humanitarian refugees' who come under the 'extended' definition of the OAU Convention is a palpably false one. The fact that a person comes, or has been recognized under, the 'extended' definition of a refugee does not necessarily put him or her outside the purview of the definition of a refugee under the 1951 Convention.

The Significance of the 'Extended' Definition

Perhaps the most apt way to describe the significance of the OAU Convention in relation to the issue of the definition of a refugee is that it facilitated the recognition of status for persons from the specified circumstances. This was done in two ways. Firstly, by avoiding the use of the politically charged term 'persecution', the extended definition made it possible for a country receiving asylum-seekers to recognize them as refugees without making a determination as to whether they had been persecuted, which was tantamount to passing judgement on the

---

[47] *Ibid.*, 168.   [48] *Ibid.*   [49] *Ibid.*, 179.

conduct of the countries of origin and possibly thereby straining relations with that country of origin.

This approach to ascribing refugee status was particularly important considering that many of the refugees were fleeing from independent African countries to other such states, and therefore a more politicized approach to determining refugee status threatened one of the primary objectives of the then OAU, which was to maintain fraternal relations among Member States.

Secondly, the grounds for which a person could be recognized as a refugee under the extended definition made it easier to accord refugee status to groups of refugees on grounds that could be easily established based on objective circumstances in the country of origin, in contrast with the cognizable grounds under the definition of a refugee under the 1951 Convention, which essentially could only be established through an individualized and costly assessment of refugee claims. This pragmatic approach to determination of protection needs was important in the context of mass influxes, another feature of refugee arrivals in Africa. Not only was this approach cost effective, it also enabled persons to receive protection and assistance within the shortest time possible.

The Limitations of the 'Extended' Definition

Although the OAU Convention facilitated the recognition of refugee status, it also has limitations that should not be underestimated. Firstly, as Alice Edwards rightly notes, the cognizable grounds in Article 1(2) of the Convention, namely, 'aggression', 'occupation', 'foreign domination' and 'events disturbing public order' in the context of refugee claims, were not elaborated.[50] This did not pose a problem in the open-door policy era when refugee claims were dealt with on a humanitarian basis with minimal regard to legal intricacies. Ironically, this 'humanitarian approach' to the application of the extended definition contributed to stunting the development of jurisprudence on concepts in Article 1(2) referred to earlier and, in particular, as to how they related to the concept of persecution under the 1951 Convention definition of refugees.

On a number of factors, including the demise of the open-door policy, states have in recent times increasingly resorted to individualized

---

[50] A. Edwards, 'Refugee Status Determination in Africa', *Revue Africaine de droit international et comparé* 14 (2006), 204, 212.

procedures to determine eligibility for recognition of refugee status, even in situations of mass influx. This includes, perforce, making determination as to whether an asylum claimant has fled his or her country as a result of one of the situations prescribed in Article 1(2) of the OAU Convention. However, these situations are described through concepts which are not easy to apply to particular factual scenarios in which mass influxes of refugees in Africa currently occur.[51]

It is also worth noting in this regard that the cognizable grounds under Article 1(2) of the OAU Convention were, with the exception of 'events seriously disturbing public order', developed in the context of decolonization. The perpetrators were presumed to be colonial states within their territories or in neighbouring independent countries. Thus, a determination could be made that aggression, occupation or foreign domination had taken place without fear of raising political tensions with another Member State of the OAU.

With the process of decolonization complete and asylum-seekers coming from independent African countries or as a result of actions by independent African countries in other states, the determination that acts such as 'aggression', 'occupation' and 'foreign domination' have taken place is likely to result in the grant of asylum to be treated as political, the very situation which the OAU Convention intended to avert. The possibility of this occurring could be minimized by developing guidelines regarding the interpretation of these concepts in an individualized status-determination procedure.

The second limitation of the extended definition is the lack of standards for refugee status determination. Many commentators on the OAU Convention give an impression that it provides facility for status determination on a group basis in mass-influx situations. However, as Okoth-Obbo rightly notes, this is not the case. The truth is that 'in relation to an elaborate or even only *essential* set of *standards* pursuant to which the *process* of refugee status determination could be devised and status determination operations better structured, organised and delivered in *mass influx* or so-called *group situations*, the OAU Convention is entirely silent. As, indeed, is international refugee law in general.'[52]

---

[51] *Ibid.*, 211.
[52] Okoth-Obbo, 'Thirty Years On', 18. For a concurrent opinion, see B. Rutinwa, 'Prima Facie Status and Refugee Protection, New Issues in Refugee Research', working paper no. 69, Evaluation and Policy Analysis Unit, UNHCR (2002), 6–7.

The Executive Committee of the UNHCR has adopted a number of conclusions addressing the question of procedures for status determination. However, as noted elsewhere, none of these conclusions has adequately dealt with the issue of standards for attribution of refugee status in the context of mass influx.[53] In the absence of international standards, some states have attempted to devise their own procedures for recognition of refugees on a prima facie basis under their domestic legislation or in state practice. However, these procedures have not adequately addressed certain important issues in status determination, such as exclusion from refugee status, and terminal issues in refugee protection, such as cessation of status on grounds of ceased circumstances.

Rights of Refugees Recognized under the 1969 OAU Convention

One of the most important aspects of the problem of refugees which preoccupied African countries at the time of the development of the OAU Convention was provision of assistance to refugees to enable them to meet their basic needs. This issue featured in virtually all refugee-specific resolutions of the Council of Ministers adopted between 1964 and 1969. Thus, in CM/Res. 19(II) of February 1964, the Council tasked the Commission formed thereunder to examine, among other things, 'ways and means of maintaining refugees in their country of asylum'.[54] In CM/Res. 36(III), the Council recommended that 'the African Group at the United Nations, with the help of the Asian and other interested parties, submit a resolution requesting an increase in the assistance given to African refugees by the United Nations High Commissioner for Refugees'.[55] In CM/Res. 52(IV),[56] the Council of Ministers mandated that African members of the Executive Board of the United Nations High Commissioner for Refugees bring to the attention of the Board 'the case of African refugees and to support the efforts of the High Commissioner in increasing the assistance given to these refugees'.[57]

In CM/Res. 104(IX) of September 1967, the Council went beyond calling for African refugees to be given just assistance to expressing a desire to take 'the necessary measures to improve living conditions and ensure humane treatment for refugees, and to help them lead

---

[53] Rutinwa, 'Prima Facie Status', 6.   [54] CM/Res. 19, para. (b).   [55] CM/Res. 36, para. 4.
[56] CM/Res. 52, para. 6.   [57] CM/Res. 52(IV), para. 6.

a normal life, by putting to an end the refugee problem in general'.[58] A similar desire 'to adopt measures to improve the living conditions of the refugees and to help them to lead normal life' was expressed in CM/ Res. 149(XI) of September 1968.[59]

As noted earlier, the initial intention of the OAU was to develop an instrument that covered all aspects of the refugee problem in Africa,[60] including the rights of refugees. It was in its Seventeenth Ordinary Session in Addis Ababa, Ethiopia, held from 31 October to 4 November 1966, that the Council of Ministers expressed its desire that the African instrument should govern the specifically African aspects of the refugee problem and that it should come to be the effective regional complement to the 1951 Convention. Looking at the provisions of earlier drafts of the African Convention,[61] which were eventually dropped, most of these provisions related to the conditions of sojourn or, in modern parlance, the rights of refugees. So it must be assumed that these are some of the matters which, when it came to dealing with African refugees, the point of reference would be the relevant provisions of the 1951 Convention.

That refugees recognized under Section I(2) of the OAU Convention were entitled to the same standards of treatment as those recognized under the 1951 Convention was confirmed by the 1979 Arusha Conference on the African Refugee Problem, which recognized the definitions of the term 'refugee' contained in Article I, paragraphs 1 and 2, of the OAU Convention as the basis for determining refugee status in Africa and stressed 'the essential need for ensuring that African refugees are identified as such, so as to enable them to invoke the rights established for their benefit in the 1951 Refugee Convention and the 1967 Refugee Protocol and the 1969 OAU Refugee Convention'.[62]

The decision to leave out the issue of refugee rights from the OAU Convention and to leave this matter to the 1951 Convention meant that the ability of refugees in Africa to enjoy refugee rights became dependent on the ratification of the 1951 Convention by African states. As it turned out, many African countries did indeed ratify the

---

[58] CM/Res. 104, preamble para. 6.

[59] Organization of African Unity (Council of Ministers), Resolution on the Problems of Refugees in Africa (OAU, Algiers, September 1968), CM/Res. 149(XI).

[60] See CM/Res. 36, para. 6, which 'invites the Commission to draw up a draft Convention covering *all aspects* of the problem of refugees in Africa'.

[61] For which, see Jackson, *The Refugee Concept*, 180–1, n. 87.

[62] See 'Recommendations of the Arusha Conference on the African Refugee Problem', adopted at the Arusha Conference on the African Refugee Problem, 7–17 May 1979, Arusha, Tanzania, para. 2.

instrument. However, many of them, if not the majority, entered reservations on very important rights, including freedom of movement, gainful employment and access to education.

Apparently, African states entered reservations on the provisions relating to refugee rights because they did not regard them as being attuned to the realities of refugee problems in Africa. For example, African states found it difficult to sign onto the gainful employment provisions of the 1951 Convention. The mass-influx nature of refugee arrivals in Africa meant that in some cases the number of refugees in host countries was far higher than that of the local host populations.

In the first two decades of the adoption of the OAU Convention, the effect of this legal lacuna was not felt because of the open-door policy of many African countries and the international community's strong commitment to burden-sharing that enabled refugees to enjoy standards of treatment provided for under the 1951 Convention without being compelled to invoke its provisions. However, from the 1990s onwards, the open-door policy and commitment to burden-sharing were replaced with protection fatigue. As a result, refugees in Africa became increasingly unable to enjoy refugee rights, particularly those to which they were not entitled as a matter of law. Consequently, the treatment of refugees has fallen short of standards prescribed even for survival. As Okoth-Obbo rightly surmises, the elaboration of standards of treatment for refugees, including particularly social and community rights, was important then, but it is even more compelling today.[63] To redress this situation, 'fundamental and far-reaching changes are required on this matter, which only the force of law can bring about.'[64]

One option to bring about these legal changes is to get states to withdraw reservations regarding refugee rights under the 1951 Convention. In recent times, UNHCR has been pursuing this option with much vigour. One of the recent initiatives in this regard was the 'states pledges process' organized by UNHCR in 2011 as part of the events to mark the sixtieth anniversary of the 1951 Convention and the fiftieth anniversary of the 1961 Convention on the Reduction of Statelessness. Under the initiative, UNHCR invited states to make pledges in relation to these instruments, including withdrawal or review of reservations to the 1951 Convention. Eventually, however, only two African countries, namely, Burundi and Malawi, appear to have made specific pledges to review

[63] Okoth-Obbo, 'Thirty Years On', 21.   [64] *Ibid.*

reservations to the 1951 Convention.[65] It would appear that the majority of African states are still reluctant to sign up to the provisions relating to refugee rights in their present form. Therefore, there is a need to look for other legal devices for ensuring that refugee rights become part of the corpus of refugee law in Africa.

Another option that is theoretically possible is to seek the revision of the OAU Convention in order to incorporate refugee rights perhaps in an adapted form. However, as was concluded during the global consultations on international protection in the early 2000s, any attempt to revise any refugee instrument is not advisable. In the present political climate, an amendment could result in the watering down or expunging of important provisions, such as those on *non-refoulement* as a trade-off for inclusion of new provisions such as those on refugee rights. The most feasible approach is to develop some guidelines on access to specific rights of refugees in situations of mass influx, drawing on the provisions of refugee instruments, human rights, humanitarian and constitutional law.

Conclusions and Recommendations

From the discussion in the preceding sections, it can be reasonably concluded that the development of the OAU Convention was not motivated by dissatisfaction with the scope of the application of the 1951 Convention. Its primary purpose was to address special problems that African countries faced when hosting refugees generated by situations of armed conflict and generalized violence. The development of the OAU Convention should probably also be seen in the context of the trend in the human rights field to have regional instruments governing specific issue areas notwithstanding the existence of international instruments covering the same matters.

Also, it has been shown that the 'extended' definition of a refugee introduced by Article I(2) of the OAU Convention was an innovative way of legally defining the beneficiaries of international protection. However, it did not constitute a radical departure from the definitions of a refugee under the then-existing instruments, namely, the 1951 Convention and the Statute of UNHCR of 1950. In fact, the extended definition

---

[65] See UNHCR, 'Compilation and Analysis of Pledges at the Ministerial Meeting in Geneva, 7–8 December 2011, to Mark the 60th Anniversary of the 1951 Convention and the 50th Anniversary of the Convention on the Reduction of Statelessness' (entered into force 13 December 1975), 989 UNTS 175.

overlapped significantly with the existing definitions under these instruments. The value and positive contribution of the extended definition were not the introduction of a new and wider definition of a refugee. Its qualities lie in defining a 'refugee' in such terms as would make it easier to make a determination that a person seeking asylum indeed did qualify as a refugee. Therefore, there is no reason to presume that persons fleeing armed conflict and other situations of violence fall outside the ambit of the definition of a refugee under the 1951 Convention. However, guidelines are needed as to when and how the definitions of a refugee under the two instruments should be applied as well as how the provisions of both instruments should be applied in situations of mass influx.

Refugees recognized under any of the limbs of the definition of a refugee under the OAU Convention are in principle entitled to the rights of refugees under the 1951 Convention. However, most African states entered reservations on some of the most important rights related provisions of the 1951 Convention, particularly those relating to gainful employment and freedom of movement. This has limited the ability of refugees in Africa to enjoy these rights.

UNHCR has made efforts to get states to remove the reservations. However, this initiative has not produced satisfactory results, with states still reluctant to sign up to some of the provisions in their present form. Another option is to seek to incorporate refugee rights in the OAU Convention itself. However, under the current political climate, this move is neither desirable nor achievable. Therefore, the most feasible approach is to develop guidelines on refugee rights in situations of mass influx that draw on the provisions of the 1951 Convention and other branches of law such as human rights, humanitarian law and constitutional law. How well these guidelines are crafted and the way they operate may, over time, induce states to consider removing reservations on the relevant provisions of the 1951 Convention.

4

The 1969 OAU Refugee Convention in the
Context of Individual Refugee Status
Determination

MARINA SHARPE

Introduction

This chapter analyses the interpretation and application of the regional refugee definition contained in the 1969 Organization of African Unity Convention Governing the Specific Aspects of Refugee Problems in Africa[1] ('OAU Convention') in the context of individual refugee status determination (RSD) conducted by states in Africa.[2] It was commissioned by UNHCR to inform a roundtable on, and the development of international protection guidelines regarding, people fleeing armed conflict and other situations of violence across borders. Given the changes in the causes, character and effects of armed conflict and other situations of violence in Africa since the adoption of the OAU Convention, this chapter is primarily interested in how the OAU Convention's regional refugee definition is applied by states in individual RSD procedures in the contemporary context.

The section that follows this introduction describes the study's research methodology. The third section provides a brief background on the OAU Convention. The fourth section discusses procedural and substantive aspects of RSD practice of African countries with a focus on the latter. This includes a consideration of the relationship between the OAU Convention and its universal counterpart – the 1951

---

[1] Organization of African Unity Convention Governing the Specific Aspects of Refugee Problems in Africa (adopted 10 September 1969, entered into force 20 June 1974), 1001 UNTS 45 ('OAU Convention').

[2] NB: References to Article 1A(2) of the 1951 Convention and to Articles I(1) and I(2) of the OAU Convention should in most contexts be taken to refer equally to these provisions as incorporated into domestic laws.

Convention Relating to the Status of Refugees[3] ('1951 Convention') – in African state practice, the relative importance of objective and subjective considerations in decision-making under the OAU Convention's regional refugee definition and the importance and meaning of the definition's 'events seriously disturbing public order' clause. The final section concludes by summarizing the main trends that emerge from the analysis.

Methodology

The research methodology for this chapter was a desk-based review of primary and secondary sources conducted for the most part in 2013. Primary sources consisted of, among other things, a questionnaire[4] which was distributed with an explanatory cover letter to thirty-five UNHCR country offices across sub-Saharan Africa. The questionnaire approach was necessary because African refugee decisions are rarely reported, and detailed information on national refugee protection frameworks in Africa is not readily accessible.[5] The questionnaires elicited information on the legislative or formal legal framework for RSD, in particular, with respect to individuals who fled armed conflict and/or generalized violence. Completed questionnaires and/or documents responsive to requests made in the questionnaire were received from twenty-four UNHCR country offices.[6] Summary information on responsibility for and the legal basis of RSD was provided in these twenty-four responses; information about nineteen further countries[7] was derived from a table compiled by UNHCR's Regional Bureau for Africa. Additional information on certain states in southern Africa[8] was

---

[3] Convention Relating to the Status of Refugees (adopted 28 July 1951, entered into force 22 April 1954), 189 UNTS 137 ('1951 Convention').

[4] Lee Anne de la Hunt authored the questionnaire.

[5] Though it should be noted that Refworld has an impressive collection of African state legislation, including national refugee acts. All URLs last checked on 27 February 2013.

[6] In West Africa, Benin, Burkina Faso, Chad, Gabon, Ghana, Guinea, Guinea-Bissau, Liberia, Mali, Niger, Nigeria, Senegal and Togo; in southern Africa, Angola, Mozambique, Zambia and Zimbabwe; and in East Africa and the horn of Africa, Burundi, Djibouti, the Democratic Republic of Congo (note that at the time of the research in 2013 there was no RSD in the DRC), Ethiopia, Kenya, South Sudan and Tanzania.

[7] Botswana, Cameroon, Cape Verde, Central African Republic, Côte d'Ivoire, Eritrea, Gambia, Madagascar, Malawi, Mauritius, Namibia, the Republic of Congo, Rwanda, Sierra Leone, Somalia, South Africa, Sudan, Swaziland and Uganda.

[8] Angola, Botswana, Malawi, Mozambique, Namibia, South Africa, Zambia and Zimbabwe.

drawn from a UNHCR report.[9] In addition to completed question-naires, other primary research sources used – which were generally but not always provided by UNHCR country offices in response to the questionnaire – included decisions on refugee status, national refugee legislation (primary and secondary), forms used by decision-makers in adjudicating refugee status, minutes of refugee status eligibility committee meetings and sample RSD interview reports. Secondary sources included academic articles, books, book chapters, reports and UNHCR's online country profiles.[10] Of Africa's fifty-four states, some information – whether responsive to a questionnaire or otherwise and whether primary or secondary – was available for fifty. Because the same range of information was not available for all fifty countries, the study cannot generalize. This chapter generalizes only to the extent permitted by the information available; the states on whose practice key conclusions are based are clearly identified.

In many cases, the primary information available was very limited and/or did not include much detail on how individuals fleeing conflict and/or violence are protected. An effort was made to supplement the information gathered pursuant to the questionnaire with additional primary research, particularly regarding RSD decisions. However, as noted earlier, most states in Africa do not report their RSD decisions. Two notable exceptions are Benin and South Africa.[11] Moreover, even where decisions are available, they tend to contain limited legal reason-ing that might reveal how Article I(2) of the OAU Convention is understood and applied.[12] Owing presumably to this limited range of primary research material, the range of secondary sources on the interpretation of Article I(2) of the OAU Convention is also very narrow. Few academic papers have been published on the OAU Convention's regional refugee definition specifically.[13] Similarly rare

---

[9] UNHCR, Regional Office for Southern Africa, 'Refugee Status Determination in Southern Africa: Best Practices and Gaps Analysis', 2010.

[10] See www.unhcr.org/pages/49c3646c206.html.

[11] South Africa is the only African country with a page on www.refugeecaselaw.org, a site maintained by the University of Michigan Law School, where judicial decisions are available. Judicial decisions have also been compiled by the University of Cape Town's Refugee Rights Project and made available online. First instance administrative decisions have at times been made available to researchers. Benin's decisions are available online at www.cnarbenin.bj.

[12] See the section, 'Substantive Aspects of State Refugee Status Determination'.

[13] T. Schreier, 'An Evaluation of South Africa's Application of the OAU Refugee Definition', Refuge 25 (2008), 53. Exceptions are A. Edwards, 'Refugee Status Determination in

are recent general analyses of African domestic legal frameworks for refugee protection,[14] despite initiatives to promote scholarship on this topic.[15]

As a result of the limited nature of the primary information available, the lack of reported RSD decisions, the absence or inadequacy of the legal reasoning in decisions that are published and the dearth of secondary source material, this chapter's conclusions on how people fleeing conflict and/or violence are protected under the OAU Convention are necessarily limited. Further empirical research into asylum procedures and refugee decision-making in Africa should be pursued. This chapter's conclusions reflect what themes emerged from the research material that was available, with a number of country-specific examples. These conclusions are placed in context with the following background on the OAU Convention and the general refugee situation in Africa.

The OAU Convention and the Refugee Context in Africa

Regional-level work on the issue of refugee protection in Africa began very soon after the Organization of African Unity's (OAU) 1963 formation, as evidenced by a 1964 resolution of the body's Council of Ministers.

Africa', *Afr J Intl Comp L* 14 (2006), 204; M. B. Rankin, 'Extending the Limits or Narrowing the Scope? Deconstructing the OAU Refugee Definition Thirty Years On', *S Afr J Hum Rts* 21 (2005), 406; T. Wood, 'Expanding Protection in Africa? Case Studies of the Implementation of the 1969 African Refugee Convention's Expanded Refugee Definition', *IJRL* 26 (2015), 555. It should be noted that the first two works are based on principled legal reasoning rather than on an extensive review of jurisprudence.

[14] Exceptions are R. Amit, 'No Refuge: Flawed Status Determination and the Failures of South Africa's Refugee System to Provide Protection', *IJRL* 23 (2011), 458; R. Amit, 'All Roads Lead to Rejection: Persistent Bias and Incapacity in South African Refugee Status Determination, African Centre for Migration and Society Research Report', 2012, available online; K. Kamanga, 'The (Tanzania) Refugees Act of 1998: Some Legal and Policy Implications', *JRS* 18 (2005), 100; T. S. Nkhoma, 'The Institution of Asylum in Malawi and International Refugee Law: A Review of the 1989 Refugee Act', *Malawi LJ* 4 (2010), 97; M. Sharpe and S. Namusobya, 'Refugee Status Determination and the Rights of Recognised Refugees under Uganda's Refugee Act, 2006', *IJRL* 24 (2012), 561.

[15] In November 2010, the University of Oxford's Refugee Studies Centre convened in Kampala a two-day workshop on RSD and refugee rights in east and southern Africa. The workshop papers and its report are available online at: www.rsc.ox.ac.uk/events/refugee-status-determination-and-rights. The Rights in Exile Programme of the International Refugee Rights Initiative (www.refugeelegalaidinformation.org) has also sought to foster scholarship on domestic refugee protection frameworks in the global south.

The resolution established an ad hoc commission consisting of OAU ambassadors from Burundi, Cameroon, Congo-Léopoldville (today the Democratic Republic of the Congo (DRC)), Ghana, Nigeria, Rwanda, Senegal, Sudan, Tanganyika (today Tanzania) and Uganda to examine '(a) the refugee problem in Africa and make recommendations to the Council of Ministers on how it can be solved; [and] (b) ways and means of maintaining refugees in their country of asylum'.[16]

The drafting process this resolution ultimately gave rise to is the subject of varied and conflicting accounts in part because there are no official *travaux préparatoires* for the OAU Convention. These accounts can, for ease of exposition, essentially be divided into two categories. On the one hand are commentators who address the OAU Convention's drafting history only briefly, without reference to primary sources such as OAU resolutions and archival material. They tend to note that the OAU's interest in a regional refugee instrument was the result of the persecution-based universal refugee definition's failure to reflect African realities,[17] such as displacement resulting from colonialism and racist regimes. On the other hand are a handful of writers who have addressed the OAU Convention's drafting history in some depth.[18] Such accounts have consistently attributed the motivations behind the OAU Convention to two factors: 'The first of these was the problem of subversive activities and the other the date line contained in Article 1A(2) of the 1951 Convention. The latter meant that whatever was the legal scope of application of the 1951 Convention, it did not apply to the new refugee situations which had arisen in Africa.'[19]

[16] Organization of African Unity (Council of Ministers), Resolution on the Problem of Refugees in Africa (OAU Lagos, 24–29 February 1964), CM/Res 19 (II).

[17] G. Okoth-Obbo, 'Thirty Years On: A Legal Review of the 1969 OAU Convention Governing the Specific Aspects of Refugee Problems in Africa', *RSQ* 20 (2001), 79, 109; see e.g. O. Goundiam, 'African Refugee Convention', *Migr News* 3 (1970), 8; J. L. Turner, 'Liberian Refugees: A Test of the 1969 OAU Convention Governing the Specific Aspects of Refugee Problems in Africa', *Geo Immigr LJ* 8 (1994), 281, 286; J. Hyndman and B. V. Nylund, 'UNHCR and the Status of Prima Facie Refugees in Kenya', *IJRL* 10 (1998), 21, 34–5.

[18] See L. Holborn, *Refugees: A Problem of Our Time – The Work of the United Nations High Commissioner for Refugees, 1951–1972*, Vols. I and II (Lanham, MD: Scarecrow Press, 1974); I. Jackson, *The Refugee Concept in Group Situations* (Leiden: Martinus Nijhoff, 1999); Okoth-Obbo, 'Thirty Years On: A Legal Review of the 1969 OAU Convention', 109–12.

[19] Okoth-Obbo, 'Thirty Years On: A Legal Review of the 1969 OAU Convention', 109–10. Article 1A(2) of the 1951 Convention limited the instrument's applicability to flight from events occurring before 1 January 1951. Under Article 1B, states have the option of further limiting its applicability to events occurring in Europe. Among African states,

The historical record is consistent with this latter account.[20] In particular, that four of the five drafts of the OAU Convention include only the 1951 Convention refugee definition (without the dateline) confirms that dissatisfaction beyond the dateline question was simply not a factor initially motivating the adoption of a regional instrument. Until the time the 1967 Protocol Relating to the Status of Refugees[21] ('1967 Protocol') was adopted, work on the OAU Convention was directed at making the 1951 Convention applicable in Africa; only later would addressing refugee issues particular to Africa – concern that refugees should not be a source of friction between states and that individuals fleeing particularly African situations such as colonialism and white racist regimes should receive refugee protection – become an explicit objective.

The legal instrument these concerns ultimately gave rise to has – alongside the 1951 Convention[22] – governed the protection of refugees in Africa since its entry into force in 1974. In defining a refugee, the OAU Convention's Article I provides two sub-provisions. The first adopts the refugee definition found in Article 1A(2) of the 1951 Convention minus the 1 January 1951 date limit that most states later agreed, by way of the 1967 Protocol,[23] not to apply. This definition applies to those outside their country of origin (or habitual residence in the case of stateless refugees) who cannot return there because of 'a well-founded fear of being persecuted for reasons of race, religion, nationality, membership of a particular social group or political opinion'.[24] The second sub-provision provides: '[T]he term refugee shall also apply to every person who, owing to external aggression, occupation, foreign domination or events seriously disturbing public order in either part or the whole of his country of origin or nationality, is compelled to leave his [or her] place of habitual residence in order to seek refuge in another place outside his [or her] country of origin or nationality'.[25]

---

only Madagascar and the Democratic Republic of Congo recognize this geographical limitation.

[20] For detailed exposition of this record, see M. Sharpe, 'Organization of African Unity and African Union Engagement with Refugee Protection: 1963–2011', *Afr J Intl Comp L* 21 (2013), 50.

[21] Protocol Relating to the Status of Refugees (entered into force 4 October 1967), 606 UNTS 267 ('1967 Protocol').

[22] See part III of M. Sharpe, 'The 1969 African Refugee Convention: Innovations, Misconceptions, and Omissions', *McGill LJ* 58 (2012), 95.

[23] 1967 Protocol, Art. 1(2).   [24] 1951 Convention, Art. 1A(2).

[25] OAU Convention, Art. I(2).

In moving away from the 1951 Convention's emphasis on individua-lized persecution linked to Convention grounds in favour of a focus on disruptive conditions in the country of origin or nationality, the Article I(2) refugee definition stresses protection from what might be more broadly applicable conditions. According to Hathaway, it 'acknowledges that fundamental forms of abuse may occur not only as a result of the calculated acts of the government . . . but also as a result of that government's loss of authority'.[26] This outward orientation has led to the conclusion among most scholars of the OAU Convention that the Article I(2) refugee definition is 'based solely on objective criteria'[27] and therefore mandates an objective test of refugee status.[28] This consensus is overstated for two reasons. Firstly, focus on the objectivity of the Article I(2) refugee definition over-estimates the subjectivity of the 1951 Convention definition[29] and under-estimates the extent to which the universal definition can equally apply to victims of war and civil strife.[30] Secondly, views of the Article I(2) refugee definition as entirely objective overlook elements of the definition that mandate an assessment of the nexus between the individual and the disruptive situation in the country of origin or nationality: that the individual must have been 'compelled' to leave his or her 'place of habitual residence'[31] and that such flight must have been 'owing to' external aggression, occupation, foreign domination or events seriously disturbing public order. These aspects of Article I(2) and their impact on RSD under the OAU Convention are addressed in detail later in this chapter.

---

[26] J. Hathaway, *The Law of Refugee Status* (Toronto: Butterworths, 1991), 17.

[27] E. O. Awuku, 'Refugee Movements in Africa and the OAU Convention on Refugees', *J Afr L* 39 (1995), 79, 81.

[28] See e.g. E. Arboleda, 'Refugee Definition in Africa and Latin America: The Lessons of Pragmatism', *IJRL* 3 (1991), 185, 195; Okoth-Obbo, 'Thirty Years On: A Legal Review of the 1969 OAU Convention', 112; P. Weis, 'The Convention of the Organization of African Unity Governing the Specific Aspects of Refugee Problems in Africa', *Revue des droits de l'homme* 3 (1970), 449, 455; W. J. E. M. van Hövell tot Westerflier, 'Africa and Refugees: The OAU Refugee Convention in Theory and Practice', *NQHR* 7 (1989), 172, 175.

[29] Rankin, 'Extending the Limits or Narrowing the Scope?', 411.

[30] Jackson, *The Refugee Concept in Group Situations*, 178; Okoth-Obbo, 'Thirty Years On: A Legal Review of the 1969 OAU Convention', 117; see V. Holzer, 'The 1951 Refugee Convention and the Protection of People Fleeing Armed Conflict and Other Situations of Violence', UNHCR Legal and Protection Policy Research Series, 2012, 12; W. Kälin, 'Refugees and Civil Wars: Only a Matter of Interpretation?', *IJRL* 3 (1991), 435.

[31] Edwards, 'Refugee Status Determination in Africa', 228; Okoth-Obbo, 'Thirty Years On: A Legal Review of the 1969 OAU Convention', 116; Rankin, 'Extending the Limits or Narrowing the Scope?', 412.

To date, the OAU Convention has been ratified by forty-six of the African Union's fifty-four member states. Morocco is party to the Convention; however, it withdrew from the OAU in 1985 after the Saharawi Arab Democratic Republic (which has neither signed nor ratified the OAU Convention) was admitted as a member state. Djibouti, Eritrea, Madagascar, Mauritius, Namibia, Sao Tomé and Principé and Somalia have signed but not ratified the OAU Convention. The Comoros, Eritrea, Libya, Mauritius and South Sudan have neither signed nor ratified the 1951 Convention nor its 1967 Protocol. Madagascar is a party to the 1951 Convention but not its 1967 Protocol, and it and the Republic of Congo continue to recognize the 1951 Convention's geographical limitation.[32] Cape Verde is party to the 1967 Protocol but not the 1951 Convention. Despite the fact that most African countries have ratified the international and regional refugee instruments, the situation for the almost 3 million[33] refugees in Africa is difficult, with their rights regularly violated.[34] Many refugees in Africa will have fled as a result of conflict and other situations of violence at home. Indeed, as of the end of 2010, the vast majority of refugees in Africa were recognized under the OAU Convention, not the 1951 Convention.[35] How its Article I(2) is applied to protect individuals from return to conflict and violence is considered next.

Procedural Aspects of State Refugee Status Determination

Some information on RSD was available for the forty-three states from which questionnaire or tabular responses were received and for two

---

[32] See note 19.

[33] According to UNHCR's *2013 Statistical Yearbook*, 13th edn (Geneva: UNHCR, 2013), at end of 2013, 25 per cent of the global refugee population of 11.7 million was in sub-Saharan Africa.

[34] See, among other works, E. Abuya, 'From Here to Where? Refugees Living in Protracted Situations in Africa', in A. Edwards and C. Ferstman (eds.), *Human Security and Non-Citizens: Law, Policy and International Affairs* (Cambridge University Press, 2010); J. Crisp, 'No Solutions in Sight: The Problem of Protracted Refugee Situations in Africa', in I. Ohta and Y. Gebre (eds.), *Displacement Risks in Africa: Refugees, Resettlers and Their Host Population* (Kyoto University Press, 2005); R. Ramcharan, 'The African Refugee Crisis: Contemporary Challenges to the Protection of Refugees and Displaced Persons in Africa', *Afr YB Intl L* 8 (2000), 119; B. Rutinwa, 'The End of Asylum? The Changing Nature of Refugee Policies in Africa', *RSQ* 21 (2002), 12; G. Verdirame and B. Harrell-Bond, *Rights in Exile: Janus Faced Humanitarianism* (Oxford, UK: Berghan Books, 2005).

[35] UNHCR statistics, on file with the author. Note that UNHCR no longer collects information on the definition pursuant to which refugees in Africa are recognized.

further states, namely, Algeria and Egypt.[36] Of these forty-five states, thirty-five have state-run RSD systems, while ten feature RSD conducted by UNHCR under its mandate. This discussion of individual RSD as conducted by states begins with a brief consideration of procedural aspects.

The national legislation of African states with domestic refugee laws generally incorporates the 1951 Convention Article 1A(2) definition and the OAU Convention Articles I(1) and I(2) refugee definitions, whether by reproducing these definitions in full or, less often, by referring to the relevant provisions of the international and regional refugee instruments (examples of the latter approach include Benin, Gabon, Ghana and Senegal). Exceptions are Botswana, Djibouti, Morocco and Zambia. Botswana has not incorporated the OAU Convention within its 1968 Refugees (Recognition and Control) Act; however, the country's Refugee Advisory Committee has recognized individual applicants from neighbouring countries on the basis of OAU Convention principles.[37] Djibouti's 1977 refugee law does not incorporate the OAU Convention, which it only signed in 2005 and which it has yet to ratify. In practice, however, Djibouti applies Article I(2) to individuals fleeing south and central Somalia, whom it recognizes on a prima facie basis.[38] Morocco's 1957 refugee law pre-dates the OAU Convention and so does not reflect its Article I(2).[39] In Zambia, refugee status is declaratory[40]; thus, while the OAU Convention has not been incorporated, the government has the discretion to recognize refugees from conflict and/or violence.[41]

When African states adjudicate refugee claims individually, which is the normal practice in the absence of a situation of mass influx,[42] the decision on refugee status is generally made by an administrative eligibility committee on which a variety of government departments are represented. UNHCR usually has advisory observer status on this committee, as in Benin, Chad, Ethiopia, Gabon, Mozambique, Niger,

---

[36] The author has firsthand experience in Egypt, and information on Algeria was found on that country's UNHCR country profile.

[37] UNHCR Regional Office for Southern Africa, 'Refugee Status Determination in Southern Africa', 21.

[38] Djibouti questionnaire, on file with the author.

[39] For more information on the situation in Morocco, see C. Lindstrom, 'Report on the Situation of Refugees in Morocco: Findings of an Exploratory Study', 2002, available online.

[40] Refugees (Control) Act 1970 (Zambia), Cap 120, sec. 3.

[41] Zambia questionnaire, on file with the author.

[42] Review of all questionnaires, which are all on file with the author.

Tanzania and Zambia,[43] for example. In rare cases, UNHCR has a decision-making role. Eligibility committees approach RSD in three principal ways. The first approach is for the committee itself to interview the refugee, as in the case of Chad.[44] Under the second approach, another state official conducts the status-determination interview, and the eligibility committee makes a decision on the basis of notes or a transcript taken during the interview. This is the situation in Uganda, where the police interview the applicant,[45] and in Tanzania, where an 'authorized officer' conducts the interview.[46] In the third and final approach, an eligibility official from the government's refugee or immigration department conducts the interview and provides the eligibility committee with a transcript and a reasoned recommendation, on which the committee bases its decision. This is the approach in Angola, Mozambique and Zambia.[47] Some states combine elements from two or more of these approaches. Whatever the approach, detailed written reasons for the decision seem generally not to be provided.[48]

Appeals are generally, though not always, available. In some cases, the same eligibility committee that decided the first instance case – though sometimes featuring new members – hears and decides on the appeal. This is the approach in Uganda, for example.[49] In other countries, a separate administrative appeals body exists. This is the case in, for example, Malawi and Tanzania.[50] Rarely is judicial review available, whether at the appeal level or as a third tier of review. It is legally possible in, for example, South Africa and Zambia.[51] It has never actually occurred in Zambia,[52] while in South Africa it has occurred to a limited

---

[43] Review of all questionnaires, which are all on file with the author.

[44] Chad questionnaire, on file with the author.

[45] Sharpe and Namusobya, 'Refugee Status Determination and the Rights of Recognised Refugees under Uganda's Refugee Act'.

[46] C. Nyonka, 'Refugee Status Determination and Refugee Rights in Tanzania', paper contributed to University of Oxford Refugee Studies Centre Workshop on RSD and Rights in East and Southern Africa, 2010, 9, available online at: www.rsc.ox.ac.uk/events/refugee-status-determination-and-rights.

[47] Review of all questionnaires, which are all on file with the author.

[48] Review of all questionnaires, which are all on file with the author.

[49] Sharpe and Namusobya, 'Refugee Status Determination and the Rights of Recognised Refugees under Uganda's Refugee Act'.

[50] Review of all questionnaires, which are all on file with the author.

[51] Review of all questionnaires, which are all on file with the author.

[52] C. Chitupila, 'The Administration of Refugees in Zambia', paper contributed to University of Oxford Refugee Studies Centre Workshop on RSD and Rights in East and Southern Africa, 2010, 9, available online at: www.rsc.ox.ac.uk/events/refugee-status-determination-and-rights.

extent, though this has been on procedural rather than substantive grounds.[53]

Substantive Aspects of State Refugee Status Determination

The research for this chapter did not reveal any jurisprudence interpreting the OAU Convention's Article I(2). One might expect this to have emerged from South Africa, which has a relatively well-developed legal system. However, this has not been the case. Of the four available reviews of South African refugee jurisprudence,[54] none revealed an authoritative interpretation of section 3(b) of South Africa's Refugees Act, which reflects Article I(2) of the OAU Convention. Indeed, Amit notes that section 3(b) 'has been largely absent from South Africa's status determination process'.[55] Moreover, all four studies noted the poor quality of South African refugee decision-making, three with specific reference to section 3(b). In Wood's survey of 307 South African decisions on refugee status from 2009, 185 characterized the applicant's claim as involving conflict or violence. Fifty-five of these made reference to section 3(b) of South Africa's Refugees Act; however, in all but three decisions, the reference to section 3(b) was cursory, consisting only of a statement such as 'the applicant does not have a refugee claim under section 3(b).' The reasoning in the three decisions where such could be said to exist was, according to Wood, very short.[56] Amit remarks that none of the 324 decisions she reviewed demonstrated a correct application of section 3 (b), 'effectively negating its role in the law'.[57] Schreier attributes poor-quality RSD decisions to limited resources, which lead to a lack of training and low-quality country-of-origin information.[58]

The Relationship between the 1951 and OAU Conventions

While no authoritative interpretation of Article I(2) has emerged from the case law, there do seem to be three distinct approaches regarding the

---

[53] Input from UNHCR's Regional Office for Southern Africa.
[54] Amit, 'No Refuge'; Amit, 'All Roads Lead to Rejection'; Schreier, 'An Evaluation of South Africa's Application of the OAU Refugee Definition'; Wood, 'Expanding Protection in Africa?'.
[55] Amit, 'All Roads Lead to Rejection', 45.   [56] Wood, 'Expanding Protection in Africa?'.
[57] Amit, 'No Refuge', 474.
[58] Schreier, 'An Evaluation of South Africa's Application of the OAU Refugee Definition', 56.

instrument under which refugee status is adjudicated. The first is to begin by applying Article 1A(2) of the 1951 Convention and to move on to Article I(2) of the OAU Convention only if the individual does not qualify under the 1951 Convention. This is the approach in Benin[59] and Burkina Faso. In the latter country, decisions are rendered on a form that instructs the decision-maker to proceed according to this sequence.[60] This approach is supported by paragraph 9 of the preamble to the OAU Convention, which recognizes the 1951 Convention as 'the basic and universal instrument relating to the status of refugees', as well as by the ordering of the two refugee definitions in Article I of the OAU Convention. Furthermore, this approach aligns with the practice of resettlement countries, which often make resettlement contingent on Article 1A(2) refugee status; assessing refugee status under the 1951 Convention first therefore ensures that the greatest number of refugees will qualify for resettlement.

An alternative approach is employed in Angola, Chad, Mozambique, Tanzania, Zambia and Zimbabwe,[61] as well as in South Africa[62] and Uganda,[63] where the instrument applied is a function of the nature of the claimant's flight. Where the nature of flight dictates the application of Article I(2), individual circumstances of persecution are not considered. In Chad and Zambia,[64] as well as in South Africa,[65] if it is clear that the claimant fled conflict, then the assessment proceeds on the basis of Article I(2). Van Beek explains the South African approach, which 'depends on whether it is "obvious" that an applicant is a refugee, based on the danger and instability within a part of the applicant's country of origin'.[66] In Angola and Mozambique, there is an observed tendency to

---

[59] Benin questionnaire, on file with the author.

[60] 2009 Burkina Faso decision, on file with the author.

[61] Angola, Chad, Mozambique, Tanzania, Zambia and Zimbabwe questionnaires, on file with the author.

[62] Schreier, 'An Evaluation of South Africa's Application of the OAU Refugee Definition', 54.

[63] Remarks of Douglas Asiimwe (Senior Protection Officer, Office of the Prime Minister, Republic of Uganda) at UNHCR Expert Roundtable, Cape Town, 14 September 2012.

[64] Chad and Zambia questionnaires, on file with the author.

[65] Schreier, 'An Evaluation of South Africa's Application of the OAU Refugee Definition', 54.

[66] I. van Beek, 'Prima Facie Asylum Determination in South Africa: A Description of Policy and Practice', in J. Handmaker, L. A. de la Hunt and J. Klaaren (eds.), *Perspectives on Refugee Protection in South Africa* (Pretoria, South Africa: Lawyers for Human Rights, 2001), 18, cited by Schreier, 'An Evaluation of South Africa's Application of the OAU Refugee Definition', 54.

conduct most RSD under the OAU Convention's Article I(2),[67] even when the 1951 Convention Article 1A(2) refugee definition would equally apply. In Zimbabwe, RSD always occurs under Article I(2), even though the 1983 Refugees Act incorporates both the 1951 Convention and the OAU Convention definitions.[68] This tendency in Angola and Mozambique to employ – and in the case of Zimbabwe to automatically resort to – Article I(2) likely relates to the nature of flight to the three countries, which according to UNHCR is better reflected by Article I(2) than by the 1951 Convention definition.[69]

It is not always, however, a case of either a sequential or fact-based 'nature of flight' approach. The application of the 1951 Convention and/ or the OAU Convention is sometimes pragmatic. According to Okoth-Obbo, the Article I(2) refugee definition is easier to apply in situations of large-scale influx than is Article 1A(2) of the 1951 Convention,[70] in particular, because of its compatibility with RSD conducted on a prima facie basis. Moreover, many states consider applying Article I(2) to be generally more expedient and less resource intensive than applying Article 1A(2) of the 1951 Convention.[71] Zambia, for example, has a policy of conducting RSD on a prima facie basis under the OAU Convention in the borderlands, where most refugees arrive. Those whose claims are more aligned with the 1951 Convention are referred to the capital, Lusaka, for individual determination under Article 1A(2).[72] Those who arrive in Lusaka without having transited through the borderlands also have their claims processed under the 1951 Convention.[73]

In still other cases, the approach seems unsystematic. In Nigeria, where the refugee legislation includes both the 1951 Convention and the OAU Convention refugee definitions, a case based on flight from unspecified insecurity was rejected under Article 1A(2) without any subsequent consideration of Article I(2).[74] The same was true of a decision from

---

[67] Angola and Mozambique questionnaires, on file with the author.

[68] Zimbabwe questionnaire, on file with the author.

[69] UNHCR Regional Office for Southern Africa, 'Refugee Status Determination in Southern Africa', 21. The nature of flight to countries beyond Angola, Mozambique and Zimbabwe may also be best reflected by Article I(2) of the OAU Convention; however, the available information was limited to these three.

[70] Okoth-Obbo, 'Thirty Years On', 120.   [71] Input from UNHCR's RSD Unit.

[72] Chitupila, 'The Administration of Refugees in Zambia', 8.

[73] Zambia questionnaire, on file with the author.

[74] *Nigerian Decision No. 5*, in April 2010 report of the Nigerian Eligibility Committee, on file with the author.

Guinea regarding a woman who fled the conflict in Liberia in 1992.[75] Even worse than an unsystematic approach, a number of decisions evidenced a misunderstanding of the distinct nature of the two refugee definitions. In two Guinean cases, the reasoning combined the 1951 Convention's 'membership of a particular social group' ground with the OAU Convention's ground of 'events seriously disturbing public order'.[76] This conflation was also evident in a decision from Liberia.[77]

The Test for Refugee Status under Article I(2)

In addition to the order in which the OAU Convention is invoked relative to its 1951 counterpart, another issue salient to the African instrument's application is the extent to which the personal circumstances of the applicant, as opposed to the objective circumstances prevailing in the country of origin, inform the test for refugee status under Article I(2).[78] Article I(2) has traditionally been regarded as susceptible to an entirely objective application largely disconnected from personal circumstances. However, it is far from clear that refugee status under Article I(2) should be assessed entirely on an objective basis for two primary reasons. Firstly, the Article I(2) refugee definition is framed in terms of individual status. Edwards argues that 'this necessitates inquiring into the individual or subjective reasons for flight of each applicant.'[79] The second reason is textual, beginning with the use of the word 'compelled'. The 'compelled' aspect of the Article I(2) refugee definition seems to have much in common with the 'fear' aspect of the 1951 Convention definition, which necessitates the consideration of individual aspects of the case: particular events that may compel one person to flee his or her place of habitual residence may not result in such compulsion in another individual whose calculation of the risk of the events differs. Indeed, Okoth-Obbo notes that Article I(2) 'is predicated mainly on the compulsion to leave the place of habitual residence in order to seek refuge ... [This] reintroduces the

---

[75] Undated *Guinean Decision No. 1*, on file with the author.
[76] Undated *Guinean Decisions No. 2 and 3*, on file with the author.
[77] *1 February 2010 Liberian Decision*, on file with the author.
[78] This section draws largely on Sharpe, The 1969 African Refugee Convention: Innovations, Misconceptions, and Omissions; i.e. much of this section condenses part of an article in the *McGill Law Journal*.
[79] Edwards, 'Refugee Status Determination in Africa', 228.

problematic question of motive for flight which it is otherwise credited with having disabused from the refugee definition.'[80]

The reference to compulsion in Article I(2) seems to mandate an assessment of whether the disruptive situation in question caused the individual refugee's flight, as opposed to a test ignorant of personal circumstances that looks solely for the existence in fact of a disruptive situation in the refugee's country of origin or nationality. Yet, commentary on the OAU Convention has rarely explicitly addressed whether a nexus between the disruptive situation and flight is required. Rather, there seems to be an implicit interpretive consensus presuming that an individual would not flee a disruptive situation but for a nexus between such a situation and his or her compulsion to leave. Indeed, according to Hathaway, 'because the African standard emphasizes assessment of the gravity of the disruption of public order rather than motives for flight, individuals are largely able to decide for themselves when harm is sufficiently proximate to warrant flight.'[81] Implicit in this view is the assumption that in the determination of refugee status, flight itself is sufficient evidence of compulsion. While in most cases this assumption will be borne out, it obfuscates the importance of, firstly, the words 'owing to' and, secondly, the fact that the individual must be compelled to leave his or her 'place of habitual residence'. Indeed, the inclusion of 'owing to' and 'place of habitual residence' further suggests that, in principle, the nexus between the disruptive events and flight ought to be more than merely presumptive.

The ordinary meaning of 'owing to' is analogous to 'as a result of', 'because of' or 'due to'. Accordingly, under the Article I(2) definition, a refugee is someone who, as a result of, because of or due to a disruptive situation, flees his or her place of habitual residence. Put this way, it becomes clear that flight must be the direct consequence of a risk of harm to the individual stemming from the disruptive situation; the words 'owing to' are an additional textual element of the Article I(2) refugee definition that mandates a subjective test of refugee status because they suggest the requirement of a nexus between the disruptive situation and flight. Furthermore, the Article I(2) refugee definition specifically provides that a refugee must have fled his or her 'place of habitual residence', as opposed to his or her 'country of origin or nationality'. According to

---

[80] Okoth-Obbo, 'Thirty Years On', 116 (emphasis added); see also Edwards, 'Refugee Status Determination in Africa', 228.

[81] Hathaway, *The Law of Refugee Status*, 18.

Rankin, this clause is used to focus 'attention on those who face danger because of the state of their communities', resulting in 'an implied relationship or geographic nexus between an OAU event and a person's place of habitual residence'.[82] That the Article I(2) definition requires physical proximity between the putative refugee and the disruptive situation further suggests that the regional refugee definition demands that a nexus between the risk of harm and reasons for flight be established. Indeed, this was the approach taken in a South African refugee appeal board decision analysed by Schreier.[83]

The requirement that flight be from the place of habitual residence also explains why the fact that the harm may be in 'either part or the whole of' the country of origin or nationality does not expand the refugee definition as much as might initially appear. The specific mention that the harm may be in 'part or the whole of' the country of origin or nationality makes it at least initially plausible that an individual may be recognized as a refugee if his or her flight is prompted by a situation anywhere in his or her homeland. However, in context, it becomes clear that there is 'a necessary link between the asylum seeker and the OAU event ... the nexus is created by the fact that an asylum seeker is compelled to leave his or her place of habitual residence.'[84] Moreover, the clause, 'either part or the whole of his country of origin or nationality' likely applies only to 'events seriously disturbing public order'. This is so for interpretive reasons – the lack of a comma between 'events seriously disturbing public order' and 'in either part or the whole of' and the result of applying the doctrine *ejusdem generis*[85] – and because the necessity of specifying 'either part or the whole of' attaches only to 'events seriously disturbing public order'. Occupation and foreign domination, even if physically affecting only one part of a state, will politically affect the country as a whole, as explained by Edwards: 'the international requirement associated with the ... three terms suggests

---

[82] Rankin, 'Extending the Limits or Narrowing the Scope?', 432.
[83] Schreier, 'An Evaluation of South Africa's Application of the OAU Refugee Definition', 60.
[84] Rankin, 'Extending the Limits or Narrowing the Scope?', 434; see also J. van Garderen and J. Ebenstein, 'Regional Developments: Africa', in A. Zimmermann (ed.), *The 1951 Convention Relating to the Status of Refugees and Its 1967 Protocol* (Oxford University Press, 2011), 191.
[85] This doctrine specifies that 'general words following special words are limited to the genus indicated by the special words' (I. Sinclair, *The Vienna Convention on the Law of Treaties*, 2nd edn. (Manchester University Press, 1984), 153).

that they are experienced throughout the whole of the territory de jure, even if the actions are limited to specific parts of the territory de facto.'[86] The inclusion of 'either part or the whole of his [or her] country of origin or nationality' thus implies that a refugee cannot justifiably flee events that are not directly connected to him or her.

In summary, the terms 'compelled' and 'owing to' and the requirement that an individual have fled his or her 'place of habitual residence', coupled with the limited applicability of 'either part or the whole of his [or her] country of origin or nationality', suggest that in cases where the effects of the disruptive situation in question are not felt country-wide, a nexus between such a situation and flight must be established, as opposed to merely presumed. In addition to establishing nationality, it would therefore be necessary to examine the particular facts of the case. Determining refugee status under Article I(2) of the OAU Convention is not a purely objective test involving a mere assessment of whether a disruptive situation is affecting the country of origin or nationality; it also requires – at least in cases where the disruptive situation is not experienced country-wide – an assessment of the risk of harm the disruptive situation actually posed to the individual concerned and his or her compulsion to flee.

In situations in which the disruptive situation does affect the whole of the country from which the individual has fled, the existence of such a nexus may, as a purely procedural matter, be presumed; any other approach would belabour the obvious and, particularly in large-scale influxes, risks overwhelming already strained RSD processes. This approach finds support in the OAU Convention's 'Preamble'. Preamble paragraph 1 notes 'with concern the constantly increasing numbers of refugees in Africa and desirous of finding ways and means of alleviating their misery and suffering as well as providing them with a better life and future'. Paragraph 2 recognizes 'the need for an essentially humanitarian approach towards solving the problems of refugees'. Moreover, the presumption of a nexus between a disruptive situation and flight is clearly the basis on which RSD conducted on a prima facie basis – a common practice in Africa – rests, and this has been the approach in individual claims in South Africa at least.[87] There decision-makers have relied on

---

[86] Edwards, 'Refugee Status Determination in Africa', 227.

[87] A. Tuepker, 'On the Threshold of Africa: OAU and UN Definitions in South African Asylum Practice', *JRS* 15 (2002), 409, 418; Schreier, 'An Evaluation of South Africa's Application of the OAU Refugee Definition', 55.

'implicit "white lists" of refugee producing countries' and focused on 'merely confirming the nationality of an asylum seeker'.[88]

Observers have, however, raised concerns about the 'white list' approach,[89] in particular, because 'white lists' may be unduly circumscribed. Indeed, Schreier notes that the South African practice 'may include generalized and hence incorrect assumptions about what constitutes an OAU or section 3(b) event and a lack of appropriate consideration of the other elements of the definition'.[90] A related problem is that applicants who are not from listed countries may find it comparatively difficult to have their refugee status recognized. Tuepker explains, 'What is troubling is the frequent link to a converse practice of rejecting applicants on the basis of nationality.'[91] It seems that 'white lists' – and the use of presumptions more generally – constitute an efficient mode of determining refugee status in certain contexts, as long as 'white lists' and presumptions are not construed restrictively and do not lead to scepticism about the claims of individuals not from listed countries or countries other than those about which a presumption has been invoked.

The Importance and Meaning of 'Events Seriously Disturbing Public Order'

The ground of 'events seriously disturbing public order' in Article I(2) of the OAU Convention appears to be the primary element of the definition under which refugee status is determined today.[92] It seems that the other grounds of refugee status under Article I(2) – external aggression, occupation and foreign domination – are now largely irrelevant.[93] This is not surprising given that they were conceived when much of Africa was still

---

[88] Schreier, 'An Evaluation of South Africa's Application of the OAU Refugee Definition', 55. See also L. A. de la Hunt, 'Refugee Law in South Africa: Making the Road of the Refugee Longer', in Legal Resources Foundation, *A Reference Guide to Refugee Law and Issues in Southern Africa* (Lusaka, Zambia: Legal Resources Foundation, 2002), 34.

[89] Tuepker, 'On the Threshold of Africa', 418; Schreier, 'An Evaluation of South Africa's Application of the OAU Refugee Definition', 55; De la Hunt, 'Refugee Law in South Africa', 34.

[90] Schreier, 'An Evaluation of South Africa's Application of the OAU Refugee Definition', 61.

[91] Tuepker, 'On the Threshold of Africa', 418.

[92] Review of all primary materials, which are all on file with the author. In 2008, for example, both Beninese decisions under Article I(2) were based on 'events seriously disturbing public order'.

[93] B. T. M. Nyanduga, 'Refugee Protection under the 1969 OAU Convention Governing the Specific Aspects of Refugee Problems in Africa', *German YB Intl L* 47 (2004), 85, 92.

under colonial rule. The predominant use of the ground of 'events seriously disturbing public order' may also reflect the changing character of war in Africa, with fewer international and more internal armed conflicts.

Conflict appears to be the most common situation constituting 'events seriously disturbing public order'. This was particularly evident in decisions from Benin, Chad and South Africa. These decisions did not distinguish between conflicts among clans or rebels and conflict between the government on the one hand and clans or rebels on the other. Examples of conflicts deemed by the Beninese, Chadian and South African jurisprudence to constitute 'events seriously disturbing public order' are the 2010 post-election violence in Côte d'Ivoire, the conflict between the forces of General Laurent Nkunda and the DRC Army in the Kivu region, the 2002 civil war in Côte d'Ivoire, the Angolan civil war, the Rwandan genocide and clan fighting in Kismayo and Mogadishu, Somalia.

Two South African cases seen by Schreier further qualify the meaning of 'events seriously disturbing public order'. The first notes that it implies the government's loss of control.[94] The second expands upon this notion, noting that

> [w]here law and order has broken [down] and the government is unwilling or unable to protect its citizens, it can be said that there are events seriously disturbing public order. To determine when a disturbance had taken place involves weighing the degree and intensity of the conduct complained of against the degree and nature of the peace which can be expected to prevail in a given place at a given time. The test should be objective.[95]

Thus, it is not the loss of governmental control that is salient but rather that such loss of control threatens the civilian protection.

It should also be noted that none of the primary materials revealed a reliance upon the definition of 'armed conflict' employed in international humanitarian law (IHL). Moreover, limiting the scope of how conflict is understood under the 'events seriously disturbing public order' ground of the OAU Convention to the IHL definition of armed conflict risks limiting the range of situations to which the OAU Convention can be applied, which would be inconsistent with the

---

[94] Schreier, 'An Evaluation of South Africa's Application of the OAU Refugee Definition', 60.
[95] Ibid., 61.

instrument's humanitarian object and purpose. Finally, while international armed conflict was not explicitly referenced in any of the primary materials reviewed, there is no principled reason why 'events seriously disturbing public order' should not include international armed conflict.

In summary, then, 'events seriously disturbing public order' as understood in the primary materials in at least three jurisdictions implies conflict – not strictly in the IHL sense of the term, whether international or non-international and whether among non-state actors or between non-state actors and the government – leading to loss of governmental control and the inability or unwillingness of the government to regain such control.

There are, however, other situations that are considered 'events seriously disturbing public order'. Nigerian case law appears to consistently absorb generalized violence within Article 1(2) of the OAU Convention. All OAU Convention Nigerian decisions available – of which there were four, three related to applicants from the DRC and one from Somalia – noted that '[t]he applicant is outside of her country of nationality or habitual residence and is unable to return there owing to serious and indiscriminate threats to life, physical integrity or freedom resulting from generalized violence or events seriously disturbing public order.'[96] This language mirror's UNHCR's broader refugee definition, which it applies when conducting RSD under its mandate. In its mandate RSD operations, UNHCR has adopted a wider refugee definition based on the definitions in the OAU Convention and the 1984 Cartagena Declaration on Refugees. In practical terms, this has extended UNHCR's mandate to a variety of situations of forced displacement resulting from conflict, indiscriminate violence or public disorder. In light of this evolution, UNHCR considers that serious (including indiscriminate) threats to life, physical integrity or freedom resulting from generalized violence or events seriously disturbing public order warrant international protection under its mandate.[97] In applying the OAU Convention, the Nigerian decisions make the existence of 'serious and indiscriminate threats to life, physical integrity or freedom' the threshold consideration for recognition under Article I(2), whether such threats stemmed from generalized violence or events seriously disturbing public order. It is unclear why

---

[96] Nigerian decisions in April 2010 report of the Nigerian Eligibility Committee, on file with the author.

[97] UNHCR, *MM (Iran)* v. *Secretary of State for the Home Department – Written Submission on Behalf of the United Nations High Commissioner for Refugees*, 3 August 2010, Case No. C5/2009/2479, para. 10, available online.

Nigerian practice 'operationalizes' Article I(2) via UNHCR's broadened refugee definition; this may be an incorrect conflation of what are two similar, though actually distinct, legal criteria for refugee status.

Such varied state approaches to Article I(2)'s 'events seriously disturbing public order' clause have led academics to attempt to come to a principled interpretation of it.[98] The understandings of the term that have emerged from their analysis should supplement interpretations of the term based on state practice. Edwards' inquiry into the meaning of 'events seriously disturbing public order' proceeds on the basis of three guiding questions. Firstly, she asks whether the term encompasses events of a non-international character. She bases this question on the interpretive rule *noscitur a sociis*, which mandates that words be interpreted in the context of surrounding language. 'External aggression', 'occupation' and 'foreign domination' clearly have international connotations; it is on this basis that she surmises that 'events seriously disturbing public order' might also have been drafted with such in mind, with the result that they would not encompass purely internal situations. She concludes, however, that since states in their practice have demonstrated willingness – and, as evidenced above, indeed a tendency – to protect people in flight from internal disturbances, the term should not be taken to include only events of an international nature.[99]

In response to her second question, what is meant by 'disruption of public order', Edwards surveys various international law contexts in which 'public order' has been employed, concluding that the term has administrative, social, political and moral meanings.[100] Rankin focuses on the use of 'public order' in the 1951 Convention, where the term was 'intended to be a reference to acts prejudicial to the "peace and tranquillity of society at large" and was imbued with a broad sense of a threat to state authority'.[101] He concludes that in the sense in which it was used in the 1951 Convention, 'public order was only thought to be at stake when there was a threat "to an uncertain number of persons carrying out their lawful occupations ... or to society at large, as in the case of riots and unrests"',[102] though he cautions that 'public order should not be conceived in the context of threats alone, but also in relation to the obligations owed by the state to its citizens'.[103]

---

[98] Edwards, 'Refugee Status Determination in Africa', 216–21; Rankin, 'Extending the Limits or Narrowing the Scope?', 423–8.
[99] Edwards, 'Refugee Status Determination in Africa', 218.   [100] *Ibid.*, 220.
[101] Rankin, 'Extending the Limits or Narrowing the Scope?', 425.   [102] *Ibid.*   [103] *Ibid.*

Edwards' third question is, 'What would qualify as serious?' In response, she finds that to meet the Article I(2) 'serious' threshold, the events in question must be 'prolonged, on a massive scale, or harmful to life, freedom or security'.[104] Examples of events that would meet this requirement are 'civil conflicts, coups d'états, militia or rebel group insurgencies and other similar actions'.[105] Rankin poses the same question and frames his response in terms of three thresholds: non-international armed conflict as understood in IHL, internal disturbances and tensions that threaten an indeterminate number of people and the widespread violation of non-derogable human rights. According to Rankin, events meeting any one of these three thresholds would qualify under Article I(2) as 'events seriously disturbing public order'.[106]

Both Edwards and Rankin speculate as to whether 'events seriously disturbing public order' might have been intended to function as a residual clause that would capture all events that would not qualify as 'external aggression', 'occupation' or 'foreign domination'. Rankin concludes that the term functions 'as a basket clause capturing a generic set of refugee producing situations'.[107] Edwards is more cautious in her analysis. While conceding that a literal interpretation of 'events seriously disturbing public order' would tend to support conclusions such as that suggested by Rankin, she notes that this would conflict with UNHCR interpretive methodology regarding the 1951 Convention's 'particular social group' ground.[108] The organization has cautioned against reading the 'social group' category as a catch-all that would render the other four grounds of refugee status superfluous. In a later discussion with Edwards, she reflected further that interpreting the OAU Convention in line with UNHCR's approach to the 1951 Convention is not required where the OAU Convention terms have their own particular meaning or context. What remains important instead, she indicated, was that the terms be given their proper meaning within the context of the convention as a whole.

Insofar as their inquiries can be summarized, Edwards' and Rankin's analyses suggest that 'events seriously disturbing public order' is not a catch-all but rather a term that provides refugee protection to individuals in flight from internal or international events that threaten life, freedom or security. This analysis, coupled with the state practice

---

[104] Edwards, 'Refugee Status Determination in Africa', 220. [105] Ibid., 221.
[106] Rankin, 'Extending the Limits or Narrowing the Scope?', 426–7. [107] Ibid., 423.
[108] Edwards, 'Refugee Status Determination in Africa', 217–18.

outlined earlier, yields an understanding of 'events seriously disturbing public order' in which the term refers to conflict – whether internal or international and whether among non-state actors or between non-state actors and the government – and other situations of violence that threaten civilian protection or, in other words, life, freedom or security.

Other Issues

Two further issues of note regarding state practice of individual RSDs emerged from the research. The first was whether the Article I(2) refugee definition specifically precludes a so-called internal flight alternative. Article I(2) mentions that the harm may be in 'part or the whole of' the country of origin or nationality, thereby precluding any onus on the individual to seek safety within his or her homeland. Indeed, in a 2006 Benin case, the possibility of internal flight was considered and ultimately rejected.[109] Later, in 2008, Benin's eligibility board made a principled decision not to consider whether protection might have been found within the country of origin.[110] Similarly, the template/checklist that assists decision-makers with RSD in Burkina Faso instructs them not to consider the possibility of internal flight. This approach reflects UNHCR's guidelines on internal flight or relocation alternative, which assert that based on a plain reading of Article I(2), such an analysis is not relevant under the OAU Convention.[111]

The second issue of note was that in 2009 a decision from Benin recognized a refugee *sur place* under Article I(2) of the OAU Convention,[112] making no distinction as to whether the asylum-seeker was, at the time of the public disorder event, inside or outside his or her country of origin or nationality. Uganda has in certain cases adopted an analogous approach.[113] Contrary opinion, however, has emerged from South Africa. According to the chairperson of its

---

[109] 2006 Benin decision, on file with the author.
[110] 2008 Benin decision, on file with the author.
[111] UNHCR, 'Guidelines on International Protection No 4: "Internal Flight or Relocation Alternative" within the Context of Article 1A(2) of the 1951 Convention and/or 1967 Protocol Relating to the Status of Refugees', 2003, UN Doc. HCR/GIP/03/04, at para. 5. Rankin rejects any obligation of internal flight under the OAU Convention on a more complex basis, arguing that throughout internal relocation there may still be a 'continuing compulsion' to flee. See Rankin, 'Extending the Limits or Narrowing the Scope?', 433–4. South African state practice is apparently the opposite. See Schreier, 'An Evaluation of South Africa's Application of the OAU Refugee Definition', 56.
[112] 2009 Benin decision, on file with the author.   [113] Input from UNHCR.

Refugee Appeal Board, 'the OAU Convention ... cannot apply to a *sur place* case because of the wording of the definition ... you must be compelled to leave your habitual place of residence.'[114] While in line with the language of Article I(2), this restrictive approach contradicts the OAU Convention's 'Preamble', which stresses the need for an essentially humanitarian approach to refugees, as well as its underlying rationale: the OAU Convention was, after all, drafted in part with a view to protecting individuals fighting colonialism and racist regimes from outside their countries of origin. Moreover, the restrictive approach would create a protection gap for individuals visiting the putative host country when conflict erupted.

Conclusion

This chapter focused on how Article I(2) of the OAU Convention is interpreted and applied in African state practice of individual RSDs. The conclusions resulting from such assessment were limited by the dearth of primary information; the lack of reasoned jurisprudence was a particular problem. The findings were further limited by the difficulty of drawing general conclusions about the region from uneven information. Nevertheless, it is possible to identify the following trends, which shed light on African state practice relating to the protection of individuals fleeing armed conflict and other situations of violence:

1. Refugee status has generally been adjudicated pursuant to Article I(2) of the OAU Convention either

   • Sequentially, after status under Article 1A(2) of the 1951 Convention has been considered;
   • Because it is clear that Article I(2) is more aligned with the conditions or situation in the individual's country of origin or nationality at the time of flight (the 'nature of flight' approach); or
   • For pragmatic reasons such as efficiency, particularly during mass influx.

2. In some other situations, the basis on which refugee status was adjudicated either under Article 1A(2) of the 1951 Convention or under Article I(2) of the OAU Convention was unclear.

---

[114] Schreier, 'An Evaluation of South Africa's Application of the OAU Refugee Definition', 56.

3. Article I(2) of the OAU Convention is at times misapplied; for example, it is sometimes conflated with Article 1A(2) of the 1951 Convention rather than applied as a separate definition.

4. In cases where the disruptive situation is limited to a specific part or parts of the country of origin, refugee status under Article I(2) requires that a nexus between the disruptive situation and flight be established. By contrast, in situations where the disruptive situation affects the whole of the country of origin or nationality, the existence of such a nexus may, purely as a matter procedure, be presumed. Drawing up 'white lists' of countries in respect of which such a presumption can be applied constitutes good practice, provided that this is not done restrictively and that negative effects on the claims of persons not from listed countries are mitigated.

5. The 'external aggression, occupation and foreign domination' grounds of refugee status under Article I(2) of the OAU Convention seem rarely to be invoked. The most commonly applied ground for refugee status under Article I(2) seems generally to be 'events seriously disturbing public order'.

6. The ground of 'events seriously disturbing public order' is most commonly applied by decision-makers and interpreted by scholars as relating to persons from situations of conflict – whether internal or international and whether among non-state actors or between non-state actors and the government – and other situations of violence that threaten civilian protection or life, freedom or security.

These conclusions must be read with the chapter's methodological limitations in mind. This chapter's most important conclusion is not, however, subject to any caveat. It is clear that Article I(2) of the OAU Convention, its 'events seriously disturbing public order' ground in particular, has provided African states with the flexibility to offer protection to the many individuals and groups forced to flee conflict and other situations of violence on the continent. That Article I(2) is not applied consistently across the region is a problem of legal certainty and hence due process rather than a fundamental problem of protection.

5

The Cartagena Declaration on Refugees and the Protection of People Fleeing Armed Conflict and Other Situations of Violence in Latin America

MICHAEL REED-HURTADO

Introduction

The 1984 Cartagena Declaration on Refugees (Cartagena Declaration)[1] is heralded as one of the greatest accomplishments in the development of the refugee protection regime in Latin America. It is most frequently invoked as the source of a broad definition of who should be considered a refugee. Beyond the definition contained in Article 1(A) of the 1951 Convention Relating to the Status of Refugees (1951 Convention) and the 1967 Protocol Relating to the Status of Refugees (1967 Protocol)[2] (hereafter referred to as the '1951 Convention definition'), the Cartagena Declaration also extends to 'persons who have fled their country because their lives, safety or freedom have been threatened by generalized violence, foreign aggression, internal conflicts, massive violation of human rights or other circumstances which have seriously disturbed public order' (hereafter referred to as the 'regional refugee definition').[3]

---

[1] Declaración de Cartagena sobre Refugiados, adopted during the Coloquio Sobre la Protección Internacional de los Refugiados en América Central, México y Panamá: Problemas Jurídicos y Humanitarios, held in Cartagena, 19–22 November 1984 (hereinafter 'Cartagena Declaration').

[2] Convention relating to the Status of Refugees (adopted 28 July 1951, entered into force 22 April 1954), 189 UNTS 137 (1951 Convention); Protocol Relating to the Status of Refugees (entered into force 4 October 1967), 606 UNTS 267 (1967 Protocol).

[3] Cartagena Declaration, Conclusion No. 3. The original document was drafted in Spanish. The official translation reads: 'persons who have fled their country because their lives, safety or freedom have been threatened by generalized violence, foreign aggression, internal conflicts, massive violation of human rights or other circumstances which have seriously disturbed public order'. The original Spanish text of the definition reads: 'la definición o concepto de refugiado recomendable para su utilización en la región es aquella que además de contener los elementos de la Convención de 1951 y el Protocolo de 1967,

The Colloquium on the International Protection of Refugees in Central America, Mexico and Panama and the Cartagena Declaration were the result of a pragmatic and protection-motivated process that began in the early 1980s as a reaction to the inadequate response of the Organization of American States (OAS) to the Central American refugee crisis. This process focused on creating and maintaining an effective humanitarian response based on solidarity, political will and respect for basic human rights.[4] The expanded conception and definition of a refugee was only one element of this initiative, which had its antecedents in the Tlatelolco Colloquium of 1981[5] and in the reiterated alerts formulated by the Inter-American Commission on Human Rights (IACommHR). By drawing from international refugee law, human rights law and international humanitarian law (IHL), the Cartagena Colloquium launched what would eventually become a dynamic atmosphere of protection and humanitarianism.

The Cartagena Declaration did not establish binding law; it is after all the final text of a gathering of academics and practitioners. When the Cartagena Declaration was adopted, most Latin American states had neither national legal frameworks to deal with refugee matters nor refugee status determination (RSD) systems in place. Thus, the Cartagena Declaration definition became a 'common language' of sorts that encapsulated contemporary protection concerns.

As part of this process, the Cartagena refugee definition has gained legal force through its widespread incorporation into national legal frameworks across the region. Nevertheless, today the Cartagena Declaration is mostly invoked only to recall the origin of the regional refugee definition, ignoring the fundamental humanitarian and legal protection principles that the Cartagena process championed, including active inter-state cooperation to satisfy humanitarian needs, the non-political nature of asylum and the principle of *non-refoulement*. Paradoxically, the Cartagena Declaration has been seldom applied in practice, guidance on its interpretation is undeveloped and national

considere también como refugiados a las personas que han huido de sus países porque su vida, seguridad o libertad han sido amenazadas por la violencia generalizada, la agresión extranjera, los conflictos internos, la violación masiva de los derechos humanos u otras circunstancias que hayan perturbado gravemente el orden public.'

[4] Recall that at the time, some of the main hosting countries (e.g. Mexico and Honduras) were not parties to the international refugee instruments.

[5] Colloquium on Asylum and the International Protection of Refugees in Latin America, Tlatelolco, Mexico, 11–15 May 1981.

authorities rarely consult its provisions when providing international refugee protection.

Methodology and Structure

This chapter is a legal study on the interpretation and application of the regional refugee definition in seventeen Latin American countries,[6] thirteen of which currently include a Cartagena-inspired refugee definition in their national laws. The desk-based review includes examinations of national constitutions, laws and policies; administrative decisions; case law and national news on refugee issues.[7] In analyzing administrative practice, this chapter surveys decisions formally adopted by administrative bodies responsible for determining asylum claims in each country. These findings were enriched by fieldwork conducted in four countries that were considered to have the heaviest caseload of asylum applications: Argentina, Brazil, Ecuador and Mexico.

Refugee matters in most Latin American countries have very little salience in law and politics: production of academic writing on the subject is limited, and specialized audiences are rare; thus, interested parties tend to speak amongst themselves. Public discussion of refugee matters is meagre, and most events or developments go unnoticed and unreported. For this reason, I am especially grateful to those who agreed to be interviewed for this study and generously shared their knowledge, guidance, opinions and enthusiasm for the protection of refugee rights.[8] The interviews with individuals who were directly involved in the Cartagena process were especially important to this analysis.

---

[6] The countries surveyed are Argentina, Bolivia, Brazil, Chile, Colombia, Costa Rica, Ecuador, El Salvador, Guatemala, Honduras, Mexico, Nicaragua, Panama, Paraguay, Peru, Uruguay and Venezuela. These countries share common legal traditions. None of the Caribbean countries were considered.

[7] I thank Viviana Tacha, a Colombian attorney and colleague, for her assistance in the desk review and particularly in compiling and systematizing the laws and regulations, news stories and academic pieces in the seventeen countries. I am also indebted to Amanda Lyons for her careful review of the original study.

[8] I am indebted to all professionals whom I interviewed – retired UNHCR staff members, officials, members of NGOs and academics – who openly shared their opinions and readily made materials available for my review. Without their contribution, this study would not have been possible. I am deeply grateful to colleagues in the Department of International Protection (DIP), the Regional Legal Support Unit in the Costa Rica Office and the UNHCR offices in Argentina, Mexico, Brazil and Ecuador, particularly all protection officers. Their opinions, positions and work were a great source of knowledge.

Following the introduction, the second section of this chapter reviews the Cartagena Declaration, including the process leading to its adoption, its content and the way it was initially understood and applied. This review reveals that practitioners in Latin America often overlook this background, generating significant consequences for adequate protection. This section is also an important contribution because most of the documentation and analysis of this historical content are not available in English.

The third section provides an overview of the extent and manner in which Latin American countries have formally incorporated the regional refugee definition into their national legal frameworks. The regional refugee definition has gained wide acceptance in national jurisdictions, although in some cases substantive variations have been made overall, but by and large, national legal frameworks have preserved the main elements of the regional definition.

The fourth section describes the core findings of state practice in relation to the regional refugee definition. The first subsection analyses the administrative legal context in which the definition is applied. Refugee law is considered to be part of administrative law in the jurisdictions surveyed. As a result, RSD procedures are unregulated, unchecked and driven by discretional delegation. These qualities substantively affect how the regional refugee definition is – or often is not – applied. These contextual elements are necessary to a proper reading of how the regional refugee definition is applied, which is presented in the second subsection.

Finally, this chapter presents in its concluding fifth section a short reflection for future initiatives aimed at reinvigorating international protection and reviving some of the aspirations that made the Cartagena-inspired process so important throughout the region.

The Cartagena Declaration: A Process Driven by Protection Needs

The events leading to adoption of a regional refugee definition are critical in explaining its scope and reach today. This chapter does not intend to fully document this process, but a brief overview is especially important given that much of the literature on the subject is available only in Spanish.[9] This section sets out the basic regional context that led

---

[9] For a comprehensive overview and analysis of the process leading to the adoption of the Cartagena Declaration, see L. Franco and J. Santistevan de Noriega, 'La contribución del proceso de Cartagena al desarrollo del derecho internacional de los refugiados en América Latina', in United Nations High Commissioner for Refugees (UNHCR), *Memoria del vigésimo*

to adoption of the Cartagena Declaration, the main accomplishments of the Cartagena process and the main legal elements of the regional refugee definition according the 'Principles and Criteria for the Protection of and Assistance to Central American Refugees, Returnees and Displaced Persons in Latin America', in short, the 'CIREFCA Legal Document'.[10] As will be shown, this text is an outdated legal document that continues to guide state practice today.

Regional Backdrop Leading up to the Cartagena Declaration

Latin American countries have a rich tradition of providing asylum to individuals facing political persecution; this has been especially true for members of the political, academic and artistic elite.[11] By the late nineteenth and early twentieth centuries, in response to turbulent events in the region, countries had consolidated this practice and even began promoting international instruments that espoused asylum as a protection measure.[12] The 1948 American Declaration of the Rights and Duties of Man stipulated the right to receive asylum as '[e]very person has the right, in case of pursuit not resulting from ordinary crimes, to seek and receive asylum in foreign territory, in accordance with the laws of each country and with international agreements.'[13]

aniversario de la Declaración de Cartagena sobre los Refugiados (San José, Costa Rica, Editorama, 2005), 79–138. See also F. G. Velez, 'Protección de refugiados, repatriados y desplazados centroamericanos, 1981–1999', in UNHCR, Comisión Nacional de los Derechos Humanos (CNDH) and Universidad Iberoamericana, Protección y asistencia a refugiados en América Latina. Documentos regionales 1981–1999 (Mexico, 2002), 21–50.

[10] 'Principles and Criteria for the Protection of and Assistance to Central American Refugees, Returnees and Displaced Persons in Latin America', prepared at the International Conference on Central American Refugees (CIREFCA), Ciudad de Guatemala, 29–31 May 1989, January 1990.

[11] See Franco and Santistevan, 'La contribución del proceso de Cartagena al desarrollo del derecho internacional de los refugiados en América Latina', 79, 86.

[12] For example, specific regulation of the asylum-refugee regime took place under the Treaty on Asylum and Political Refuge (adopted 4 August 1939). See also the Treaty on International Penal Law (adopted 23 January 1889) at the First South American Congress on Private International Law, Montevideo, Uruguay. The treaty regulated asylum in its Title II (Arts. 15–18), in close connection to extradition (addressed under Title III of the treaty).

[13] American Declaration of the Rights and Duties of Man, adopted by the Ninth International Conference of American States (1948), reprinted in Basic Documents Pertaining to Human Rights in the Inter-American System, OEA/Ser. L V/II.82 Doc. 6 Rev. 1 at 17 (1992), Art. XXVII.

The early development of this regime therefore underscored the connection to fundamental rights and liberties and the predominance of political asylum for individuals.

This regional protection scheme faced a major crisis in the 1960s. The mass exodus of Cubans beginning in 1959 and the plight of thousands of exiles from Bolivia, Haiti, Honduras, Nicaragua and Paraguay generated questions as to the capacity of states to absorb and integrate refugees. In 1965, the IACommHR reported on this changing situation:

> The problem of the American political refugees has fundamentally changed over the last years. The situation is no longer characterized by the refugees of former times, who were generally few in numbers and were fundamentally constituted by leaders that had some source of wealth. Currently the problem lies in that, as a result of the political movements that have taken place in the majority of American countries and the absence of democratic stability in some of them, a large amount of persons, most of them without means of any sort, are transferring to the territory of other American Republics as a result of being the object of persecution.
>
> This reality, which is compounded by extended periods of exile, has not been adequately addressed by international law or by national legislation of the States; and thus, the situations faced by the American political refugees are disquieting.[14]

Upon determining that the situation was not being adequately addressed by international law or national legislation, the IACommHR recommended the preparation of a regional instrument for the protection of refugees. In 1966, the Inter-American Juridical Committee elaborated a draft Inter-American Convention on Refugees,[15] but it was never formally considered by any of the political bodies of the OAS.

The assessment that international law did not adequately address the predicament of refugees in the Americas in 1965 is explained in part by the fact that for the two decades prior, Latin American states had not participated in developing the global refugee regime. Governments in the region were reticent to sign the 1951 Convention. American states asserted that the flow of refugees was not something that concerned the

---

[14] Cited in Inter-American Commission on Human Rights (IACommHR), Informe Anual de la Comisión Interamericana de Derechos Humanos 1981–1982, 20 September 1982, OEA/Ser. L/V/II.57, Doc. 6 Rev.1. See chap. IV, sec. B ('Los refugiados y el sistema interamericano'), para. 3. Available only in Spanish online at: www.cidh.org/annualrep/81.82sp/indice.htm (translation by the author). All URLs last checked on 5 June 2012.

[15] Ibid., para. 4.

region. Franco and Santistevan suggest instead that the most likely explanation for this resistance was a general unwillingness of Latin American states to be subject to any type of international control.[16]

In the decade that followed, the Central American refugee situation deteriorated severely as governments stepped up violent actions against the civilian population. Thousands were murdered and disappeared, and hundreds of thousands of peasants, indigenous populations and impoverished urban-dwellers fled to neighbouring countries.

The refugee situation in the region worsened as a result of the growing flight of persons escaping the coups d'état in the Southern Cone. These displaced persons had a different profile than the Central American refugees; nonetheless, they were in dire need of protection. By the end of the 1970s, refugees were scattered en masse, and the protection scheme was failing. The depiction provided by the IACommHR is extremely useful to understand the state of affairs:

> [T]he events that took place in the 1970s and the first years of the 1980s have signified a change of circumstances in relation to the old tradition of awarding political asylum, as follows:
>
> a) the number of persons in need of political asylum is several times greater than in any other moment of the history of the region;
>
> b) the composition of the groups that are requesting political asylum has changed from individual political figures to large groups of persons with a well-founded fear of persecution given the conditions of generalized violence and their involvement in politically vulnerable sectors of society, though they have not necessarily participated in individual political acts;
>
> c) while the old exiles were generally persons of economic means and a certain level of education, the asylum seekers of recent years are overwhelmingly persons without financial resources, that usually lack education and job skills;
>
> d) amongst the countries that have traditionally offered refuge to political exiles, some are not only refusing to accept Latin American

---

[16] See generally Franco and Santistevan, 'La contribución del proceso de Cartagena al desarrollo del derecho internacional de los refugiados en América Latina', 90–3. The authors provide several illustrations of the lack of interest in the 1951 Convention, the sense of regional segregation and the guarding of the regional asylum regime; only four regional governments (Brazil, Colombia, Cuba and Venezuela) participated in the Conference of Plenipotentiaries on the Status of Refugees and Stateless Persons; the 1951 Convention was not mentioned (even once) in the preparation of the OAS Convention on Diplomatic Asylum (adopted 29 December 1954) Treaty Series No. 18; and only four Latin American states ratified the 1951 Convention during its first decade in force (Ecuador, 1955; Brazil, 1960; Colombia, 1961; and Argentina, 1961).

refugees, but are also, additionally, becoming a main source of refugees in the region;

e) national legislation and regional treaties related to refugees and exiles
are inadequate to address the situations of mass asylum;

f) the economic conditions experienced by a large portion of the hemi-
sphere, generally poor, make the resettlement of thousands of foreign
nationals very difficult; and

g) many governments of the region are not willing to receive refugees for
ideological or political motives, as they consider them a threat to
national security.[17]

The IACommHR documented the changed circumstances and the
flaws in protection practice as related to the Inter-American asylum
regime and urged states to comply with their human rights obligations
in relation to refugees. The IACommHR recommended that the OAS
consider establishing an inter-American authority in charge of assisting
and protecting refugees on the continent, to work in close association
with UNHCR.[18] States remained impassive.

The lack of official response from both the OAS and individual states
led a group of regional experts to come together in 1981 in Tlatelolco,
México, under the auspices of the Universidad Autónoma de México to
examine the relation between the regional asylum regime and the global
refugee regime. Formally an academic exercise, the group intended
to address the protection gaps that had become apparent.[19] UNHCR
discreetly accompanied the exercise. The colloquium supported and
promoted basic principles of international refugee law – including *non-
refoulement* and the humanitarian and non-political nature of granting
asylum – and called for an incorporation of both inter-American and
global efforts to adequately protect refugees.[20]

Notably, the 1981 Colloquium concluded that it was necessary to
extend protection in Latin America 'to those persons that flee their
country as a result of aggression, foreign occupation or domination,

---

[17] IACommHR, Informe Anual de la Comisión Interamericana de Derechos Humanos
1981–1982, para. 9.

[18] *Ibid.*, para. 12.

[19] See e.g. the introductory remarks presented by the then-director of the Department of
International Protection of UNHCR, Michel Moussalli. Instituto de Investigaciones
Jurídicas, 'Asilo y protección internacional de los refugiados en América Latina', 25–32.

[20] Conclusions and Recommendations of the Colloquium on Asylum and the International
Protection of Refugees in Latin America, Tlatelolco, Mexico, 11–15 May 1981, Instituto
de Investigaciones Jurídicas, 'Asilo y protección internacional de los refugiados en
América Latina', 205–8.

massive human rights violations, or events that seriously disturb public order, in either part or the whole of the territory of the country of origin'.[21]

Despite these efforts and the IACommHR's insistence, countries proved unwilling to confront new manifestations of forced migration and referred instead to the region's traditional definition of asylum. In the meantime, refugee flows and internal displacements grew unabated.

'Refugees under Cartagena': Regional Refugee Definition and Other Achievements

As can be drawn from the context described earlier, the 1984 Cartagena Colloquium developed out of the ongoing need to establish and con-solidate the 'humanitarian practices and principles' to provide protection to a growing number of Central Americans compelled to leave their home countries.[22] The Cartagena Declaration is the pronouncement resulting from that 1984 Colloquium. It is not a legally binding instru-ment or an officially sanctioned statement. Nonetheless, its value rests on pragmatism and commitment to the application of protection principles as has been endorsed by a large number of states, including in their domestic law.

Therefore, the Cartagena Declaration must be understood as part of a process of developing a roadmap for protection practices that would prove crucial in addressing the Central American humanitarian crisis of the 1980s and which laid the foundation for much of the work conducted in relation to internally displaced persons (IDPs).[23] The significance of the Cartagena Declaration must not be limited to the adoption of

---

[21] *Ibid.*, Conclusion No. 4. This early proposal clearly reflects the influence of the African treaty addressing the issue of refugees. See Organization of African Unity Convention Governing the Specific Aspects of Refugee Problems in Africa (entered into force 20 June 1974), 1001 UNTS 45 (OAU Convention), Art. 1.2.

[22] Franco and Santistevan, 'La contribución del proceso de Cartagena al desarrollo del derecho internacional de los refugiados en América Latina', 113.

[23] The processes and synergies that grew out of the Cartagena Declaration best depict the accomplishments of the Cartagena Round Table. Nearly thirty years later, the Cartagena Declaration is still invoked to motivate humanitarian action and protection in the region. This process has been well documented through the accounts of the colloquia that have taken place ten and twenty years after Cartagena. See e.g. Instituto Interamericano de Derechos Humanos (IIDH) and UNHCR, *Memoria del Coloquio Internacional. 10 Años de la Declaración de Cartagena sobre Refugiados* (San José, Costa Rica, Imprenta Nacional, 1995); and UNHCR, *Memoria del vigésimo aniversario de la Declaración de*

a regional refugee definition. Before a more concentrated discussion of the definition, at least five accomplishments of the Cartagena Colloquium and Declaration should be highlighted.

First and foremost, the process accomplished what it set out to do: it promoted the establishment and consolidation of the humanitarian practices and principles that were necessary to respond to the Central American refugee crisis. A key element of this was the confirmation of 'the peaceful, non-political and exclusively humanitarian nature of [the] granting of asylum or recognition of the status of refugee'.[24] Above all, the Cartagena Declaration was described by the leading humanitarian actors of the time as a practical framework that contributed to make humanitarian action possible on a daily basis, even under adverse conditions, particularly given that there were more people in need of protection and humanitarian assistance than those covered by the 1951 Convention and the 1967 Protocol.

Second, the consensus reached in the process underscored the centrality of existing international norms[25] and the need to establish a basic agreement backing the 1951 Convention and the 1967 Protocol. This consensus was especially important given that countries in the region were giving the inter-American asylum regime importance and precedence as opposed to participating in global legal developments. Recall that some of the principal asylum countries were not parties to the international refugee instruments, and thus the Cartagena Declaration became common ground.

Third, the Cartagena Colloquium promoted the dynamic interaction of international human rights law, international humanitarian law and international refugee law in the areas of displacement.[26] The Cartagena proponents asserted that the convergence of these three branches of public international law (and their respective protection bodies) offered the best conditions for providing the necessary protection.[27]

Cartagena sobre los Refugiados (San José, Costa Rica, Editorama, 2005). UNHCR, academics and specialized NGOs are currently preparing 'Cartagena Plus Thirty'.

[24] Cartagena Declaration, Conclusion No. 4.

[25] See e.g. Cartagena Declaration, Conclusions Nos. 2, 3 and 8.

[26] Franco and Santistevan, 'La contribución del proceso de Cartagena al desarrollo del derecho internacional de los refugiados en América Latina', 118–19.

[27] See the seminal work by Antonio Cançado Trindade that underscored this interaction ten years after the Cartagena Declaration. A. Cançado Trindade, 'Aproximaciones o convergencias entre el derecho internacional humanitario y la protección internacional de los derechos humanos', in IIDH and UNHCR, *Memoria del Coloquio Internacional. 10 Años de la Declaración de Cartagena sobre Refugiados*, 79–168, contained also in

Fourth, the Cartagena Declaration accentuated the principle of *non-refoulement* as one of the key protection principles.[28] It was seen as emerging from the interaction between international refugee law and international human rights law to safeguard the right to receive protection when a person faces the risk of being exposed to persecution as well as the right to be free from harm to life, liberty or person.[29] Based on this principle and general human rights obligations, governments were persuaded that persons should not be returned to places where their life, freedom or safety might be at risk.

Fifth, the Cartagena Declaration also called on countries to use a definition of 'refugee' that, in addition to those covered by the 1951 Convention and its 1967 Protocol, also included 'persons who have fled their country because their lives, safety or freedom have been threatened by generalized violence, foreign aggression, internal conflicts, massive violation of human rights or other circumstances which have seriously disturbed public order'.[30]

This definition drew heavily from the 1969 OAU Convention Governing the Specific Aspects of Refugee Problems in Africa (OAU Convention), which states, 'the term "refugee" shall also apply to every person who, owing to external aggression, occupation, foreign domination or events seriously disturbing public order in either part or the whole of his [or her] country of origin or nationality, is compelled to leave his [or her] place of habitual residence in order to seek refuge in another place outside his [or her] country of origin or nationality.'[31]

Despite the striking similarity between the two definitions, the drafters of the Cartagena Declaration did not leave record of any weighty comparative exercise in relation to the African instrument. The record does not indicate that analysis of the definitional component went beyond imitation and adaptation to the Latin American reality. An interview conducted with one of the central drafters of the text supports this finding.[32]

Seminario interamericano sobre la protección de la persona en situaciones de emergencia (San José, Costa Rica: Instituto Interamericano de Derechos Humanos, 1995), 33, at 40–5.

[28] Cartagena Declaration, Conclusion No. 5, emphasizing the value of *non-refoulement* as a principle of *ius cogens*. See also Franco and Santistevan, 'La contribución del proceso de Cartagena al desarrollo del derecho internacional de los refugiados en América Latina', 119–20.

[29] Cançado Trindade, 'Aproximaciones o convergencias entre el derecho internacional humanitario y la protección internacional de los derechos humanos', 180–1.

[30] Cartagena Declaration, Conclusion No. 3.   [31] OAU Convention, Art. I(2).

[32] Interview of Leonardo Franco, Buenos Aires, Argentina, 18 May 2012.

The refugee definition proposed in the Cartagena Declaration was designed to narrow the protection gaps faced by thousands of persons who were forced to flee their countries of origin but were not deemed to be covered under the 1951 Convention definition of refugee. As one of the principal actors behind the Cartagena Declaration recalls

> The adoption of the new definition arose out of a protection need: problems arose and solutions had to be found ... Given that it was obvious that persons should not be differentiated so severely as a result of varying causes of their forced displacement, the solution adopted in the African context became very interesting ... The success of [the definition adopted by the] Cartagena [Declaration] is that it served to protect persons who had fled in mass numbers. What is surprising now is that practice has evolved and the Cartagena definition is applied to individuals seeking asylum.[33]

In interviews, several of the participants in the events leading up to the Cartagena Declaration emphasized another development from the process that has been marginalized from practice today. The regional refugee definition was a shift in focus from the subjective and individualized element – fear of persecution of the 1951 Convention – to the objective elements leading to flight: 'generalized violence, foreign aggression, internal conflicts, massive violation of human rights or other circumstances which have seriously disturbed public order'. In the regional context, this shift allowed for greater expediency in awarding protection and facilitated work with different population groups to search for solutions. Less concerned with individual RSD procedures, the main purpose was to offer a point of reference that justified humanitarian engagement.

Today, and as will be detailed later, most of the prevailing interpretations of the regional refugee definition have lost sight of these purposes. The regional refugee definition cannot be detached from the process that launched it. Moreover, the true significance of the Cartagena Declaration is not limited to the definition that emerged. Ensuring humanitarian protection was the objective and the most important accomplishment. Unfortunately, both in practice and in academic consideration, the Cartagena Declaration has been reduced to the regional refugee definition. This has led to a misunderstanding of its purpose and scope.

[33] *Ibid.*

Interpretative Guidelines: The CIREFCA Legal Document

In response to states' requests for legal guidance on the refugee protection obligations after adoption of the Cartagena Declaration, the United Nations sponsored the International Conference on Central American Refugees (CIREFCA) in Guatemala City in 1989. The conference adopted a series of documents, including the benchmark 'CIREFCA Legal Document'.[34]

States' insistence on establishing clear legal guidelines was a double-edged sword. The explicit restatement of international obligations was a positive contribution, but it was ultimately used in a legalistic fashion to limit state engagement and commitment to refugees and others in need of protection. The group of experts commissioned by the 1988 Preparatory Committee of CIREFCA (San Salvador) favoured a generous interpretation that would afford the greatest level of protection. This focus was consistent with the 'spirit' of the Cartagena Colloquium and Declaration but in tension with the governments' push for legal precision throughout the process.[35] The CIREFCA Legal Document that the conference adopted was therefore a compromise. It insisted on principled protection but provided definitions that were interpreted in a legalistic fashion.

Arguably the most important assertion or clarification in the CIREFCA Legal Document is that the elements of the regional refugee definition 'were intentionally depicted in a broad fashion in order to ensure that those persons whose need for international protection is evident are covered, and they may be protected and assisted as refugees'.[36] The group of experts explicitly called for flexibility and leeway in applying and interpreting the regional definition in order to ensure its adequate scope for protection

---

[34] 'Principles and Criteria for the Protection of and Assistance to Central American Refugees, Returnees and Displaced Persons in Latin America'. In addition to attempting to explain the reach of the regional refugee definition, it insisted on the centrality of the 1951 Convention definition for international protection (sec. IV, para. 24); underscored the non-political and humanitarian nature of asylum and the value of *non-refoulement* for protection and established minimum ground rules for the treatment of refugees (sec. V, paras. 42–52); laid down the framework of durable solutions (sec. VI, paras. 56–66); explicitly presented the challenges and the need for action in favour of IDPs (sec. VII, paras. 67–9) and stressed the role of NGOs and human-rights bodies in the protection of refugees and IDPs (secs. VIII and IX, paras. 70–3).

[35] During the second Preparatory Committee of CIREFCA (Antigua), governments insisted on 'the need to refine, even more, the [content and] reach of the definition contained in the Cartagena Declaration'. *Ibid.*, para. 3. As is recognized in the approved document, the group of experts did not incorporate this commentary.

[36] *Ibid.*, para. 26 (emphasis added).

purposes. The list of situations provided in the regional refugee definition was intended to be evocative of all situations that existed or could arise to generate refugee flows. It was not intended or seen as a restrictive legal formula; rather, it was a wide-ranging, blanket formulation that allowed humanitarian actors to conduct their operations in favour of persons who were experiencing the consequences of the situation in the region.

The CIREFCA drafters observed that the regional refugee definition contained in the Cartagena Declaration includes 'the objective situation prevailing in the country of origin and the particular situation of the individual or group of persons who are seeking protection and assistance as refugees'.[37] The document thus asserts that the definition requires two features: 'on the one hand, the existence of a threat to life, safety or freedom; and on the other, that the threat is the result of one of the five elements enumerated in the text'.[38]

The first element – the existence of a threat to life, safety or freedom – was addressed in the CIREFCA Legal Document through a rights-based approach. Threats to life, safety and freedom should be deduced from infringements on human rights. However, the document goes no further than reasoning that international protection had the purpose of safeguarding physical integrity and was thus triggered as a result of a threat to the right to life, safety and liberty.[39]

For the second element – the five objective situations foreseen by the regional refugee definition – the document provides restrictive and confused interpretative guidance. The drafters grouped together four of the five situations asserting guidance under IHL i.e. internal conflicts, foreign aggression, generalized violence and other circumstances that seriously disturb public order. These were interpreted in the following ways:

> The guidance that provided for 'internal conflicts' was only a reference to IHL applicable to non-international armed conflicts, namely, Article 3 common to the Geneva Conventions (1949) and Additional Protocol II (1977).[40]

---

[37] *Ibid.*   [38] *Ibid.*   [39] *Ibid.*, para. 27.

[40] *Ibid.*, paras. 28–30; Geneva Convention for the Amelioration of the Condition of the Wounded and Sick in Armed Forces in the Field (entered into force 21 October 1950), 75 UNTS 31 (First Geneva Convention); Geneva Convention for the Amelioration of the Condition of Wounded, Sick and Shipwrecked Members of Armed Forces at Sea (entered into force 21 October 1950), 75 UNTS 85 (Second Geneva Convention); Geneva Convention Relative to the Treatment of Prisoners of War (entered into force 21 October 1950), 75 UNTS 135 (Third Geneva Convention); Geneva Convention Relative to the Protection of Civilian Persons in Time of War (entered into force

'Foreign aggression' was considered in light of the 1974 UN General Assembly Resolution on the subject as 'the use of armed force by a State against the sovereignty, territorial integrity or political independence of another State, or in any other manner inconsistent with the Charter of the United Nations'.[41]

'Generalized violence' was considered to refer 'to armed conflicts as defined by international law, whether international or non-international in nature. For violence to be generalized it must be continuous, general and sustained.'[42] The drafters' interpretation mistakenly linked this phrase to armed conflict so narrowly as to make the inclusion of 'generalized violence' superfluous as a separate objective situation.

The group of experts also turned to IHL to interpret 'other circumstances that seriously disturb public order'. The document determined that the expression did not include natural catastrophes and referred only to man-made acts, including 'internal disturbances and tensions, such as riots, isolated and sporadic acts of violence and other acts of a similar nature as long as they seriously disturb public order'.[43] The document remitted to the 1951 Convention *travaux préparatoires* for further interpretation of the notion of public order.[44]

After describing the IHL grouping, the document instructed that 'massive violations of human rights' would be satisfied when internationally recognized rights are subject to widespread or large-scale

21 October 1950), 75 UNTS 287 (Fourth Geneva Convention); Protocol Additional to the Geneva Conventions of 12 August 1949, and Relating to the Protection of Victims of Non-International Armed Conflicts (entered into force 7 December 1978), 1125 UNTS 609 (Protocol II).

[41] UN GA Res. 3314 (XXIX), 14 December 1974 (cited in the CIREFCA Legal Document, para. 32).

[42] CIREFCA Legal Document, para. 32.

[43] *Ibid.*, para. 33. The limits between internal armed conflict and 'internal disturbances and internal tensions' generated a lot of interest at the end of the 1980s. Several draft declarations were being discussed to address situations that were perceived to not be fully covered by IHL or human-rights law. Similarly, protection concerns in the inter-American human rights protection system and academic production of the time concentrated on exploring themes related to the convergence of IHL and human-rights law. See e.g. 'Declaration of Minimum Humanitarian Standards' (adopted 2 December 1990), by an expert meeting convened by the Institute for Human Rights, Åbo Akademi University, in Turku/ Åbo Finland; or T. Meron, 'Model Declaration on Internal Strife', *Int'l Rev. Red Cross* 262 (1988), 59. See also 'Internal Disturbances and Tensions: A New Humanitarian Approach?', *Int'l Rev. Red Cross* 28 (1988), 262.

[44] CIREFCA Legal Document, para. 33.

violations – situations of 'gross and systematic denial of civil, political, economic and social and cultural rights'.[45] To address situations of human rights violations, the document made reference to individuals whose cases were under consideration by special international mechanisms at the time of the drafting.[46]

Based on the case law reviewed and interviews conducted, decision-makers are uncomfortable with the flexibility and breadth of the definition and for political reasons appear to have chosen instead to interpret it conservatively. This has led to the CIREFCA Legal Document being treated as a strict legalistic guide for applying the regional refugee definition in individual RSD proceedings.

In its interpretations of the objective situations, especially in light of the evolution of international law, the CIREFCA Legal Document does not adequately restate the law. Firstly, the exclusive reliance on IHL for guidance on situations of generalized violence, foreign aggression, internal armed conflicts and other circumstances that seriously disturb public order is problematic. In principle, IHL only addresses situations that qualify as international or non-international armed conflicts, a designation that is specifically for the purpose of applying the laws of war. Situations that do not fall within the expression 'armed conflict' can be construed or inferred through other sources of international law or even comparative law. Situations such as 'generalized violence' and 'other circumstances that seriously disturb public order' are precisely those types of situations which reveal the gaps in protection and the need for other branches of international law to be considered in order to afford appropriate protection to people in need.[47]

Modern-day interpreters of the regional refugee definition should be mindful that the drafters of the Cartagena Declaration and the CIREFCA Legal Document were unsystematic in the usage of terms to describe the gravity of situations. A great variety of qualifiers with no specific or

---

[45] *Ibid.*, para. 34. The Spanish uses the expression '*a gran escala*'.

[46] *Ibid.* The document makes explicit reference to the mechanism established by UN ECOSOC Res. 1503 that established a confidential review of complaints alleging serious violations. The procedure was considered under the guise of the Sub-Commission on the Prevention of Discrimination and the Protection of Minorities.

[47] Recent exercises have drawn attention to the intersection of the different branches of international law and could inform this exercise. See e.g. UNHCR and International Criminal Tribunal for Rwanda (ICTR), 'Summary Conclusions, Expert Meeting on Complementarities between International Refugee Law, International Criminal Law and International Human Rights Law', Arusha, Tanzania, 11–13 April 2011.

technical meaning attached to them was often employed interchangeably, including 'grave', 'gross', 'flagrant', 'systematic', 'generalized', 'widespread', 'serious', 'numerous' and 'massive'.[48] Knowledge of IHL was limited in the region, and its interaction with human rights law was not common. Unlike today, the IACommHR in the 1980s would use terms such as 'generalized violence,' 'mass' or 'massive' as general descriptors for egregious violations rather than technical terms of art with established parameters or thresholds.

Consequently, the list of objective situations leading to flight should not be interpreted as an exhaustive set that would exclude situations not specifically contemplated. The final clause – 'other circumstances that seriously disturb public order' – is meant to encompass unforeseen situations that produce similar effects. However, in practice, this ground has been the least used by refugee adjudicators despite the fact that the regional refugee definition was *intentionally drafted to promote inclusion* by recognizing that there were those in need of international protection who do not satisfy the refugee criteria of the 1951 Convention. This intent has been widely ignored or misinterpreted in the current practice and usage.

Beyond these definitions, no further guidance is provided. Even for the late 1980s, these interpretations are conservative at best and did not explore all relevant sources of law. Nonetheless, since that time, the CIREFCA Legal Document has been held to be a sort of unassailable dogmatic manual. The document has transcended unabated and without critique and continues to be the most frequently, if not the only, source cited by most national authorities to interpret the regional refugee definition in current-day practice.[49] Given the limited doctrinal development of the regional refugee definition, this document from the 1980s has been wrongly elevated in importance by practitioners eager for guidance. As one practitioner stated, 'It is difficult. We do not have a manual; all we have is CIREFCA. There are no tools. Each one of us moves or advances through the cases as [he or] she can. For those that are

---

[48] See e.g. IACommHR, *1980-1 Annual Report*, chap. V; or IACommHR, *1984-5 Annual Report*, chap. IV; IACommHR, *1985-6 Annual Report*, chap. IV.

[49] Every operator interviewed for this study in the context of RSD in Argentina, Brazil, Mexico and Ecuador cited the CIREFCA Legal Document as the source of their current-day interpretation of the objective situations laid out in the Cartagena Declaration. This text is promoted by UNHCR regionally, and as will be demonstrated in the next section, it is also cited as the source of interpretation in RSD administrative resolutions.

just starting it is very difficult, especially for those of us who are not lawyers. What do you read? You read CIREFCA. It is all there.'[50]

The uncritical reliance on the CIREFCA Legal Document compounded by a general ongoing absence of appropriate guidelines is a key factor in explaining the slow development of the regional refugee definition.

The CIREFCA Legal Document should be recalled primarily as an historical reference. Contemporary interpretation should recover the 'spirit' of Cartagena and invoke the basic principles of protection. The demand for guidance as to the interpretation and application of the Cartagena Declaration could be met more meaningfully through deeper analysis, modern hermeneutical practice and reference to up-to-date developments of IHL, international human rights law, international refugee law and comparative constitutional law.

Formal Adoption of the Regional Refugee Definition in National Legal Frameworks: Reproduction and Variations

The regional refugee definition has been widely adopted in national laws. Seven of the seventeen countries – Argentina, Bolivia, Chile, El Salvador, Guatemala, Mexico and Nicaragua – have directly imported the definition contained in the Cartagena Declaration into their national regimes, with six other countries using slightly different wording.[51] Only three countries, Costa Rica, Panama and Venezuela, have not incorporated the regional refugee definition into their national regime in any way.[52] Prior

---

[50] Interview with a member of one of the national commissions conducted between May and June 2012, on file with the author.

[51] Ley No. 26.165 de 2006, Ley General de Reconocimiento y Protección al Refugiado, Art. 4b (Argentina); Ley 215 de 2012, Ley de protección a personas refugiadas, Art. 15(I)(b) (Bolivia); Ley 20430 de 2010, Establece disposiciones sobre Protección de Refugiados, Art. 2.2 (Chile); Decreto 918 de 2002, Ley para la determinación de la condición de las personas refugiadas, Art. 4c (El Salvador); Acuerdo gubernativo 383 de 2001, Reglamento para la protección y determinación del estatuto de refugiado en el territorio del Estado de Guatemala, Art. 11c (Guatemala); Ley sobre Refugiados y Protección Complementaria, Se reforman, adicionan y derogan diversas disposiciones de la Ley General de Población, 2011, Art. 13 (II) (Mexico); and Ley 655 de 2008, Ley de Protección a Refugiados, Art. 1c (Nicaragua).

[52] See Ley 8764 de 2009, Ley General de Migración y Extranjería, sec. V (Costa Rica); Decreto ejecutivo 23 de 1998, Por el cual se desarrolla la Ley No. 5 del 26 del octubre de 1977 que aprueba la Convención de 1951 y Protocolo de 1967 sobre el Estatuto de Refugiados, se derogan el Decreto No. 100 del 6 de julio de 1981 y la Resolución Ejecutiva No. 461 del 9 de Octubre de 1984, y se dictan nuevas disposiciones en materia de protección temporal por

to a May 2012 retrogressive modification to its legal regime, Ecuador had included the regional refugee definition in its national legislation, and it was widely applied.[53] In fact, Ecuador was the first Latin American country to introduce the regional refugee definition in 1987 into domestic law. Given the particularities of this case, it will be addressed independently in a following section.

Though all national legislative frameworks present specific characteristics, some trends or groupings can be underscored. In the first place, four countries – Brazil, Colombia, Paraguay and Peru – have limited the definition of refugee to persons who are 'forced' or 'obligated' to leave their country as a result of the objective situation. This modification adds the element of compulsion, duress or obligation to the impetus of flight.[54] In contrast, the regional refugee definition recommended by the Cartagena Declaration requires only that flight be a consequence of the (generic) threat to life, safety or freedom generated by one of the five objective situations contemplated.

Secondly, some national laws have introduced changes to the objective situations defined in the Cartagena Declaration that lead to the person's flight or status as a refugee. These include the national laws of Brazil, Honduras, Peru and Uruguay. For example, the Uruguayan framework incorporates the list from the regional refugee definition but adds the situation of terrorism.[55] Peru varies from the definition by excluding generalized violence and adding 'foreign occupation or domination',[56] following the formulation contained in the OAU Convention.

Honduran legislation includes 'generalized violence' and adds that such violence must be 'grave and continuous'. It incorporates an antitechnical formula referring to 'mass, permanent and systematic violence of human rights', and Honduran legislation does not include 'other

---

razones humanitarias (Panama); and Ley orgánica sobre refugiados o refugiadas y asilados o asiladas, 13 de septiembre de 2001 (Venezuela).

[53] Decreto 3301 de 1992, Reglamento para la Aplicación en el Ecuador de las normas contenidas en la Convención de Ginebra de 1951 sobre el Estatuto de los Refugiados y en su Protocolo de 1967, Art. 2 (Ecuador).

[54] Lei no. 9.474, de 22 de julho de 1997, Define mecanismos para a implementação do Estatuto dos Refugiados de 1951, e determina outras providências, Art. 1 (III) (Brazil); Ley 27.891 de 2002, Ley del Refugiado, Art. 3b (Peru); Decreto 4513 de 2009, Por el cual se modifica el procedimiento para el reconocimiento de la condición de refugiado, se dictan normas sobre la Comisión Asesora para la determinación de la condición de refugiado y se adoptan otras disposiciones, Art. 1b (Colombia); and Ley 1938 de 2002, Ley General sobre Refugiados, Art. 1b (Paraguay).

[55] Ley 18076 de 2006, Estatuto del Refugiado, Art. 2b (Uruguay).

[56] Ley 27.891 de 2002, Ley del Refugiado, Art. 3b (Peru).

circumstances that seriously disturb public order'. Honduras' extended definition also recognizes persons who flee from 'persecution derived from sexual violence or other forms gender-based violence'. Finally, Honduras included definitional elements for 'foreign aggression' and 'internal armed conflicts'.[57]

Brazil has arguably most drastically varied the original wording proposed in the Cartagena Declaration. The regionally inspired definition was incorporated into Brazilian legislation in 1992 – a time when only a few countries in South America had included the regional refugee definition in their legislation (namely, Bolivia, Colombia and Ecuador). Brazilian legislation includes recognition of refugees as defined by the 1951 Convention and further articulates that recognition shall be granted to any individual who 'due to gross and generalized violations of human rights is forced to leave his/her country of nationality to seek refuge in another country'.[58]

In addition to these variations, Mexican practice is worth underscoring. Mexico initially incorporated the regional refugee definition without variation in 1990, even before acceding to the international refugee instruments and incorporating the universally recognized definition into its legislative framework. Through its recently enacted legislation, it has adopted both the universal and regional refugee definitions.[59] Mexico is the only state that has produced and adopted internal interpretive guidelines. The executive branch adopted a decree with administrative regulations for the national Law on Refugees and Complementary Protection in February 2012.[60] Its provisions include general definitions of the concepts contained in the regional refugee definition:

> VII. Generalized violence: confrontations in the country of origin or habitual residence (of the asylum seeker) of continuous, general,

---

[57] Ibid. 'Foreign aggression is understood as the use of force by one state against the sovereignty, territorial integrity or political independence of the country of origin [of the asylum seeker]'. Ibid., Art. 42.3b. 'Internal armed conflicts' are those that take place among 'the armed forces of the country from where flight originates and (other) armed forces or groups'. Ibid., Art. 42.3c.

[58] Lei no. 9.474, de 22 de julho de 1997, Define mecanismos para a implementação do Estatuto dos Refugiados de 1951, e determina outras providências, Art. 1 (III) (Brazil).

[59] Ley sobre Refugiados y Protección Complementaria, Se reforman, adicionan y derogan diversas disposiciones de la Ley General de Población, 2011, Art. 13 (Mexico).

[60] Presidencia de los Estados Unidos Mexicanos, Reglamento de la Ley sobre refugiados y protección complementaria, 21 February 2012 (Mexico).

and sustained nature, in which force is used in an indiscriminate manner.

VIII. Foreign aggression: the use of armed force by one state against the sovereignty, territorial integrity, and political independence of the country of origin or of habitual residence of the asylum seeker.

IX. Internal conflicts: the armed confrontations that take place in the territory of the country of origin or habitual residence (of the asylum seeker) between its armed forces and organized armed groups or among those groups.

X. Mass violations of human rights: conduct that violates human rights and fundamental freedoms in the country of origin, taking place on a wide scale and according to a determined policy.

XI. Other circumstances that have gravely disturbed public order: the situations that gravely alter public peace in the country of origin or habitual residence of the asylum seeker and that result from acts attributable to mankind.[61]

As they were only recently adopted, these internal interpretative guidelines have yet to be used, and decision-makers with whom the author spoke are split on their efficacy.

Although variations of the regional definition in national legislation have been substantive, their impact on state practice has been limited. This is so because, as will be seen in the next section, the actual use of the regional refugee definition itself is minimal, and there are problems in practice when it is applied.

State Practice in Applying the Regional Refugee Definition: Far from the 'Spirit' of Cartagena

The main findings of this chapter regarding state practice and the development of the regional refugee definition in Latin American countries are overwhelmingly negative. Generally speaking, the national systems are poorly regulated and developed. Although the regional refugee definition formally exists in law, it is seldom applied. Officers generally consider asylum requests on what is deemed the 'principal bracket' or 'primary fragment or clause' of the national refugee definition, which is the definition of the 1951 Convention. The statement of one practitioner is illustrative: 'There is no hierarchy between the two variants included in the law; it would be a mistake to consider one over the other. However,

---

[61] *Ibid.*, Art. 4 (translation by the author).

we do haul custom into the equation and probably give greater weight to the definition based on the Convention.'[62]

Furthermore, its occasional application is not guided or supported by doctrinal or jurisprudential development. Its use is subject to arbitrary, unchecked administrative delegation and a lack of due-process protections. The application of the regional refugee definition is intimately linked to the overall protection regime in Latin America. Conclusions regarding how the regional refugee definition is applied cannot be isolated from more general practices. Thus this section addresses concerns of the overall protection regime in order to contextualize the findings.

To implement national law, most countries in the region (fifteen of seventeen) have established an inter-institutional body supported by some sort of secretariat or administrative direction to conduct RSDs. The two other countries, Colombia and Honduras, address refugee status requests through intra-institutional agencies linked with the regulation of migration. The operation of these bodies varies in terms of resources, independence, influence of the supporting technical bodies and the role granted to UNHCR. As administrative bodies, these organs apply a branch of national administrative law, thus incorporating practices that are far from a rights-based approach. Practices observed in RSD procedures are not exclusive to refugee frameworks but are part of the idiosyncrasy of administrative law in general in Latin America – mechanical application of the law, incorporation of wide margins of discretion (as a result of the way delegation of authority is perceived), evasion of due-process standards and departure from oversight mechanisms.

Claims under the 1951 Convention and the regional refugee definition share the same procedural practice in relation to national RSD procedures. Though variations exist in each country and some better practices will be underscored, RSD in the region is generally conducted in the penumbra of an administrative setup that equates confidentiality with concealment – out of sight – and operates with little or no public interest – out of mind.[63]

---

[62] Interview with CONARE officials, Buenos Aires, Argentina, 17 May 2012. Similar statements were recorded in interviews with officials in Brazil and Mexico.

[63] Few writings explore the practical implications of the way refugee law is applied in national regimes. Importantly, Martin Lettieri and others edited a text on international protection of refugees in the countries of the southern region of South America. V. Abramovich et al., *Protección internacional de refugiados en el sur de Sudamérica* (Buenos Aires: De la UNLa – Universidad de Lanús, 2012).

The commendable acceptance of the regional refugee definition through formal incorporation into national laws is met with less commendable practices in the administrative sphere that debilitates its meaningful application at the national level. These issues are raised in the following five subsections and include inadequate and often arbitrary application of the law, mistaken understanding of confidentiality, the arbitrary application of the law and the use of unclear evidentiary standards. Finally, in the six subsection, the Ecuadorean experience is presented as an outstanding exception to the application of the regional refugee definition. However, that exception is now part of the past, as Ecuador has recently changed its national regime, devaluating many of the protection standards, including the explicit exclusion of the regional refugee definition.

The Regional Definition Is Seldom Used

Despite formal adoption of the regional definition in national legislation, administrative authorities infrequently apply it in RSD. Cases that could easily be addressed through the regional refugee definition are assessed instead under complementary forms of protection without any analysis of the regional refugee definition's applicability.

The practice in Mexico best illustrates this finding. Although the Mexican Commission for the Assistance of Refugees (COMAR) considers that certain asylum-seekers merit protection because they would be exposed to threats against their right to life, safety or freedom if returned to their home countries, it does not analyse the cases according to the requirements of the second segment of the national legislation which relies on situations listed in the regional refugee definition. Instead, the COMAR recommends complementary protection. In one decision,[64] the administrative body concluded that the applicant did have a well-founded fear of persecution but found no causal link with one of the protected grounds. However, it did not analyse the case under the regional refugee definition, even though state protection was not adequate; it proceeded to award complementary protection under the relevant national regime. This practice was documented in several decisions.[65]

---

[64] COMAR, Dirección de Protección y Retorno, EXP-20121001-5065XXX.
[65] See e.g. Dirección de Protección y Retorno, EXP-20122111-5019XXX (concerning a Salvadoran national) and EXP-20122507-54836XXX (concerning a Nicaraguan national).

One of the main reasons given by national RSD officers for not applying the regional refugee definition as a basis for refugee recognition is political in nature. As one expert commented, 'The definition requires us to qualify a particular situation as one of generalized violence or manifest that a particular country is a gross human-rights violator. There are some political considerations. The Ministry of Foreign Affairs is vigilant.'[66] This statement is illustrative of others recorded in Argentina and Brazil and most evidently in Mexico, where the RSD process includes consideration of a country-situation report issued by the Ministry of Foreign Affairs. This practice demonstrates that the task of analyzing the objective situations contained in the regional refugee definition is interpreted in a way that contradicts the non-political and humanitarian nature of refugee protection and strays far from the intention of the drafters of the Cartagena Declaration.

As stated by an Argentinean authority, 'We do not necessarily go through all the possible elements of the definition contained in the national regime. You just look at the case and you work it, according to where you believe it fits.'[67] This type of practice reinforces the lack of use of the regional refugee definition. For example, in Argentina and Mexico, where humanitarian protection is extended to minors or other forms of complementary protection are granted to asylum-seekers, RSD skips over consideration of the regional definition and proceeds to the 'best fit', according to the respective officer.[68] While complementary forms of protection at least provide some assistance, they never offer more than refugee protection.

The end result is that the regional refugee definition is used scarcely. Despite the rhetorical attention given to the regional refugee definition, these findings suggest that it is not adequately considered as an independent source of law to grant protection to refugees.

Conflating Claims under the Regional Refugee Definition and the 1951 Convention Definition

One of the greatest obstacles in the development of the regional refugee definition (and its national variations) as an authoritative source of law

---

[66] Interview with academic and public official, Mexico City, Mexico, 19 June 2012, on file with the author.

[67] Interview, Buenos Aires, Argentina, May 2012, on file with the author.

[68] Ley sobre Refugiados y Protección Complementaria, Se reforman, adicionan y derogan diversas disposiciones de la Ley General de Población, 2011, Arts. 16, 28–32 (Mexico).

and an autonomous basis for extending protection for persons fleeing one of the objective situations is that authorities do not interpret the definitional elements on their own terms. Instead, they subsume a finding of protection after deciding that the person is covered under 1951 Convention grounds. It is possible that a person can satisfy requirements under both the 1951 Convention and regional grounds; this finding is not problematic.

However, regional standards that uniquely apply to refugee flight in Latin America and more broadly cover circumstances of flight that are not included in the 1951 Convention definition are not developed; rather, they are conflated with 1951 Convention grounds, which has several deleterious effects. Firstly, in many cases the default is to use the least inclusive (i.e. 1951 Convention definition) rather than most inclusive definition (i.e. Cartagena definition). Secondly, when officials purport to use the Cartagena definition, they often do so only if the case falls within the scope of the 1951 Convention definition, thereby depriving the regional definition of unique authority or region-specific applicability. Thirdly, by using both definitions together, the regional definition can become an additional qualification to be eligible for protection rather than a separate, extended legal process.

Several adopted decisions illustrate this inappropriate aggregation of the elements to determine whether a person merits protection. One repeated pattern is for officials to use generalized violence or armed conflict to provide contextual reinforcement to a person's narrative arguing a well-founded fear of persecution. As an Argentinean national RSD officer explained, 'The Cartagena situations help to contextualize claims. It is something we explore, but in relation to petitions under the traditional definition.'[69] In practice, this type of 'contextualization' is nothing different than using country-of-origin information to evaluate an application under 1951 Convention grounds. It is not, however, use of the regional refugee definition as an independent source of law.

Another common practice observed in several countries is to provide rather meaningless recognition according to the regional refugee definition in conjunction with 1951 Convention grounds. The Salvadoran case involving an Iranian national is illustrative: 'The Commission for Determination of Refugee Status, according to [the Constitution, international law], and items a and c of article 4 [referring to the 1951

[69] Interview with CONARE officials, Buenos Aires, Argentina, 17 May 2012.

Convention and the regional refugee definitions, among others] of the Law on Determination of the Status of Refugees DECIDES: 1. To recognize refugee status to [the applicant].'[70]

Despite this language, the decision is based on grounds squarely and solely found in 1951 Convention RSD. There is no analysis or legal reasoning to support the conclusion that the individual qualified under the regional refugee definition.

This practice was also detected in Brazil, which has received some attention for purportedly using the regional refugee definition as autonomous grounds for protection. However, I have observed the practice in Brazil of subsuming recognition according to the regional variant only if status is granted under the 1951 Convention grounds. In its variation of the regional refugee definition, the only objective situation that Brazil includes in its national definition relates to 'gross and generalized violations of human rights'.[71] A past coordinator general of the Brazilian refugee committee (CONARE) suggested in published writings that there are specific conditions used to determine whether such a situation exists.[72] However, this appears to be his own personal approach as there is no evidence that these conditions ever constituted an institutional practice, particularly now that the author has left his post. Committee members and attorneys interviewed for this chapter expressed their concern over the regional refugee definition and reported that it is rarely used as an autonomous source for recognition. One senior member confirmed, 'The expression "gross and generalized violations" is indeterminate. It is difficult to apply. It is not clear what the definition means. The criteria presented by [the ex-coordinator] are far from desirable, and they represent his personal opinion.'[73] Instead of using the ambiguity of 'gross and generalized violations' to develop legal doctrine and guidance, the office dismissed its use.

---

[70] Comisión para la Determinación de la Condición de Personas Refugiadas (CODER), decisión de 2009 (El Salvador).

[71] Lei no 9.474, de 22 de julho de 1997, Define mecanismos para a implementação do Estatuto dos Refugiados de 1951, e determina outras providências, Art. 1 (III) (Brazil).

[72] See R. Zerbini Ribeiro Leão, 'O reconhecimento dos refugiados no Brasil no início do Século XXI', in L. P. Teles Ferreira Barreto et al. (eds.), Refúgio no Brasil. A proteção brasileira aos refugiados e seu impacto nas América (Brasilia: UNHCR and Ministry of Justice: 2010), 72–96, at 89. The former co-ordinator also asserted that several cases had been determined based on these conditions and the variant of the regional refugee definition.

[73] Interviews in Brasilia and Rio de Janeiro, May 2012, on file with the author.

A review of the available decisions confirms the failure to properly apply the definition.[74] As an example of the application of the regional definition variant in Brazil, the ex-coordinator cites a case in which the committee found that as a result of the climate of gross and generalized violations in Colombia, some persons were more prone to suffer discrimination and persecution than were others.[75] In light of this finding, the committee found that the Colombian context gave way to arbitrary action by drug dealers, and it therefore extended protection under 1951 Convention grounds for persecution experienced as a result of a politically imputed opinion. The committee ultimately recognized the applicant as a refugee under both the 1951 Convention and the variation of the regional refugee definition contained in Brazilian law. This oft-cited case does not in fact show a meaningful application of the regional refugee definition but is instead an example of the application of the 1951 Convention, implicitly subsuming protection under the regional definition.

Confidentiality as Concealment

Confidentiality is unquestionably a basic right of the applicant and 'is essential to creating an environment of security and trust for asylum seekers'.[76] However, state practice in the region has unfortunately misinterpreted confidentiality and equated it with concealment.[77] The primary consequence of this mistaken understanding and use of

---

[74] Four cases in particular are repeatedly mentioned as examples of the autonomous application of the regional refugee definition. Independent review of these decisions for this chapter revealed that two applications were in fact granted according to analysis of the 1951 Convention and not the regional refugee definition. See Brazil, CONARE, Processes Nos. MJ 08400.015093/2000–84 (regarding an applicant from Sierra Leona); MJ 08505.024796/2006–11 (regarding an applicant from Iraq); MJ 08000.013694/2006–51 (regarding an applicant from the DRC); and MJ 08460.024984/2004–41 (regarding an applicant from Colombia). The co-ordination of the committee did not provide any additional cases decided using the regional refugee definition variant.

[75] Case no. MJ 08460.024984/2004–41 (regarding an applicant from Colombia), cited in Zerbini Ribeiro Leão, 'O reconhecimento dos refugiados no Brasil no início do Século XXI', 77.

[76] UNHCR, 'Procedural Standards for Refugee Status Determination under UNHCR's Mandate', 20 November 2003, Unit 2.1.1, 'The Applicant's Right to Confidentiality'.

[77] This issue has been briefly addressed in the Latin American context by Lettieri. See M. Lettieri, 'Procedimientos de determinación del estatuto de refugiado y cuestiones de prueba', in V. Abramovich et al. (eds.), Protección internacional de refugiados en el sur de Sudamérica, 110.

confidentiality is that one key aspect of due-process standards is not fully respected. A second important and related consequence is that the national process is isolated from interaction with the legal community (including national practitioners in the same jurisdiction), as well as the basic democratic controls and oversight mechanisms of public administration. Lawyers working in the field of refugee protection cannot easily or officially access decisions that might instruct them as to the way the law is being applied in their country. This has directly affected the lack of development of a coherent practice and application of the elements of the regional refugee definition and related standards of proof.

The insulation resulting from confidentiality (mistakenly interpreted as concealment) was demonstrated by the obstacles faced during the conduct of this study. The bulk of decisions reviewed were made available under restricted terms. The remaining decisions were acquired through informal means. The sense of secrecy also conditioned the content and quality of the interviews, and most interviewees asked not be identified. This general attitude of concealment and mystery is contrary to the principles of justice, equality and transparency that should characterize administrative acts. Moreover, it demonstrates that the development of the law and practice is taking place outside the scope of any meaningful guidance or oversight.

The effects of the prevailing confidentiality-as-concealment attitude are compounded by other practices that violate due process and hinder the development of a coherent body of law and practice around the regional refugee definition. These include ad hoc procedures and standards, incoherency and inconsistency of decisions, absence of proper substantiation of decisions (lack of legal reasoning) and use of inexplicit standards and burdens of proof.

Argentina presents a potential reversal of this trend. There the UNHCR is working with national authorities to publish systematized excerpts of administrative RSD decisions. The extracts provide sufficient information to understand a given case without disclosing information regarding the applicant. The extract includes the reasoning of the decisions to document the interpretation and application of national and international law, standards of proof and other procedural aspects. The project in Argentina is an exceptional, positive development that should be considered by all countries in the region as a step towards promoting a proper understanding of the regional refugee definition and an application of refugee law that is in accordance with due-process standards.

Structural Due-Process Violations Lead to Arbitrary Application of the Law, Including the Regional Refugee Definition

Adequate development of the law – including implementation of the regional refugee definition – goes hand-in-hand with a strong adherence to due-process standards. I have identified serious and interrelated deficiencies in administrative practices that contribute to the arbitrary application of the regional refugee definition.

Firstly, decision-makers in Latin America generally label RSD as an ad hoc and unique procedure. In practice, this means that status determination responds to arbitrary criteria as opposed to a coherent body of law. For example, one RSD official described her assessment of cases in the following way: 'There is no method; it is done on a case-by-case basis.'[78] This is a mistaken understanding of specificity or speciality. The case-by-case analysis should not be understood as a wide margin of flexibility or foster unwanted discretionary practices. This approach is contrary to international standards[79] set out in the inter-American human rights system, 'The process of determining who is or is not a refugee involves making case-by-case determinations that may affect the liberty, personal integrity, and even the life of the person concerned ... [T]he basic principles of equal protection and due process reflected in the American Declaration *require predictable procedures and consistency in decision-making at each stage of the process.*'[80]

The case-by-case analysis called for in RSD cannot be taken as a license for arbitrary decisions removed from reference to a consistent set of procedures. The lack of a coherent understanding of the regional refugee definition is both a consequence and a contributing factor to the predominance of this so-called ad hoc approach observed in this survey of state practice.

Secondly, and intimately related to the first, refugee determinations in the region are generally not backed by documented, reasoned legal decisions. The international standards and importance of this for due

---

[78] Records of interviews are on file with the author.

[79] These standards have been studied and analysed in a recent publication in relation to RSD in southern Latin America. See M. Ezequiel Filardi et al., 'El debido proceso en el reconocimiento de la condición de refugiado de niños y niñas no acompañados o separados de sus familias', in V. Abramovich et al. (eds.), *Protección internacional de refugiados en el sur de Sudamérica*, 227–54.

[80] IACommHR, 'Report on the Situation of Human Rights of Asylum Seekers within the Canadian Refugee Determination System', 28 February 2000, OEA/Ser. L/V/II.106, Doc. 40 Rev., para. 52 (emphasis added).

process are clear. The Inter-American Court of Human Rights (IACourtHR) has repeatedly ruled that all administrative decisions with the potential to affect human rights need to be grounded in law and include proper reasoning.[81]

Chilean practice is illustrative. Despite acceptable procedures established in domestic legislation, in practice, the decisions do not include sufficient legal grounds to discern the consideration made in a given case.[82] I reviewed 211 decisions[83]; in fewer than ten cases did decisions take up two pages. The rest were one page in length, and none provided the *rationes decidendi* of the administrative act. The 114 decisions denying refugee status reflected the use of a boilerplate template. The lack of specific consideration of individual cases and the absence of legal reasoning tailored to the individual claim for protection gravely affect asylum-seekers' rights and the quality of the decisions. Although Chile stood out as an example of particularly problematic practice (perhaps because of the number of decisions made available for study), decisions adopted by the Bolivian, Colombian, Guatemalan, Honduran, Peruvian and Salvadoran authorities demonstrated similar shortcomings.

---

[81] '[T]he reasons given for a judgment must show that the arguments by the parties have been duly weighed and that the body of evidence has been analyzed ... [W]hen the decision is subject to appeal, it affords them the possibility to argue against it, and of having such decision reviewed by an appellate body.' See e.g. *Case of Apitz Barbera et al. ('First Court of Administrative Disputes')* v. *Venezuela*, 5 August 2008, Inter-American Court of Human Rights, Ser. C No. 182, para. 78 (internal citations omitted). This holding has been reiterated by the court on several occasions: *Case of Tristán Donoso* v. *Panamá*, 27 January 2009, Inter-American Court of Human Rights, Series C No. 193, para. 153; *Case Yvon Neptune* v. *Haiti*, 6 May 2008, Inter-American Court of Human Rights, Ser. C No. 180, para. 108; *Case of Chaparro Álvarez and Lapo Íñiguez* v. *Ecuador*, 21 November 2007, Inter-American Court of Human Rights, Ser. C No. 170, para. 107; *Case of Claude-Reyes et al.* v. *Chile*, 19 September 2006, Inter-American Court of Human Rights, Ser. C No. 151, para. 120; *Case of Palamara Iribarne* v. *Chile*, 22 November 2005, Inter-American Court of Human Rights, Ser. C No. 135, para. 216; *Case of Yatama* v. *Nicaragua*, 23 June 2005, Inter-American Court of Human Rights, Ser. C No. 127, para. 152; and *Case of Ivcher Bronstein*, 6 February 2001, Inter-American Court of Human Rights, Ser. C No. 74, para. 105.

[82] The Chilean framework sets out a reasonable procedure for the decision of asylum claims that grants proper consideration to due process. See generally chap. III of the national law. Ley 20430 de 2010, Art. 29–37 (Chile).

[83] All decisions were issued by the Ministry of the Interior of Chile, Sub-Secretary of the Interior, Department of Immigration and Emigration in 2011. Of the 211 decisions, 14 closed the case without consideration of the merits; 2 involved cessation of refugee status; 46 extended temporary visas; 114 rejected asylum requests; 9 rejected requests for reconsideration of initial rejection; 14 rejected administrative appeals and 12 recognized refugee status.

A third factor that has led to informal and less than consistent practice and scarce legal development of this branch of administrative law is that asylum-seekers are discouraged from using legal counsel.[84] Most public officials who conduct RSD resist the exercise of the right to counsel by asylum-seekers. In opinions expressed through the interviews, public servants assert that they can properly weigh and represent the various interests involved, including those of the asylum-seeker and of the administration (whether technical or political).

Evidentiary Standards: Treading Mysterious Grounds

A final and related concern with the proper consideration of claims under the regional refugee definition is the use of unclear and changing evidentiary standards. A few national normative frameworks have established particular probative or evidentiary regimes for RSD. For example, Argentinean law refers to 'sufficient indicia' to consider facts to be proven.[85] Similarly, Chilean law refers to 'sufficient material proof' as the ideal standard but allows decisions to be based on 'indicia, presumptions, and general credibility of the asylum seeker'.[86] Most normative schemes include a general principle of interpretation to favour asylum.[87] In line with UNHCR's *Handbook on Criteria and Procedures for Determining Refugee Status*, Peruvian law's normative scheme explicitly states that where there is doubt, the adjudicator should apply the interpretation most favourable to the asylum-seeker.[88] Although these are not

---

[84] In the early 1990s, Roger Zetter warned about the risks of 'bureaucratic labelling' in RSD proceedings and demonstrated the 'extreme vulnerability of refugees to imposed labels'. The fact that refugees cannot use counsel and that officials are provided with ample discretion to act illustrate the powerlessness of refugees and their lack of protection in the course of 'latent and manifest processes of institutional action'. See R. Zetter, 'Labelling Refugees and Forming and Transforming a Bureaucratic Identity', *JRS* 4 (1991), 39.

[85] Ley No. 26.165 de 2006, Art. 46 (Argentina). [86] Ley 20430 de 2010, Art. 34 (Chile).

[87] The Argentinean law makes direct reference to the *pro homine* principle (Ley No. 24.165, Art. 2); in other jurisdictions, such as Brazil and Bolivia, it has been included through practice.

[88] The Peruvian regime is illustrative of this type of principle. The refugee commission 'can adopt a decision in favour of an asylum seeker in cases in which doubts arise in relation to the assessment of probative elements required to be considered a refugee', Ley 27.891 de 2002, Art. 16 (Peru). Venezuela is another positive example: 'If doubt arises in the interpretation or the application of any norm, that which is most favourable to the exercise of the rights of the (claimant) will be applied'; Ley orgánica sobre refugiados o refugiadas y asilados o asiladas, 13 de septiembre de 2001, Art. 4 (Venezuela). See UNHCR, *Handbook on Procedures and Criteria for Determining Refugee Status under the 1951 Convention and the 1967 Protocol Relating to the Status of Refugees*, HCR/IP/4/Eng/

rules of evidence but rather guidelines for legislative interpretation, most decision-makers point to these provisions as qualifying the evidentiary regime.

Most legal regimes base their operation on a flexible model for assessment that is part of Latin American legal culture – known as *sana crítica* – in which evidence is considered according to the general rules of logic and experience and based on the totality of the circumstances. Although there is no inherent problem with this model, in practice, judicial and administrative authorities often incorrectly interpret this model of assessment as giving them a wide margin of discretion to decide. Instead of basing decisions on the relevant law and the rules of evidence, practitioners revealed the primacy given to intuition: 'We really do not have a standard' or 'The standard is sufficient indicia, but it is a standard that is *sui generis*.' The lack of rigor in analyzing the cases has meant that the well-intentioned interpretation clauses designed to favour the claimant lose their desired impact in practice.

With only a few exceptions, it is impossible to assess the standards used to evaluate credibility of asylum claims or of the information backing the claim. One exception is the Argentinean National Refugee Commission (CONARE), whose authorities employ the most extensive evidentiary considerations in their decisions supported by reports from secretariat staff members. Consideration is largely based on the 1951 Convention and often refers to suggested parameters on standards and burden of proof, including application of legal criteria to the facts, explicit setting out of the standard of proof applied and inclusion of an explanation of the way the factual elements were weighed to reach a decision. However, this is not the case for petitions considered under the regional refugee definition, for which the final decisions are not specific. Regardless, Argentina represents the best practice observed in this study in relation to these matters.

Mexico is another exception in terms of considering matters of proof in RSD decisions. However, the standard set out in the decisions adopted by the Mexican Commission for the Assistance of Refugees (COMAR) is problematic. Recent decisions (2011 and 2012) for claims under the 1951

Rev. 2, paras. 34, 73, 196 and 203–204, January 1992, regarding the application of the benefit of the doubt in favour of the applicant. Additionally, according to UNHCR, 'Where the adjudicator considers that the applicant's story is on the whole coherent and plausible, any element of doubt should not prejudice the applicant's claim; that is, the applicant should be given the "benefit of the doubt"'. See UNHCR, 'Note on Burden and Standard of Proof in Refugee Claims', 16 December 1998.

Convention or regional refugee definitions repeat a standard paragraph referring to a 'conviction of certainty' that needs to be established.[89] It is not clear whether 'certainty' is the standard being used in practice or what the administrative body understands 'certainty' to be. However, it is clear that the 'certainty' standard found in the public record is not consistent with international rules[90] and raises scrutiny to a level that is similar to demanding a level of conviction beyond a reasonable doubt, as is the practice in criminal law.

These decisions demonstrate a misunderstanding of the nexus between the flight and the objective situation under the regional refugee definition. Correctly, decision-makers point to the need to link the objective situations to the cause of the flight, derived from threat to life, safety or freedom of the person (according to the regional refugee definition); interviewees repeatedly asserted that in addition to the existence of the objective situation, 'something else' has to be demonstrated. When asked about the nature of the threat to which the regional refugee definition refers, national RSD officers offered a full variety of responses including, among others: 'The life of the person must be unbearable'; 'Whether the person would face serious risk if he [or she] were to return to his [or her] home country'; and 'A specific intent to cause him [or her] harm'.[91]

The misunderstanding or misinterpretation of the nexus element is often intentional so as to avoid granting international protection to individuals who come from countries exposed to situations of generalized violence or armed conflict. There is an eagerness to avoid a type of prima facie standard that would extend protection simply because a person fled from a particular country presenting one of the prescribed situations. This has had the perverse result of national authorities raising the bar of required elements under the regional refugee definition and

---

[89] The paragraph states 'the information (available) analyzed as a whole must assemble a discernment that generates certainty within the authority that the applicant would be exposed to experience harm against his life, liberty, safety and personal integrity if he were to return to his country of origin'. The original Spanish reads: 'información que al ser analizada en su conjunto debe constituir razonamientos que generen en la autoridad, la certeza de que el solicitante sería expuesto a sufrir daño contra su vida, libertad, seguridad e integridad personal en caso de regresar a su país de origen'.

[90] It is worth reiterating that this analysis is permitted because of Mexico's practice of issuing decisions that are somewhat reasoned. The secrecy and opacity of other national bodies have made it impossible to evaluate whether they comply with proper probative standards.

[91] Interviews conducted in Brazil, Argentina and Mexico 2012, on file with the author.

making direct victimization a necessary criterion for obtaining protection. The regional refugee definition standard being applied to evaluate refugee applications may be arbitrarily higher than that assigned to the 1951 Convention definition, in direct opposition to the intent and purpose of the Cartagena Declaration – particularly given that the regional refugee definition was promoted to extend international protection to more people by using a lesser threshold (threat to life, safety and freedom rather than well-founded fear of persecution).

Two respondents stood out by providing understandings of the nexus that are consistent with the spirit of the regional refugee definition. The first, a relatively senior member of a foreign relations ministry, stated: 'We do not look for particular harm. We do need to look at the situation of the particular individual in relation to the objective situation.'[92] Along the same lines, a director of the secretariat of one of the national commissions asserted that 'the person does not have to have suffered any harm. All we need to establish is some link between the flight and the objective situation. We are looking for some sort of effect on a person's ability to conduct a normal life as a result of the objective situation. And we use a human-rights lens to detect this situation.' Although these are personal responses and not institutional parameters, they are examples of a proper understanding of the regional refugee definition.

Overall, decisions-makers of national refugee regimes who were interviewed for this study are not certain of any standard to assess threats to life, safety and liberty for the purposes of applying the regional refugee definition. To avoid over-inclusion, they are adopting positions that are not based in law. The interviewees instead confirmed that it was in fact their subjective values (or those of the policy-makers) that guide the system.

The drafters of the Cartagena Declaration sought to avoid this type of subjective and individualized finding. The historical context resoundingly refutes any suggestion that the regional refugee definition should be limited only to those who can demonstrate some type of individualized or direct harm. The Cartagena Declaration and, in particular, the regional refugee definition contained therein sought precisely to cover persons who fled turmoil and insecurity in an attempt to protect their rights. The main objective was to protect those fleeing the indiscriminate effects of various levels of violence by recognizing that there were far more

---

[92] Interview, 2012, on file with the author.

people in need of international protection than those able to fulfil the requirement of the 1951 Convention refugee definition with its five persecution grounds. As the examples from this chapter reveal, the requirements being assigned to the regional refugee definition are in effect higher than those under the 'well-founded fear' standard of the 1951 Convention. The prevailing, asylum-influenced interpretation that requires a person to demonstrate victimization prior to flight defeats the protective purpose of the refugee regime and goes against the primary purpose of the regional refugee definition.

A Good Practice Gone Awry: Ecuador's Experience with the Extended Registry

Ecuador is the only country in the region that has used the regional refugee definition in a fashion envisaged by those who promoted the Cartagena Declaration. This practice faced an abrupt change in May 2012 when national law was modified by presidential decree.[93] For twenty-five years (1987–2012), Ecuador included the extended regional refugee definition as part of its national law, though the definition was not readily used.[94] However, for a slight window of time, international protection was extended in an unprecedented modern-day application of the Cartagena regime. A confluence of factors that were internal to the refugee-protection logic and also external influences (namely, the deteriorating Ecuador–Colombia relations) led Ecuador to realize the need to respond in a humanitarian way to Colombians in its territory. UNHCR was undoubtedly instrumental in advocating for such a decision.

Colombian nationals had fled to neighbouring Ecuador for years, especially as a result of the escalation of the armed conflict and other sources of violence (generalized violence, massive violation of human rights and other circumstances that seriously disturb public order) in Colombia after the year 2000. The worsening of the situation in areas along the border generated greater trans-national flight, and by

---

[93] Presidente Constitucional de la República, Decreto Ejecutivo No. 1182 del 30 de mayo de 2012 (Ecuador).

[94] Decreto 3293 de 1987, Reglamento para la aplicación en el Ecuador de las normas contenidas en la Convención de 1951 sobre el Estatuto de los refugiados y en su Protocolo de 1967, 30 de septiembre de 1987, Art. 2 (Ecuador); Decreto 3301 de 1992, Reglamento para la Aplicación en el Ecuador de las normas contenidas en la Convención de Ginebra de 1951 sobre el Estatuto de los Refugiados y en su Protocolo de 1967', Art. 2 (Ecuador).

mid-2000, the number of Colombians in Ecuador in need of international protection was growing steadily and was estimated to be in the tens of thousands. For one year (March 2009–March 2010) Ecuadorean authorities worked together with UNHCR, NGOs and refugee groups to conduct an 'Extended Registry' of Colombians who were on Ecuadorean soil fleeing the conflict and violence in their country. This initiative recognized nearly 30,000 Colombians as refugees. However, this application of the regional refugee definition ended in May 2012 when the Ecuadorean government modified the refugee regime through a presidential decree.[95] Nevertheless, the exercise merits special consideration as the only recorded regional experience where international protection practices have echoed the practices and concepts contained in the regional refugee definition.

In September 2008, the Ministry of Foreign Affairs, Commerce, and Integration adopted the 'Asylum Policy of Ecuador'.[96] Though the document purported to be the general refugee policy, it explicitly focused on addressing the situation of approximately 180,000 Colombians.[97] The policy mandated the implementation of a 'mixed model' addressing the situation of the mass influx of Colombians into Ecuadorean territory while responding to individual asylum claims.

A major concern at the time was the overwhelming backlog of cases that had never been considered by the National Commission for the Determination of the Status of Refugees in Ecuador and the infrequent application of the regional refugee definition.[98] Accordingly, a streamlined procedure granted international protection to all those who qualified under the regional refugee definition.[99] Starting in 2000, Ecuadorean policy explicitly recognized the need to address the situation of many persons who had not contacted authorities because of a lack of knowledge or trust and in 2008 were considered 'invisible' asylum-seekers.

---

[95] Presidente Constitucional de la República, Decreto Ejecutivo No. 1182 del 30 de mayo de 2012 (Ecuador). The reasons for Ecuador's regressive move go beyond the scope of this chapter and are deeply political, including concerns expressed by the Ecuadorean security sector, confusion regarding the application of the regional refugee definition, political pacts related to upcoming electoral bouts and changing regional politics, particularly in relation to the government of Colombia.

[96] Ecuador, Ministerio de Relaciones Exteriores, Comercio e Integración, Dirección General de Refugiados, Política del Ecuador en Materia de Refugio, Quito, 2008.

[97] Ibid. Palabras Preliminares de la Ministra.

[98] Contained in Art. 2 of Decree No. 3301 of 1992.

[99] See Presidente Constitucional de la República, Decreto Ejecutivo No. 1182 del 30 de mayo de 2012, para. 33.

In addition to addressing such RSD concerns, Ecuador's policy document also set out basic assistance policies that would require long-term integration efforts by the Ecuadorean authorities. It outlined the intention to establish a 'co-responsibility' scheme with Colombian authorities rather than burden-/responsibility-sharing mechanisms with the international community. Relevant stakeholders in Ecuador called the document ground-breaking for putting into motion institutional efforts and resources not previously seen.

Without renouncing individual asylum requests, authorities implemented a special mechanism that would address the backlog of cases as well as the new requests. This streamlined mechanism was termed the 'Extended Registry' (*registro ampliado*), and as an important part of the process, the Ecuadorean government designed a manual for operation together with UNHCR.[100]

The manual set out the relevant protection principles and standards as well as guidelines for streamlining procedure. Relevant adjustments were made to local legislation to facilitate the implementation of this policy and Extended Registry.[101]

The special procedure made the elements of the regional refugee definition operational by establishing a series of geographical and thematic criteria that were used to codify and evaluate the asylum request of each applicant. Based on the asylum-seeker's interview, a series of geographical references were drawn in order to establish the applicant's place of residence and work.[102] This information was then cross-checked with country-of-origin information including specific regional breakdowns according to objective threats and risk factors (human-rights violations, presence of armed groups, combat and other sources of violence).

The manual also presented a series of thematic criteria in order to properly assess the objective situations set out in the regional refugee definition.[103] The following twelve elements were adopted for establishing the 'reasons that motivated the person's flight':[104]

---

[100] See generally Ministerio de Relaciones Exteriores, Comercio e Integración, Dirección General de Refugiados and UNHCR, Manual de Registro Ampliado, January 2009. The final version was adopted 15 April 2009.

[101] Presidential Decree No. 1635, 25 March 2009.

[102] 'Manual de Registro Ampliado', 26–7, addressing the verification of the regional criteria for purposes of recognizing refugee status.

[103] Ibid., 27–32, including guides to interpret and verify the thematic criteria.

[104] Ibid., 32.

1. Military or warring activity;
2. Attacks against civilian infrastructure;
3. Forced recruitment;
4. Anti-personnel mines and other explosive devices;
5. Intimidation and threats;
6. Victims of forced labour (including coca production);
7. Kidnapping, extortion and other forms of confiscation of property;
8. Attacks on civilians, massacres, killings and other acts aimed at producing terror;
9. Enforced disappearances;
10. Lack of state protection and effective access to justice;
11. Aerial aspersion of chemicals conducted by the Colombian government in order to eradicate illicit crops; and
12. Forced displacement, confinement or other forms of restriction of freedom of movement.

Based on the juxtaposition of the geographical and thematic criteria in each individual application, the interviewer would make a recommendation to the commission, which would then consider each petition and make a final decision. The streamlined procedure did not imply the meting out of collective or generic decisions; rather, the commission considered individual cases and made individualized decisions for each and every applicant. The process was swift but provided substantiated decisions in each case. At the end of each day, the commission would compile all decisions and adopt an official administrative act. The record for each decision included a summary of the facts, the recommendation of the official who conducted the interview, the motivation (outlining the geographical and thematic criteria applied) and the resolution (either recognizing refugee status or deferring the case to the ordinary proceeding).[105]

The Extended Registry became operational on 23 March 2009 and ended on 31 March 2010. A total of 28,909 Colombians were registered, and 27,740 were recognized as refugees. Rejection or denial of refugee status was not an option under the streamlined mechanism; if applications generated doubt, they were sent to the ordinary proceeding but not rejected. Nearly 1,200 cases were sent to the ordinary proceeding for reconsideration.

---

[105] Several of the administrative acts of the Ecuadorean Commission are on file with the author.

This extraordinary process exemplified and implemented the nature and spirit of the regional refugee definition recommended by the 1984 Cartagena Declaration. Unfortunately, the experience came to a close with much opposition and little understanding. Though the situation of Colombians recognized under the streamlined process was by no means perfect, the documented efforts and recognition rates have made this experience one of the most successful in recent history. The humanitarian space has been reduced in Ecuador since the end of the programme. This experience serves as a reminder of the importance of political will and the need to support protection efforts worldwide.

Conclusion

The regional refugee definition appears to have a greater existence in rhetoric than in practice. Thirty years after its adoption, the best acknowledgement of the value of the Cartagena Declaration would be to reinvigorate the commitment to cover persons in need of international protection by promoting policies that are inclusive rather than exclusive in nature. Protection is above all a mindset and a reflection of political will.

Today, with a few exceptions, the mindset and political will in Latin America are at odds with the primary objective of the Cartagena Declaration 'to promote that countries in the region establish a regime including the basic treatment for refugees, based on the precepts contained in the 1951 Convention and the 1967 Protocol, and the American Convention on Human Rights'.[106]

The regional refugee definition in the Cartagena Declaration was meant to provide a concise reference point to expand protection while swiftly responding to the growing plight of refugees who did not fulfil the 1951 Convention definition. Almost thirty years later, the failure of many Latin American states to champion the regional refugee definition, to take concrete steps to make it operable and to faithfully apply its contents

---

[106] Cartagena Declaration, Conclusion No. 8. Conclusion 8 of the Cartagena Declaration also states, 'To ensure that the countries of the region establish a minimum standard of treatment for refugees, on the basis of the provisions of the 1951 Convention and 1967 Protocol and of the American Convention on Human Rights, taking into consideration the conclusions of the UNHCR Executive Committee, particularly No. 22 on the Protection of Asylum Seekers in Situations of Large-Scale Influx'. This statement reflects the notion that there are more people in need of international protection, who deserve protection, though they do not satisfy the refugee criteria of the 1951 Convention.

has implications that go far beyond the sidelining of the regional refugee definition. Officials processing asylum claims do not appear to know how to apply the regional refugee definition in a consistent and coherent manner. This element remains an important regional challenge for the protection of refugees in Latin America. The issues that are at stake are the loss of solidarity towards persons fleeing generalized violence or conflict in the region and the overshadowing of the refugee protection regime by the growing focus on security.

Regardless of the superficial esteem given to this definition, it has been set aside and left undeveloped. Although the regional refugee definition has been incorporated in a number of national legal frameworks, it still falls short of being part and parcel of day-to-day practice in domestic jurisdictions.

As has been demonstrated throughout this chapter, doctrinal development of the regional refugee definition remains necessary. In developing these parameters, particular attention should be paid to the type of relation that needs to exist between the flight of a person and the objective situations that cause the flight, according to the regional refugee definition. Proper interpretation of the cause of flight – namely, the prevailing situation in the country of origin and a threat to life, safety or freedom – is key to the appropriate application of the regional refugee definition. Likewise, procedural standards need to be adopted to ensure respect for due process. Lastly, a central element in reversing the improper application of the regional refugee definition is confronting the lack of transparency in adjudication of refugee cases in national settings.

As things currently stand in Latin America, refugee law is being applied 'out of sight and out of mind', subject to the whims of administrative bureaucracies. What is clear is that refugee law deserves more than rhetorical allegiance, but its place on the public agenda in Latin America remains uncertain.

PART III

Refugee Status and Special Groups

6

Women and Girls Fleeing Conflict

Gender and the Interpretation and Application of the 1951 Refugee Convention

VALERIE OOSTERVELD*

Introduction

Women, girls, men and boys all suffer when exposed to the effects of conflict. Sometimes women and girls have similar experiences in these situations as men and boys. Many times, however, they have different experiences. They may be subjected to different violations because they are women and girls, or they may be subjected to the same types of violations as men and boys but experience or perceive these harms in a different manner. One obvious example is sexual violence committed during war; the United Nations reports that '[s]exual violence, and the long shadow of terror and trauma it casts, disproportionately affects women and girls.'[1] This different female experience stems from pervasive global gender inequality: around the world, women and girls tend to be poorer and receive less education and are often less mobile as a result of traditional family and care-giving responsibilities, all of which nega- tively compound their experiences during conflict.[2] While women and girls may have common experiences based on their gender, sometimes girls suffer additional targeted harm as a result of their young age. For

* I thank Alexandra MacKenzie for her valuable research assistance and UNHCR's Sanne Andersen, Alice Edwards and Gisela Thater, as well as Margaret Martin, for their helpful suggestions. Any errors are my own. A more detailed version of this chapter is available in UNHCR's RefWorld online database.
[1] UN Secretary-General, 'Conflict-Related Sexual Violence: Report of the Secretary-General', 13 January 2012, UN Doc. S/2012/33, para. 6.
[2] Committee on the Elimination of Discrimination against Women, 'Concept Note: General Discussion on the Protection of Women's Human Rights in Conflict and Post-Conflict Contexts', 18 July 2011, 6–7.

example, girls forcibly recruited to serve as fighters may serve in combat (like boys) but may also be subjected to conjugal slavery (unlike boys).

When women and girls fleeing conflict seek asylum, are their gender-differentiated experiences recognized by decision-makers? It is not immediately obvious that they would be, given that neither the terms 'sex' nor 'gender' appear in the definition of 'refugee' set out in the 1951 Convention Relating to the Status of Refugees (1951 Convention), as amended by the 1967 Protocol Relating to the Status of Refugees (1967 Protocol).[3] However, over the past twenty years, there has been a significant focus at the international level on ensuring a gender-sensitive interpretation of the refugee definition. These efforts include UNHCR's issuance of a number of groundbreaking guidance documents[4] and state adoption of legislation including 'sex' or 'gender' in the list of 1951 Convention grounds[5] or of guidelines on female asylum-seekers.[6]

Given this guidance, one would expect gender-sensitive determinations of asylum claims by women and girls fleeing conflict. However, numerous studies show that deep flaws still exist in the domestic consideration of refugee claims by women and girls and that both policy and practice need

---

[3] Convention Relating to the Status of Refugees (adopted 28 July 1951, entered into force 22 April 1954), 189 UNTS 137 (1951 Convention), Art. 1A(2); Protocol Relating to the Status of Refugees (entered into force 4 October 1967), 606 UNTS 267 (1967 Protocol), Art. 1(2). On the history of this, see A. Edwards, 'Transitioning Gender: Feminist Engagement with International Refugee Law and Policy 1950-2010', *RSQ* 29(2) (2010), 21, 22-3.

[4] Recent examples include UNHCR, 'Handbook for the Protection of Women and Girls', January 2008; UNHCR, 'Sexual and Gender-Based Violence against Refugees, Returnees and Internally Displaced Persons: Guidelines for Prevention and Response', May 2003; and UNHCR, 'Guidelines on International Protection: Gender-Related Persecution within the Context of Article 1A(2) of the 1951 Convention and/or Its 1967 Protocol Relating to the Status of Refugees', 7 May 2002, HCR/GIP/02/01, para. 6 (UNHCR, 'Guidelines on International Protection No. 1').

[5] For example, Refugee Act of 1996 (Ireland), sec. 1 (in defining membership of a particular social group).

[6] For example, 'Guidelines on Gender Issues for Decision Makers 1996' (Australia); and 'Gender Guidelines 2012' (Australia); 'Guidelines for Women Refugee Claimants Fearing Gender-Related Persecution 2003' (Canada) ('Guidelines for Women Refugee Claimants'); 'Gender Guidelines for Asylum Determination 1999' (South Africa); 'Asylum Gender Guidelines 2000' (United Kingdom) ('Asylum Gender Guidelines') and 'Gender Issues in the Asylum Claim 2006' (United Kingdom); and 'Considerations for Asylum Officers Adjudicating Asylum Claims from Women 1995' (United States) and 'Gender Guidelines for Overseas Refugee Processing 2000' (United States) ('Considerations for Asylum Officers').

improvement.[7] To date, this analysis has not concentrated specifically on women and girls who have fled conflict. This chapter therefore aims to bring some focus to this subset of female refugee claimants.[8] It does so by analyzing a group of forty-six cases decided between 2004 and 2012 in Australia, Canada, New Zealand, the United Kingdom and the United States involving women and girls who seek asylum based on claims related to conflict. These cases come from various levels of the refugee determination process. In addition to this group of recent cases, this chapter also considers certain relevant earlier cases, as well as reports on and academic discussions of the female refugee experience that include contemplation of conflict-related claims.

The second section of this chapter begins by exploring when conflict-related ill-treatment has been recognized as persecution and when it has not. This section also examines whether ill-treatment in conflict can be considered to be targeted at individual women and girls. The third section examines the 1951 Convention grounds most often used in refugee claims made by women and girls fleeing conflict: membership of a particular social group, political opinion, race and religion. The fourth section discusses how lack of state protection has been considered in female conflict-related refugee claims. The fifth section discusses procedural and evidentiary problems that arise in such asylum claims, especially with respect to credibility gaps on sexual violence and lack of gender-specific country-of-origin information. The final section concludes with observations on the need for a deeper understanding of persecution, expanded conceptions of the 1951 Convention grounds as they relate to women and girls fleeing conflict and recognition that women and girls fleeing conflict face problems similar to those making peacetime-related claims *and* specific conflict-related evidentiary and procedural hurdles.

---

[7] For example, C. Querton, "'I Feel Like as a Woman I'm Not Welcome": A Gender Analysis of UK Asylum Law, Policy and Practice', Asylum Aid, January 2012; H. Muggeridge and C. Maman, 'Unsustainable: The Quality of Initial Decision-Making in Women's Asylum Claims', Asylum Aid, January 2011; H. Cheikh Ali, C. Querton and E. Soulard, 'Gender-Related Asylum Claims in Europe: Comparative Analysis of Law, Policies and Practice Focusing on Women in Nine EU Member States', GENSEN, May 2012; and UNHCR, 'Improving Asylum Procedures – Comparative Analysis and Recommendations for Law and Practice: Key Gender-Related Findings and Recommendations', March 2010.

[8] This chapter does not focus on some related areas that deserve greater scrutiny, such as gender-related refugee claims by men and boys fleeing conflict and the reliance on subsidiary or complementary protection as a 'safety valve' for gender and conflict cases (on this, see, Cheikh Ali et al., 'Gender-Related Asylum Claims in Europe', 57).

Persecution

The 1951 Convention requires that the refugee claimant possess a well-founded fear of a form of harm that qualifies as persecution.[9] The term 'persecution' is not defined in the 1951 Convention, though there is agreement that 'a threat to life or freedom on account of race, religion, nationality, political opinion or membership of a particular social group' and other serious violations of international human rights constitute persecution.[10] There are a number of gender-related forms of harm that are currently considered to fit within these parameters – such as rape, dowry-related violence, female genital mutilation, domestic violence and trafficking – because they inflict severe pain and suffering (both mental and physical), whether perpetrated by state or non-state actors.[11] However, only some gender-related forms of ill-treatment common in the context of conflict have been recognized as rising to the level of persecution. The conflict-related harm that is most well established as a form of gendered persecution is rape.

Rape in Conflict

Rape is committed during conflict for many reasons.[12] These reasons may range from opportunistic 'sexual looting', to strategic design, to a combination of the two.[13] These reasons may overlap and coexist in a given conflict and may also change over time. Rape can also be committed in many ways, such as brutal gang rapes, the insertion of various objects into victims' genitalia, the raping of pregnant women and forced sexual intercourse between male and female civilian abductees.[14] Rape is an

---

[9] 1951 Convention, Art. 1A(2).

[10] UNHCR, 'Handbook on Procedures and Criteria for Determining Refugee Status under the 1951 Convention and the 1967 Protocol Relating to the Status of Refugees', January 1992, HCR/1P/4/Eng./Rev.1, para. 51. Such human rights would include those listed in the 1981 Convention on the Elimination of All Forms of Discrimination against Women (entered into force 3 September 1981), 1249 UNTS 13 (CEDAW).

[11] UNHCR, 'Guidelines on International Protection No. 1', para. 9.

[12] OCHA Policy Development and Studies Branch, 'Sexual Violence and Conflict: Understanding the Motivations', 20 June 2008.

[13] X. Agirre Aranburu, 'Sexual Violence beyond Reasonable Doubt: Using Pattern Evidence and Analysis for International Cases', Leiden Journal of International Law (2010), 609, at 613–14, 622.

[14] For example, as carried out by the Revolutionary United Front during the civil war in Sierra Leone: Prosecutor v. Sesay et al., Case No. SCSL-04-15-T, Trial Judgement, 9 March 2009, paras. 1181, 1185, 1193–4, 1205–7, 1289 and 1347, n. 2509 (Sesay Trial Judgement).

expression by the perpetrator of control and power[15] and therefore is effective in not only physically and psychologically harming the victims but also in tearing apart social units (such as families and communities).[16] This is why rape has been acknowledged as a particularly effective tool of genocide,[17] as a crime against humanity (including the crime against humanity of persecution)[18] and as a war crime.[19] Rape has also been recognized as a human rights violation.[20]

Given the serious harm created by rape, it is therefore not surprising that rape has been identified within international and domestic refugee law as a form of persecution. UNHCR has stated that '[t]here is no doubt that rape is an act which inflicts severe pain and suffering (both mental and physical) and which has been used as a form of persecution by States and non-State actors.'[21] Various country guidelines, directed at refugee claim adjudicators, also specify rape as a form of persecution.[22] Domestic refugee case law has also recognized rape in conflict as a form of persecution.[23] In my examination of twenty recent cases involving claims of rape (of the claimant or a family member) or fear of rape as persecution,[24] eight claims or appeals were accepted on the evidence of

---

[15] M. Eriksson, *Defining Rape: Emerging Obligations for States under International Law?* (Boston: Martinus Nijhoff, 2011), 171.

[16] *Ibid.* 126; *Sesay* Trial Judgement, paras. 1349–50.

[17] *Prosecutor* v. *Akayesu*, Case No. ICTR-96-4-T, Judgement, 2 September 1998, at para. 731 (*Akayesu* Trial Judgement).

[18] For example, *Prosecutor* v. *Krstić*, Case No. IT-98-33-T, Judgement, 2 August 2001, paras. 617–18.

[19] Rape is explicitly listed as a crime against humanity and sometimes also as a war crime in international criminal statutes: e.g., Rome Statute of the International Criminal Court (entered into force 1 July 2002), 2187 UNTS 90 (Rome Statute), Arts. 7(1)(g), 8(2)(b)(xxii) and 8(2)(e) (vi).

[20] UNGA Res. 48/104, 20 December 1993, Art. 2.

[21] UNHCR, 'Guidelines on International Protection No. 1', para. 9.

[22] For example, Canada, 'Guidelines for Women Refugee Claimants', Art. B 'Assessing the Feared Harm'; United Kingdom, 'Asylum Gender Guidelines', Art. 2A.16–8; and United States, 'Considerations for Asylum Officers', 9.

[23] *SS (Burundi) CG*, [2004] UKIAT 00290 (29 October 2004) (United Kingdom), para. 16 (*SS* (United Kingdom)).

[24] *1203764*, [2012] RRTA 312 (18 May 2012) (Australia) (*1203764* (Australia)); *TA6-00022*, [2007] RPDD No. 233 (29 October 2007) (Canada) (*TA6-00022* (Canada)); *JXV (Re)*, [2008] RPDD No. 3 (23 January 2008) (Canada) (*JXV* (Canada)); *VA8-01482*, [2010] RPDD No. 105 (8 March 2010) (Canada) (*VA8-01482* (Canada)); *VA9-00148*, [2010] RPDD No. 512 (30 June 2010) (Canada) (*VA9-00148* (Canada)); *MA8-07482*, [2010] RPDD No. 145 (17 September 2010) (Canada) (*MA8-07482* (Canada)); *Kika* v. *Minister of Citizenship and Immigration*, [2011] FC 1039 (2 September 2011) (Canada) (*Kika* (Canada)); *Refugee Appeal Nos. 73894, 73895, 73896, 73897*, (24 January 2005) (New Zealand) (*73894 et al.* (New Zealand)); *Refugee Appeal Nos. 76464 and 76465*,

past rape and/or future feared rape.[25] For example, in a New Zealand case involving the Democratic Republic of the Congo (DRC), the female applicant's husband was sexually assaulted in detention, her mother and sister were raped during a visit to their house by soldiers and other women in her house were sexually assaulted. This, and other treatment during conflict, was considered to amount to a well-founded fear of persecution.[26]

However, it must be noted that several of the eight positive decisions presented troubling histories in the lower courts, only remedied on appeal. For example, in the Canadian case of *Kika*, the claimant had been raped by soldiers in the DRC in 2006.[27] Her claim was initially denied on the basis of lack of evidence of persecution but was ordered to be reassessed, as 'the officer apparently did not consider the possibility that Ms. Kika had a gender-based claim for refugee protection as a result of her sexual assault in 2006.'[28] As in *Kika*, the claimant in the case of *NS* (United Kingdom) was originally denied asylum in part because the adjudicator had found that her rape occurred 'because the assailant found her attractive, and therefore that the attack was a purely personal one, and no more than a common crime'.[29] On appeal, the Immigration Appeal Tribunal stated that this 'finding was not based on the evidence before [the adjudicator]'.[30] The evidence was that the applicant's

(28 June 2010) (New Zealand) (*76464 & 76465* (New Zealand)); *AB*, [2011] NZIPT 800019 (24 August 2011) (New Zealand) (*AB* (New Zealand)); *SS* (United Kingdom); *NS* Afghanistan CG, [2004] UKIAT 00328 (30 December 2004) (United Kingdom) (*NS* (United Kingdom)); *In re B (FC) (Appellant) (2002) Regina* v. *Special Adjudicator (Respondent) ex parte Hoxha (FC) (Appellant)*, [2005] UKHL 19 (10 March 2005) (United Kingdom) (*In re B (FC)* (United Kingdom)); *BK* DRC CG, [2007] UKAIT 00098 (September 2007) (United Kingdom) (*BK* (United Kingdom)); *LM* Republic of Congo (Congo-Brazzaville) CG, [2008] UKAIT 00064 (4 August 2008) (United Kingdom) (*LM* Congo (United Kingdom)); *PS (Sri Lanka)* v. *Secretary of State for the Home Department*, [2008] EWCA Civ. 1213 (23 October 2008) (United Kingdom) (*PS* (United Kingdom)); *AMM and others* Somalia CG, [2011] UKUT 00445 (IAC) (15 July 2011) (United Kingdom) (*AMM and Others* (United Kingdom)); *Mohammed* v. *Attorney General*, [2005] 400 F.3d 785 (10 March 2005) (United States) (*Mohammed* (United States)); *Mambwe* v. *Attorney General*, [2009] 572 F.3d 540 (16 July 2009) (United States) (*Mambwe* (United States)); and *Kante* v. *Attorney General*, [2011] Fed. App. 0014N (6th Cir.) (7 January 2011) (United States) (*Kante* (United States)).

[25] *Kika* (Canada); *73894 et al.* (New Zealand); *AB* (New Zealand); *NS* (United Kingdom); *In re B (FC)* (United Kingdom); *LM* Congo (United Kingdom); *PS* (United Kingdom); and *AMM and Others* (United Kingdom).

[26] *73894 et al.* (New Zealand), paras. 35, 43 and 97 (it was unclear whether the applicant herself had been raped).

[27] *Kika* (Canada), para. 5.   [28] *Ibid.*, para. 14.   [29] *NS* (United Kingdom), para. 16.

[30] *Ibid.*

husband had been detained by the militia of an Afghan warlord on suspicion of supporting the warlord's enemy.[31] The warlord's nephew took advantage of her husband's detention and the applicant's vulnerability[32] and demanded that the applicant become his fourth wife; when she refused, he raped, beat and threatened her with death.[33] The tribunal concluded that 'to take as a wife, by force, the wife of one's enemy, after first imprisoning him, is not an uncommon act in the course of war or other conflict, as an act of aggression against the enemy.'[34] The applicant was granted refugee status.[35]

In another case, PS (United Kingdom), the applicant, a Tamil woman from Jaffna, had been raped on three occasions in her home by Sri Lankan soldiers.[36] The first time, she was raped by two soldiers.[37] Five days later, one of those soldiers returned, accompanied by a different soldier, and both of them raped her. A week or so after, these latter two soldiers returned, held her father at gunpoint so that he could witness the act and raped her again.[38] She subsequently tried to kill herself and failed and then discovered that she was pregnant.[39] The immigration judge classified these soldiers as 'rogue', comparing them to three civilian criminals, and concluded that these past rapes had no relevance to the potential for future persecution.[40] This decision was rejected on appeal: the soldiers were clearly able to act with impunity, given the repetition of the rapes, and therefore there was a real risk that she would again be targeted for rape by Sri Lankan soldiers in the vicinity.[41] In a similar decision, in the case of LM Congo (United Kingdom), the court accepted, on appeal, that the applicant, who was from the Republic of Congo, had been raped in 1997 and that she had 'a real risk of something similar happening to her on return'.[42] Finally, in In re B (FC), the House of Lords considered an appeal by a female Kosovar Albanian applicant who had been raped in front of her husband, sons and twenty to thirty neighbours due to suspected involvement in the Kosovo Liberation Army. Baroness Hale of Richmond found that the Court of Appeal had failed to realize that 'the persecution of Mrs. B was expressed in a different way from the persecution of her husband and sons', through rape, and that rape may be a weapon or strategy of war.[43]

---

[31] Ibid. Paras. 26, 28.
[32] Ibid. para. 29 (she was still being harassed by the militia, who killed her sister).
[33] Ibid. Paras. 31 and 68.   [34] Ibid. para. 69.   [35] Ibid. para. 101.
[36] PS (United Kingdom), para. 1.   [37] Ibid.   [38] Ibid.   [39] Ibid.   [40] Ibid., para. 7.
[41] Ibid., paras 15 and 16.   [42] LM Congo (United Kingdom), paras. 1, 2 and 114.
[43] In re B (FC) (United Kingdom), para. 30.

These examples demonstrate that rape claims stemming from conflict face some common obstacles. The first obstacle is in the characterization of the rape. Some adjudicators – such as the initial adjudicator in *NS* (United Kingdom) – view sexual violence in conflict as a matter of personal sexual gratification rather than as a method of terrorizing, controlling or punishing civilians.[44] In the UK case of *Najjemba*, the court held that a woman from Northern Uganda who had suffered rape at the hands of government soldiers was the victim of 'simple and dreadful lust' and not persecution.[45] This was despite her connection to her son, who was suspected of involvement with a rebel group opposed to the Ugandan government and had 'disappeared'.[46]

A related concern is that those who commit sexual violence in conflict are sometimes viewed by adjudicators as having committed the act in their private capacity and are therefore analogous to common criminals rather than persecutors, which was the original reasoning in *PS* (United Kingdom) and the reasoning in the Canadian case of *VA9-00148*.[47] Both the 'conflict rape as lust' and the 'conflict rape as a common crime' approaches demonstrate a profound misunderstanding of the context of rape in conflict. As Macklin puts it, 'some decision-makers have proven unable to grasp the nature of rape by State actors [and non-state fighters, too] as an integral and tactical part of the arsenal of weapons deployed to brutalise, dehumanise, and humiliate women and demoralise their kin and community.'[48] The characterization of rape as lust incorrectly creates the impression that sexuality, rather than an exercise of power and gender-based discrimination, is at play. It also completely ignores the coercion, overarching violence and impunity created by the conflict. In other words, even if the perpetrator's motive happens to be entirely sexual, it does not follow that the perpetrator did not target the victim for persecutory reasons or that his conduct does not cause severe pain and suffering to the point of persecution. Similarly, the characterization of rape as a 'common' criminal activity instead of

---

[44] *NS* (United Kingdom), para. 16.
[45] *Najjemba* v. *Secretary of State for the Home Department*, [2002] EWCA Civ. 1082 (15 July 2002) (United Kingdom), para. 9.
[46] *Ibid.*, para. 2.
[47] *PS* (United Kingdom), at para. 7; *VA9-00148* (Canada), para. 16. More generally, see H. Crawley and T. Lester, 'Comparative Analysis of Gender-Related Persecution in National Asylum Legislation and Practice in Europe', May 2004, EPAU/2004/05, para. 167.
[48] A. Macklin, 'Refugee Women and the Imperative of Categories', *Human Rights Quarterly* 17(2) (1995), 213, 226.

persecution assumes that the rape in conflict is somehow random or private – and therefore unconnected to the state and lacking the discriminatory or rights-violating character required by the refugee definition.[49] This is despite the fact that the rape occurs in the context of overarching violence and impunity granted by weak or misdirected state authority and enhanced by vulnerability and gender-based discrimination. Both types of (mis)characterizations of rape are not exclusive to refugee claims involving conflict,[50] but the fact that they occur means that decision-makers are failing to adequately consider the environment surrounding the rape. On a positive note, these characterizations were correctly dismissed in *In re B (FC)* and the UK case of *N.*[51]

The second common obstacle identified in the cases is that, sometimes, adjudicators (and the applicant's counsel) do not recognize the importance of considering the after-effects of past rape in order to consider the risk of future persecution.[52] These after-effects commonly include societal stigma, which considers raped women and girls to be somehow 'tainted'.[53] This stigma is a form of discrimination, and it can create social, cultural and economic exclusion for the victim and her children and lead to increased vulnerability to sexual and other forms of violence, as well as death.[54] For example, the US case of *Mambwe* considered the claim of a young Angolan woman who had fled from National Union for the Total Independence of Angola (UNITA) forces as a child, was raped in a Zambian refugee camp (and gave birth as a result) and was kidnapped from Zambia by UNITA and repeatedly raped.[55] Her appeal was

---

[49] T. Spijkerboer, *Gender and Refugee Status* (Burlington, VT: Ashgate, 2000), 94–5, 97–9. The assumption that rape is 'private' can lead to three incorrect assumptions: a denial that the rape amounts to persecution, that it is not linked to the conflict and that it has no state connection. H. Crawley, *Refugees and Gender: Law and Process* (Bristol, UK: Jordan Publishing, 2001), 89.

[50] Crawley, *Refugees and Gender*, 44.

[51] *In re B (FC)* (United Kingdom), para. 30; and *N (FC)* v. *Secretary of State for the Home Department*, [2005] UKHL 31 (5 May 2005) (United Kingdom), para. 58 (*N* (United Kingdom)).

[52] For example, even though *NS* (United Kingdom) contains strong gender analysis, the Immigration Appeal Tribunal did not consider the specific future risk of further victimization (including stigmatization) raised by the applicant's previous rape. However, it did consider the risk to the applicant and her children of living in Kabul on her own without family or community support. See *NS* (United Kingdom), paras. 64–5, 93–4, 96.

[53] For example, in societies where virginity is highly valued, 'loss of virginity for women often means loss of marriage opportunities, which can have severe social-cultural repercussions for them and their families'. International Centre for Transitional Justice, 'Across the Lines: The Impact of Nepal's Conflict on Women', December 2010, 27.

[54] Crawley, *Refugees and Gender*, 43.   [55] *Mambwe* (United States), 2.

denied on the basis that the conflict in Angola had ended.[56] However, it appears that the court (and earlier decision-makers) did not consider the lasting stigma (and therefore discrimination) she would likely face in post-conflict Angola as a lone young woman with no relatives who had been a past victim of rape by rebels, raising a child conceived through rape.[57] However, in *In re B (FC)*, Baroness Hale of Richmond states, 'To suffer the insult and indignity of being regarded by one's own community (in Mrs. B's words) as "dirty like contaminated" because one has suffered the gross ill-treatment of a particularly brutal and dehumanizing rape directed against that very community is the sort of cumulative denial of human dignity which to my mind is quite capable of amounting to persecution' as 'the victim is punished again and again for something which was not only not her fault but was deliberately persecutory of her, her family and her community.'[58] She did note, however, that these issues should have been identified by earlier decision-makers but were overlooked.[59] An evaluation of the risk created by the after-effects of rape should be a standard consideration in conflict-related cases in order to better understand potential sources of future persecution.

Other common obstacles to conflict-related refugee claims based on rape – such as rape being considered to be part of indiscriminate conflict, rape being found not to relate to a 1951 Convention ground, rape evidence being considered as not credible and a lack of relevant country-of-origin information on rape in conflict – will be dealt with in the sections that follow.

Other Forms of Sexual Violence in Conflict

While case law and academic analysis to date have largely focused on rape as a form of persecution common in conflict, other forms of sexual violence may qualify as forms of persecution.[60] International criminal

---

[56] *Ibid.*, 7.

[57] Rape victims with children are often severely stigmatized and ostracized (as are their children). See M. Turshen, 'Women's War Stories', in M. Turshen and C. Twagiramariya (eds.), *What Women Do in Wartime: Gender and Conflict in Africa* (New York: Zed Books, 1998), 1, at 16.

[58] *In re B (FC)* (United Kingdom), para. 36.   [59] *Ibid.*, para. 39.

[60] For example, trafficking for sexual slavery or enforced prostitution: UNHCR, 'Guidelines on International Protection: The Application of Article 1(A)(2) of the 1951 Convention and/or 1967 Protocol Relating to the Status of Refugees to Victims of Trafficking and Persons at Risk of Being Trafficked', 7 April 2006, HCR/GIP/06/07, para. 15; United Kingdom, 'Asylum Gender Guidelines', para. 2A.18, which lists, apart from rape,

law provides some assistance in enumerating examples of such sexual violence. Sexual slavery, enforced prostitution, mutilation of sexual organs or breasts and forced nudity have all been recognized as forms of sexual violence amounting to crimes against humanity and/or war crimes.[61] Given their comparability to rape, it can be expected that the same obstacles outlined earlier would apply to other forms of sexual violence.

Other Forms of Gender-Related Ill-Treatment in Conflict

There are a number of gender-related forms of ill-treatment that occur in conflict that may qualify as persecution. These include conjugal slavery (also referred to as 'forced marriage' in conflict),[62] forced pregnancy,[63] forced sterilization[64] and forced abortion/miscarriage.[65] The latter three violations are likely the easiest to understand as gender-related crimes because they are targeted at reproductive organs. Conjugal slavery, which is comprised of sexual slavery plus domestic slavery, is also clearly a gender-related crime: the perpetrators enforce a norm of 'femaleness' on the victims, expecting them to submit to sex and cook and clean on demand.

Other forms of gender-related persecution in conflict may be more difficult to identify for two reasons. Firstly, applicants may describe seemingly gender-neutral forms of ill-treatment, such as torture, enslavement and imprisonment, but underneath those descriptions may lie a gendered form of the harm particularly targeted at or affecting women

---

'enforced nakedness, mechanical or manual stimulation of the erogenous zones; the insertion of objects into the body openings; the forced witnessing or commission of sexual acts; forced masturbation; fellatio and oral coitus; a general atmosphere of sexual aggression, the loss of the ability to reproduce plus threats of the above'.

[61] For example, Rome Statute, Arts. 7(1)(g), 8(2)(b)(xxii) and 8(2)(e)(vi); *Sesay* Trial Judgement, paras 143–72, 1205–8, 1291–7, 1465–75, 1579–83; *Prosecutor* v. *Tadić*, Case No. IT-94-1-T, Opinion and Judgement, 7 May 1997, paras. 45, 198, 206; *Akayesu* Trial Judgement, para. 697.

[62] *Prosecutor* v. *Taylor*, Case No. SCSL-03-01-T, Trial Judgement, 18 May 2012, paras. 427–30 (*Taylor* Trial Judgement); *Sesay* Trial Judgement, paras 1154–5, 1178–9, 1291–7, 1406–13, 1459–75, 1579–83. See also *NS* (United Kingdom), paras. 31 and 69, on attempted forced marriage.

[63] Rome Statute, Arts. 7(1)(g), 8(2)(b)(xxii) and 8(2)(e)(vi); *Mambwe* (United States), 2, containing facts related to pregnancy resulting from rape.

[64] Rome Statute, Arts. 7(1)(g), 8(2)(b)(xxii) and 8(2)(e)(vi).

[65] M. Deen, 'Pregnant Girls Forced to Abort', The Lubanga Trial, Open Society Justice Initiative, 18 March 2009.

and girls: torture through threatened or actual sexual touching or rape,[66] enslavement by forced domestic labour[67] and imprisonment by the opposing side in a conflict so as to create easily available female 'entertainment' for troops.[68] Another example is terrorizing civilians; this may be achieved through a variety of methods, including rape, sexual slavery and conjugal slavery.[69] In other words, while some ill-treatment will be gender related on its face (like rape), other ill-treatment may only be revealed as such after gathering further information from the applicant. In the cases studied for this chapter, there appeared to be missed chances to discover potential gendered ill-treatment when ill-treatment was simply described as 'torture' or 'beatings' without further explanation of how these acts were carried out.[70]

Secondly, the way in which women view harm may be gender differentiated. For example, 'preliminary empirical research suggests that loss of a child, separation from children, and witnessing harm to children or family members are particularly viewed by women as primary harms to the self, often as or more egregious than a severe violation of their own bodies'.[71] Since female applicants may experience various harms as intertwined, they may not be able to easily compartmentalize the harms they face into conflict- and non-conflict-related harms for the purposes of describing past and feared persecution.[72] Similarly, given their experience of persecution as a physical-social-economic whole, they may not see sexual violence as the sole or central part of their claim.[73] Thus,

---

[66] *Prosecutor* v. *Furundžija*, Case No. IT-95–17/1-T, Trial Judgement, 10 December 1998, para. 163.

[67] *Taylor* Trial Judgement, paras. 1066, 1072–5, 1094, 1098, 1108, 1144–6, 1828, 1833.

[68] *Prosecutor* v. *Kunarac et al.*, Case No. IT-96–23-T and IT-96–23/1-T, Judgement, 22 February 2001, paras. 747–55, 760–6.

[69] *Sesay* Trial Judgement, paras 1347–52; and *Taylor* Trial Judgement, paras 2034–8, 2051–2, 2175–8.

[70] See *73894 et al.* (New Zealand), para. 41; and *EB (Ethiopia)* v. *Secretary of State for the Home Department*, [2007] EWCA Civ. 809 (31 July 2007) (United Kingdom), para. 8 (*EB* (United Kingdom)).

[71] F. Ní Aoláin, D. F. Haynes and N. Cahn, *On the Frontlines: Gender, War, and the Post-Conflict Process* (New York: Oxford University Press, 2011), 48, 154. This is illustrated in the observation that '[f]emale claimants may also fail to relate questions about "torture" to the types of harm which they fear': UNHCR, 'Guidelines on International Protection No. 1', para. 36(vii).

[72] Ní Aoláin et al., *On the Frontlines*, 46.

[73] H. Baillot, S. Cowan and V. Munro, '"Hearing the Right Gaps": Enabling and Responding to Disclosures of Sexual Violence within the UK Asylum Process', *Social and Legal Studies* 21(3) (2012), 269, 289.

applicants should be given the opportunity to identify the full range of conflict-related harms from their perspective in order for the harms to be evaluated cumulatively as persecution. Such an approach is more likely to uncover a wider range of gender-related persecutory acts.

Both reasons require those working with refugee claimants to listen closely to the stories told, to consider whether what is said reveals potential gendered ill-treatment and to ask appropriate questions to gain further insight.[74] In the cases studied, adjudicators tended to focus on the most obvious individual gender-related violation when considering whether persecution is gender related[75] rather than evaluating the harms as a whole, although there were exceptions.[76] However, sometimes gender aspects were simply never raised or examined by the applicant (or her representative) or the decision-makers, or the adjudicator decided to focus on the non-gender-related aspects of the claim.[77] This has been identified as a particular problem in cases involving sexual violence – 'a tendency among some asylum professionals to marginalize, trivialize or ignore accounts of rape'.[78]

Indiscriminate versus Targeted Gender-Related Ill-Treatment

This section concludes by discussing a major obstacle for female refugee claimants fleeing conflict: the categorization of gender-related violence as

---

[74] See *ibid.* Proper listening requires training: UNHCR, 'Improving Asylum Procedures – Gender', 10.

[75] For example, *SS* (United Kingdom); *HH & Others*, Somalia CG, [2008] UKAIT 00022 (November 2007) (United Kingdom) (*HH* (United Kingdom)); *LM Congo* (United Kingdom); *Mohammed* (United States); and *Mambwe* (United States).

[76] For example, *NS* (United Kingdom), paras. 60–4; and *NA* Iraq CG, [2008] UKAIT 00046 (2 January 2008) (United Kingdom), paras. 91–9 (*NA* (United Kingdom)).

[77] For example, *In re B (FC)* (United Kingdom), paras 30–9; *N* (United Kingdom), paras 56–8 (the only issue considered was whether the appellant would be able to access treatment for HIV but not the fact that she had been kidnapped by the Lord's Resistance Army and then raped by government soldiers); *JXV* (Canada), para. 91; *0901064*, [2009] RRTA 373 (4 May 2009) (Australia), para. 54 (*0901064* (Australia)) (unclear whether her torture was gendered despite country of origin information on gendered abuse in detention, and whether she was chosen to deliver the parcels because of a gendered assumption that a woman would attract less attention or would be less at risk); *1010754*, [2011] RRTA 320 (4 May 2011) (Australia), para. 30 (the gendered aspects of the applicant's status as a widow and of the harassment were not explored) (*1010754* (Australia)); and *EB* (United Kingdom), note 70 above, para. 8 (the potentially gendered aspects of torture were not explored); *AB* (New Zealand), note 24 above, paras. 6, 7, 14 62–4; and *73894 et al.*, (New Zealand), paras. 35, 43, 97–104.

[78] Baillot et al., 'Gaps', 270, 289–91.

part of the general indiscriminate consequences of conflict and not targeted at the claimant. This classification occurred in a significant number of the cases studied.[79] For example, in the Canadian case of *VA9-00148*, an applicant from the DRC described an attack in 2008 in which rebels came to her home demanding money because they knew that her family had a business.[80] Her family was beaten and tortured, and the applicant was raped.[81] The rebels stole $40,000 and abducted her husband and stepson – she has not seen them since.[82] The rebel violence subsequently increased, and her neighbour and her children were beheaded, while others had body parts amputated or were killed.[83] While the adjudicator found that a nexus to a 1951 Convention ground does exist due to the sexual violence, he characterized the beatings, rape and torture of her and her family as 'localized crime', and even if the rebels had targeted them, it was for money and not for any other reason.[84] This led to a decision that '[a]lthough conditions in the DRC certainly involve a degree of risk and violence', the applicant and her family would not face a personalized risk to their lives if returned.[85] This decision is particularly striking because it lacks any consideration of the significant political and ethnic dimensions of the conflict in the DRC, including the political and ethnic choices by the various rebel groups of where, how and who they attack.[86] As Goodwin-Gill and McAdam note, 'A closer look at the background to the conflict ... and the ways in which it was fought, will often establish a link to the [1951] Convention.'[87]

The classification of gender-related ill-treatment in conflict as indiscriminate leads to the assumption that the applicant was not

---

[79] *1002652*, [2010] RRTA 557 (15 July 2010) (Australia), para. 68 (*1002652* (Australia)); *TA8-00963*, [2009] RPDD No. 395 (22 September 2009) (Canada), para. 7 (*TA8-00963* (Canada)); *TA8-18792*, [2010] RPDD No. 374 (17 June 2010) (Canada), para. 36 (*TA8-18792* (Canada)); *VA9-00148* (Canada), para. 20; *Kika* (Canada), para. 9; *PS* (United Kingdom), para. 7; *Camara* v. *Attorney General*, [2009] 580 F.3d 196 (4 September 2009) (United States), 8 (*Camara* (United States)); *SS* (United Kingdom), para. 22.3; and *Gomez* v. *Immigration and Naturalization Service*, 947 F.d 660; 1991 US App. LEXIS 25697 (28 October 1991) (United States), 6604 (*Gomez* (United States)).

[80] *VA9-00148* (Canada), para. 10.   [81] *Ibid.*   [82] *Ibid.*   [83] *Ibid.*, para. 11.

[84] *Ibid.*, paras. 15 and 16.   [85] *Ibid.*, para. 20.

[86] There are numerous reports by international organizations and NGOs detailing varying political and ethnic reasons for militia violence. For example, on motives for sexual violence by the Mai Mai, see J. Kelly, 'Rape in War: Motives of Militia in DRC', United States Institute of Peace, June 2010. The adjudicator did not appear to refer to any country-of-origin information in making this decision.

[87] G. S. Goodwin-Gill and J. McAdam, *The Refugee in International Law*, 3rd edn. (New York: Oxford University Press, 2007), 126.

personally targeted for past persecution and/or that she can be returned to her country of origin because any future risk she would face is a risk faced by everyone in that country. While the facts of every case are individual, these underlying assumptions can be legitimately questioned. On the issue of personal targeting, it is crucial that decision-makers examine both the narrow and the wider context in which the violations occurred. In the case of *VA9-00148* outlined earlier, the narrow focus reveals a potential case of targeting: the applicant was raped during the rebel attack, while her husband and son were abducted.[88] Both forms of mistreatment are gendered: the applicant may have been targeted for rape because she is female,[89] while the men may have been targeted for abduction because they are men (perhaps to become forced fighters). Furthermore, if one examined the wider context of militia movements in the applicant's area at the time of the attack,[90] one might be able to discern other cross-cutting ways in which the applicant and her family were targeted – perhaps due to the (presumed) ethnicity or (presumed) political affiliation of the individuals in that area. These narrow and wider inquiries into the conflict would also inform analysis of the risk of future targeting for gender-related persecution (including persecution of a different type than originally suffered).[91] These deeper inquiries – both gender sensitive and intersectional – are crucial to more accurately determining whether violence is indiscriminate or targeted.

---

[88] *VA9-00148* (Canada), para. 10.

[89] There are many layers to this: she may have been targeted for rape because she is of the female sex (and therefore has the genitalia to rape); because of her gender (e.g. due to patriarchal assumptions by the perpetrators that women are there to serve the needs of men); to punish her in a psychological and physical manner without the use of physical weapons; to humiliate her male family members (that they cannot protect her, that the enemy has power); and/or to humiliate her community.

[90] This requires detailed country-of-origin information. For more on this, see the part on country-of-origin information later.

[91] For example, *AA (Uganda)* v. *Secretary of State for the Home Department*, [2008] EWCA Civ. 579 (22 May 2008) (United Kingdom), para. 17 (*AA* (United Kingdom)), in which in humanitarian protection (but not refugee status) was granted to the applicant based on a future risk that the applicant (originally from northern Uganda and a victim of rape) would be forced into prostitution if returned to Kampala: 'Even if it is the fate of many of her countrywomen, I cannot think that either the AIT or the House of Lords that decided *AH (Sudan)* would have felt able to regard enforced prostitution as coming within the category of normal country conditions that the refugee must be expected to put up with.'

Lessons Learned

During war, gender norms often take on even greater socio-political significance than during peacetime. For example, 'the role of women in the biological and social reproduction of group identity places them in a position of particular vulnerability.'[92] Thus, gender-related acts in conflict, such as the rape of women and girls, often take on deeper meanings or have broader repercussions (for families, for communities), thereby creating differentiated experiences. However, the significance of these meanings or repercussions is 'currently rarely recognized in the asylum determination process'.[93] This is evidenced by the common obstacles faced by women and girls in proving that they were persecuted in gender-related ways in the past and/or that they risk gender-related persecution in the future. Within rape claims, there are continuing difficulties with the incorrect characterization of rape in conflict as a 'private' act. Additionally, not enough attention is paid to the after-effects of past rape in creating future risks of persecution. While the cases studied did not shed much light on other types of ill-treatment in conflict that might be considered as gender-related persecution, there are clearly many more (less obvious) forms.

Another, rather significant obstacle is that a number of decision-makers classify gender-related violence as part of the general indiscriminate consequences of conflict. It appears that this is done without necessarily considering potential gender-related reasons for targeting (e.g. the various ways in which rape is used as a weapon of war) or the wider political and other dimensions of the conflict. If this contextual and gender-sensitive analysis is done, it is suggested that fewer cases of gender-related ill-treatment would be categorized as untargeted.[94]

Refugee decision-makers must listen carefully for, and draw out, gender-related ill-treatment while at the same time respecting that women or girls may identify harm in gender-differentiated ways. Unfortunately, the analysis of persecution in the cases studied suggests that this careful listening is not always happening.

[92] Crawley, *Refugees and Gender*, 88.
[93] *Ibid.* This comment is from 2001, but the analysis in this section demonstrates that it is still applicable.
[94] This does not directly answer the question of whether violence directed against women and girls during conflict can ever be described as indiscriminate. The discussion suggests that many more forms of ill-treatment in conflict may be considered gender based and that the fact that the ill-treatment is gendered may reflect at least a modicum of targeting of the victim on the basis of gender, sex or both.

1951 Convention Grounds

Under the 1951 Convention, only those who can demonstrate a 'well-founded fear of being persecuted for reasons of race, religion, nationality, membership of a particular social group or political opinion' can qualify as refugees.[95] As gender is not explicitly listed as a persecutory ground, women and girls fleeing conflict for gender-related reasons must fit their claims within one of the other grounds.[96] There are many different ways in which gender relates to the 1951 Convention grounds. If the persecutor would not have persecuted the victim had the victim not been female, 'then an inference may be drawn that one of the motivations for persecution was the victim's gender.'[97] For example, a party to a conflict may impose specific forms of conformity on women and girls based on a particular ideological view of how they should act.[98] When the reason underlying the persecution is the victim's gender, then 'membership of a particular social group' may be the best category.[99] Where the gender of the victim dictates the manner of persecution (i.e. the persecution is carried out in a gender-specific manner, such as through rape and other forms of sexual violence, forced marriage, forced abortion, forced sterilization or forced pregnancy) but is not necessarily the reason for the persecution itself, then other 1951 Convention grounds might be more applicable.[100]

Membership of a Particular Social Group

In practice, claims by women and girls tend to be considered under – and, indeed, funnelled into – the category of 'membership of a particular

---

[95] 1951 Convention, Art. 1A(2).

[96] UNHCR, 'Guidelines on International Protection No. 1', paras. 22–34. Note that 'sex' may be relevant as a category: A. Edwards, 'Distinction, Discretion, Discrimination: The New Frontiers of Gender-Related Claims to Asylum', remarks presented at Gender, Migration and Human Rights Conference, Florence, Italy, 18–19 June 2012, 11–12. Where sex is a factor, gender may also simultaneously be a factor. There are often socially constructed assumptions accompanying the choice of biologically female individuals for persecution.

[97] A. Roberts, 'Gender and Refugee Law', Australian Yearbook of International Law 22 (2002), 159, 185.

[98] Goodwin-Gill and McAdam, The Refugee in International Law, 82.

[99] T. Inlender, 'Status Quo or Sixth Ground? Adjudicating Gender Asylum Claims', in S. Benhabib and J. Resnick (eds.), Migrations and Mobilities: Citizenship, Borders, and Gender (New York University Press, 2009), 359.

[100] Ibid.

social group' (MPSG).[101] The cases studied confirmed this. MPSG was the most common 1951 Convention ground, with political opinion, race and religion the next most common grounds (in that order). Thus, conflict-related cases appear to reflect the more general trend in female cases, which suffer from the disproportionate use of MPSG.[102]

UNHCR has defined 'particular social group' as 'a group of persons who share a common characteristic other than their risk of being persecuted, or who are perceived as a group by society. The characteristic will often be one which is innate, unchangeable, or which is otherwise fundamental to identity, conscience or the exercise of one's human rights.'[103] Within the cases studied, there were examples in which 'women' within a particular country were identified as such a group,[104] for example, Iraqi,[105] Afghani[106] and Somali women.[107] However, in other cases, this category was not considered to provide enough differentiation.[108] In these other cases, the group was defined both by gender and by other characteristics, for example, Tamil women whose husbands are missing or dead,[109] Afghan women and girls related to a particular male,[110] lone Somali Ashraf woman with children,[111] widows of former members of the Iraqi Ba'ath Party and lone women with children,[112] single Somali women with

---

[101] This is the tendency in all claims by women and girls and not only conflict-related claims: see Querton, 'I Feel Like', 32–3; Cheikh Ali et al., 'Gender-Related Asylum Claims in Europe', 58–60; C. Querton, 'The Interpretation of the Convention Ground of "Membership in a Particular Social Group" in the Context of Gender-Related Claims for Asylum', Refugee Law Initiative, January 2012, 4; and Edwards, 'Transitioning Gender', 28.

[102] Chiekh Ali et al, 'Gender-Related Asylum Claims in Europe', 55.

[103] UNHCR, 'Guidelines on International Protection: "Membership of a Particular Social Group" within the Context of Article 1A(2) of the 1951 Convention and/or Its 1967 Protocol Relating to the Status of Refugees', 7 May 2002, HCR/GIP/02/02, para. 11 (UNHCR, 'Guidelines on MPSG'). Note that some countries require both or add an additional requirement: Querton, 'I Feel Like', 35–6; Cheikh Ali et al., 'Gender-Related Asylum Claims in Europe', 62; and Crawley and Lester, 'Comparative Analysis of Gender-Related Persecution', para. 388.

[104] UNHCR has indicated that 'women' can be a valid group: UNHCR, 'Guidelines on MPSG', para. 12.

[105] 1002091, [2010] RRTA 469 (7 June 2010) (Australia), para. 69 (1002091 (Australia)).

[106] NS (United Kingdom), para. 79

[107] HM Somalia, [2005] UKIAT 00040 (26 January 2005) (United Kingdom) para. 35 (HM (United Kingdom)).

[108] HH (United Kingdom), para. 352: 'On the evidence, being a woman, without more, is not a sufficient differentiator to place her at such risk.'

[109] 1203764 (Australia), para. 85.

[110] JDG (Re), [2007] RPDD No. 33 (10 July 2007) (Canada), para. 133 (JDG (Canada)).

[111] HH (United Kingdom), para. 369.   [112] NA (United Kingdom), paras. 93 and 97.

children with no clan or family protection[113] and family of senior Iraqi government employees with the additional factors of being in a mixed Sunni/Shia marriage and having liberal views.[114]

The cases studied demonstrate that there are differing approaches as to whether and when it is appropriate to adopt the broad category of 'women' as a particular social group in a given country in conflict. For example, the UK case of *HM* indicated that women in Somalia form a particular social group 'not just because they are women, but because they are extensively discriminated against'.[115] However, in the UK case of *HH & Others*, a narrower approach was adopted, in order, it appears, to be able to accept one female claimant and exclude others. Thus, the analysis did not focus, as it had in *HM*, on the overarching situation of women in Somalia. Rather, the focus was on clans and sub-clans because '[o]n the evidence, being a woman, without more, is not a sufficient differentiator' to place her at individualized risk on return to a city 'which is in a situation of armed conflict'.[116] Thus, the successful claimant was classified as part of the social group 'lone Ashraf woman with children', while the analysis of the others focused on clan (and not gender).[117] In this case, the narrowness of the social group seemed to be a decision-making device rather than an analysis of intersectionality. Intersectionality, in and of itself, can be positive and necessary because it recognizes the lived realities of female members of a society – who are not only female but also of a particular age, religion, race and so on.[118] However, if one is able to establish that a woman is being persecuted because she is a woman, or for reasons of gender, then 'women' may be the more accurate particular social group.[119]

A default to the MPSG category sometimes also means that the nature of the conflict from which the applicant is fleeing is not analysed

---

[113] *AMM and Others* (United Kingdom), para. 631.

[114] *1110871*, [2012] RRTA 131 (6 March 2012) (Australia), paras. 90–1 (*1110871* (Australia)).

[115] *HM* (United Kingdom), para. 35.   [116] *HH* (United Kingdom), para. 352.

[117] *Ibid.*, paras. 349, 355 and 369.

[118] For example, the intersection of sex and age in the case of girls can compound the harm suffered: A. Edwards, 'Age and Gender Dimensions in International Refugee Law', in E. Feller, V. Turk and F. Nicholson (eds.), *Refugee Protection in International Law: UNHCR's Global Consultations on International Protection* (Cambridge University Press, 2003), 46, at 47. For cases involving girls, see *Mohammed* (United States); and *AA* (United Kingdom).

[119] Edwards, 'Distinction', 10–11.

at all or not in depth.[120] It is not clear from the cases why this is so, but it may be because many MPSG gender-related cases typically deal with 'private' harms in peacetime,[121] such as domestic violence, forced marriage and female genital mutilation.[122] As with these other sorts of harms, sometimes the MPSG analysis in conflict-related cases focused closely on the ill-treatment and less so on the wider (and more 'public') religious, national or political aspects of the conflict and their gendered components.[123] As a result, potential social groups or other applicable 1951 Convention grounds may be missed. There is also the concern that conflict-related cases raising non-typical gender issues (e.g. outside of the realm of sexual violence) may mistakenly be considered as not qualifying as MPSG. Within the cases studied, the decisions that did consider the nature of the conflict in some depth tended to be more thorough in their consideration of the various facets of MPSG *and* the other 1951 Convention grounds.[124]

It is well accepted that the social group cannot be solely defined by the type of current persecution.[125] However, this does not mean that the form of persecution is irrelevant. Those who have suffered past gender-related persecution such as rape 'are linked by an immutable characteristic which is at once independent of and the cause of their current ill-treatment'.[126] A characteristic or an attribute expressed visibly may reinforce a finding that the individual belongs to a particular social group, but it is not a pre-condition for recognition of the group,

---

[120] For example, *MZXQS* v. *Minister for Immigration and Citizenship*, [2009] FCA 97 (17 February 2009) (Australia) (see original decision, para. 24) (*MZXQS* (Australia)); *1010754* (Australia); *AHU (Re)*, [2007] RPDD No. 189 (AHU (Canada)); *TA8-00963* (Canada); *VA9-00148* (Canada); *Kika* (Canada) (original decision, para. 9); *EB* (United Kingdom); *AA* (United Kingdom); *SH (Palestinian Territories)* v. *Secretary of State for the Home Department*, [2008] EWCA Civ. 1150 (22 October 2008) (United Kingdom); *Mohammed* (United States); *Lopez* v. *Attorney General*, [2007] 504 F.3d 1341 (25 October 2007) (United States) (*Lopez* (United States)); *Mambwe* (United States).

[121] Baillot et al., 'Gaps', 274–5.

[122] For example, see the topics covered in K. Musalo, J. Moore and R. Boswell, *Refugee Law and Policy: A Comparative and International Approach*, 4th edn. (Durham, NC: Carolina Academic Press, 2011), 689–820; and Crawley, *Refugees and Gender*, 79–198.

[123] In one case, the analysis changed from being about ill-treatment in conflict to female genital mutilation, perhaps because the decision-maker felt it was more well established as a gender-related form of harm falling within MPSG: *Mohammed* (United States).

[124] *1002091* (Australia); *1110871* (Australia); *1203764* (Australia); *JDG* (Canada); *Camara* (United States); and *Kante* (United States).

[125] For example, *In re B (FC)* (United Kingdom), para. 37; and UNHCR, 'Guidelines on MPSG', paras. 2 and 14.

[126] *In re B (FC)* (United Kingdom), para. 37.

especially given that those targeted for persecution may take pains to remain as invisible as possible.[127] Thus, 'persecutory action toward a group may be a relevant factor in determining the visibility of a group in a particular society.'[128] This may be of special assistance in cases dealing with gender-related harm in conflict because women and girls who suffered war-related sexual violence or were conjugal slaves ('bush wives') may be stigmatized within society and therefore become part of a visible group. That said, some adjudicators seem to struggle with drawing the line between when a proposed particular social group is defined improperly by reference to conflict-related persecution and when a past form of conflict-related persecution might be a relevant factor in creating visibility for the immutable characteristic.[129]

Contrary to these concerns, MPSG may also be a good category in which to analyse the types of conflict-related social and cultural harms identified by many women as central to their persecution.[130] This is illustrated, for example, in cases identifying relational social groups, especially family.[131] That said, women and girls should not be essentialized as solely social and cultural beings[132] – obviously their lives are complex, and their suffering in conflict is also complex. It is for this reason that it is also important to consider the applicability of other 1951 Convention grounds in conflict-related refugee claims by women and girls.[133]

Political Opinion and the Remaining Convention Grounds

The 1951 Convention ground of political opinion is particularly useful in conflict-related claims. Nine of the cases studied seriously considered

---

[127] UNHCR, 'Matter of Valdiviezo-Galdamez, Amicus Curiae Brief in Support of Respondent', 10 August 2012, 17–18.

[128] UNHCR, 'Guidelines on MPSG', paras 2 and 14. This approach was applied in *LM* Congo (United Kingdom), para. 111 (applicant's current vulnerability increased by fact of past rape in Congo).

[129] *Kante* (United States), 26–7; and *Gomez* (United States), 663–4.

[130] Ní Aoláin et al., *On the Frontlines*, 48 and 154.

[131] *MZXQS* (Australia), paras. 23–4; *1010754* (Australia), para. 68; *1110871* (Australia), para. 90; *TA3-24983 and TA3-24984*, IRB Canada (2 February 2005) (Canada), 6–7 (*TA3-24983 and TA3-24984* (Canada)).

[132] Edwards, 'Transitioning Gender', 27–8.

[133] The importance of this was demonstrated in some cases in the case set: e.g. *NA* (United Kingdom), paras. 91–7, which considered that being an ethnic Palestinian, former member of Ba'ath party and widow of former Ba'ath member, an academic and a lone woman with children in Iraq were risk factors (the first was enough, but the immigration judge looked at other risk factors for completeness). See also *1203764* (Australia), para. 85.

political opinion as an applicable 1951 Convention ground.[134] This ground captures different ways in which a woman or girl may have political opinion imputed to her by a party to the conflict. This may occur when the claimant worked with, or for, a political party or a politician in her country of origin. For example, in the case of *LM Congo* (United Kingdom), the applicant had served as secretary for youth and in other roles for an opposition group.[135] Persecutors may also impute political opinion based on familial relationships. In the Australian case of *MZXQS*, the applicants claimed a well-founded fear of persecution because of their link to their sister, a well-known Tamil opposition Member of Parliament in Sri Lanka representing an LTTE-controlled area.[136] The original tribunal considered this claim as falling under MPSG and dismissed the claim on this ground.[137] The court found that the tribunal had incorrectly characterized the claim, which was actually a claim of imputed political opinion on the basis of their relationship with their sister.[138] Another way in which political opinion may be imputed to a woman or a girl is for appearing to hold views different from those of the warring factions.[139] In the UK case of *LM Iraq*, the applicant was perceived by Iraqi militia as supporting or collaborating with the West in part because she was a high-profile working woman who did not wear the hijab at work.[140] In addition, political opinion has been deemed to be imputed based on racial or ethnic identity. In the Australian case of *1203764*, the tribunal found that there was a real risk that the applicant, a Tamil from the north, would be sexually assaulted or otherwise harmed if she returned to Sri Lanka for reasons of the political opinion imputed to her (membership of or sympathy for the LTTE).[141]

The applicant herself may not classify her actions as political. It is therefore important for refugee decision-makers to recognize when

---

[134] *MZXQS* (Australia); *0901064* (Australia); *1012015*, [2011] RRTA 245 (1 April 2011) (Australia) (*1012015* (Australia)); *1203764* (Australia); *TA3-24983 and TA3-24984* (Canada); *73894 et al.* (New Zealand); *LM Iraq* CG, [2006] UKAIT 00060 (26 July 2006) (United Kingdom) (*LM* Iraq (United Kingdom)); *LM Congo* (United Kingdom); but see *Lopez* (United States).

[135] *LM Congo* (United Kingdom), para. 107. In this case, the political opinion of the applicant's political superior was imputed to her: para. 114.

[136] *MZXQS* (Australia), para. 4.   [137] *Ibid.*, para. 11.

[138] *Ibid.*, para. 24. The tribunal was therefore asked to deal with the political opinion claim: para. 28.

[139] *LM Iraq* (United Kingdom), paras 73–5.

[140] *Ibid.*, paras 67, 71, 73 and 75. This was considered as perceived political opinion (rights of Iraqi women): para. 73.

[141] *1203764* (Australia), para. 84. See also *1012015* (Australia).

a claim is, in fact, based on political opinion by examining the applicant's actions. For example, in the case of *73894 et al.*, the female applicant, who was from the DRC, indicated that she 'has not been interested in politics'.[142] However, she and her husband disagreed with the government's policy of persecuting Rwandan Tutsis, and the applicant therefore helped to shelter Rwandan Tutsis (while her husband helped them to flee).[143] The Refugee Status Appeals Authority characterized this as 'an overt political act opposing the policies of the Kabila regime'.[144] As a result of her actions and those of her husband, her home was searched several times, and the female members of her family were raped and sexually abused.[145] Despite the conclusion that sheltering Rwandan Tutsis was a political act, the authority felt that the applicant's case was derivative of her husband's and based its grant of refugee status on imputed political opinion (due to her husband's actions).[146]

Women's political activity during conflict may take forms different from that associated with male political activity – and the political activity by women must be recognized as such. In the US case of *Lopez*, the applicant joined the Colombian Liberal Party, providing humanitarian assistance to residents of poor communities and conducting seminars on the principles of the Liberal Movement.[147] She was subsequently attacked by the FARC in retaliation for these activities.[148] The immigration judge found that these activities were 'community-based and not political in nature', and therefore the 1951 Convention ground of political opinion did not apply.[149] This categorization of women's political activities as something other than political, such as community work, is also recognized as a serious problem for non-conflict-related female refugee claims.[150]

Finally, the cases demonstrated that in the context of racially or religiously motivated conflicts, the 1951 Convention grounds of race and religion are particularly helpful.[151] While the 1951 Convention

---

[142] *73894 et al.* (New Zealand), para. 15.   [143] *Ibid.*, paras. 95 and 96.
[144] *Ibid.*, para. 96.   [145] *Ibid.*, paras. 41–5.
[146] *Ibid.*, paras. 100–4. The grant of status is found in para. 106. There appears to be a typographical error in the first sentence of para. 106, as the second sentence refers to a grant of refugee status.
[147] *Lopez* (United States), 1343.   [148] *Ibid.*
[149] *Ibid.*, 1344. Petition for review on this point not granted.
[150] Crawley, *Refugees and Gender*, 79–83.
[151] On race, see *1203764* (Australia), para. 85; *NA* (United Kingdom), para. 91; on religion, see *JXV* (Canada), para. 89.

ground of nationality was not represented in the cases studied, it also would be a useful ground in the context of nationality-driven conflicts.

Lessons Learned

This section has explored the hazards associated with over-reliance on MPSG in cases dealing with both gender and conflict, such as a tendency towards creating artificial subgroups of women rather than relying on 'women' generally.[152] Additionally, there appears to be a focus on the 'private' side of the gender-related harms to the detriment of an analysis of the nature of the conflict. It is important for adjudicators to avoid an automatic reliance on MPSG and instead consider the other 1951 Convention grounds, especially political opinion. Race, religion and nationality may also be useful grounds when considering cases stemming from racial, religious or nationality-driven conflicts. However, there are benefits to using MPSG, as it draws attention to social and cultural harms.

Lack of State Protection

When adjudicators evaluate the risk of future persecution in gender-related claims, one issue they assess is whether the applicant can benefit from state protection against the actions of non-state actors. The cases studied revealed some gender-sensitive analysis of whether or not state protection is available, especially consideration of the dangers faced by a lone woman (sometimes with children) returning to a conflict-ridden society rife with discrimination against women, in which women (and girls) may be common targets for gender-related violence (such as rape, forced prostitution and trafficking).[153] However, there were also disturbing examples of non-sensitivity. In the UK case of PS, the second immigration judge found that the Tamil applicant's rapists, despite being Sri Lankan soldiers, were comparable to 'three civilian criminals'.[154] The judge concluded that

---

[152] Edwards, 'Distinction', 10.

[153] For example, NA (United Kingdom), paras. 97–8; AA (United Kingdom), paras. 9–10; and AMM and Others (United Kingdom), para. 631. See also, Judgement W2K11.30330, Administrative Court of Würzburg (Germany), 16 February 2012, available online (in German) at: www.asyl.net/fileadmin/user_upload/dokumente/19769.pdf, in which the fact that a woman was single and lacked protection of a male family member led to a serious and individual threat for the applicant in Afghanistan, and there was no meaningful internal protection alternative.

[154] PS (United Kingdom), para. 7.

there was no threat of future persecution and that, in the event the applicant had difficulties from them again, she could seek state protection from the Sri Lankan government.[155] This was overturned on appeal, with the judges finding that '[t]he whole point was that, unlike ordinary criminals, the soldiers were in a position to commit and repeat their crime with no apparent prospect of detection or punishment.'[156] The lesson from this case is that the analysis of future risk must be undertaken in a gender-sensitive manner with a full appreciation of the nature of the conflict, including whether the state permits impunity for gender-related violations.

One key issue arising in the cases studied related to the impact the end of a conflict had on consideration of the risk of future persecution and state protection. This is demonstrated in the US case of *Mambwe*, in which the end of the civil war in Angola was considered to eliminate any future risk of persecution.[157] This was despite the applicant's assertion that the civil war 'was not put to rest' by the peace accord and disarmament of UNITA.[158] Rather than consider persecutory risks in Angola facing young female rape victims of UNITA with a child by rape who have no relatives, the court instead only considered whether UNITA is still a military threat.[159] Thus, state protection from sources of persecution other than UNITA were not considered, even though the applicant is likely to face severe societal stigma from those on both sides of the conflict.[160] It is important to recognize that the timelines of persecution do not necessarily accord with the timelines of cease-fires or peace agreements. One court explained, 'Regime changes may be less effective in protecting women from such dangers [as rape] than they are for men.'[161] The Canadian guidelines correctly state, 'A change in country circumstances, generally viewed as a positive change, may have no impact, or even a negative impact, on a woman's fear of gender-related persecution.'[162] Peace processes may marginalize women's concerns and may not touch deep-seated discrimination directed against women and girls.[163] When considering risk of future persecution in cases where

---

[155] *Ibid.*   [156] *Ibid.*, para. 8.   [157] *Mambwe* (United States), 4.   [158] *Ibid.*

[159] *Ibid.*, 4–5.

[160] See also *AA* (United Kingdom), para. 17, noting that the future persecution feared (in this case, forced prostitution) can be of a different category from that on which the original claim was based.

[161] *N* (United Kingdom), para. 58.

[162] Canada, 'Guidelines for Women Refugee Claimants', Art. C(3), 'Evidentiary Matters'.

[163] Ní Aoláin et al., *On the Frontlines*, 46.

conflict has ceased, it is relevant for an adjudicator to consider whether conflict-related sexual violence has been addressed in any cease-fire or peace agreement in the country of origin.[164] If it has not, then this is a potential indicator of state unwillingness to counter sexual violence.

Procedural and Evidentiary Issues

Procedural and evidential barriers 'often inhibit women's access to the determination process and may serve to limit the quality of information gathered about the claim and, in turn, the quality of the decision-making process'.[165] This proved true in the cases reviewed. The most challenging issue arising in conflict- and gender-related claims appears to be lack of gender-sensitive country-of-origin information, followed closely by an inability to establish credibility.

Country-of-Origin Information

The lack of gender-sensitive country-of-origin information is an overarching problem affecting all gender-related claims,[166] but the problem seems to be compounded in conflict-related claims. Where there was adequate gender- and conflict-related country-of-origin information available to decision-makers, the analysis of the cases tended to be more thorough and sensitive.[167] Where such information seemed to be lacking, the analysis was less thorough and more speculative, and the female applicants had serious difficulties proving their cases.[168]

Female claimants typically would benefit from pre-conflict information on the legal, political, social, cultural and economic position of

---

[164] For examples of how this might be done, see UN Department of Political Affairs, 'Guidance for Mediators: Addressing Conflict-Related Sexual Violence in Ceasefire and Peace Agreements', January 2012, 5.

[165] Crawley, *Refugees and Gender*, 199.

[166] Querton, 'I Feel Like', 32; Crawley and Lester, 'Comparative Analysis of Gender-Related Persecution', para. 653; H. Crawley, 'Thematic Review on the Coverage of Women in Country of Origin Information (COI) Reports', Centre for Migration Policy Research, 19 September 2011, 133–44.

[167] For example, *110871* (Australia), para. 86; *NS* (United Kingdom), 10–17; *LM* Iraq (United Kingdom), paras 38–9 and 63–4; *HH* (United Kingdom), paras. 187, 188 and 192; *NA* (United Kingdom), paras 31 and 40; *LM* Congo (United Kingdom), para. 77; and *SS* (United Kingdom), paras. 22.4–8.

[168] For example, *AHU* (Canada); *TA8-00963* (Canada); *VA9-00148* (Canada); *Kika* (Canada); *Lopez* (United States); *Camara* (United States); and *Kante* (United States).

women and girls and the consequences for non-adherence to socio-cultural gender norms; information on how these aspects have changed for women and girls during the conflict; the incidence and forms of reported violence (in both the private and public spheres) against women and girls pre-conflict and during the conflict; the protection available to them during the conflict or post-conflict; any penalties imposed on those who perpetrate the violence and detailed information about the nature of the conflict and the parties to the conflict.[169] It is not always possible to collect this information on countries at peace, but getting accurate, up-to-date information on the situation of women and girls during a conflict can be extremely difficult, and if it is collected, it likely reflects under-reporting and therefore underestimation.[170]

The cases studied tended to rely on specific types of country-of-origin information, especially from UNHCR,[171] so it is crucial that UNHCR continue to provide as much guidance in this respect as possible.[172] Other sources included international NGOs[173] and certain UN reports.[174] There is certainly scope for improving country-of-origin information on both gender and conflict issues to include a wider range of UN documents, such as Security Council resolutions referring to gender-related ill-treatment,[175] reports of the UN Secretary General written pursuant to Security Council resolutions 1889 (and its indicators) and 1960[176] and other UN reports providing qualitative and quantitative

---

[169] Ní Aoláin et al., *On the Frontlines*, 45–6; Crawley, 'COI', 133–4.

[170] Chiekh Ali et al., 'Gender-Related Asylum Claims in Europe', 89; and UN Women, '2011–2012 Progress of the World's Women: In Pursuit of Justice', 83.

[171] For example, *NS* (United Kingdom), 13–14.

[172] For example, UNHCR, 'Interim Eligibility Guidelines for Assessing the International Protection Needs of Asylum-Seekers from Côte d'Ivoire', 15 June 2012, HCR/EG/CIV/ 12/01, 28–32.

[173] For example, *NS* (United Kingdom), 13–15: Amnesty International and International Commission of Jurists.

[174] For example, reports from the UN Commission on the Status of Women: *ibid.*, 13–14.

[175] Since the adoption of Resolution 1325, the Security Council has made reference in its country-specific resolutions to gender-based violence directed against women and girls (UNSC Res. 1325 (2000), 31 October 2000). For example, in 2012: UNSC Res. 2035 (2012), 17 February 2012, op. para. 8; UNSC Res. 2040 (2012), 12 March 2012, preamble para. 7.

[176] The indicators are set out in UN Secretary-General, 'Women and Peace and Security: Report of the Secretary-General', 28 September 2010, UN Doc. S/2010/498, Annex. Each year, the Secretary-General addresses one-third of these indicators in his reports: e.g. UN Secretary-General, 'Report of the Secretary-General on Women and Peace and Security', 29 September 2011, UN Doc. S/2011/598. The Secretary-General's reports pursuant to Resolution 1960 include a discussion of conflicts in which sexual violence

information on women and girls in conflict settings. Finally, reports from international and domestic nongovernmental women's organizations (including those located in the country of origin) should be considered.[177] All refugee-receiving countries should aim to systematically collect and make available to applicants and their representatives up-to-date and accurate information on the situation and experiences of women and girls, including in conflict.[178] Where there is a lack of information, decision-makers should be cautioned against drawing speculative conclusions or assuming lack of persecution.[179]

Credibility

The second most challenging procedural barrier relates to credibility. Within the cases studied, a number of claims were not accepted due to rulings of lack of credibility, either at the initial stages or on appeal.[180] This was due to a number of factors, most often inconsistencies[181] or perceived implausibilities in testimony, 'incorrect' demeanour (e.g. being matter-of-fact when the adjudicator expects an applicant to be distressed)[182] or lack of corroborative country-of-origin information. When found credible, it was often due to a combination of 'correct' demeanour,[183] relative consistency in the applicant's story[184] and

---

has been documented: UN Secretary-General, 'Conflict-Related Sexual Violence: Report of the Secretary-General', 13 January 2012, S/2012/33, paras. 17–57 and Annex.

[177] Crawley, 'COI', 137, 142.   [178] Ibid., 134.

[179] Ibid., 139; Cheikh Ali et al., 'Gender-Related Asylum Claims in Europe', 91.

[180] For example, 0901064 (Australia) (found credible on appeal); 1002652 (Australia); 1203764 (Australia) (on rape); TA3-24983 and TA3-24984 (Canada); JDG (Canada); MA5-05605, [2007] RPDD No. 26 (26 October 2007) (Canada); TA6-00022 (Canada); MA8-00516, [2009] RPDD No. 148 (6 May 2009) (Canada); VA8-01482 (Canada); TA8-18792 (Canada); MA8-07482 (Canada); Kika (Canada), para. 14; EB (United Kingdom) (found credible on appeal); BK (United Kingdom); HH (United Kingdom); AMM and Others (United Kingdom); Mohammed (United States) (at initial stage); and Mambwe (United States).

[181] In one case involving a claim of sexual violence, the decision-maker accepted that women can have valid reasons for giving unclear evidence about rape but felt that the applicant's inconsistencies were too large: BK (United Kingdom), paras. 524 and 527.

[182] For example, Refugee Appeal No. 75410, (7 March 2005) (New Zealand), paras 54–7 (75410 (New Zealand)); the applicant presented evidence about her fiancé's disappearance in a matter-of-fact manner, but the adjudicator felt that she should have been distressed and so found her not credible.

[183] For example, 1110871 (Australia), para. 86; and TA3-24983 and TA3-24984 (Canada), 4 (gave evidence in a straightforward and consistent manner).

[184] Complete consistency is not expected: 0901064 (Australia), para. 63.

corroborative country-of-origin information.[185] The cases mirror concerns expressed about similar experiences with claims by women and girls more generally.[186] For example, previous studies have shown that most female claimants are simply not believed at first instance.[187] This is due to many factors: a hostile environment negatively affecting how detailed the applicant can be in explaining her case,[188] undue concentration on perceived inconsistencies without consideration for the impact of trauma and dislocation on memory or for culturally different ways of expression,[189] disincentives for women and girls to reveal sexual violence (due to being traumatized, feelings of shame or fear of stigma) with late disclosure of sexual violence sometimes being held against the applicant,[190] difficulty in evidencing gender-specific forms of harm and the absence of state protection[191] and incorrect assumptions about the meaning of an applicant's demeanour.[192] Credibility findings are clearly affected by gender-insensitive refugee claim processes and procedures.

Lessons Learned

The cases revealed two major procedural problems facing women and girls making refugee claims based on a combination of gender- and conflict-related harms. The first challenge for these applicants was in accessing and presenting accurate and up-to-date country-of-origin information containing relevant facts about the conflict and its gender dimensions. The second difficulty was in establishing credibility in the claim procedure. These problems are not exclusive to conflict-related

---

[185] For example, *1012015* (Australia); *1010754* (Australia); *1110871* (Australia); *JXV* (Canada); *73894 et al.* (New Zealand); *75410* (New Zealand); *76464 and 76465* (New Zealand); and *AB* (New Zealand).

[186] For example, Muggeridge and Maman, 'Unsustainable', 34–43; Querton, 'I Feel Like', 55–63; and Cheikh Ali et al., 'Gender-Related Asylum Claims in Europe', 77–88.

[187] Muggeridge and Maman, 'Unsustainable', 5.

[188] Human Rights Watch (HRW), 'Fast-Tracked Unfairness: Detention and Denial of Women Asylum Seekers in the UK', 42.

[189] Querton, 'I Feel Like', 38–9. For example, HRW, 'Fast-Tracked', 41, recounts the case of Jane S., who was told that her accounts of being raped and the killing of her family in Sierra Leone were not believed because she could not remember the dates.

[190] Cheikh Ali et al., 'Gender-Related Asylum Claims in Europe', 81; Querton, 'I Feel Like', 41–4.

[191] Cheikh Ali et al, 'Gender-Related Asylum Claims in Europe', 77, 172.

[192] Querton, 'I Feel Like', 41; and HRW, 'Fast-Tracked', 40–1.

claims, but the fact that a claim involves conflict heightens these challenges.

Conclusions

Women and girls fleeing conflict clearly face a number of obstacles to presenting a successful claim for refugee status. In the second section, this chapter indicated that some forms of gender-related ill-treatment in conflict have been found to amount to persecution, especially rape. And yet many applicants have difficulty establishing conflict-related rape as persecution for two reasons. Firstly, some adjudicators incorrectly characterize rape in conflict as a 'private' act and therefore outside the realm of persecution, and secondly, not enough attention is paid by decision-makers to the after-effects of past rape in creating related yet different future risks of persecution. Another challenge relates to the current relatively narrow perception of what qualifies as a gender-related form of persecution in conflict. Rape and some other forms of sexual violence are recognized, but it is less common for decision-makers to recognize non-sexual but still gendered violations. A third obstacle is that some decision-makers classify gender-related violence as part of the general indiscriminate consequences of conflict and therefore not targeted enough to amount to past persecution or present a risk for future persecution. However, refugee decision-makers may be less likely to classify such violence as untargeted if they have an in-depth understanding of both the gendered nature of the conflict and the nature of gender-related discrimination before, during and after the conflict, provided through country-of-origin information. While it is not clear whether there are forms of gender-related ill-treatment in conflict that may properly be considered as indiscriminate, it is evident that more cases of such ill-treatment should be considered as targeted (rather than indiscriminate) than is currently the case.

The third section continued the discussion of obstacles, focusing on the 1951 Convention grounds. As with all gender-related claims, there is a tendency for adjudicators to rely on MPSG as the main ground for analysis. The use of MPSG can be acceptable, but it can also be problematic. For example, while some decision-makers have accepted that 'women' can be a valid particular social group, others create narrower, sometimes artificial, subgroups, which can distort the resulting analysis. As well, some adjudicators focus on the 'private' side of the gender-related harms to the detriment of an analysis of the nature of the conflict.

These obstacles may be overcome in conflict-related cases with a more fulsome focus on the other 1951 Convention grounds, such as political opinion.

The fourth section considered obstacles arising with the consideration of whether or not there is state protection in the country of origin. There is some positive case law considering the risks to lone females returning to conflict-affected countries of origin. However, there are also cases in which the judges failed to understand the actual vulnerabilities of women and girls in relation to their own conflict-affected or post-conflict state. Additionally, some positive case law recognizes that a cease fire or peace agreement does not necessarily mean the end of gender-related persecution in a country of origin, but other case law demonstrates that some decision-makers do not pay enough attention to the actual post-conflict circumstances of women and girls. Women and girls fleeing conflict therefore face more difficulties than they should in demonstrating lack of state protection and risk for future persecution.

Finally, the last section examined procedural and evidentiary difficulties arising in conflict- and gender-related claims. Women and girls face significant hurdles in accessing and presenting accurate and up-to-date country-of-origin information containing relevant facts on the conflict and its gender dimensions; this has a significant impact on their ability to demonstrate persecution, a 1951 Convention ground, and lack of state protection and therefore their credibility. On the latter, some decision-makers took into account the effects of conflict-related trauma on memory or demeanour, but others unfortunately did not.

In conclusion, while there are welcome developments in international and domestic refugee law under which claims by women and girls fleeing conflict have been accepted, there is also significant room for improvement. There is a need for a deeper understanding of gender-related persecution and its future risks, such that seemingly indiscriminate and/or seemingly gender-neutral ill-treatment of women and girls is more correctly recognized as persecution. There is also a need for expanded conceptions of the 1951 Convention grounds as they relate to women and girls fleeing conflict. Lastly, while women and girls fleeing conflict face problems similar to those making peacetime-related claims, they may also face specific conflict-related evidentiary and credibility hurdles. There have been many recent studies outlining proposed improvements to domestic refugee determination processes involving either women and girls or gender-based claims more generally.[193] The hurdles identified in this chapter might be (partly) removed by implementing the recommendations in these studies, but it may be necessary for decision-makers to be provided with (more) conflict- and gender-specific guidance on persecution, applicable 1951 Convention grounds and state protection to assess country-of-origin information and credibility.

[193] For example, Cheikh Ali et al., 'Gender-Related Asylum Claims in Europe'; Querton, 'I Feel Like'; Muggeridge and Maman, 'Unsustainable'; HRW, 'Fast-Tracked'; UNHCR, 'Improving Asylum Procedures – Gender'.

7

Children Fleeing Conflict

Age and the Interpretation and Application of the 1951 Refugee Convention

RACHEL BRETT, MARGARET BRETT AND HAIFA RASHED

Introduction

Over half the world's refugees are children, and 2014 saw an unprecedented number of asylum applications by unaccompanied or separated children.[1] Article 1(A)2 of the Convention Relating to the Status of Refugees (1951 Convention)[2] defines a 'refugee' as anyone who 'owing to well-founded fear of being persecuted for reasons of race, religion, nationality, membership of a particular social group or political opinion, is outside the country of his [or her] nationality and is unable or, owing to such fear, is unwilling to avail himself [or herself] of the protection of that country'.[3] This definition applies to all individuals regardless of their age but has traditionally been interpreted in light of adult experiences with the result that many refugee claims made by children (defined as all those below eighteen years of age) have been assessed incorrectly or overlooked altogether.[4] A lack of awareness and/or understanding of the reasons that children may flee also creates a risk of over-reliance on the use of complementary/subsidiary protection regimes, which can deny potential 1951 Convention refugee children the protection they require and deserve.[5]

---

[1] UNHCR, 'Global Trends: Forced Displacement in 2014', June 2015.

[2] Convention Relating to the Status of Refugees (adopted 28 July 1951, entered into force 22 April 1954), 189 UNTS 137 (1951 Convention).

[3] *Ibid.*, Art. 1(A)2.

[4] UNHCR, 'Guidelines on International Protection No. 8: Child Asylum Claims under Articles 1(A)2 and 1(F) of the 1951 Convention and/or 1967 Protocol Relating to the Status of Refugees', 22 December 2009, HCR/GIP/09/08, para. 1 (UNHCR, 'Guidelines No. 8: Child Asylum Claims').

[5] See e.g. the reference to the immigration judge's assertion that the 1951 Convention is 'not engaged' due to the appellant's being adequately protected by leave to remain in the United Kingdom in *LQ (Age: Immutable Characteristic) Afghanistan* v. *Secretary of State for the*

In establishing their claim to refugee status, children fleeing conflict face both those problems shared by all child asylum-seekers and those of individuals fleeing conflict or violence, in particular, the problem of demonstrating that they are fleeing persecution rather than 'only' fleeing because of generalized violence. Although the issue of children's asylum claims has been addressed generally in UNHCR's *Handbook and Guidelines on International Protection on Child Asylum Claims*,[6] and has been covered by several UNHCR executive committee conclusions,[7] there has been little international attention to the distinctive situation of children fleeing conflict.[8]

This chapter aims to address this gap by exploring the substantive aspects of refugee status determination (RSD) in relation to children fleeing conflict and violence.[9] It considers the nature of persecution,

---

Home Department, [2008] UKAIT 00005, United Kingdom: Asylum and Immigration Tribunal / Immigration Appellate Authority, 15 March 2007.

[6] UNHCR, *Handbook and Guidelines on Procedures and Criteria for Determining Refugee Status under the 1951 Convention and the 1967 Protocol Relating to the Status of Refugees*, December 2011, HCR/1P/4/ENG/REV. 3, paras. 213–19; UNHCR, 'Guidelines No. 8: Child Asylum Claims'.

[7] See UNHCR ExCom, 'Refugee Children', 12 October 1987, No. 47 (XXXVIII) 1987, UN Doc. A/42/12/Add.1; UNHCR ExCom, 'Refugee Children', 13 October 1989, No. 59 (XL) 1989, UN Doc. A/44/12/Add.1; UNHCR ExCom, 'Refugee Children and Adolescents', 17 October 1997, No. 84 (XLVIII) 1997, UN Doc. A/52/12/Add.1; UNHCR ExCom, 'Conclusion on Children at Risk', 5 October 2007, No. 107 (LVIII) 2007, UN Doc. A/AC.96/1048.

[8] A notable exception: E. M. Ressler, N. Boothby and D. J. Steinbock, *Unaccompanied Children: Care and Protection in Wars, Natural Disasters and Refugee Movements* (Oxford University Press, 1988). It is also worth noting that child refugees are protected under Article 22 of the Convention on the Rights of the Child (entered into force 2 September 1990), 1577 UNTS 3 (CRC), which given its near universal ratification means in some states that they are protected despite the state not being a party to the 1951 Convention.

[9] The procedural issues arising in all considerations of child asylum claims, such as questions of age determination, interviewing children (including interviewing children of different ages), different ways of expressing/manifesting 'well-founded fear' due to age, sex, culture and so on are equally relevant in these situations, but an examination of these problems is beyond the scope of this chapter. Similarly, there may be factors to consider which are peculiar to their status as children, such as their lack of legal status to bring cases. See e.g. the cases in Ireland of *Marina Djimbonge (a minor)* v. *Refugee Appeals Tribunal, Minister for Justice and the HSE* (Unreported, High Court, 16 Oct. 2006, No. 1293 JR) and *Jamal Nourali (a minor)* v. *The HSE and the Legal Aid Board* (Unreported, High Court, 2006, No. 768 JR), discussed in D. O'Connell, D. Griffin and P. Kenna, 'Fundamental Rights Agency: Thematic Study on Child Trafficking – Ireland', European Union Agency for Fundamental Rights, 2009, at para. 221. Both cases are reported in S. Mullally, 'Separated Children in Ireland: Responding to "Terrible Wrongs"', *IJRL* 23(4) (2011), 632–55, at 641–2.

including child-specific forms, agents of persecution, the nexus between the persecution and a 1951 Convention ground and, briefly, issues arising in relation to internal flight alternatives and the specific considerations that arise in relation to the exclusion of children from refugee status. Particular attention is paid to the situation of children who have been actively involved in the conflict or violence (as child soldiers or child gang members)[10] and those who flee to avoid recruitment. These cases present a number of problems which are specific to child asylum-seekers and to the background of conflict or violence. In most other cases, the conflict or violence is not central to the persecution suffered by the child, although it may encourage, facilitate or exacerbate it.

Persecution

'Children are no longer just innocent bystanders caught in the crossfire of armed conflict, but are subject to calculated genocide, forced military conscription, gender-based violence, torture and exploitation.'[11] Conflict is a major cause of child displacement. Much of the existing literature on forced displacement of children has been written through the prisms of mental health and psychology,[12] with the practical intention of creating effective child protection mechanisms. This perspective fits with the widely held concept of the child as victim and as recipient of humanitarian assistance. Such an attitude depoliticizes the child's potential reasons for fleeing[13] and assumes that the child is neither an active participant in the conflict nor a deliberate target, but only a collateral victim of the actions and decisions of adults. Although it

---

[10] The situation of child members of 'terrorist organizations' is not addressed as a separate category. It is unclear that there are distinctive features of such groups which would prevent cases involving child members fitting within the frameworks outlined here in relation to armed groups (where the organization is a party to an armed conflict) or gangs (where its activities are criminal in nature).

[11] J. Bhabha, 'Minors or Aliens? Inconsistent State Intervention and Separated Child Asylum-Seekers', *European Journal of Migration and Law* 3 (2001), 283, 288.

[12] See M. Hodes, 'Three Key Issues for Young Refugees' Mental Health', *Transcultural Psychiatry* 39(2)(2002), 196; D. Summerfield, 'Childhood, War, Refugeedom and "Trauma": Three Core Questions for Mental Health Professionals', (2000) 37(3) *Transcultural Psychiatry* 417; and for a comprehensive analysis of research in this area, see T. Thomas and W. Lau, 'Psychological Well-Being of Child and Adolescent Refugee and Asylum Seekers: Overview of Major Research Findings of the Past Ten Years', Australian Human Rights Commission, 2002.

[13] G. Doná and A. Veale, 'Divergent Discourses, Children and Forced Migration', *Journal of Ethnic and Migration Studies* 37(8) (2011), 1273, at 1274.

may recognize the need to provide displaced children with protection, such an approach can wrongly deny them refugee status due to a failure to identify their experience as persecution for a 1951 Convention reason.[14]

The particular importance of the family for children and (usually) their reliance on adult care-givers render children particularly susceptible to persecution. The child may be deliberately targeted because he or she is assumed to share the characteristic that is the basis of the persecution (e.g. imputed political opinion) or in order to punish or put pressure on the parents or family members.[15] Measures targeting a parent or family member may also persecute a child.

However, it is also important to remember that the child may be the victim of persecution in his or her own right and on the grounds of his or her own race, nationality, ethnicity, religion, (real or imputed) political opinion or membership in a particular social group. The persecution may, but need not, be shared by the other members of the family. In this context, it is useful to recall that the child may differ from the parents with regard to any or all relevant grounds of persecution. Whatever the context, the child has a right to a separate claim 'regardless of whether s/he is accompanied or unaccompanied'.[16]

Child-Related Manifestations of Persecution

Threatened or actual harm that would amount to persecution for an adult in a particular situation will also be persecution for a child in that situation. However, threatened or actual harms that would not amount

---

[14] This point is considered in *ZK (Afghanistan)* v. *Secretary of State for the Home Department*, [2010] EWCA Civ. 749, 4, where on appeal the initial finding that the applicant was not entitled to refugee status as he had already been granted leave to remain was overturned.

[15] See e.g. *RRT Case No. 1214575*, [2012] RRTA 1139, Australia: Refugee Review Tribunal, 19 December 2012, where a young man fleeing religious persecution in Afghanistan was granted refugee status due to his 'religion and his membership of a particular social group of members of a family whose head is a member of the Afghan National Army'; *ZK (Afghanistan)* v. *Secretary of State for the Home Department* (United Kingdom), where a young man feared being targeted by Afghan and American officials because of his father's involvement in the Taliban and also feared exposure to general risk of harm because of his status as an orphaned minor; and *AA (unattended children) Afghanistan* v. *Secretary of State for the Home Department CG*, [2012] UKUT 00016 (IAC).

[16] UNHCR, 'Guidelines No. 8: Child Asylum Claims', para. 6.

to persecution for adults may be persecutory for children due to their age, lack of maturity or vulnerability.[17] This could include aggressive questioning, the use of handcuffs, forced separation from parents, malnutrition (food deprivation) and deprivation of education.[18] For children fleeing conflict or violence, the psychological and physical impacts of the conflict may render them still more vulnerable, with the result that lesser harms or threats will amount to persecution.

Child-Specific Persecution

'The fact that the refugee claimant is a child may be a central factor in the harm inflicted or feared. This may be because the alleged persecution only applies to, or disproportionately affects, children or because specific child rights may be infringed.'[19] Actions that would not be considered harm or would not in themselves amount to persecution if applied to adults may be recognized as such when they affect children. Child-specific forms of persecution include forced child marriage,[20] female genital mutilation,[21] child sale or trafficking,[22] child labour and child

---

[17] See e.g. US Bureau of Citizenship and Immigration Services, 'Guidelines for Children's Asylum Claim', 21 March 2009, 37, noting that 'the harm a child fears or has suffered, however, may be relatively less than that of an adult and still qualify as persecution.' This has been reinforced by the US Seventh Circuit: '[A]ge can be a critical factor in the adjudication of asylum claims and may bear heavily on the question of whether an applicant was persecuted or whether she [or he] holds a well-founded fear of future persecution', in *Liu* v. *Ashcroft*, 380 F.3d 307, 314 (7th Cir. 2004). See also *Chen Shi Hai* v. *The Minister for Immigration and Multicultural Affairs*, [2000] HCA 19, Australia: High Court, 13 April 2000, where the Court found that 'what may possibly be viewed as acceptable enforcement of laws and programmes of general application in the case of the parents may nonetheless be persecution in the case of the child', para. 79.

[18] Save the Children noted that more than 80 per cent of those affected by sexual violence in conflict are children (especially, but not exclusively, girls). See Save the Children, 'Unspeakable Crimes against Children: Sexual Violence in Conflict', 2013.

[19] UNHCR, 'Guidelines No. 8: Child Asylum Claims', para. 18.

[20] See e.g. *Arrêt No. 131 887*, Belgium: Conseil du Contentieux des Etrangers, 23 October 2014; *Hong Ying Gao* v. *Alberto Gonzales*, 04-1874-ag, United States Court of Appeals for the Second Circuit, 3 March 2006, deals with the case of an adult women but nonetheless finds that forced marriage amounts to persecution. Similarly, the prevalence of rape as a weapon of war gives rise to the possible persecution of the children born as a result and of their mothers who may themselves be children.

[21] See e.g. *Abay* v. *Ashcroft*, 368 F.3d 634, 640 (6th Cir. 2004), which overturned, on the basis of age, the immigration judge's finding that a nine-year-old applicant had not adequately expressed a fear of future persecution relating to female genital mutilation.

[22] UNHCR ExCom, 'Conclusion on Children at Risk', 5 October 2007, No. 107 (LVIII) 2007, UN Doc. A/AC.96/1048, para. (g)(viii).

abuse.[23] Such persecution is not generally the result of direct action by the government but may result from the failure to criminalize or enforce prohibitions on cultural or social practices that are of a persecutory nature. The following section will focus on two related forms of child-specific persecution: military recruitment and gangs.

Military Recruitment of Children

According to the Paris Principles, a child associated with an armed force or armed group (child soldier) is 'any person below 18 years of age who is or who has been recruited or used by an armed force or armed group in any capacity, including but not limited to children, boys and girls used as fighters, cooks, porters, messengers, spies or for sexual purposes. It does not only refer to a child who is taking or has taken a direct part in hostilities.'[24] Child Soldiers International further elaborates: '[s]ince 2000, the participation of child soldiers has been reported in most armed conflicts and in almost every region of the world.'[25]

In assessing their asylum claims, it is important to be aware of the range of functions carried out by child soldiers and the reasons for which they may be recruited. However, these different roles often are not separated from each other, and children, including girls recruited for sexual slavery or forced marriage, will usually be expected to be fighters as well, either on a regular basis or as a last resort.[26] Full consideration of an asylum claim should explore all the possibilities rather than assuming that only one (gendered) role will be relevant.

All military recruitment and use in hostilities of children under the age of fifteen is prohibited in all circumstances.[27] In both international and

---

[23] M. Crock, *Seeking Asylum Alone: A Study of Australian Law, Policy and Practice Regarding Unaccompanied and Separated Children* (Sydney, Australia: Themis Press, 2006).

[24] UN Children's Fund (UNICEF), 'The Paris Principles: Principles and Guidelines on Children Associated with Armed Forces or Armed Groups', February 2007, definition 2.1.

[25] Child Soldiers International, 'About the Issues: Who Are Child Soldiers?'. Although there are no exact figures, and numbers continually change, based on data collected by Child Soldiers International, tens of thousands of children under the age of eighteen continue to serve in government forces or armed opposition groups. Some of those involved in armed conflict are under ten years old.

[26] See R. Brett and I. Specht, *Young Soldiers – Why They Choose to Fight* (Boulder, CO: ILO/ Lynne Rienner, 2004), 85–104.

[27] Convention on the Rights of the Child, Art. 38; International Committee of the Red Cross (ICRC), Protocol Additional to the Geneva Conventions of 12 August 1949, and Relating to the Protection of Victims of International Armed Conflicts (Protocol I), 8 June 1977 (entered into force 7 December 1978), 1125 UNTS 3, Art. 77(2); Protocol Additional to

non-international armed conflicts, voluntary or compulsory recruitment or active use in hostilities of children under age fifteen is a war crime.[28] As such, the recruitment of children under age fifteen constitutes a serious violation of both international human rights and international humanitarian law and therefore amounts to persecution in itself.[29] The fact that voluntary recruitment of children under the age of fifteen is prohibited means that the child is unable to consent to recruitment, so recruitment will amount to persecution even if the child believes that he or she volunteered. For children between fifteen and eighteen years of age, the situation is less clear-cut because there is not one single universal standard but a patchwork of different ones. The standards also differ depending on whether the child is being recruited into government armed forces or a non-state armed group.

The Optional Protocol to the Convention on the Rights of the Child on the involvement of children in armed conflict (CRC-OPAC) prohibits all recruitment and use in hostilities of children under age eighteen by 'armed groups that are distinct from the armed forces of the State'.[30] Notably, there is no requirement that there be an armed conflict, nor that the groups are armed *opposition* groups. This means that in a state that has ratified the CRC-OPAC, children under age eighteen are incapable of consenting to join an armed group, which makes a distinction between voluntary and forced recruitment irrelevant.

The International Labour Organization (ILO) Worst Forms of Child Labour Convention prohibits 'forced or compulsory labour, including

the Geneva Conventions of 12 August 1949, and Relating to the Protection of Victims of Non-International Armed Conflicts (Protocol II) (entered into force 7 December 1978), 1125 UNTS 609, Art. 4(3)(c). It is also prohibited as a norm of customary international law: J.M. Henckaerts and L. Doswald-Beck, *Customary International Humanitarian Law*, Vol. I (Cambridge University Press, 2005), rules 136–7, 482–8.

[28] Rome Statute of the International Criminal Court (entered into force 1 July 2002), 2187 UNTS 90 (Rome Statute), Art. 8(2)(b)(xxvi) and (e)(vii). This war crime is also included in the Statute of the Special Court for Sierra Leone, UN Security Council, Statute of the Special Court for Sierra Leone, 16 January 2002, Art. 4(c). See also the decision of the Special Court for Sierra Leone in *Prosecutor* v. *Sam Hinga Norman*, Case No. SCSL-2003-14-AR72(E), Decision on preliminary motion based on lack of jurisdiction (child recruitment), 31 May 2004, finding that child recruitment is a crime under customary international law.

[29] UN Committee on the Rights of the Child, 'General Comment No. 6: Treatment of Unaccompanied and Separated Children Outside Their Country of Origin', 1 September 2005, CRC/GC/2005/6, paras. 58–9.

[30] UN General Assembly, Optional Protocol to the Convention on the Rights of the Child on the Involvement of Children in Armed Conflict, 25 May 2000 (entered into force 12 February 2002), UNGA Res. A/RES/54/263 (CRC-OPAC), Art. 4.

forced or compulsory recruitment of children for use in armed conflict'.[31] This prohibition applies to both armed groups and state armed forces. The CRC-OPAC also prohibits the compulsory recruitment (conscription) of under-eighteens into government armed forces.[32] As one of the worst forms of child labour, forced or compulsory recruitment of children under age eighteen amounts to persecution per se.[33]

In general, the age between fifteen and eighteen at which a child can legally volunteer to join the government armed forces is established by national law. However, three regional treaties set a minimum age. The Organization of African Unity's African Charter on the Rights and Welfare of the Child[34] and the African Union Protocol to the African Charter on Human and Peoples' Rights on the Rights of Women in Africa[35] prohibit all recruitment of under-eighteens, including voluntary recruitment, into government armed forces.

The Ibero-American Convention on Young People's Rights requires state parties to 'undertake to assure youth under 18 years of age that they shall not be called up or involved, in any way, in military hostilities'.[36] At the international level, the CRC-OPAC only requires state parties to (1) raise the minimum age (in years) from that specified in the 1951 Convention itself, in other words from fifteen to at least sixteen years, (2) submit a binding unilateral declaration specifying the minimum age and (3) have safeguards to ensure that any such recruitment is genuinely voluntary.[37] The minimum age declared by the unilateral declaration can subsequently be raised but cannot be lowered and is legally binding as part of the CRC-OPAC for that state.[38] In this respect, the CRC-OPAC

---

[31] International Labour Organization (ILO), Worst Forms of Child Labour Convention, 1999 (C-182) (entered into force 19 November 2000), Art. 3(a).

[32] CRC-OPAC, Art. 2.

[33] UNHCR, 'Guidelines No. 8: Child Asylum Claims', paras 21–2; *RRT Case No. 071959605*, [2008] RRTA 256, Australia: Refugee Review Tribunal, 27 June 2008.

[34] Organization of African Unity (OAU), African Charter on the Rights and Welfare of the Child (entered into force 29 November 1999), CAB/LEG/24.9/49, Art. 22(2).

[35] African Union (AU), Protocol to the African Charter on Human and Peoples' Rights on the Rights of Women in Africa (entered into force 25 November 2005), CAB/LEG/66.6, Art. 11(4), with a particular but not exclusive reference to girls.

[36] Ibero-American Convention on Young People's Rights (entered into force 1 March 2008), Art. 12(3).

[37] CRC-OPAC, Art. 4. There are 159 state parties as of 5 July 2015.

[38] According to Child Soldiers International, seventeen-year-olds can enlist in the armed forces of twenty-four states. Eighteen states continue to permit voluntary recruitment at sixteen years of age, and in five states there is no minimum age or it has been set below sixteen years. Child Soldiers International, 'Our Work: Straight-18'.

represents an awkward compromise between the desire to raise the minimum age from fifteen and the reluctance to universalize an age lower than eighteen.

The (illegal) recruitment of a child under the age limit set by national law amounts to forced recruitment (as national law does not permit the child to volunteer; i.e. he or she is unable to consent to recruitment) and as such is persecution. This will be the case even if the child could legally have been recruited in another state, including that in which he or she is applying for asylum.

Legal voluntary recruitment (i.e. the voluntary recruitment into governmental armed forces of children over the minimum age set by national law, which does not conflict with the state's treaty obligations) does not per se amount to persecution. In assessing asylum claims relating to such recruitment, it is essential to establish that the recruitment was genuinely voluntary. In this respect, the CRC-OPAC requires the informed consent of the child's parents or legal guardians, that the child is fully informed of the duties involved in such military service, and that the child provide reliable proof of age prior to acceptance into national military service. Where these conditions are not met, the recruitment is not considered to be genuinely voluntary and therefore amounts to forced recruitment under international law. This can still be the case when the child (and indeed the recruiter) considers that he or she volunteered.

Finally, the conditions or treatment encountered by a child soldier may amount to persecution, even if the recruitment was genuinely voluntary. The CRC-OPAC requires states to 'take all feasible measures to ensure that members of their armed forces who have not attained the age of 18 years do not take a direct part in hostilities'.[39] Failure to respect this provision itself constitutes a serious breach of international law. Child recruits may also be required to kill or harm their own parents, to execute prisoners or other children trying to escape and be used as spies, messengers, porters, servants, sex slaves or to lay or clear landmines.[40]

The ILO's case law on forced labour may be relevant in establishing that either the recruitment or the continuing military service of a child

---

[39] CRC-OPAC, Art. 1. Article 4 prohibits the use of under-eighteens in hostilities by armed groups. The Ibero-American Convention on Young People's Rights, Art. 12(3); OAU Charter on the Rights and Welfare of the Child, Art. 22(2); and AU Protocol on the Rights of Women in Africa, Art. 11(4) also all explicitly prohibit the use of children in hostilities.

[40] UNHCR, 'Guidelines No. 8: Child Asylum Claims', para. 23.

amounts to forced labour. In its considerations on forced labour, the ILO Committee of Experts on the Application of Conventions and Recommendations has identified a range of relevant factors that render labour forced. These include misleading contracts, ill-treatment of the workers, long working days and no or unreasonable restrictions on freedom to terminate employment. In relation to children, they also refer to removal from home and family, isolation, worse conditions than those they had been led to expect, dependence on their employer and becoming prisoners at the work site (risking their lives if they attempt to flee).[41]

Children and Gangs

There is no universally accepted definition of the term 'gang'. Here it is used to mean an organized group which engages in criminal activities and violence and for which these are an integral part of its identity.[42] Most gang members are male, but girls may also be involved, sometimes forming their own gangs. Gang membership may result in persecution of a child member through forced recruitment, harm or threats that prevent the child from leaving, risk of harm from others due to the child's association with the gang and harmful treatment of the child gang member by the gang.

Where a gang uses violence or threats to force a child to join, these in themselves are a form of harm, which may amount to persecution.[43] The violence or threats may be directed against the child or against family members.[44] In other instances, the pressure to join may be indirect, resulting from harm to others who refused to join or the need for protection from other gangs. In such cases, there may still be a genuine fear of harm amounting to persecution due to the reality of the threats feared. In some instances, threats related to not joining the gang may not

---

[41] See R. Brett and I. Specht, *Young Soldiers*, 112–14, citing ILO case law in relation to the ILO Forced Labour Convention (entered into force 1 May 1932), C29. The ILO does not appear to have addressed the question of establishing the voluntariness of recruitment under the Worst Forms of Child Labour Convention.

[42] This definition is largely derived from that used in UNHCR, 'Guidance Note on Refugee Claims Relating to Victims of Organized Gangs', 31 March 2010, para. 4 ('UNHCR, Guidance Note: Gangs'). A similar definition is established in American law; see Criminal Street Gangs Statute, 18 US Code § 521.

[43] UNHCR, 'Guidance Note: Gangs', para. 21.

[44] *Maydai Hernandez-Avalos* v. *Loretta E. Lynch, Attorney General*, 14-1331, United States Court of Appeals for the Fourth Circuit, 30 April 2015 (death threats to a mother who refused to permit her son to join a gang).

amount to persecution on their own but in conjunction with other factors, such as ill-treatment once a gang member, may reveal a pattern of harm or threat of harm amounting to persecution.

In other cases, the child's association with the gang may be voluntary. However, as with the recruitment of child soldiers, it may be relevant to consider how genuinely voluntary the choice was. For instance, children who have a credible fear of the consequences of not joining because of the treatment of those who refused to join in the past may nevertheless consider themselves to have volunteered. A further factor is the extent to which children are aware of the purposes and activities of the gang and have the necessary maturity to make an informed decision regarding their association with it.

When a child gang member is unable to leave the gang (whether or not he or she was originally forced to join) due to threat of harm to himself or herself or to others, this threatened harm is likely to amount to persecution. If the harm threatened does not amount to persecution, it is unlikely to be effective in deterring members from leaving and/or seeking the protection of the state. Situations in which the gang has a reputation for punishing those who leave or attempt to leave and/or the gang members are aware of past cases in which those who attempted to leave have suffered serious harm as a result can constitute an implied threat and give rise to a genuine fear of persecution even if the individual has not personally been threatened.

In addition to the direct threat of harm if he or she leaves, the fact that a child has been abducted and/or is forced to remain a gang member may be considered slavery or practices similar to slavery or forced or compulsory labour.[45] Using children to carry out criminal activities, especially those related to the production or trafficking of drugs, violates the Worst Forms of Child Labour Convention and should on that basis be considered persecutory.[46] Treatment to which child gang members are subjected may violate other human rights, including child-specific rights such as access to education and family, and thus be relevant in assessing whether the child has suffered harm amounting to persecution.

A serious risk of harm from others (including the state authorities) due to the child's association with the gang may also amount to persecution. In general, the fact that law enforcement personnel target gang members would not be considered persecution. However, a response that is disproportionate or treatment of child gang members that fails to take into

---

[45] *Ibid.*, para 22.   [46] Worst Forms of Child Labour Convention, Art. 3(c).

account their status as children may rise to the level of persecution.[47] State authorities treating former gang members (who may for that reason be at risk of reprisals from the gang they have left) as though they were still members of the gang may also inflict harm amounting to persecution. Finally, a child who is identified as belonging or having belonged to a gang may be targeted by other gangs or by members of society for that reason, and where such behaviour inflicts harm on the child, it may amount to persecution. This may be a particular problem where gang members are clearly identified by distinctive tattoos or other body markings.[48]

Agents of Persecution

As the preceding sections show, the asylum claims of children fleeing conflict or violence may result from a range of situations. In some, the harm from which the child is fleeing emanates directly from the state authorities e.g. where the state forcibly recruits children. In other cases the persecutor is a non-state actor, and it will be necessary to show that the state authorities are unable or unwilling to protect the child in order to ground an asylum claim.[49] In situations of armed conflict, the capacity of the state to protect individuals, including children, from persecution by non-state actors may be significantly reduced.

When children are actively involved in conflict or violence as members of armed forces, armed groups or gangs, the actions of the state, non-state actors and the community may interact in ways that result in the state and/or non-state actors becoming the agent of persecution. A child forcibly recruited by an armed group or gang may be a victim of persecution by that group, with the state unable or unwilling to prevent the recruitment or harm resulting from membership.[50] A child may be targeted by the community because of his or her real or imputed association with an armed group or gang, and the state is unable or unwilling to protect him or her.[51] Finally, a child may suffer persecution at the

---

[47] UNHCR, 'Guidance Note: Gangs', para. 23.   [48] Ibid., para. 13.

[49] See UNHCR, Handbook and Guidelines for Determining Refugee Status, para. 65, which states that '[w]here serious discriminatory or other offensive acts are committed by the local populace, they can be considered as persecution if they are knowingly tolerated by the authorities, or if the authorities refuse, or prove unable, to offer effective protection.'

[50] See e.g. Hernandez-Avalos v. Loretta E. Lynch, Attorney General, discussing evidence that the state is unable or unwilling to provide protection.

[51] See e.g. Lukwago v. Ashcroft, Attorney General, 02-1812, US Court of Appeals for the Third Circuit, 14 May 2003.

hands of the state authorities because of his or her (real or imputed) association with an armed group or gang. For instance, this could occur where law enforcement measures targeting gangs are unduly violent. In this case, the child may be a victim of both the armed group or gang and the state authorities or of the authorities alone.

Situations of conflict or violence may also cause an increase in persecutory behaviour by family members, which the state has a weakened capacity to prevent. A decreased capacity of the state to enforce laws prohibiting persecutory behaviour may directly facilitate such behaviour. Families may also attempt to provide protection which the state cannot. For instance, forced child marriage[52] may be more prevalent during times of conflict or displacement because some parents see it as a protective strategy, in particular, for girls.[53] Finally, there may be forms of persecution that are not directly related to the decreased capacity of the state to offer protection but nonetheless are facilitated by it e.g. an increase in child labour as a result of the separation of families during conflict.[54]

Nexus to a Convention Ground

In order to be a refugee, the well-founded fear of persecution must be 'for reasons of race, religion, nationality, membership of a particular social group or political opinion'. Where the agent of persecution is a non-state actor, the nexus to a 1951 Convention ground can relate to either the reason for the persecution by the non-state actor or to the reason the state is unable or unwilling to provide protection.[55]

---

[52] C. Turner, 'Out of the Shadows – Child Marriage and Slavery', Anti-Slavery International, April 2013.

[53] World Vision UK, 'Untying the Knot: Exploring Early Marriage in Fragile States', March 2013, Research Report UK-RR-RE-01, 7, 11; Save the Children, 'Too Young to Wed: The Growing Problem of Child Marriage among Syrian Girls in Jordan', 2014; UNHCR, 'Protection of Refugee Children in the Middle East and North Africa', October 2014. In addition, particular problems may arise for children seeking asylum because their status as a minor may not be recognized because they are married; see e.g. Council Regulation (EC) No. 343/2003 of 18 February 2003, establishing the criteria and mechanisms for determining the Member State responsible for examining an asylum application lodged in one of the Member States by a third-country national, [2003] OJ L. 50/1-50/10, Art. 2(h), which defines an unaccompanied minor as an *unmarried* person below the age of eighteen years (emphasis added).

[54] See e.g. UNHCR, 'The Future of Syria – Refugee Children in Crisis', November 2013.

[55] See UNHCR, *Handbook and Guidelines for Determining Refugee Status*, para. 65.

The asylum claims of children fleeing conflict or violence may involve a nexus to any one of the 1951 Convention grounds or to several of the grounds. However, membership of a particular social group as a ground deserves particular attention as it is the one in which the fact that the applicant is a child is most likely to be directly relevant and where the differences from the claims of adult asylum-seekers are most likely to be prominent. Membership of a particular social group may also be a key factor in demonstrating that the individual faces a particular risk of persecution as distinct from the general hardship faced by the population during times of conflict or violence.

Race, Nationality, Ethnicity

Many of today's conflicts include a racial or ethnic dimension. In such cases, civilians, including children, of the opposing ethnicity may be deliberately targeted by armed forces or armed groups. This may also be a factor in the recruitment of children by armed forces or armed groups or in their persecution because members of a particular race or ethnicity are assumed to be in sympathy with and/or actively supporting the opposing forces. Children of mixed ethnicities, including children conceived as a result of rape by the armed forces, may be particularly vulnerable, being perceived as enemies by both sides. Some gangs may also be formed on ethnic grounds, with the result that ethnicity is a factor when children are forced to join the gang or are assumed by other gangs to be members of the community or the authorities to be associated with the gang.

Religion

As with race, nationality or ethnicity, religion may be a factor in armed conflicts or in violence. In such instances, the ways in which this may relate to the persecution of children discussed earlier will also be relevant. A specific form of religious persecution relates to the failure to conform to religious codes of behaviour. For instance, attacks on schools because they do not conform with religious teachings could, in themselves, amount to persecution on grounds of religion; the attacks on civilians and civilian buildings are a war crime and may violate the child's right to an education, while the motivation for the persecution is religious (the school and/or the students fail to comply with religious teachings).

Political Opinion

The UNHCR guidelines highlight that political opinion should be defined broadly 'as any opinion on any matter in which the machinery of State, government, society or policy may be engaged'.[56] The political opinion forming the basis of the persecution may be real or imputed. Children may be particularly likely to suffer from the assumption that they share the political opinions of parents or family members. However, if a child is targeted in order to put pressure on a family member because of that family member's political opinion rather than because the child is assumed to share the opinion, the relevant 1951 Convention ground for the child would not be political opinion but might be membership in the family considered as a particular social group.[57]

Children may also be politically active and hold political opinions in their own right (and these opinions may or may not coincide with those of other members of their families). A clear example is the 2011 uprising in Syria against President Bashir Al-Assad's government, which started with the outrage caused by the arrest and torture of a group of school-children for writing anti-government graffiti on the wall of their school.[58] Children have subsequently continued to be involved and have been subjected to persecution by the authorities, as Human Rights Watch asserts: 'In many cases, security forces have targeted children just as they have targeted adults.'[59] In assessing the asylum claims of children, it is therefore essential not to assume that political activity is solely the realm of adults and that any asylum claim by a child on this ground is derivative. In times of conflict, the fact that children are members of the armed forces or of armed groups may be related to their political opinions or cause others to assume that their political opinions align with those of the group for which they are fighting.

Finally, the question arises as to whether resistance to joining a gang or resistance to gang activities can constitute a political opinion. Where the gang has a political ideology or agenda and resistance to the gang stems from a disagreement with that political position, the situation is relatively

---

[56] UNHCR, 'Guidance Note: Gangs', para 45, citing UNHCR, 'Guidelines on International Protection No. 1: Gender-Related Persecution within the Context of Article 1A(2) of the 1951 Convention and/or Its 1967 Protocol Relating to the Status of Refugees', 7 May 2002, para. 32.

[57] *AA (unattended children) Afghanistan CG*, which considers both the child applicant's political opinion and his [or her] persecution as a member of the family on the basis of his [or her] family's political opinions.

[58] 'Deraa Protests: Organiser Recalls Start of Syrian Uprising', *BBC News*, 15 March 2013.

[59] Human Rights Watch, 'Syria: Stop Torture of Children', 3 February 2012.

clear (although it will still be necessary to show that the persecution relates to the political opinion).[60] More complex issues arise when the opposition is to the criminal activities of the gang. Asylum authorities have generally taken the position that opposition or resistance to criminal activities is not an expression of a political opinion.[61] A stronger argument for persecution on grounds of political opinion can be made in relation to the inability or unwillingness of the state to protect a child who resists gang membership or activities. The UNHCR 'Guidance Note on Refugee Claims Relating to Victims of Organized Gangs' points out that '[t]he activities of gangs and certain State agents may be so closely intertwined that gangs exercise direct or indirect influence over a segment of the State or individual government officials. Where criminal activity implicates agents of the State, opposition to criminal acts may be analogous with opposition to State authorities.'[62]

Particular Social Group

As stated in UNHCR's guidelines, a 'particular social group is a group of persons who share a common characteristic other than their risk of being persecuted, or who are perceived as a group by society. The characteristic will often be one which is innate, unchangeable, or which is otherwise

---

[60] UNHCR, 'Guidance Note: Gangs', para. 48, citing *Klinko* v. *Canada (Minister of Citizenship and Immigration)*, 3 F.C. 327 [2000] F.C.J. No. 228, Federal Court, 22 Feb. 2000 (Canada). Although the applicant in this case was an adult, the same considerations could apply in the case of a child.

[61] *Vassilev* v. *Canada (Minister of Citizenship and Immigration)*, 1997, CanLII 5394 (F.C.), 131 F.T.R. No. 128, Canada, Federal Court, 4 July 1997 (citing previous decisions of the Canadian Federal Court); *Emilia Del Socorro Gutierrez Gomez* v. *The Secretary of State for the Home Department*, 00/TH/02257, UK Asylum and Immigration Tribunal/ Immigration Appellate Authority, 24 Nov. 2000 (United Kingdom); in *Tobias Gomez* v. *Canada (Citizenship and Immigration)*, 2011 F.C. 1093, although the Court held on judicial review that the tribunal had erred in failing to consider whether the applicant was 'a member of a particular social group on the basis of his status as . . . a youth who refused to join a gang' (para. 29); the Court found that his refusal to comply with escalating extortion demands and [his] resistance to recruitment were acts of economic and personal preservation, not a political stance' (para 26). However, an American court took the opposite view in *Matter of Orozco-Polanco (Re)*, No. A75-244-012, US Executive Office for Immigration Review, 18 December 1997, characterizing 'believing in following the rule of law and earning an honest living and of opposing gang life and its accompanying illegal activities' as a political opinion.

[62] UNHCR, 'Guidance Note: Gangs', para. 47, citing *Vassilev* v. *Canada (Minister of Citizenship and Immigration)* and *Emilia Del Socorro Gutierrez Gomez* v. *The Secretary of State for the Home Department* (United Kingdom).

fundamental to identity, conscience or the exercise of one's human rights.'[63] Although the age of an individual changes constantly, it is not within that individual's power to change it at any given time. It may therefore be considered an immutable characteristic in itself?[64] and thus form the basis for recognition as a member of a particular social group for asylum purposes.[65] In some circumstances, the relevant group may be narrower, including elements such as ethnicity or gender as well as age. However, the fact that age is not always the sole identifying factor of a particular social group does not mean that it cannot be in some circumstances.

In considering child asylum claims, the concept of a 'particular social group' must be interpreted in a child-sensitive manner. It should, for instance, take into consideration the particular importance of the family unit for children. This might lead to identification of the family itself as a particular social group.[66] However, it could also include recognizing that orphans[67] or children living with a single parent or children born out of wedlock constitute a particular social group. Factors such as place of education or place of residence[68] could also be relevant to the identification of social groups to which child asylum-seekers belong.

---

[63] UNHCR, 'Guidelines on International Protection: No 2: "Membership of a Particular Social Group" within the Context of Article 1(A) 2 of the 1951 Convention and/or Its 1967 Protocol Relating to the Status of Refugees', 7 May 2002, HCR/GIP/02/02, para. 11 (UNHCR, 'Guidelines No. 2: MPSG'.

[64] In *LQ (Age: Immutable Characteristic) Afghanistan* v. *Secretary of State for the Home Department*, para. 6, it was found that 'age is immutable. It is changing all the time, but one cannot do anything to change one's own age at any particular time.'

[65] Guidelines on International Protection No. 8, para. 49. *Re B(PV)*, [1994] CRDD No. 12 (10 May 1994); *Canada (Minister of Citizenship and Immigration)* v. *Lin*, (2001) FCA 306, 17 Imm. L.R. (3d) 133, [21]. But see e.g. *Escobar* v. *Gonzales*, 417 F.3d 363, 368 (3d Cir. 2005), rejecting the argument that 'youth' is a particular social group; *Gomez* v. *INS*, 947 F.2d 660, 664 (2d Cir. 1991).

[66] *Hernandez-Avalos* v. *Loretta E. Lynch, Attorney General*, involving death threats to a mother who refused to permit her son to join a gang considered persecution on account of her membership in a particular social group formed by the nuclear family; *Wildon Manfredo Aquino Cordova* v. *Holder, Attorney General*, 13-1597, US Court of Appeals for the Fourth Circuit, 18 July 2014; although this case did not involve a child, it discusses the family as a particular social group in the context of gang attacks on the family of members of a rival gang.

[67] *LQ (Age: Immutable Characteristic) Afghanistan* v. *Secretary of State for the Home Department*, para. 7; *ZK (Afghanistan)* v. *Secretary of State for the Home Department*; *DS (Afghanistan)* v. *Secretary of State for the Home Department*, [2011] EWCA Civ. 305, UK Court of Appeal (England and Wales), 22 March 2011, discussing age and the applicants' status as orphans with regard to the risks faced if returned to Afghanistan.

[68] *Matter of Orozco-Polanco*, but see e.g. *Ayala Sosa and Others* v. *Canada (Minister of Citizenship and Immigration)*, 2014 F.C. 428, Canada Federal Court, 6 May 2014, arguing

Former child soldiers and gang members may themselves be 'particular social groups' as the experience of having been child soldiers or child gang members are immutable and provide a shared characteristic of the group.[69] Gang affiliation indicated by marks such as tattoos may be a particular problem as former members are unable to disguise their association with the gang. Furthermore, former child soldiers and former child gang members may remain members of a child-based social group even once they themselves are no longer children, as their previous age-related status is immutable and the consequences may continue.[70] When former gang members are not considered a particular social group because the group is too amorphous[71] or does not share characteristics other than the fact of being persecuted,[72] it may be important to consider the underlying factors of age, gender and socio-economic status, which make individuals susceptible to joining gangs. Of course, such factors may also include ethnicity, religion and political opinion which can ground an asylum claim in themselves.

UNHCR has taken the view that 'voluntary membership in organized gangs normally does not constitute membership of a particular social group within the meaning of the 1951 Convention. Because of the criminal nature of such groups, it would be inconsistent with human rights and other underlying humanitarian principles of the 1951 Convention to consider such affiliation as a protected characteristic.'[73] However, in applying this position, three points deserve attention. Firstly, as the guidance note highlights, this primarily concerns current rather than former gang members, especially if the former member has

---

that lack of money, lack of education and lack of a place of live are not immutable and therefore did not render the applicants members of a particular social group.

[69] *Lukwago* v. *Ashcroft, Attorney General*, regarding child soldiers; see *Rolando Augustin Castellano Chacon* v. *Immigration and Naturalization Service*, 18 August 2003, 341 F.3d 533 (6th Cir. 2003), para. 65: '[I]t is possible to conceive of the members of MS 13 as a particular social group . . . sharing for example the common immutable characteristic of their past experiences together, their initiation rites, and their status as Spanish-speaking immigrants in the United States.' See also *Jose Luis Urbina-Mejia* v. *Holder*, 597 F.3d 360 (6th Cir. 2010); *Nelson Benitez Ramos* v. *Holder*, 589 F.3d 426 (7th Cir. 2009); and *Julio Ernesto Martinez*. v. *Holder, Attorney General*, US Court of Appeals for the Fourth Circuit, 23 January 2013.

[70] UNHCR, 'Guidelines No. 8: Child Asylum Claims', para. 51.

[71] *Arteaga* v. *Mukasey*, 511 F.3d 940 (9th Cir. 2007); *Matter of W-G-R-*, US Board of Immigration Appeals, 7 February 2014.

[72] *Matter of S-E-G- et al.*, 24 I. & N., Dec. 579 (US BIA 2008), 30 July 2008.

[73] UNHCR, 'Guidance Note: Gangs', para. 43.

clearly renounced association with the gang.[74] Secondly, the association must have been genuinely voluntary. In assessing the voluntariness of such association, children's greater vulnerability and susceptibility to pressure as well as the possibility that they were not aware of or lacked the maturity to understand the nature of the gang's activities should be considered. In particular, a child under the age of criminal responsibility would not normally be considered legally responsible for committing a criminal offence. As the reason for not considering gang membership as a particular social group relates directly to the criminal activities of such groups, it would be illogical to apply this standard to children under the age of criminal responsibility.

Finally, UNHCR has stated that young people 'who live in communities with a pervasive and powerful gang presence but who seek to resist gangs may constitute a particular social group for the purposes of the 1951 Convention'.[75] However, the case law suggests that it may be difficult to convince decision-makers that those who resist gang membership constitute a distinct group without other shared characteristics.[76] For instance, in one case, the particular social group was narrowed from those opposing gang practices to young 'students who expressly oppose gang practices and values and wish to protect their family members against such practices'.[77] Family members of individuals who oppose gang practices and are targeted because of that resistance may themselves be considered as part of a particular social group that resists the gang, or, as noted earlier, the family may be considered a particular social group once the persecution of one member by the gang has been established.[78]

---

[74] Ibid., para 44. A similar position is taken in Martinez. v. Holder, Attorney General, which distinguishes between present and former gang members and recognizes former gang membership as an immutable characteristic which could only be changed by rejoining the gang. In this context it notes that requiring individuals to rejoin such gangs to avoid persecution would be perverse.

[75] Ibid., para. 65.

[76] Matter of S-E-G- et al. Bonilla-Morales v. Holder, 607 F.3d 1132 (6th Cir. 2010); Mendez-Barrera v. Holder, 602 F.3d 21 (1st Cir. 2010); Marroquin-Ochoma v. Holder, 574 F.3d 574 (8th Cir. 2009); Ramos-Lopez v. Holder, 563 F.3d 855 (9th Cir. 2009); Contreras-Martinez v. Holder, 346 F. App'x. 956, 958 (4th Cir. 2009), but, however, Tobias Gomez v. Canada (Citizenship and Immigration) considered either the applicant's status as a young Salvadoran male living in San Salvador or as a youth who refused to join a gang could constitute membership of a particular social group.

[77] Anonymous, US Executive Office for Immigration Review, 3 May 2007, ES.013, 11.

[78] See references in note 66.

Internal Flight Alternative

In general, internal flight is considered a valid alternative if the individual could live safely in another part of the country. This will generally not be the case where the state is the persecutor.[79] Where persecution is by a non-state actor, consideration needs to be given to both the relevance and the reasonableness of such an option and to whether internal relocation would give rise to other violations of the child's rights.[80] In order for an internal flight alternative to be relevant, the individual must be able to access the place of relocation practically, safely and legally.[81] In order to be reasonable, it should enable the claimant to lead a relatively normal life without facing undue hardship.[82]

The basic assessment of the reasonableness of the internal flight alternative will be the same for children as for adults. However, greater consideration should be given to factors such as contact with family and access to education, which are more important for children than for adults. In particular, for a child to live a 'relatively normal life' would usually mean living with a parent or other primary care-giver.[83] Where the internal flight alternative would involve separating the child from his or her previous primary care-giver, the impact of this separation will need to be considered along with the manner in which the child will live and be supported in the new location. The greater susceptibility of children to psychological trauma may also be a factor, especially where remaining in the country of origin may leave the child feeling unprotected. In all assessments of the internal flight alternative, the best interest of the child should be paramount.

An ongoing armed conflict or ongoing situation of violence will also be an element in assessing the reasonableness of the internal flight alternative. Some of the issues arising from this situation will be the (possible) decreased ability of the state to provide protection, the increased sense of insecurity as a result of the conflict, the individual's diminished sense of

---

[79] UNHCR, 'Guidelines on International Protection No. 4: "Internal Flight or Relocation Alternative" within the Context of Article 1A(2) of the 1951 Convention and/or 1967 Protocol Relating to the Status of Refugees', 23 July 2003, HCR/GIP/03/04, paras. 13–14 ('UNHCR, Guidelines No. 4: IFA').

[80] UNHCR, 'Guidelines No. 8: Child Asylum Claims', paras. 53–7.

[81] UNHCR, 'Guidelines No. 4: IFA', para. 7.   [82] Ibid.

[83] See e.g. RRT Case No. 071959605, whereby two teenage children fleeing probable forced recruitment by armed groups in Colombia were deemed to have a valid claim under the 1951 Convention, with internal flight alternative dismissed on account of the fact that they 'had only ever lived in one place and only had relatives there'.

security and the lack of certainty that the internal flight location will remain safe.

Finally, in assessing the reasonableness of an internal flight alternative, it is important to consider safety from all relevant agents of persecution. In cases involving gang membership, the possibility of threats from rival gangs and vengeance by the gang of which the child was a member are relevant.[84] This problem was vividly demonstrated in the case of a child judged to have an internal flight alternative in Guatemala who was unable to disguise his former gang membership and was killed for that reason seventeen days after his return to a 'safe' part of the country.[85]

Exclusion

Child applicants are not exempted from the application of the exclusion clauses (Article 1F) of the 1951 Convention and thus may be excluded from refugee status if it is established that they committed, or participated in the commission of, acts within the scope of this provision in a manner that gives rise to individual responsibility. The same general considerations relating to content and application of the exclusion clauses, including relevant defences, will apply to children as to adults.[86] In applying these considerations to children, their generally low status in hierarchies and their greater vulnerability and susceptibility to coercion should be borne in mind. In particular (as with acts amounting to persecution), acts which would not necessarily be considered to amount to coercion or duress for an adult may

---

[84] See e.g. *Matter of Orozco-Polanco*, in which the threats from both rival gangs and the gang whose membership the applicant avoided by fleeing were taken into account, with the former not being considered to pose a threat in other parts of the country but the latter being likely to use their national connections to persecute the applicant if returned.

[85] American Immigration Lawyers Association (AILA), 'Sign-On Letter Advocating Reforms for Children Seeking Asylum', 1 July 2004, InfoNet Doc. No. 04070265.

[86] UNHCR, 'Guidelines on International Protection No. 5: Application of the Exclusion Clauses: Article 1F of the 1951 Convention Relating to the Status of Refugees', 4 September 2003, HCR/GIP/03/05, ('UNHCR, Guidelines No. 5: Article 1F'); and UNHCR, 'Background Note on the Application of the Exclusion Clauses: Article 1F of the 1951 Convention Relating to the Status of Refugees', 4 September 2003. See M. Happold 'Excluding Children from Refugee Status: Child Soldiers and Article 1F of the Refugee Convention', *American University Int'l. Law Rev* 17(6) (2002), 1131–76, for a detailed discussion of issues around the exclusion of child soldiers who have committed war crimes with a particular focus on the availability of duress as a defence.

do so for a child.[87] Similarly, considerations relating to the proportionality of exclusion may be affected by the fact that the individual is a child. The specificities of applying the exclusion clause to children relate mostly to the age and maturity of the child and assessments of how these affect his or her criminal responsibility for the acts committed.

Age of Criminal Responsibility

As the exclusion clause is concerned with responsibility for the commission of criminal acts, it ought not to be applied to an individual who was under the age of criminal responsibility at the time he or she committed the acts for which he or she might be excluded. In the absence of an agreed age for criminal responsibility in international law, the relevant age will be that fixed in national law.

Where the relevant age differs between the child's country of origin and the country in which he or she is applying for asylum, the higher age must apply.[88] If the child was under the age of criminal responsibility of the state in which he or she is applying for asylum, he or she was considered incapable of committing an offence by that state. To exclude the child because of his or her involvement in criminal acts would not only be contrary to the national law in question but also violate the principle of equality before the law (as a national of the asylum state of the same age and having carried out the same act would not have committed a criminal offence). However, if the child was below the age of criminal responsibility in the country of origin (or the country in which he or she carried out the act, if different), he or she did not legally commit a crime, and the principle of legal certainty should preclude his or her exclusion on such grounds. Furthermore, in this second instance, exclusion of the child does not serve the purpose of ensuring that perpetrators of serious crimes do not use the institution of asylum in order to evade legal accountability, which is a primary purpose of the exclusion clause[89]; if returned to his or her country of origin, the child could not be prosecuted given his or her lack of criminal responsibility.

---

[87] It is, however, by no means clear that such factors are considered in practice in reaching decisions on the exclusion of children.

[88] UNHCR, 'Guidelines No. 8: Child Asylum Claims', para. 60.

[89] UNHCR, 'Guidelines No. 5: Article 1F', para. 2.

Maturity and Mental Capacity

When a child asylum-seeker is over the age of criminal responsibility in both the country of origin and the country of asylum at the time he or she committed the acts for which he or she might be excluded, his or her maturity and mental capacity will still be relevant in assessing whether or not he or she had the necessary understanding of the nature and effect of the acts to be held criminally responsible. Where voluntary association with an organization known to engage in criminal acts which render members liable to exclusion is a factor in determining the excludability of the child, it will be important to consider the age, maturity and mental capacity of the child both at the time that he or she was involved in criminal acts and when he or she first became involved with the organization. In particular, the factors affecting the voluntariness of such association (discussed earlier)[90] and the extent to which he or she knew and understood the nature of the organization's activities may be relevant. In assessing such cases, Canadian courts have suggested that a child below the age of twelve would not generally be considered to have the relevant mental capacity to understand the nature of a terrorist organization or gang which he or she joined.[91] This is in line with the position taken by the Committee on the Rights of the Child that twelve should be

---

[90] Although the fact that the initial recruitment was forced cannot in itself absolve the child of responsibility for actions carried out while a member of the armed group or gang. See e.g. *Gracias-Luna* v. *Canada (Minister of Citizenship and Immigration)*, IMM-1139-92, 25 May 1995; *Bah* v. *Ashcroft*, 341 F.3d 348 (5th Cir. 2003), at 351; *N1998/532 and Minister for Immigration and Multicultural Affairs*, [1999] AATA 116 (5 March 1999); *N96/12254*, [1997] RRTA 492 (17 February 1997). In contrast *Moreno* v. *Canada (Minister of Employment and Immigration)*, (1994), 1 F.C. 298 (F.C.A.), considered the individual's forcible recruitment and desertion in reaching the conclusion that his standing guard outside a cell while a prisoner was tortured did not render him excludable.

[91] *Poshteh* v. *Canada (Minister of Citizenship and Immigration)*, (F.C.A.) 2005 F.C.A. 85, [2005] 3 F.C.R. 487; *Decision A7-00299*, 2007 CanLII 47735 (I.R.B.), Immigration and Refugee Board of Canada, 31 May 2007 (citing *Poshteh*), finding a fourteen-year-old to have been aware of the criminal activities of the gang he joined and capable of distinguishing right and wrong. *Canada (Minister of Public Safety and Emergency Preparedness)* v. *Ronald Antonio Castellon Viera*, VB0-04891, Immigration and Refugee Board of Canada, 24 November 2011, finding that an individual who joined a gang at age twelve at oldest (there were some doubts about the age at which he joined) was not able to form the intent to join a criminal organization but that he had gained the requisite mental capacity before leaving the gang at age fifteen or sixteen and (in the absence of evidence of duress preventing him leaving the gang) could be considered a member of a criminal organization. While other courts have not clearly indicated such a cut-off age, the cases in which exclusion is considered generally relate to older children.

the minimum age for criminal responsibility, while inviting states to set a higher age.[92]

Conclusion

Concern over the special problems facing refugee children during and following war prompted the submission of the original draft of the Geneva Declaration of the Rights of the Child of 1924[93] to the League of Nations.[94] In contrast with this historical concern for these children, this chapter has overviewed the various substantive challenges that children currently fleeing armed conflict and violence may face. In addition to being persecuted under one of the five 1951 Convention grounds either in their own right or in relation to their parent/other family member, a number of different forms of child-specific persecution exist. Courts need to be aware of these and take them into consideration when assessing a claim.

For young people who may have participated in armed conflict or violence, it is important to consider all relevant factors, including whether or not the child's recruitment into an armed force or group is genuinely 'voluntary'. Flawed assessments of the possibility of an internal flight alternative and harsh judgements of a child's character based on past criminal behaviour may prove fatal for the individual child. The fact that many cases of those fleeing gang violence are made on the ground of the applicant belonging to a 'particular social group' can lead to varied interpretations of whether such a group exists, even within one country's case law. Children fleeing armed violence and conflict will, like other refugee children, also face substantial procedural issues. When assessing their asylum claims, it is important that child-specific factors are considered alongside the rigorous application of the general provisions of the 1951 Convention.

---

[92] CRC, 'General Comment No. 10: Children's Rights in Juvenile Justice', 25 April 2007, CRC/C/GC/10, para. 32.

[93] League of Nations, Geneva Declaration of the Rights of the Child of 1924 (adopted 26 September 1924), LoN, Official Suppl. No. 21 October 1924), 43.

[94] G. S. Goodwin-Gill, 'Unaccompanied Refugee Minors: The Role and Place of International Law in the Pursuit of Durable Solutions', *International Journal of Children's Rights* 3 (1995), 405, at 413, cited by J. Bhabha, 'Minors or Aliens? Inconsistent State Intervention and Separated Child Asylum-Seekers', *European Journal of Migration and Law* 3 (2001), 283.

PART IV

Subsidiary Protection

8

Protection in the European Union for People Fleeing Indiscriminate Violence in Armed Conflict

Article 15(c) of the EU Qualification Directive

MADELINE GARLICK*

Introduction

The European Union (EU)'s Qualification Directive[1] is the first supranational instrument in Europe to provide for a specific form of protection for people fleeing indiscriminate violence in situations of armed conflict. Article 15(c) of the Directive, first adopted in 2004,[2] establishes a right to a complementary form of protection known as 'subsidiary protection' for those at risk of 'serious and individual threat to a civilian's life or person by reason of indiscriminate violence in situations of international or internal armed conflict'.

While the national law of several EU Member States had previously contained a form of protection for people fleeing indiscriminate or generalized forms of violence, including in armed conflict situations,[3]

---

* This chapter is based on research undertaken as part of a contribution to S. Peers, V. Moreno-Lax, M. Garlick and E. Guild (eds.), *EU Immigration and Asylum Law*, 2nd edn., Vol. 3 (Leiden, Netherlands: Brill, 2015). It expresses the opinions of the author and does not represent the views of UNHCR or the United Nations.

[1] Directive 2011/95/EU of the European Parliament and of the Council of 13 December 2011 on Standards for the Qualification of Third-Country Nationals or Stateless Persons as Beneficiaries of International Protection, for a Uniform Status for Refugees or for Persons Eligible for Subsidiary Protection, and for the Content of the Protection Granted (recast), OJ L 337/9, 20/12/2011 ('Qualification Directive'). References to the Qualification Directive hereafter will refer to the '2011 Directive', unless otherwise specified.

[2] Council Directive 2004/83/EC of 29 April 2004 on Minimum Standards for the Qualification and Status of Third Country Nationals or Stateless Persons as Refugees or as Persons Who Otherwise Need International Protection and the Content of the protection granted, OJ L 304, 30/09/2004 P. 0012–0023 ('2004 Qualification Directive').

[3] These included Belgium, Germany, the Netherlands and Sweden, among others.

no such obligation existed in a binding form at the regional level. The pre-existing national provisions and practice in Europe differed in their criteria, duration and associated rights.

The Qualification Directive, including Article 15(c), represents an important and innovative element in the EU's Common European Asylum System (CEAS), which sets common legal standards binding upon EU Member States in relation to protection criteria, the treatment of asylum-seekers and refugees, procedures for determining asylum claims and other matters. The legal instruments forming part of the CEAS were adopted after the EU Member States decided to transfer legal competence for asylum matters – until then exclusively under national jurisdiction – to the European Union pursuant to the Treaty of Amsterdam,[4] which entered into force in 1999. Ten years later, in 2009, the Treaty on the Functioning of the European Union (TFEU)[5] established a new and more ambitious legal basis for the European Union's asylum laws, requiring the adoption of a 'common policy on asylum' along with a 'common asylum procedure' and 'uniform status' of asylum and of subsidiary protection across the European Union.[6] These objectives formed the EU legal basis for amendments to the Qualification Directive adopted in its 2011 'recast', which also aimed to achieve 'a higher level of approximation of the rules on the recognition ... of international protection on the basis of higher standards'.[7] While aiming to promote greater consistency in the legislation and practice of the Member States, the amended Directive nevertheless still permits Member States to depart from the EU norms if they wish to adopt higher standards than those defined in its terms.[8]

'Serious Harm' and Various Forms of Subsidiary Protection

Subsidiary protection, according to its definition in Article 2(g) of the Qualification Directive, must be granted to persons fleeing 'serious harm'. Its personal scope, as for other provisions in the Directive, is

---

[4] Treaty of Amsterdam amending the Treaty on European Union, the Treaty Establishing the European Communities and Certain Related Acts, [1997] OJ C 340/1 (entered into force 1 May 1999) (Treaty of Amsterdam). See in particular Title IV on visas, asylum, immigration and other policies related to the free movement of persons.

[5] Consolidated version of the Treaty on the Functioning of the European Union, [2008] OJ C 115/47 (TFEU) ('Lisbon Treaty').

[6] *Ibid.*, Art. 78.   [7] Qualification Directive, Recital 9.

[8] Qualification Directive, Art. 3, on 'more favourable standards'.

limited to non-EU citizens, under the definitions in Article 2(d)–(i) inclusive, which confine eligibility for such protection to 'third country nationals or stateless persons'.[9] There are three forms of 'serious harm' warranting the grant of subsidiary protection: risk of application of the death penalty or execution (under Article 15(a) of the Directive); torture, inhuman or degrading treatment or punishment (Article 15(b))[10] and individual threats from indiscriminate violence in a situation of internal or international armed conflict under Article 15(c).

Aims of Article 15(c)

The other forms of subsidiary protection under Article 15(a) and (b) of the Directive are derived from human rights instruments which bind European states. Article 15(c), by contrast, expresses a novel concept that is not linked directly to Member States' prior regional or international obligations and extends beyond their scope to broaden the categories of people entitled to protection under EU law. According to the Directive's drafting history, the European Commission proposed the adoption of Article 15(c) as a means of providing protection to a wider category of persons than those covered by the refugee definition under Article 1A of the 1951 Convention Relating to the Status of Refugees (1951 Convention).[11] In its 2001 'Explanatory Memorandum to the Proposal for the Original Qualification Directive', the Commission stated that the new provision should enable states to grant longer-term status to persons who would fall within the definition of a 'mass influx', as

---

[9] This limitation of personal scope reflects the Protocol on Asylum attached to the EU Treaties Protocol No. 24 on Asylum for Nationals of Member States of the European Union, [2010] OJ C 83/305. The instrument is also known as the 'Aznar Protocol', informally named after the former Spanish Prime Minister who proposed its adoption.

[10] In addition to the constraints of its personal scope to non-EU nationals, there is also a geographical limitation on Article 15(b), providing for subsidiary protection for those fleeing torture, inhuman or degrading treatment or punishment. Such threats will qualify an applicant for subsidiary protection only if the alleged mistreatment will take place in his or her country of origin. For a detailed discussion of the geographical scope of Art. 15(b), see H. Battjes, *European Asylum Law and International Law* (Leiden, Netherlands: Martinus Nijhoff, 2006), 235; and J. McAdam, 'The Qualification Directive: An Overview', in K. Zwaan, *The Qualification Directive: Central Themes, Problem Issues, and Implementation in Selected Member States* (Oisterwijk, Netherlands: Wolf Legal Publishers, 2007), 7, at 19–20.

[11] Convention relating to the Status of Refugees (adopted 28 July 1951, entered into force 22 April 1954), 189 UNTS 137 ('1951 Convention').

envisaged under the EU's Temporary Protection Directive,[12] in case such people would arrive individually, rather than in a group, without qualifying for refugee protection.[13]

It is thus apparent that the Commission's original goal was to fill a gap in the European protection framework, namely, for people fleeing indiscriminate violence in conflict who may not for various reasons fulfil the criteria for refugee status. Other regional instruments in different parts of the world had addressed this need – in Africa, through the Organization of African Unity (OAU) Convention, providing for protection for persons who 'owing to external aggression, foreign domination or events seriously disturbing public order',[14] and in Latin America in the Cartagena Declaration, which calls for recognition of persons 'who have fled their country because their lives, safety or freedom have been threatened by generalized violence, foreign aggression, internal conflicts, massive violation of human rights or other circumstances which have seriously disturbed public order'.[15] The adoption of subsidiary protection can thus be seen as a move to extend Europe's protection framework in line with wider international developments in refugee law.

At the same time, it would appear that the desire of some Member States to expand the scope of their protection obligations was limited. Article 15(c) was subject to lengthy debate during the 2004 Qualification Directive's negotiation, with some Member States unwilling to adopt a very broad concept that could create extensive obligations towards a wide category of people, unpredictable in scale and nature, who might flee unforeseeable situations of indiscriminate violence occurring in conflict.[16] The interpretation and application of Article 15(c) in

---

[12] Council Directive 2001/55/EC of 20 July 2001 on Minimum Standards for Giving Temporary Protection in the Event of a Mass Influx of Displaced Persons and on Measures Promoting a Balance of Efforts between Member States in Receiving Such Persons and Bearing the Consequences Thereof, [2001] OJ L 212/12.

[13] European Commission, Proposal for a Council Directive on Minimum Standards for the Qualification and Status of Third Country Nationals as Refugees or as Persons Who Otherwise Need International Protection, COM (2001) 510, 12.9.2001, 26.

[14] Organization of African Unity Convention Governing the Specific Aspects of Refugee Problems in Africa (entered into force 20 June 1974), 1001 UNTS 45 ('OAU Convention'), Arts. 1(1) and 1(2).

[15] 1984 Cartagena Declaration on Refugees (adopted 22 November 1984) ('Cartagena Declaration'), Organization of American States, Art. III(3).

[16] Council Doc. No. 9038/02 of 17 June 2002, Outcome of Proceedings from Asylum Working Party on 4–5 June 2002. See also an account of the legislative history of Article 15(c) in K. Hailbronner, 'Articles 11–19: Council Directive 2004/83/EC of 29 April 2004 on Minimum Standards for the Qualification and Status of Third

practice in EU Member States since its adoption, moreover, demonstrate significantly diverging approaches to its constituent elements which appear to signal different understandings at a national level of its objectives. These differences in interpretation and use appear to have undermined the potential for Article 15(c) to fill the gap in the European legal framework that it aimed to address.

The following analysis examines, firstly, the relationship between refugee status and subsidiary protection under Article 15(c). It notes that the primacy that refugee status should enjoy, under the terms of the Directive and leading jurisprudence, could be placed into question by some national practices, according to which subsidiary protection may be awarded to people who would otherwise be entitled to refugee status. Secondly, it seeks to describe the approaches taken in practice and case law to key elements of Article 15(c), which have been interpreted in widely varying – and in some instances, potentially problematic – ways, which have apparently limited its application to some people fleeing violence in conflict.[17]

Primacy of the 1951 Convention

The Preamble to the Qualification Directive makes clear that subsidiary protection, including where it is granted on the basis of risks deriving from indiscriminate violence under Article 15(c), is intended to be complementary and additional to refugee status under Article 1A of the 1951 Convention.[18] In this sense, it aims to reinforce the primacy of

Country Nationals or Stateless Persons as Refugees or as Persons Who Otherwise Need International Protection and the Content of the Protection Granted', in K. Hailbronner (ed.), *EU Immigration and Asylum Law: Commentary* (Oxford, UK: Hart Legal Publishers, 2010), 1093.

[17] The first-instance practice and case law quoted herein do not represent an exhaustive account of decision-making on Article 15(c) at the national level. It seeks rather to provide some insights into the challenges and differences of approach taken in the application of the provision in recent years. For a wider analysis of the different elements of Article 15(c) and recommendations for guidance of judicial and other bodies, see the outcome of a joint project involving a working group of judges and experts convened by the European Asylum Support Office (EASO) and the International Association of Refugee Law Judges (IARLJ) and the Association of European Administrative Law Judges (AEAJ): European Asylum Support Office, 'Article 15(c) of the Qualification Directive (2011/95/EU): A Judicial Analysis', December 2014.

[18] See Qualification Directive, Recital 4: 'The Geneva Convention and Protocol Provide the Cornerstone of the International Legal Regime for the Protection of Refugees'; and Recital 6: 'rules regarding refugee status should be complemented by measures on subsidiary forms of protection.'

refugee protection rather than establishing an alternative or substitute form of protection in its place. Deference to the primary character of refugee status as defined in the 1951 Convention is consistent with the requirement in Article 78 of the TFEU, which requires asylum measures under the CEAS to be 'in accordance with' the 1951 Convention. The Court of Justice of the European Union (CJEU) has also confirmed in the case of *Salahadin Abdulla* that the Qualification Directive enshrines 'two distinct systems' of protection, 'firstly, refugee status and, secondly, subsidiary protection status, in view of the fact that Article 2(e) of the Directive (and Article 2(f) of the 2011 Directive) states that a person eligible for subsidiary protection is one "who does not qualify as a refugee"'.[19]

This secondary and, by definition, subsidiary nature of protection under Article 15 is further reinforced by Article 10(2) of the recast Asylum Procedures Directive,[20] providing that asylum authorities must first 'determine whether the applicants qualify as refugees and, if not, determine whether the applicants are eligible for subsidiary protection'.[21] This rule should ensure that authorities will not first consider whether to grant subsidiary protection, carrying more limited rights, before determining an applicant's possible eligibility for refugee status. It would be a violation of the Directive – and of the 1951 Convention – if states were to apply subsidiary protection in cases where refugee status would be warranted, for example, because subsidiary protection could be given based on a more superficial review of the case or because of the comparatively easier task of establishing the existence of violence and conflict through generally available evidence than specific individual persecution. Such practices would have the potential to undermine and limit the granting of refugee status, contrary to the requirements of Article 78 of the TFEU and the generally accepted approach to application of the 1951 Convention. This complementary view of subsidiary protection is also consistent with UNHCR's oft-repeated view that the 1951 Convention and its 1967 Protocol have afforded protection to people fleeing a variety of threats over the decades, even 'as armed conflicts rooted in ethnic and

---

[19] *Aydin Salahadin Abdulla and others* v. *Bundesrepublik Deutschland*, C-175/08, Court of Justice of the European Union, 2 March 2010 [2010], para. 78.

[20] Directive 2013/32/EU of the European Parliament and of the Council of 26 June 2013 on Common Procedures for Granting and Withdrawing International Protection (recast), [2013] OJ L 180/60.

[21] *Ibid.*, Art. 10(2).

religious differences have become increasingly prevalent'.[22] Its flexible application in changing circumstances over time, in UNHCR's view, puts 'the continuing relevance of the Geneva Convention definition ... beyond question'[23] and affirms its dominant place in the international legal framework.[24]

In the case of *El-Kott*, the CJEU underlined the supplementary role of subsidiary protection status, noting that Palestinians who would not qualify for refugee protection under Article 12(1)(a) of the Directive (which is the EU provision corresponding to Article 1A of the 1951 Convention) could be eligible for subsidiary protection under Article 15.[25] Subsequently, in the case of *HN* v. *Minister of Justice*,[26] the court recalled that subsidiary protection is 'intended for third country nationals who do not qualify for refugee status'[27] and that based on Article 78(2)(a) and (b) of the TFEU, its purpose is to 'complement and add to the protection of refugees enshrined in the Geneva Convention'.[28] In consideration of the higher level of rights attached to refugee status, the court also excluded the possibility of 'an application for subsidiary protection [being] considered before the competent authority has reached the conclusion that the person seeking international protection does not qualify for refugee status'.[29] Based on this clear ruling by the court, the pre-eminent position of refugee status should thus be reflected in the status-determination procedures implemented by Member States and the sequence of the assessment used to establish whether an applicant qualifies for international protection.

In providing guidance on the application of refugee protection criteria, UNHCR has consistently maintained that persons fleeing armed conflict will in many cases qualify for refugee protection, where they can show the existence of a threat of harm and a nexus with a 1951 Convention ground.[30] This has also been argued particularly convincingly in the case

---

[22] UNHCR, 'Safe at Last? Law and Practice in Selected EU Member States with Respect to Asylum-Seekers Fleeing Indiscriminate Violence', 27 July 2011, 16; Protocol Relating to the Status of Refugees (entered into force 4 October 1967), 606 UNTS 267 ('1967 Protocol').

[23] UNHR, Safe at Last?', 16.

[24] The risk of 'wrongly characterizing' a claim by a person who satisfied the criteria for refugee protection is examined by McAdam, 'The Qualification Directive', 16ff.

[25] *El Kott and Others* v. *Hungary*, C-364/11, Court of Justice of the European Union, 27 October 2011, paras. 66-7.

[26] *HN* v. *Minister of Justice*, C-604/12, Court of Justice of the European Union, 8 May 2014.

[27] *HN*, para. 30.   [28] *Ibid.*, paras. 31-3.   [29] *Ibid.*, para. 35.

[30] UNHCR, 'Interpreting Article 1 of the 1951 Convention Relating to the Status of Refugees', April 2001.

of Syrian refugees, many of whom since 2011 have fled situations
of violence on a massive scale in the context of the ongoing conflict,
where the vast majority of people are not only at risk of indiscriminate
violence but also targeted threats based on their race, religion, ethnicity
or actual or imputed political opinion, which could entitle them to refugee
status. UNHCR has taken the position that states should thus be prepared
to grant refugee status to those fleeing conflict and indiscriminate
violence.[31] Nevertheless, until the end of 2013, asylum decision-making
in several EU Member States on claims filed by Syrians led to grants of
subsidiary protection in a significant proportion of cases.[32] Positively, the
overwhelming majority of asylum applications by Syrians have been
recognized as needing some form of protection in most EU Member
States.[33] However, the forms of status granted have varied significantly.
While some Member States (including in 2013 Austria, Denmark,
France and the United Kingdom and increasingly Germany in 2014)
have accorded refugee status[34] to most of those recognized as needing
protection, while others granted subsidiary protection to most successful
claimants.[35] Those granting subsidiary protection differed with respect to
the protection grounds of Article 15 that were applied. The Netherlands
and Sweden, amongst others, applied Article 15(b) to most Syrians based
on the finding that they were at risk of torture, inhuman or degrading
treatment. Others, including Finland, Hungary, Spain and Switzerland,
considered the situation one of indiscriminate violence in conflict to which
large parts of the civilian population were exposed and granted protection
under Article 15(c).

   While UNHCR has welcomed the fact that an increasing proportion
of Member States recognized Syrians as refugees in 2014,[36] the widely
varying approaches to assessment and identification of protection needs
have suggested significant continuing differences in interpretation and

---

[31] UNHCR, 'International Protection Considerations with Regard to People Fleeing the Syrian Arab Republic, Update III', 27 October 2014.

[32] UNHCR reported that Syrians received protection in 91 per cent of cases decided. See also Eurostat, 'Asylum Statistics 2013'.

[33] Eurostat, 'Asylum Statistics 2013'.

[34] EASO, 'Annual Report on the Situation of Asylum in the European Union 2013', Malta, July 2014, 40.

[35] Those giving subsidiary protection in most cases included Belgium, Bulgaria, Cyprus, Czech Republic, Finland, Malta, Romania and Sweden. See EASO, 'Annual Report on the Situation of Asylum in the European Union 2013', 40.

[36] UNHCR, 'Syrian Refugees in Europe: What Europe Can Do to Ensure Protection and Solidarity', 11 July 2014, 16.

assessment of evidence in the case of people fleeing armed conflict. In the Netherlands in 2014, a short procedure was used which led to the grant of subsidiary protection status to Syrians in the majority of cases. However, it would appear that in some instances Syrians who could have presented evidence demonstrating their individual risk of persecution – and thus entitlement for refugee status – chose not to do so, as this would have led to referral to the full procedure and a potentially longer wait for recognition. Given that the rights attached to both forms of status are the same, including rights to family reunification, refugees might not see an interest in pursuing the higher form of 1951 Convention status to which they could be entitled, where subsidiary protection is available more swiftly.

The concern thus arises that subsidiary protection is being awarded through swift procedures and under a broad interpretation of its criteria, while a narrower and stricter approach is being taken to refugee status, which could potentially lead to a more limited use of the refugee definition over time. Predominant use of Article 15(c) for Syrian claims in some states is occurring despite the acknowledged primacy in law of refugee status and procedural safeguards designed to ensure its grant to those who qualify, as well as clear country-of-origin and interpretive guidance. Such a development could be characterized as signalling the emergence of a regional concept of protection which creates the risk of undermining protection under the 1951 Convention and that could have an impact on the central place of refugee status in the international protection system.[37]

It could be asked why the European Union did not, as other regions have done, simply adopt a wider refugee definition in the 2004 Qualification Directive. The most likely explanation is that when subsidiary protection was established under the Directive, Member States did not foresee that they would come to accord it similar or identical levels of rights as those attached to refugee status. Information available about the Directive's negotiation process suggests that at least some Member States saw subsidiary protection as a short-term protective measure carrying minimal entitlements.[38] Experience has regrettably shown, however, that the grave threats to life and person facing many of those fleeing violence in conflict are frequently as serious in nature and as lasting in duration as the persecution from which refugees need

---

[37] See J.-F. Durieux, 'Salah Sheekh Is a Refugee: New Insights into Primary and Subsidiary Forms of Protection', Refugee Studies Centre Working Paper No. 49, October 2008.

[38] See Hailbronner, 'Articles 11–19: Council Directive 2004/83/EC of 29 April 2004', 1093.

protection. Thus, while approaches to the application of subsidiary protection vary across Member States, it has attained wider use and a stronger set of associated rights across the European Union as a whole – even to the point, in some cases, where it may be used where refugee status would be more appropriate.

Article 15(c): Individual Nature of Threats from Indiscriminate Violence

One of the most significant areas of apparent divergence and obfuscation in approach in the interpretation of Article 15(c) relates to the degree of 'individualization' of the threat facing applicants fleeing indiscriminate violence in conflict situations which is required to qualify for protection under Article 15(c). Given the challenge of reconciling what could be seen as two conflicting concepts, it is noteworthy that some Member States have omitted one (or both) of the terms 'indiscriminate' and 'individual' in their national legislation or used terms that can be translated in different ways in different languages. In its 2010 evaluation of the Directive, the European Commission noted that eight Member States omitted the word 'individual' when transposing the term 'serious and individual threat',[39] effectively broadening the scope of the provision in national law to encompass protection for those facing a 'serious threat' without requiring them to show a specific individual form of risk.

By contrast, one Member State – Germany – had omitted altogether the concept of 'indiscriminate violence' from its transposing legislation. In this way, the German formulation apparently sought to restrict its obligations to protect only people facing threats that are individual in their character. This narrower approach is also reflected in the Preamble of the 2004 Directive, where Recital 35, reportedly inserted at Germany's request, states that 'risks to which a population of a country or a section of the population is generally exposed do normally not create in themselves an individual threat which would qualify as serious harm.'[40] It is interesting nevertheless to observe that the German Federal Administrative Court could be seen as having effectively reinserted a broader requirement to protect people fleeing violence in conflict

---

[39] Austria, Belgium, Czech Republic, Germany, Greece, Hungary, Lithuania and Spain. European Commission, Report on the Application of Directive, 2004/83/EC, COM (2010) 314, 9.

[40] Recital 35, Qualification Directive.

when it ruled in 2008 that the existence of indiscriminate violence must be taken into account in assessing eligibility for protection under the Residence Act.[41] In France, the French word for 'generalized' violence has been used in the place of 'indiscriminate'. France also added a requirement for such violence to be 'direct', raising further questions about how to reconcile this with its 'generalized' nature. [42] In its evaluation, the European Commission thus concluded that the requirement of an 'individual threat', read in conjunction with the notion of 'indiscriminate violence', has been interpreted in some Member States as requiring the applicant to demonstrate that he or she is at greater risk of harm than the rest of the population, or parts thereof, in his or her country of origin.[43]

The CJEU, since 2005, has had jurisdiction to issue binding rulings on the interpretation of EU asylum legislation based on preliminary questions referred by Member States' national courts. In *Elgafaji v. Staatssecretaris van Justitie*,[44] one of its first preliminary reference cases, the CJEU addressed the requirement for a 'serious and individual threat' in Article 15(c), finding that it was consistent and reconcilable with the obligation to grant protection to people fleeing indiscriminate violence. 'Indiscriminate', in the court's view, implied that the threat 'may extend to people irrespective of their personal circumstances'. Article 15(c) could apply in such cases where violence reaches 'such a high level that substantial grounds are shown for believing that a civilian ... would, solely on account of his [or her] presence on the territory' of the relevant country or region, 'face a real risk of being subject to the serious threat' of suffering serious harm.[45] The court considered that this interpretation was 'not invalidated' by Recital 26 of the 2004 Directive, which provides that 'risks to which a population of a country or a section of the population is generally exposed do normally not create in themselves an individual threat which would qualify as serious harm.'[46]

The CJEU in *Elgafaji* analysed the question through the use of a 'sliding scale'. As stated in the judgement, 'the more the applicant is

---

[41] *Case 10C 43/07*, Federal Administrative Court of Germany, 28 June 2008, para. 36.

[42] *Code de l'entrée et du séjour des étrangers et du droit d'asile* (CESEDA), 16 January 2015, Art. L.712.1(c).

[43] This was the case e.g. in France, Germany and Sweden. See COM (2010) 314, 9.

[44] *Elgafaji v. Staatssecretaris van Justitie*, C-465/07, Court of Justice of the European Union, 17 February 2009.

[45] *Ibid.*, paras. 34–5.   [46] Recital 35 of the 2011 Qualification Directive.

able to show that he [or she] is specifically affected by reason of factors particular to his [or her] personal circumstances, the lower the level of indiscriminate violence required for him [or her] to be eligible for subsidiary protection.'[47] Conversely, the higher the level of violence observed in the conflict, the less the importance of individual circumstances and attributes is to the assessment of risk. While the court clearly considered that this might be a useful approach to interpretation of Article 15(c), it provided limited guidance on how to apply it in practical terms. The court did not elaborate specifically on what levels of violence might correspond to a particular degree of individual targeting of violence which might be required, thus leaving it to national courts and authorities to apply the sliding scale based on their own assessments.

Following the *Elgafaji* judgement, the German Federal Administrative Court has ruled that 'a substantial individual danger . . . can be assumed only if the general danger impending in [the concerned country] is of such density or of such a high degree that practically any civilian is exposed to a serious individual threat solely on account of his or her presence there.'[48] The court has subsequently found that indiscriminate violence includes acts that do not target particular individuals or groups but which affect civilians regardless of their characteristics or circumstances.[49] In the United Kingdom, using similar reasoning, the Upper Tribunal has concluded that 'an attempt to distinguish between a real risk of targeted and incidental killing of civilians during armed conflict . . . is not a helpful exercise in the context of Article 15(c); nor does it reflect the purposes of the Directive.'[50]

Research by UNHCR has described some of the varying approaches taken by Member States to the application of this concept. France, Germany and the United Kingdom have consistently used the 'sliding scale', examining levels of general violence based on the available evidence and assessing individual factors and circumstances against this wider background. However, in the Netherlands, the Council of State has not used the sliding scale, based on its view that a claimant's individual attributes or circumstances are not relevant to the determination of whether Article 15(c) applies. The dominant question for the Netherlands is whether the situation of violence is considered to

---

[47] *Elgafaji*, para. 39.
[48] BVerwG 10 C 9.08, Federal Administrative Court of Germany, 14 July 2009.
[49] BVerwG 10 C 4.09, Federal Administrative Court of Germany, 27 April 2010.
[50] *HM & Others Iraq* v. *Secretary of State for the Home Department CG*, [2010] UKUT 331 (IAC), United Kingdom Upper Tribunal, para. 73.

be sufficiently 'exceptional' to conform to the standard set in the Luxembourg Court's *Elgafaji* ruling.

The requirement for an individualized risk of serious harm in the context of Article 3 of the European Convention on Human Rights (ECHR)[51] was also considered by the Grand Chamber of the European Court of Human Rights (ECtHR) in the case of *MSS* v. *Belgium and Greece*.[52] There the Grand Chamber found, following earlier decisions in *Salah Sheekh*[53] and *NA* v. *UK*,[54] that the fact that a large number of persons might be exposed to a similar threat did not render that threat less individual in nature. In situations where many people could face a general risk of treatment violating Article 3 of the ECHR, provided the risk faced by the applicant is 'sufficiently real and probable', according to information from reliable sources, the test will be satisfied.[55] In *MSS*, the court found that information provided by UNHCR, the Council of Europe and other expert bodies could constitute 'prima facie evidence' of such risks applying to concerned individuals in Greece at that time.[56]

Moreover, in the case of *Sufi and Elmi* v. *UK*,[57] a few months later, the Strasbourg court found that a single individual could be considered to face a 'real risk' in exceptional cases of generalized violence which reached a particularly high level of intensity. The court concluded that 'in exceptional circumstances, be attained in consequence of a situation of general violence of such intensity that any person being returned to the region in question would be at risk simply on account of their presence there'.[58] The court concluded that the violence prevalent in Mogadishu, Somalia, as evidenced in that case at the time, was of a 'sufficient level of intensity to pose a real risk to the life or person of any civilian in the capital'.[59]

This more expansive approach to the scope of protection available to people at risk in generalized violence situations has been developed

---

[51] European Convention for the Protection of Human Rights and Fundamental Freedoms, as amended by Protocols Nos. 11 and 14, ETS 5 (ECHR).

[52] *MSS* v. *Belgium and Greece*, App. No. 30696/96 (21 January 2011), ECtHR.

[53] *Salah Sheekh* v. *The Netherlands*, App. No. 1948/04 (11 January 2007), ECtHR.

[54] *NA* v. *UK*, App. No. 259/04 (17 July 2008), ECtHR.

[55] *MSS* v. *Belgium and Greece*, para. 359. See also V. Moreno-Lax, 'Dismantling the Dublin System: *MSS* v. Belgium and Greece', *EJML* 14(1) (2012), 28.

[56] *MSS* v. *Belgium and Greece*, para. 296.

[57] *Sufi and Elmi* v. *UK*, App. Nos. 8319/07 and 11449/07 (28 June 2011), ECtHR.

[58] *Sufi and Elmi*, para. 7.   [59] *Ibid.*, para. 241.

further in *Hirsi Jamaa* v. *Italy.*[60] There the Grand Chamber of the ECtHR found that a state is precluded from removing a person to a country where he or she would face the risk of treatment contrary to Article 3 of the ECHR whenever that state exercises jurisdiction over that person, including outside its territory. In *Hirsi*, the court concluded that information from UNHCR and other reliable sources demonstrated a 'sufficiently real and probable' risk that asylum-seekers and irregular immigrants would face treatment contrary to Article 3 if they were returned to Libya. In these circumstances, the court took the view that the applicant was not required to prove that he or she faced an individual threat of torture, inhuman or degrading treatment or punishment.[61]

The CJEU examined the issue of individualized versus generalized threats further in *NS and ME*,[62] a case which, like *MSS*, considered whether removal of asylum-seekers from another Member State to Greece under the Dublin Regulation was permissible. While the case did not concern the application of Article 15(c) as such, the Luxembourg Court considered the level of risk facing the concerned individuals, namely, asylum-seekers in the European Union, and concluded that removal was precluded in light of the 'systemic deficiencies' in Greece's asylum and reception systems. The CJEU determined that where there were 'substantial grounds for believing there is a real risk' of treatment contravening Article 4 of the EU Charter of Fundamental Rights,[63] removal under Dublin must be suspended. There was no need for the applicant to show that he or she would be particularly exposed to that risk because of his or her individual circumstances.[64]

It is possible that further references to the Luxembourg Court may be expected, aimed at clarifying further the interpretation of the requirement

---

[60] *Hirsi Jamaa and others* v. *Italy*, App. No. 27765/09 (23 February 2012), ECtHR (Grand Chamber).

[61] *Ibid.* paras. 118, 123, 136. For further analysis, see V. Moreno-Lax, '*Hirsi Jamaa and Others* v. *Italy* or the Strasbourg Court versus Extraterritorial Immigration Control?', *HRLR* (2012), 574, at 582ff.

[62] Joined Cases *NS* and *ME*, C-411/10 and C-493/10, Court of Justice of the European Union, [2011] ECR I-13905.

[63] Article 4 of the Charter provides that 'none shall be subjected to torture or to inhuman or degrading treatment or punishment'. Charter of Fundamental Rights of the European Union, [2000] OJ C 364/1; [2010] OJ C 83/2.

[64] For further analysis and comparison of the respective lines of reasoning of the ECtHR in *MSS* and the CJEU in *NS and ME*, see C. Costello, 'Dublin Case *NS/ME*: Finally, an End to Blind Trust Across the EU?', *Asiel et Migrantierecht* 2 (2012), 83, at 89–90.

for an individual threat in the context of indiscriminate violence under Article 15(c), including in light of the Charter of Fundamental Rights and the evolving Strasbourg jurisprudence on Article 3.

Assessing Violence: The 'Exceptionality' Test, Levels and Indicators of Violence

As noted earlier, the CJEU in *Elgafaji* concluded that a serious and individual threat to an asylum-seeker's life or person may 'exceptionally be considered ... where the degree of indiscriminate violence characterising the armed conflict taking place ... reaches such a high level that substantial grounds are shown for believing that a civilian, returned to the relevant country or, as the case may be, to the relevant region, would, solely on account of his [or her] presence on the territory of that country or region, face a real risk of being subject to that threat'.

In examining the level of violence required by Article 15(c), the court stated that 'the objective finding alone of a risk linked to the general situation in a country is not, as a rule, sufficient to establish that the conditions set out in Article 15(c) ... have been met in respect of a particular person ... its wording nonetheless allows – by use of the word "normally" – for the possibility of an *exceptional situation* which would be characterised by *such a high degree of risk* that substantial grounds would be shown for believing that that person would be subject *individually* to the risk in question.'[65]

In 2009, the UK Court of Appeal expressed the view that the *Elgafaji* judgement has not introduced an additional test of 'exceptionality' to the analysis of whether levels of violence are sufficient to justify the grant of subsidiary protection in a given situation. Rather, the word 'exceptional', as used in the judgement, was seen simply as indicating that 'it is not every armed conflict or violence situation that will attract the protection of Article 15(c), but only one where the level of violence is such that, without anything to render them a particular target, civilians face real risks to their life or personal safety.'[66]

In the Netherlands, by contrast, it has been considered that Article 15(c) applies only to 'exceptional situations' of indiscriminate violence. The Dutch State Secretary of Justice, writing to the Dutch Parliament in the wake of the *Elgafaji* decision, stated his view that the

---

[65] Emphasis added. *Elgafaji*, para 37.
[66] *AD and AH* v. *SSHD*, [2009] EWCA Civ. 620, UK Court of Appeal, para. 25.

judgement meant that Article 15(c) would apply to 'a very limited number of situations'.[67]

The Luxembourg Court in *Elgafaji* made clear that it is the responsibility of national asylum authorities to determine if the degree of indiscriminate violence rises to the level of 'exceptionality' required by Article 15(c). However, it did not provide detailed guidance as to how to make the necessary assessment. The concept of an 'exceptional' risk of serious harm is thus subject to different interpretations. UNHCR's 2011 research found that the authorities in some Member States[68] assessed levels of violence as part of their analysis of whether an international or internal armed conflict was taking place.[69] In others, they reportedly focused on whether the levels of indiscriminate violence disclosed by the evidence reached, or were likely to reach in the foreseeable future, such a level as to pose a real risk of serious harm to civilians in general.

According to UNHCR, in assessing whether such a 'real risk' is present, national authorities and courts in a number of Member States have defined a very high threshold of violence that must be reached before they consider that Article 15(c) could apply.[70] Describing the different assessments of the levels of violence in particular regions and countries in armed conflict, UNHCR reported that in 2010 and 2011, Member States receiving the largest numbers of asylum-seekers from conflict zones were able to agree on only one location where violence was considered to reach the threshold for applying Article 15(c). For Belgium, France, Germany, Sweden and the United Kingdom, Mogadishu was the only conflict zone area where the prevalence of violence was so high that it satisfied Article 15(c)'s test.[71] Based upon this analysis, UNHCR concluded that 'it is fair to ask whether the threshold of violence ... has been set so high that civilians who have a "real risk" of serious harm are unable to secure protection.' Since that time, the ECtHR has decided in the 2013 case of *KAB* v. *Sweden*[72] that Mogadishu was no longer a place where civilians were automatically at risk of torture and inhuman or degrading treatment by virtue of their mere presence. With this decision, which is very

---

[67] Letter from the Ministry of Justice to the Speaker of the Lower House of the Parliament, the Netherlands, 17 March 2009.

[68] Germany, Netherlands and the United Kingdom. See 'Safe at Last?', 32.

[69] Belgium, France and Sweden. *Ibid.*   [70] UNHCR, 'Safe at Last?', 32ff.

[71] *Ibid.*, 33. In the case of the United Kingdom, UNHCR also noted a further limitation in that the level of violence was considered high enough to satisfy 15(c) only for 'most civilians' present in Mogadishu but not for all.

[72] *KAB* v. *Sweden*, App. No. 886/11 (5 September 2013), ECtHR.

likely to influence the application of Article 15(c) by EU Member States, the Strasbourg Court has raised the bar for people coming from that city and potentially elsewhere in Somalia in seeking to establish a need for protection.

Subsequent practice in relation to asylum claims by Syrians has indicated that a wider group of Member States considers that levels of violence prevailing in Syria in 2012 and 2013 have been sufficient to trigger the application of Article 15(c).[73] But with varying approaches still being taken among Member States to the forms of protection granted to Syrians fleeing the conflict, a consistent interpretation remains elusive.

In state practice in the European Union, different indicators or factors have been applied in judging whether the requisite high level of violence has occurred. Among those which have been documented in national authorities' assessments are the general security situation in the concerned country or area, statistics on casualties and security incidents, numbers of displaced people, likely or foreseeable developments in a conflict (including prospects for resolution, socio-economic and humanitarian conditions), capacity of relevant actors to provide protection in the area and levels of humanitarian need.[74] At least one Member State in the past has focused almost exclusively on the total number of deaths within a defined geographical area – effectively reducing the analysis to a mathematical formula,[75] apparently according insufficient weight to other crucial elements determining the impact of violence on individuals, such as the prevalence of severe injury and trauma, sexual and gender-based violence, (un)availability of medical care, rates of post-traumatic stress disorder and other physical and mental illnesses. Taking a more nuanced approach, the UK Upper Tribunal in 2012 stated that 'an inclusive approach' was needed in the assessment of levels of violence for the purposes of granting subsidiary protection, subject only to the need for a 'sufficient causal nexus' between the violence and the conflict. This included having regard to 'threats to the physical safety and integrity of civilians beyond those measured in the civilian casualty rates', as well as 'indirect forms of violence such as threats, intimidation, blackmail, seizure of property, raids on homes and businesses, use of checkpoints to push out other factions, kidnapping and extortion',[76] among others.

---

[73] See European Council on Refugees and Exiles (ECRE), 'Information Note on Syrian Asylum Seekers and Refugees in Europe', November 2013.

[74] UNHCR, 'Safe at Last?', 42.   [75] Ibid., 43ff.

[76] H.M. & Ors (Article 15(c)), Iraq Country Guidance, [2012] UKUT 000409 (IAC), UK Upper Tribunal, paras. 113–14.

Internal and International Armed Conflict

A further key requirement for the application of Article 15(c) is that the relevant threat to an individual's life or person from indiscriminate violence must arise in a situation which can be characterized as 'international or internal armed conflict'. Defining these notions and determining what kind of conflict falls within the definition has proven a challenge. International humanitarian law (IHL) is used as a major point of reference by some Member States in applying Article 15(c),[77] in spite of the specific, non-international protection-related objects and purposes of IHL, which does not provide a single agreed definition of 'armed conflict'. Commentators have debated the linkage between IHL, international human rights law and international refugee law, including in relation to the criteria for subsidiary protection under the Qualification Directive.[78] An international expert roundtable organized by UNHCR in 2011 concluded that IHL, as well as international criminal law, could inform the interpretation of protection criteria in situations of indiscriminate violence and armed conflict but that its role should not be over-estimated. The determining factor should be the need for protection in such cases rather than the legal qualification of the conflict which gave rise to that need.[79]

UNHCR has noted that, in practice, the existence or otherwise of an international or internal armed conflict is considered as a decisive

---

[77] For an analysis of the contrasting approaches taken by UK and French courts on this issue, see H. Lambert and T. Farrell, 'The Changing Character of Armed Conflict and the Implications for Refugee Protection Jurisprudence', *IJRL* 22 (2010), 237, at 241–57.

[78] Storey has argued that refugee law encounters difficulties in dealing with asylum claims from those fleeing armed conflict for reasons including failure by asylum decision-makers and courts to recognize that IHL is the *lex specialis* of armed conflict. He argues for human rights law, refugee law and IHL to be applied in tandem. See H. Storey, 'Armed Conflict in Asylum Law: The War Flaw', *RSQ*. 31(1) (2012). In riposte, Durieux maintains that existing legal definitions (including as explored by Storey) fail satisfactorily to answer the question of what rights and protection needs of people threatened by armed violence fall outside the scope of refugee protection and are instead covered by Article 15(c) of the Directive. See J.-F. Durieux, 'Of War, Flows, Laws and Flaws: A Reply to Hugo Storey', *RSQ* 31(3)(2012), 161. As a response to this exchange, Storey has refined his position in H. Storey, 'The War Flaw and Why It Matters', in D. Cantor and J.-F. Durieux (eds.), *Refuge from Inhumanity? War Refugees and International Humanitarian Law* (Leiden, Netherlands: Martinus Nijhoff, 2014), 39.

[79] UNHCR, 'Expert Meeting on Complementarities between International Refugee Law, International Criminal Law and International Human Rights Law: Summary Conclusions', (July 2011), 24, available at: www.refworld.org/docid/4e1729d52.html.

element in deciding to grant Article 15(c) protection, among others in the practices of Belgium, France and Sweden. The Netherlands, by contrast, has not considered that this question holds decisive importance for the application of Article 15(c), following the *Elgafaji* judgement.[80] Member State jurisprudence has referred to various requirements drawn from IHL and international criminal law, relating, among other things, to the status of the parties to the conflict (between governmental armed forces, or between governmental forces and other armed groups, or between such groups); the need for the conflict to be sustained, concerted and ongoing; the requirement that conflicts be shown to be more than mere local disturbance or tension; the presence of functioning command and control structures and others. The widely varying approaches to these elements further confirm the ongoing lack of clarity across the European Union regarding the interpretation of Article 15(c).

The CJEU issued a preliminary ruling which addressed directly the role of IHL in 2014 in the interpretation of Article 15(c) in the case of *Aboubacar Diakité*.[81] The court held that IHL, while designed to ensure protection for citizens in a conflict zone, did not provide for *international* protection for those *outside* a conflict zone and beyond the territory of the conflicting parties.[82] The court endorsed the Advocate-General's argument that the 2004 Qualification Directive's provisions on subsidiary protection and IHL pursued 'different aims and establish[ed] quite distinct protection mechanisms'.[83] It would be impossible, without disregarding the distinct nature of these two areas, to make eligibility for subsidiary protection conditional on a finding that the conditions for applying IHL are met.[84] The court concluded that an internal armed conflict, for the purposes of Articles 2(e)[85] and 15(c), existed 'if a state's armed forces confront one or more armed groups or if two or more armed forces confront each other' and that it was not necessary for the conflict to be characterized as an 'armed conflict not of an international nature' under IHL.[86]

---

[80] NHCR, 'Safe at Last?', 65.

[81] *Aboubacar Diakité* v. *Commissaire général aux réfugiés et aux apatrides*, C-285/12, Court of Justice of the European Union, 30 January 2014.

[82] *Ibid.*, para. 23. [83] *Ibid.*, para. 24. [84] *Ibid.*, para. 26.

[85] Article 2(e) of the 2004 Directive, defining eligibility for subsidiary protection, has been replaced by Article 2(f) of the 2011 Directive.

[86] *Diakité*, para. 35. On this issue, see Bauloz, 'The (Mis)Use of International Humanitarian Law under Article 15(c) of the EU Qualification Directive', in Cantor and Durieux, *Refuge from Inhumanity?*, 247.

Recalling its previous ruling in *Elgafaij*,[87] the court affirmed that the more specific the impact of violence upon the applicant due to his or her personal circumstances, the lower the level of indiscriminate violence needed for him or her to qualify for subsidiary protection. Apart from this appraisal of the level of indiscriminate violence in the territory concerned, the court in *Diakité* decided that it was not necessary in addition to carry out a separate assessment of the intensity of the armed confrontation, nor of the level of organization of the armed forces or of the duration of the conflict.[88] In this way, the court has confirmed that the meaning of the concept of 'international or internal armed conflict' is autonomous and distinct from that of the related terms in IHL.[89]

National courts in several cases in recent years have also grappled with the notion of what constitutes an internal or international armed conflict. In a judgement of the German Federal Administrative Court, it was found that a high level of organization on the part of the military forces involved was not needed, nor far-reaching control of territory, which would enable the situation to fall within the rules of international humanitarian law under the Geneva Conventions of 1949. The German court found that other acts of violence affecting civilians on a non-selective basis, going beyond those which might violate IHL, should be taken into account in assessing the relevant level of indiscriminate violence.[90] Other judgements have also confirmed that authorities construing Article 15(c) should take IHL into account but not that the fighting in question must fall squarely within the IHL definition of armed conflict.[91] As such, most

---

[87] *Diakité*, para. 31; *Elgafaji*, para. 39.   [88] *Diakité*, para. 34.

[89] Further on this point, see V. Moreno-Lax, 'Of Autonomy, Autarky, Purposiveness and Fragmentation: The Relationship between EU Asylum Law and International Humanitarian Law', in Cantor and Durieux, *Refuge from Inhumanity?*, 295.

[90] Geneva Convention for the Amelioration of the Condition of the Wounded and Sick in Armed Forces in the Field (entered into force 21 October 1950), 75 UNTS 31 (First Geneva Convention); Geneva Convention for the Amelioration of the Condition of Wounded, Sick and Shipwrecked Members of Armed Forces at Sea (entered into force 21 October 1950), 75 UNTS 85 (Second Geneva Convention); Geneva Convention Relative to the Treatment of Prisoners of War (entered into force 21 October 1950), 75 UNTS 135 (Third Geneva Convention); Geneva Convention Relative to the Protection of Civilian Persons in Time of War (entered into force 21 October 1950), 75 UNTS 287 (Fourth Geneva Convention); Protocol Additional to the Geneva Conventions of 12 August 1949, and Relating to the Protection of Victims of Non-International Armed Conflicts (entered into force 7 December 1978), 1125 UNTS 609 (Protocol II); BVerwG 10 C 4.09, Judgement (10th Div.) of 27 April 2010, German Higher Administrative Court.

[91] BVerwG 10 C 43.07, Judgement (10th Div.) of 24 June 2010, German Higher Administrative Court.

interpretations appear to uphold a reading of the EU law on subsidiary protection as being complementary to and autonomous of other branches of law, including IHL.

Interaction between Rules on Protection for People Fleeing Torture, Inhuman and Degrading Treatment vs. Indiscriminate Violence in Conflict: Article 15(b) and (c) of the Directive

Article 15(b) of the Qualification Directive provides for protection for people at risk of 'torture, inhuman or degrading treatment or punishment', reflecting the *non-refoulement* obligation under Article 3 of the ECHR. While the distinct wording and separate provisions for subsidiary protection under paragraphs (b) and (c) of Article 15 would at first glance suggest that they are deliberately intended to define entirely separate concepts, which are to be applied to people fleeing distinct risks, the question of whether and how they differ has been debated at the highest levels of EU juridical analysis.

The CJEU in 2009 pronounced its view in the *Elgafaji* decision, where the Dutch Council of State asked whether the scope of Article 15(c) was different from or broader than Article 3 of the ECHR (the wording of which is reflected in Article 15(b)), as interpreted by the European Court of Human Rights. In case Article 15(c) would be considered broader, the referring court asked what criteria should be applied to determine when protection should be granted in cases of real risk of serious and individual threat by reason of indiscriminate violence.

Clarification was considered necessary, at least in part, because of jurisprudence from the Strasbourg Court in the case of *NA v. UK*,[92] which had found that, in principle, a situation of 'general violence' could 'be of a sufficient level of intensity as to entail that any removal to it would necessarily breach Article 3' of the ECHR. In that particular case – as in others it had decided to that point – the ECtHR did not find that the situation of violence under consideration had reached the requisite level of intensity. However, according to the CJEU in *Elgafaji*, the Strasbourg Court had left open the possibility that it could adopt such an approach, albeit 'only in the most extreme cases of general violence, where there was a real risk of ill-treatment simply by virtue of an

---

[92] *NA v. UK*, paras. 115–17.

individual being exposed to such violence on return'.[93] As the court considered possible a situation in which general violence could expose people to an Article 3 risk merely because of their presence – albeit not identified to that point in a specific case – then the question arose as to what further or additional scope Article 15(c) might have beyond that covered by Article 3 of the ECHR.

The Luxembourg Court decided in *Elgafaji* that Article 15(c) did have its own distinct area of application. It found that the provision's content 'is different from Article 3 of the ECHR, and [its] interpretation must, therefore, be carried out *independently*, although with due regard for fundamental rights' as guaranteed under the ECHR.[94] It concluded that Article 15(b), by contrast, was the provision in the Qualification Directive which corresponded in its meaning to Article 3 of the ECHR. In explaining the independent scope of Article 15(c), the court analysed the three forms of serious harm addressed by Article 15 and observed that Article 15(c)'s requirement for a serious and individual threat to life or person 'covered a more general risk of harm' than those in Article 15(a) or (b). This interpretation departed from the view of the Dutch Council of State that individual circumstances were relevant *only* in the context of Article 3 of the ECHR (and Article 15(b))–related threats of torture, inhuman or degrading treatment or punishment and were not relevant to indiscriminate violence under Article 15(c).

Despite the Luxembourg Court's clear statement that Article 15(c) should be seen as distinct in scope and content from Article 15(b), it would appear that the interpretation of the two provisions at a national level, at least in one Member State, has remained unclear.[95] The Dutch Council of State, in deciding on the merits of the *Elgafaji* case after the ruling of the CJEU, concluded that 'the material scope of . . . Article 15(c) of the Directive is, in accordance with the Luxembourg Court's ruling of

---

[93] *Ibid.* See also *Mawaka* v. *The Netherlands*, App. No. 29031/04 (1 June 2010), ECtHR, where the court found that the situation in the DRC, and in the north-eastern Kivu provinces in particular, was dire but not such as to reach the requisite level of violence (so that a real risk of ill-treatment existed simply by virtue of an individual being exposed to such violence on return).

[94] Emphasis added. *Elgafaji*, para. 27 (emphasis added). See also Opinion of Advocate-General Maduro in *Elgafaji*, para 19; and on the question of autonomy in the judgement, see R. Errera, 'The CJEU and Subsidiary Protection: Reflections on Elgafaji – and After', *IJRL* 23 (2010), 93.

[95] For a discussion of the impact and meaning of Article 15(c) by comparison with Article 15(b), see P. Tiedemann, 'Subsidiary Protection and the Function of Article 15(c) of the Qualification Directive', *RSQ* 31(1)(2012), 123.

17 February 2009, not broader than that of Article 3 [of the] ECHR.'[96] Subsequent decisions of Dutch courts and first-instance authorities, as analysed in research conducted by UNHCR,[97] have cited ECtHR jurisprudence on Article 3 in relation to conflict situations in Iraq, Afghanistan and the Democratic Republic of Congo. However, they have not concluded that Article 15(c) would apply to applicants coming from those countries. The United Kingdom's Upper Tribunal, by contrast, has cited the *Elgafaji* judgement and noted that while potential for overlap between the two provisions exists, Article 15(c) 'is an autonomous concept distinct from and broader than Article 3 of the ECHR',[98] as interpreted by the Strasbourg Court.

As noted earlier, the ECtHR in 2011 itself referred to the Luxembourg Court's *Elgafaji* decision in its Chamber judgement in the case of *Sufi and Elmi*. The court noted that its jurisdiction was limited to the ECHR and that it would therefore not be appropriate to express a view on the ambit of Article 15(c) Directive. Nevertheless, the ECtHR said that, based on the decision of the CJEU in *Elgafaji*, it was 'not persuaded that Article 3 of the [1951] Convention as interpreted in *NA* does not offer comparable protection to that afforded under the Directive. In particular, [the CJEU] noted that the threshold set by both provisions may, in exceptional circumstances, be attained in consequence of a situation of general violence of such intensity that any person being returned to the region in question would be at risk simply on account of [his or her] presence there.'[99] Given the high levels of violence prevalent in Mogadishu, it found accordingly that return to Mogadishu would amount to a violation of Article 3 of the ECHR.[100]

In seeking further guidance on the independent scope of Article 15(c) and its distinct application from that of Article 15(b), commentators have considered the Explanatory Memorandum to the European Commission's original draft of Article 15(c) in its first proposal for the Qualification Directive in 2001.[101] However, neither the explanations

---

[96] *Case 201000765/1/V2*, 10 June 2010, Council of State, the Netherlands.
[97] UNHCR, 'Safe at Last?', 55.   [98] *HM & Others Iraq*, para. 67.
[99] *Sufi and Elmi* v. *United Kingdom*, App. Nos. 8319/07 and 11449/07 (28 June 2011), ECtHR, para 226.
[100] The ECtHR has subsequently concluded that the situation in Mogadishu no longer reaches the requisite level of Article 3 risk. See *KAB* v. *Sweden*. For further analysis, see L. Tsourdi, 'What Protection for Persons Fleeing Indiscriminate Violence? The Impact of the European Courts on the EU Subsidiary Protection Regime', in Cantor and Durieux, *Refuge from Inhumanity?*, 270.
[101] COM (2001) 510.

nor available records of negotiations between Member States on the wording have been found to provide a clear distinction.[102] As a result of this uncertainty, which evidently remains despite the rulings of the two European courts on Article 3 of the ECHR and Article 15(c) of the Directive, it would appear that further clarification may be needed regarding the respective scope of the two provisions in practice, concerning situations of intense violence and risks to which people who seek asylum are exposed.[103]

The Recast Qualification Directive: A Missed Opportunity to Clarify Protection from Indiscriminate Violence?

An important opportunity arose to clarify and strengthen the Qualification Directive in 2009 when the European Commission tabled its 'recast' amendment proposals as part of a set of second-phase legislative measures to address gaps in the first EU legal instruments on asylum. While the Commission's recast proposals did foresee changes to some substantive elements[104] and proposed raising standards in the rights attached to subsidiary protection status, it did not propose any changes to the criteria for protection, including under Article 15(c) as such. This is despite the Commission's acknowledgement, in the 'Explanatory Memorandum' to the recast proposal, that stakeholders had 'stressed the need for clarification of Article 15(c)'.[105] The 2004 Directive had noted, in its Article 37(1), dealing with possible

---

[102] Hailbronner notes that the drafting history 'does not shed much light' on the interpretation of the provision. See Hailbronner, *EU Immigration and Asylum Law*, 1093, 1147. See also R. Errera, 'The CJEU and Subsidiary Protection: Reflections on *Elgafaji* and After', *IJRL* 23 (2010), 93; and H. Battjes, *European Asylum Law and International Law* (Leiden, Netherlands: Martinus Nijhoff, 2006), 239. For an argument based on the principle of effectiveness and the presumption against redundancy of legal provisions, according to which the scope of Article 15(c) must be different from, and potentially wider than, that of Article 15(b), see V. Moreno-Lax, 'Of Autonomy, Autarky, Purposiveness and Fragmentation: The Relationship between EU Asylum Law and International Humanitarian Law', in Cantor and Durieux, *Refuge from Inhumanity?*, 295, at 332–9.

[103] See further on *Diakité*.

[104] These included rules on internal protection (or internal flight) alternatives, non-state actors of protection and particular social groups. See European Commission, Proposal for a Directive of the European Parliament and of the Council on Minimum Standards for the Qualification and Status of Third Country Nationals or Stateless Persons as Beneficiaries of International Protection and the Content of the Protection Granted, COM (2009) 551, 21 October 2009.

[105] *Ibid.*, 5.

future amendments, that Article 15 was a provision for which amendments 'shall be made by way of priority'.

The Commission's decision not to table amendments to Article 15, despite evident divergences in its interpretation and application, appeared to be based on concerns that negotiations could lead to a narrowing of its scope rather than merely a clarification or even expansion of its wording. These reflected the desire expressed in negotiations on the 2004 Directive by some Member States to limit the application of Article 15's protection to people at risk in situations of violence[106] and strict approaches to its application observed in subsequent practice. Thus, the Commission elected not to open Article 15(c) up for renegotiation to avoid the risk that Member States would seek to reduce the scope of their obligations, retaining the ambiguities and scope for differing interpretations, rather than seeking to clarify them and risk the possibility of a more restrictive approach. The consequence, however, is that ambiguities and differences in application of Article 15(c) are likely to continue unless and until further guidance is provided by the European courts in the future.

From a positive perspective, the changes that were made in the recast Directive have served significantly to improve the legal and material situation of holders of subsidiary protection. Amendments to the rights associated with protected status have resulted in strengthened and improved entitlements for subsidiary protection beneficiaries, bringing their position more closely into line with that of refugees. Although some distinctions remain – notably in relation to the shorter duration of the residence permit granted to subsidiary protection holders and a right to 'core benefits' only for social assistance – other rights, including to work, health care, vocational training and integration facilities, are significantly improved. According to reports on national practice, a number of states accord identical rights to both refugee status and subsidiary protection holders. Subsidiary protection is thus a stronger form of status as a result.

Conclusion

The adoption of Article 15(c) of the Qualification Directive represents an important step by the European Union and its Member States to expand the scope of international protection under EU asylum law and practice. Extending beyond Member States' obligations under other human rights

---

[106] See e.g. Recital 26, 2004 Directive.

instruments, it has the potential to play a crucial role for many people fleeing violence stemming from national and international conflicts who do not qualify for refugee status. Its application in practice in recent years, however, has revealed significant variations in the application of key concepts by different Member States and a lack of shared understanding among national authorities of this important provision. Moreover, in at least some Member States, there appear to be cases where Article 15(c) protection might be granted through swift procedures to people who would otherwise qualify as refugees, a tendency that could threaten to undermine 1951 Convention status over time.

An opportunity to clarify Article 15(c)'s more complex elements arose in 2009, but the current formulation was retained to avoid the risk that its scope would be narrowed or limited further. It is thus likely to fall to the courts to provide further necessary guidance to ensure not only consistent outcomes across the European Union, but also broad and inclusive approaches to interpretation and application of the subsidiary protection definition to asylum-seekers fleeing violence in armed conflict in today's troubled global context.

APPENDIX I

Summary Conclusions on International Protection of Persons Fleeing Armed Conflict and Other Situations of Violence

The Office of the United Nations High Commissioner for Refugees (UNHCR) convened a roundtable on the International Protection of Persons Fleeing Armed Conflict and Other Situations of Violence in Cape Town, South Africa on 13 and 14 September 2012, hosted by the Refugee Rights Project of the University of Cape Town. The roundtable was organized as part of a broader project to develop Guidelines on International Protection[1] and to clarify the interpretation and application of international and regional refugee law instruments to persons fleeing armed conflict and other situations of violence across international borders. The background to the roundtable is a perception that the definition of a 'refugee' in the 1951 Convention Relating to the Status of Refugees ('1951 Convention')[2] and the 1967 Protocol Relating to the Status of Refugees ('1967 Protocol')[3] does not easily map on to the size,

---

[1] UNHCR, *Handbook and Guidelines on Procedures and Criteria for Determining Refugee Status under the 1951 Convention and the 1967 Protocol Relating to the Status of Refugees*, December 2011, HCR/1P/4/ENG/REV. 3, available at: www.unhcr.org/refworld/docid/4f33c8d92.html. The Guidelines complement and update the Handbook and should be read in combination with it.

[2] Convention relating to the Status of Refugees, 28 July 1951 (entered into force 22 April 1954), 189 UNTS 137 ('1951 Convention').

[3] Protocol Relating to the Status of Refugees, 31 January 1967 (entered into force 4 October 1967), 606 UNTS 267 ('1967 Protocol').

scale and character of many modern conflicts or violent situations and refugee movements. Meanwhile, a number of refugee and complementary/subsidiary protection instruments have been developed at regional and national levels to more explicitly cover persons fleeing, *inter alia*, the broader effects of armed conflict and other situations of violence. These developments raise questions about the relationship between these instruments and the 1951 Convention and the 1967 Protocol (hereafter jointly referred to as the 1951 Convention).

Participants included thirty experts from fifteen countries drawn from governments, NGOs, academia, the judiciary, the legal profession and international organizations. Four background papers and presentations by the authors, as well as two additional presentations, informed the discussion.[4]

These 'Summary Conclusions' do not necessarily represent the individual views of participants or UNHCR but reflect broadly the themes and understandings emerging from the discussion.

Understanding Contemporary Armed Conflicts and Other Situations of Violence

1. The second half of the twentieth century saw a steep rise in the number of internal armed conflicts and other forms of violent situations leading to mass displacement across borders. Since the end of the cold war, two main trends in the causes, character and impact of armed conflict and other situations of violence can be observed. Firstly, there has been a rise in non-international armed conflicts involving a diversity of armed actors along with different modes of violence, thus blurring the traditional boundaries between war and peace and between combatants and civilians. Secondly, while there has been a general decline in the lethality of armed conflicts,

---

[4] The background papers included (1) Theo Farrell and Olivier Schmitt, 'The Causes, Character and Conduct of Armed Conflict, and the Effects on Civilian Populations, 1990–2010', April 2012, PPLA/2012/03, available at: www.unhcr.org/refworld/docid/4f8c3fcc2.html; (2) Vanessa Holzer, 'The 1951 Refugee Convention and the Protection of People Fleeing Armed Conflict and Other Situations of Violence', September 2012, PPLA/2012/05, available at: www.unhcr.org/refworld/docid/50474f062.html; (3) Valerie Oosterveld, 'Women and Girls Fleeing Conflict and Generalized Violence: Gender and the Interpretation and Application of the 1951 Refugee Convention', September 2012, PPLA/2012/06, available at: www.unhcr.org/refworld/docid/504dcb172.html; (4) Marina Sharpe, 'Preliminary Assessment Report of Case Law and Other Primary Sources, 1969 OAU Refugee Convention and the Protection of People Fleeing Armed Conflict and Other Situations of Violence within the Context of Individual Status Determination Procedures', forthcoming. Presentations were also provided by Michael Reed-Hurtado on the interpretation and application of the 1984 Cartagena Declaration and Bonaventure Rutinwa on the relationship between the 1951 and the 1969 OAU Convention from an historical perspective. Both presentations will be published in due course.

there has been an increase in the targeting or terrorizing of civilians (and other forms of 'coercive violence' aimed, for example, at controlling the population). The use and availability of low-technological weaponry has also aided the spread of conflict into civilian areas, including urban settings. Meanwhile, the indirect effects of conflict – including poverty, economic decline, inflation, violence, disease, food insecurity and malnourishment and displacement – need to be taken into account.

2. Internal and external displacement can also be an indication of the intensity of the conflict, and its impacts, but it should not be seen in isolation from other factors. Depending on the situation, persons may be unable to leave their areas of habitual residence as they become trapped – sometimes periodically and sometimes cyclically – in the zone of conflict, including in situations of urban violence and warfare. Displacement has also been used as a direct military strategy in some conflicts, including in the form of 'ethnic cleansing' or genocide.

3. Quantitative data on armed conflicts remain unreliable, and systematic hidden errors in the collection and interpretation of data are not uncommon (see also paragraph 39). Such data may also be biased in favour of fatalities and may not capture harm other than deaths or other impacts such as trauma, inter-generational health problems, diminished female or minority participation in public life, disruption of education and so on. Any data should therefore be approached with great caution and should be triangulated with other information as part of an overall assessment. Quantitative data always need to be complemented by qualitative data.

4. On the causes of contemporary armed conflict and other situations of violence, it was noted that there is usually no singular explanation for a particular conflict and that there are multiple and overlapping causes, which may change over time. Different or similar causes may lead to the perpetuation of conflict or may reignite it. Reasons underlying armed conflict, or other situations of violence, range from political, ethnic or religious, to the exploitation of economic resources, to drugs trade and gang activities. Further, while the roundtable did not discuss in detail the meaning of 'other situations of violence', the phrase was used to refer to violence below the threshold of armed conflict.

5. The phenomenon of recruitment of child soldiers was mentioned explicitly as a pervasive characteristic of contemporary conflicts, including the challenges their cases present for refugee status decision-makers and adjudicators. One particular issue that arose in this context was how to assess voluntariness. While children may appear to make rational decisions to join armed groups or the armed forces, this decision cannot be determined to be voluntary in circumstances where the decision is based on fear or for the purposes of ensuring their own economic survival or safety.

The illegality of child recruitment is also an important factor in assessing their claims to refugee protection.[5]

Applying the 1951 Convention to Persons Fleeing Armed Conflict or Other Situations of Violence

6. The 1951 Convention is the primary instrument for the protection of refugees, including those fleeing armed conflict and other situations of violence. Nothing in the text, context or object and purpose of the 1951 Convention hinders its application to armed conflict or other situations of violence. In fact, the 1951 Convention makes no distinction between refugees fleeing peacetime or wartime situations. Drafted in the aftermath of the Second World War, the drafters understood that individuals fleeing from armed conflict and other situations of violence may have a well-founded fear of being persecuted for one or more 1951 Convention grounds. Yet, a wide variation in refugee recognition rates for persons from countries in conflict suggests divergences in the application of the 1951 Convention.[6] While there is some good state practice in applying the 1951 Convention to persons fleeing armed conflict and other situations of violence, there are also jurisdictions where erroneous or overly restrictive interpretations of the 1951 Convention refugee definition are commonplace. In still other countries, an over-reliance on the use of non-Convention protection is evident, for example, under complementary/subsidiary protection regimes, which can deny 1951 Convention refugees the protection they require and deserve.

7. For the purposes of applying the 1951 Convention refugee definition, classifying a particular situation as an armed conflict can be a relevant component of the background to the refugee claim, but it too frequently distorts the assessment of the basis for the claim, emphasizing issues around the generalized impact of violence rather than persecution, or around the credibility of the claim for protection. Participants noted that in every claim for refugee protection, it remains necessary to understand and analyse the factual situation in the country of origin in its proper

[5] Convention on the Rights of the Child, 20 November 1989 (entered into force 2 September 1990), 1577 UNTS 3 (CRC), Art. 38. Optional Protocol to the Convention on the Rights of the Child on the Involvement of Children in Armed Conflict, 25 May 2000 (entered into force 12 February 2002), 2173 UNTS 222, Arts. 2 and 3. Rome Statute of the International Criminal Court, 17 July 1998 (entered into force 1 July 2002), 2187 UNTS 90 (ICC Statute), Arts. 8(2)(b)(xxvi) and 8(2)(e)(vii).

[6] UNHCR, 'Safe at Last? Law and Practice in Selected EU Member States with Respect to Asylum-Seekers Fleeing Indiscriminate Violence', 27 July 2011, available at: www.unhcr.org/refworld/docid/4e2ee0022.html.

context, including the causes, character and impact of the conflict or violence on the applicant and others similarly situated and how the individual applicant is affected by the factual situation. Quality country-of-origin information should avoid generalizations about the conflict and may highlight groups that are persecuted.[7]

A Well-Founded Fear of Being Persecuted

8. A person's risk of being persecuted must be assessed in the context of the overall situation in the country of origin, taking into account general as well as individual circumstances. In armed conflict and other situations of violence, whole communities may suffer or be at risk of persecution. The fact that many or all members of particular communities may be equally at risk does not undermine the validity of any particular claim. The test is whether an individual's fear of being persecuted is well founded. In fact, at times, the impact of a conflict on an entire community strengthens, rather than weakens, the risk to any particular individual.

9. There is no basis in the 1951 Convention for holding that in armed conflict or other situations of violence an applicant needs to establish a risk of harm over and above that of others caught up in such situations (sometimes called a 'differentiated risk'). Further, there is nothing in the text of the 1951 Convention to suggest that a refugee has to be singled out for persecution, either generally or over and above other persons at risk of being persecuted. A person may have a well-founded fear of persecution that is shared by many others.

Persecution

10. Threats to life or freedom, serious human rights violations, including torture or inhuman or degrading treatment, and other forms of serious harm constitute persecution for the purposes of the refugee definition, whether committed in times of peace, armed conflict, or other situations of violence. Likewise, serious violations of international humanitarian law (IHL) can constitute persecution.[8] In the context of armed conflict and other situations of violence, no higher level of severity of harm is required

---

[7] UNHCR, 'Expert Meeting on Complementarities between International Refugee Law, International Criminal Law and International Human Rights Law: Summary Conclusions', July 2011, paras. 22–5, available at: www.unhcr.org/refworld/docid/4e1729d52.html.

[8] UNHCR, 'Expert Meeting on Complementarities between International Refugee Law, International Criminal Law and International Human Rights Law: Summary

for conduct to amount to persecution. The question is not whether persons would be treated worse in situations of conflict or violence than in times of peace, but whether the individual fears persecution on account of a protected ground.[9]

11. A risk of regular exposure to violent conduct and other consequences common in situations of conflict can amount to persecution within the meaning of Article 1(A)(2) of the 1951 Convention, either independently or cumulatively, depending on the seriousness of the conduct or its consequences. Such conduct can include more general conduct such as shelling and bombardments, cutting of food supplies, militarization of hospitals and schools and conduct – or the consequences thereof – that is more long term and indirect, such as food insecurity, poverty, collapse of the political, health care and education systems, or displacement. It can also include methods of warfare representing conduct that is more individual in nature such as security checks, house or office raids, interrogation, personal and property searches, forced evictions, sexual violence or restrictions on freedom of movement.

12. In regulating the conduct of hostilities, IHL can provide guidance to establish if certain conduct amounts to persecution for the purposes of applying the 1951 Convention refugee definition. However, there was a difference of opinion at the roundtable whether the IHL definition of 'armed conflict' was useful to the determination of refugee status and persecution. Determining whether a situation in the country of origin qualifies as an 'armed conflict' was considered to be a distraction from the refugee question, which revolves around what predicament the individual would face if he or she were returned to his or her country of origin, and in addition, many violent situations are not classed as 'armed conflicts' yet their means employed and their consequences may be just as violent or persecutory. At least one participant felt that the predicament analysis would give too wide a scope for subjective decision-making.[10]

Conclusions', July 2011, paras. 13–21, available at: www.unhcr.org/refworld/docid/4e1729d52.html.

[9] For example, see 'Guideline 1: Civilian Non-Combatants Fearing Persecution in Civil War Situations, Immigration and Refugee Board of Canada', available at: www.irb-cisr.gc.ca/eng/brdcom/references/pol/guidir/Pages/civil.aspx: 'A person taking no active part in hostilities associated with a civil war should be treated by the combatants humanely and without adverse consequences . . . The fact that the treatment feared by the claimant arises from the hostility felt, or the violence engaged in, by combatants directly involved in the civil war does not exclude the possibility that it could constitute persecution' (footnotes removed).

[10] In determining what constitutes an 'armed conflict', participants pointed to the fact there is no agreed definition, nor clarity on who decides whether an 'armed conflict' exists. Nonetheless, the International Committee of the Red Cross' Opinion Paper, 'How Is the

The Causal Link and the 1951 Convention Grounds

13. Determining which 1951 Convention ground(s) is of relevance for an applicant fleeing armed conflict and other situations of violence needs to be derived from the factual context, including the causes, character and impact of the feared harm.

14. The causal link (or nexus) required under the 1951 Convention definition refers to the refugee's predicament rather than the persecutor's mindset. Such a predicament may be affected by the motivation of the persecutor but also more broadly by the causes, character and foreseeable impact of the conflict or violence.

15. When assessing international protection for persons fleeing armed conflict and other situations of violence, each – and more than one – of the 1951 Convention grounds may be relevant. An analysis of the causes, character and impact of the conflict and/or violence is necessary to determine the relevant 1951 Convention ground(s) and the causal link with the well-founded fear of persecution. Claims from persons who have fled a conflict or violent situation can raise complex factual issues and are highly contextual, turning on the particular characteristics, attributes and background of the applicant viewed against the causes, character and impact of the conflict and violence.

16. The conflict and violence may be motivated or driven by ethnic, religious, political or social divisions or may affect people along ethnic, religious, political, social or gender lines. The conflict and violence may also have aspects that are outside the scope of the 1951 Convention, such as economic or criminal motivations, but these too are regularly interconnected with 1951 Convention grounds. These motivations, drivers and impact often imply the existence of a 1951 Convention ground for persons belonging to a certain race, nationality, religion or particular social group or having a certain political opinion.

17. In some armed conflicts or other situations of violence, harm may appear to be indiscriminate. However, the underlying causes, character and/or impact of the violence causing harm may reveal that it is in fact discriminate. For example, on the face of it, civilians in a particular conflict may appear to be at a general risk of harm from bombing, shelling, suicide attacks and/or the use of improvised explosive devices.

Term "Armed Conflict" Defined in International Humanitarian Law', March 2008, available at: www.icrc.org/eng/assets/files/other/opinion-paper-armed-conflict.pdf, was thought useful. See also UNHCR, 'Expert Meeting on Complementarities between International Refugee Law, International Criminal Law and International Human Rights Law: Summary Conclusions', July 2011, para. 22, available at: www.unhcr.org /refworld/docid/4e1729d52.html.

However, these methods of violence may also be used to target particular groups of civilians or the areas where they reside or gather because of their real or perceived ethnic, religious, political or social profiles. Where this is the case, these acts may be persecutory and linked to a 1951 Convention ground. Notably, too, violence may be both generalized (e.g. because it is experienced throughout the territory) and discriminate (e.g. because there are targeted attacks against particular groups) at the same time.

18. The question of imputed political, religious or other identities or views was also discussed, with a particular call for further research into imputed social group in the context of armed conflict and violence. There were also mixed views on whether 'civilians' could be a particular social group for the purposes of the refugee definition. Some participants considered that 'civilians' could only be a recognizable 'social group' in highly militarized societies. Others argued that the targeting of 'civilians' during a conflict ordinarily had political connotations.

19. To establish the causal link between a well-founded fear of persecution and a 1951 Convention ground, it is not necessary that the asylum-seeker is known to, or was sought out or targeted individually by, the persecutor(s). As acknowledged in UNHCR's 'Handbook on Procedures and Criteria for Determining Refugee Status', often the asylum-seeker may not be aware of the reasons for the persecution feared. It is not his or her duty to analyse his or her situation to such an extent as to identify the reasons in detail,[11] and this cannot be seen as a pre-condition for eligibility for protection.

Gender-Related Persecution in Armed Conflict

20. It was acknowledged that violence during situations of armed conflict directed at women and girls or men and boys on account of their gender, alone or in combination with other factors, can be persecutory.

21. Rape and other forms of gendered physical, sexual and psychological violence are common forms of persecution perpetrated in situations of armed conflict, particularly against women and girls and sometimes against men and boys. Rape in conflict is by definition persecutory irrespective of the purpose behind the rape or motivation of the perpetrator. The effects of rape, including social stigma and increased vulnerability to

---

[11] UNHCR, *Handbook and Guidelines on Procedures and Criteria for Determining Refugee Status under the 1951 Convention and the 1967 Protocol Relating to the Status of Refugees*, December 2011, HCR/1P/4/ENG/REV.3, para. 66, available at: www.unhcr.org/refworld/docid/4f33c8d92.html.

violence and discrimination, may also amount to persecution. Other forms of gender-related persecution common in armed conflict and other situations of violence include human trafficking, sexual slavery and conjugal slavery/forced marriage.

22. Both substantive and procedural/evidentiary issues were discussed. Five particular issues were raised. The first was the issue of credibility. In assessing the credibility of a claim for refugee status based on gender-related persecution, decision-makers need to ensure that they do not succumb to stereotyped assessments of how women or girls – or men or boys – respond (or are expected to respond) to such violence.

23. The second issue was that of the evidentiary standard of proof. For example, if rape against women and girls is widespread and/or systematic in a given conflict, a well-founded fear of persecution can be established merely by the fact of being a woman or girl (i.e. for reasons of her gender), yet research has shown that the claims of many victims or persons at risk of rape from countries in conflict are regularly rejected.[12] Gender-sensitive country-of-origin information was also highlighted: it is often not available, and at times, it may be inaccurate because of a lack of corroborative information on gender issues. It was noted that the same problem of lack of country-of-origin information was evident in children's claims as well as those based on sexual orientation and/or gender identity.

24. Third, in establishing persecution, it was noted that the after-effects or longer-term consequences of sexual and gender-based violence are often ignored or not fully taken into account. Such effects could include stigma, discrimination, social, cultural and economic exclusion, increased vulnerability to violence or threats of death. The absence of professional psychosocial services in countries of origin can be a relevant element in assessing a claim.

25. Fourth, the mischaracterization of acts of sexual and gender-based violence as committed, for example, for reasons of personal gratification rather than an exercise of power or political control, or private rather than state or political coercion, was also noted as a problem, including in respect of the relevant 1951 Convention ground. The focus on the motivations of the individual perpetrator is very difficult to assess with any accuracy and can distort and downplay the overall violence as well as

---

[12] H. Baillot, S. Cowan and V. E. Munro, 'Hearing the Right Gaps: Enabling and Responding to Disclosures of Sexual Violence within the UK Asylum Process', Social and Legal Studies 12 (2012), 269–96; H. Baillot, S. Cowan and V. E. Munro, 'Crossing Borders, Inhabiting Spaces: The (In)Credibility of Sexual Violence in Asylum Appeals', in S. Fitzgerald (ed.), Regulating the International Movement of Women: From Protection to Control (New York: Routledge, 2011), 111–31.

impunity created by the conflict. While recognizing that 'membership of a particular social group' is the typical ground applied in such cases, the other grounds – in particular, real or perceived political opinion, ethnicity and/or religion – may also apply, especially in conflicts that target women and girls as part of military strategies, or where women and girls advocate against their mistreatment during conflict.

26. Finally, it was noted that decision-makers often classify the risk of gender-related violence as part of the general indiscriminate conse-quences of conflict and therefore not persecutory in the sense of the 1951 Convention definition. This appears to be done without consis-tently considering the potential gender-related reasons for that violence (e.g. the various ways in which rape is used as a weapon of war or as 'coercive violence' to destroy the social fabric of the society) or the broader political and other dimensions of conflict.

Refugee Status under the 1969 OAU Convention and the 1984 Cartagena Declaration and the Relationship with the 1951 Convention Definition

27. While the 1951 Convention is the universal and primary legal protection instrument for refugees, regional refugee instruments complement the 1951 Convention. In particular, they incorporate the 1951 Convention refugee definition and also contain a further – extended – definition of a refugee.

28. In terms of rights or status of refugees following recognition as a refugee under the 1951 Convention or the regional refugee law instruments, there is no hierarchical relationship between the 1951 Convention definition and the regional refugee definitions contained in Article I(2) of the 1969 OAU Convention Governing the Specific Aspects of Refugee Problems in Africa and Conclusion III(3) of the 1984 Cartagena Declaration on Refugees (cf. subsidiary protection under the European Union Qualification Directive; see paragraphs 36 and 37). The 1969 OAU Convention and the 1984 Cartagena Declaration incorporate the rights granted to refugees under the 1951 Convention. The regional refugee definitions determine who is to be accorded international protection as a refugee, ensuring the widest possible exercise of fundamental rights and freedoms. The regional definitions, in particular Article I(2) of the 1969 OAU Convention, have a specific, but not exclusive, application to refu-gees in situations of mass displacement, making it easier to determine refugee status based on objective situational circumstances in the country of origin to which these definitions refer.

1969 OAU Convention

29. The 1969 OAU Convention, with a humanitarian object and purpose, was considered particularly relevant in the African context and contemporary forms of non-international armed conflict and other situations of violence. In addition to incorporating the 1951 Convention refugee definition, the 1969 OAU Convention also provides international protection to refugees on the basis of the objective situation in the country of origin, namely, 'external aggression, occupation, foreign domination or events seriously disturbing public order'. Despite this objective orientation, it was noted that the definition requires a causal link between the objective situation and the person's compulsion to leave and seek asylum. Where the objective situations referred to in the 1969 OAU Convention affect the whole of the country or territory from which the person has fled, the existence of a causal link between the situation and the compulsion to leave may be presumed to exist. In fact, recognition of refugee status on a prima facie basis – based on an objective assessment of the situation in the country of origin – developed as an accommodation technique or procedural/evidentiary shortcut for determining refugee status in mass-influx situations, although it was also noted that prima facie techniques are also applicable under the 1951 Convention (see paragraph 40).

30. Of the four 1969 OAU Convention situations, it was noted that 'events seriously disturbing public order' is the most commonly used ground, including to persons fleeing armed conflict, serious internal disturbances, gross violations of human rights or other similar situations.

31. Based on the material in the background paper,[13] and confirmed by the presentations from a number of African governments participating in the roundtable, three approaches to the relationship between the 1951 Convention and the 1969 OAU Conventions in individual refugee status-determination procedures were observed: firstly, a sequential approach in which an assessment on the basis of the criteria of the 1951 Convention refugee definition, as stipulated in Article I(1) of the 1969 OAU Convention, preceded the application of the 1969 OAU Convention's Article I(2) definition; secondly, a 'nature of flight' approach, in which the prevailing situation in the country of origin (e.g. an armed conflict) would lead to an initial application of the 1969 OAU Convention Article I(2) definition, rather than the 1951 Convention refugee definition; and thirdly, a pragmatic approach, in which the 1969 OAU Convention Article I(2) definition is applied for reasons of efficiency and ease.

[13] Marina Sharpe, 'The 1969 OAU Refugee Convention and the Protection of People Fleeing Armed Conflict and Other Situations of Violence in the Context of Individual Refugee Status Determination', forthcoming.

32. It was argued that the sequential approach more closely follows the scheme of the international and African instruments, with the 1951 Convention as the primary instrument. It was also thought to reflect the approach in other regions (Europe was mentioned specifically; see paragraph 36). At the same time, the 'nature of flight' and pragmatic approaches were also considered to be acceptable in situations where the cause of flight was clear. Also, as the rights and status of the 1969 OAU Convention Art I(2) are equivalent to those enjoyed by 1951 Convention refugees, common sense might argue in favour of the 'nature of flight' and pragmatic approaches. At the same time, further consideration needs to be given to any later disadvantage to people not assessed for protection under the 1951 Convention. Access to resettlement and cessation was noted explicitly. In relation to the latter, for example, exemption from cessation is based amongst others on establishing 'past persecution'.[14]

1984 Cartagena Declaration on Refugees

33. The 1984 Cartagena Declaration is a set of (non-binding) conclusions aimed at promoting the establishment of a protection regime in Latin America and ensuring basic treatment for refugees. It is based on the precepts contained in the 1951 Convention as well as the 1969 American Convention on Human Rights. It follows the developments in Africa, in particular, the 'objective circumstances' approach of the 1969 OAU Convention. The regional refugee definition in the 1984 Cartagena Declaration is meant to provide a concise reference point to expand humanitarian responses and develop national laws and policies.

34. The 1984 Cartagena Declaration in Conclusion III(3) calls on countries in Latin America to use a definition or concept of 'refugee' that, in addition to those covered by the 1951 Convention definition, also includes 'persons who have fled their country because their lives, safety or freedom have been threatened by generalized violence, foreign aggression, internal conflicts, massive violation of human rights or other circumstances which have seriously disturbed public order'. In the current environment in parts of the Americas, where in certain countries violence is escalating, the growth in individual refugee status-determination procedures and the

---

[14] UNHCR, 'Guidelines on International Protection No. 3: Cessation of Refugee Status under Article 1C(5) and (6) of the 1951 Convention Relating to the Status of Refugees' (the 'Ceased Circumstances Clauses'), 10 February 2003, HCR/GIP/03/03, available at: www.unhcr.org/refworld/docid/3e50de6b4.html. UNHCR, 'Guidelines on Exemption Procedures in Respect of Cessation Declarations', December 2011, available at: www .unhcr.org/refworld/docid/4eef5c3a2.html.

limited import of the CIREFCA Legal Document,[15] the need for guidelines on how the definition is to apply within individual procedures was emphasized. At least one participant encouraged caution in being too fixated on providing strict legal definitions of the separate elements in the definition, preferring instead the encouragement of a flexible 'humanitarian' approach to interpreting the elements in the definition. Others considered that this 'humanitarian' approach would not adequately respond to the needs of lawyers and adjudicators in individual refugee status-determination procedures.

35. The term 'generalized violence' contained in the 1984 Cartagena Declaration was discussed in some detail. It was felt, however, that rather than trying to settle a definition of the term, or of the other terms, it would be more helpful for a range of indicators or a 'spectrum' approach to be developed, including consideration of temporal and spatial dimensions, such as gravity/severity, intensity and effects/consequences of the violence, violations or disturbances.

Subsidiary Protection under the EU Qualification Directive and the Relationship with the 1951 Convention Definition

36. The EU Qualification Directive[16] acknowledges the primacy of the 1951 Convention and requires that it is first determined who qualifies as a refugee in accordance with the 1951 Convention before assessing subsidiary protection. It is both a sequential and a hierarchical (in terms of rights) relationship, which is different from the relationship of the 1969 OAU Convention and the 1984 Cartagena Declaration to the 1951 Convention (see paragraph 28). However, in practice, especially in the context of persons fleeing armed conflict and other situations of violence, the sequential assessments are not always undertaken adequately. Frequently, it appears that the assessment of international protection

---

[15] 'Principles and Criteria for the Protection and Assistance of Central American Refugees, Returnees and Internally Displaced in Latin America' ('CIREFCA Legal Document'), UN, CIREFCA, Ciudad de Guatemala, 29–31 May 1989, Distr. General CIREFCA 89/9, April 1989. (English version) 'Principles and Criteria for the Protection of and Assistance to Central American Refugees, Returnees and Displaced Persons in Latin America', January 1990, available at: www.unhcr.org/refworld/docid/4370ca8b4.html.

[16] European Union: Council of the European Union, *Directive 2011/95/EU of the European Parliament and of the Council of 13 December 2011 on Standards for the Qualification of Third-Country Nationals or Stateless Persons as Beneficiaries of International Protection, for a Uniform Status for Refugees or for Persons Eligible for Subsidiary Protection, and for the Content of the Protection Granted (recast)*, 20 December 2011, L337/9, available at: www.unhcr.org/refworld/docid/4f197df02.html.

needs on the basis of the 1951 Convention is rather superficial, resulting in an over-reliance on the application of Article 15(c) of the EU Qualification Directive on the basis of designating the situation in a country or region as meeting the threshold for the application of Article 15(c) of the EU Qualification Directive. According to Article 15(c) of the EU Qualification Directive, people qualify for subsidiary protection when faced with a real risk of suffering serious harm consisting of a 'serious and individual threat to a civilian's life or person by reason of indiscriminate violence in situations of international or internal armed conflict'.

37. On the meaning of 'armed conflict' in Article 15(c) of the EU Qualification Directive, it was agreed that it does not have an autonomous meaning, though IHL should be regarded as informative and not determinative. As noted earlier in paragraph 12, there are situations that may not meet the threshold of armed conflict within the meaning of IHL, yet persons displaced by those situations are nonetheless in need of international protection as a refugee or should receive subsidiary protection under the EU Qualification Directive. What should be determinative in providing international protection is the need for international protection, not the legal qualification of the conflict that generates that need.[17]

Procedural and Credibility-Related Issues

38. Armed conflict and other situations of violence often create, for entire groups, a risk of being persecuted, including in the form of threats to life, safety or freedom on one or more of the 1951 Convention grounds. As a result, each member of the group seeking international protection may be regarded prima facie as a refugee under the relevant instrument.

39. While in general the burden of proof lies on the person submitting the claim, the obligation to gather and analyse all relevant facts and supporting evidence and determining eligibility for refugee status is shared between the applicant and the decision-maker. This is particularly important if the country of origin is experiencing armed conflict or another situation of violence as this makes obtaining information and documentation in general – as well as in relation to the individual – more difficult. It is therefore also important that applicants are given the benefit of the doubt, notably in the absence of supporting evidence.

---

[17] UNHCR, 'Expert Meeting on Complementarities between International Refugee Law, International Criminal Law and International Human Rights Law: Summary Conclusions', July 2011, para. 24, available at: www.unhcr.org/refworld/docid/4e1729d52.html.

40. In practice, such evidential bars to recognition for individual applicants could be obviated by declarations or designations of entire countries or specific regions of a country as areas from which, because of the prevailing conditions, all persons who left between relevant dates, and potentially for specific reasons, are granted refugee status. Individual applicants need then only establish their identity, their country or region of origin and date of departure. In such scenarios, it still remains necessary to determine, if relevant in the individual case and to the extent possible, that exclusion provisions do not apply.

41. Decision-makers should use statistical data with great caution when assessing international protection needs. Different sources use different methodologies, often depending on their motivation for collecting statistics, resulting in substantial divergences. Statistical data can provide an indication of the impact of conflict and violence on the civilian population, but they can be inconclusive or unreliable regarding the risk, harm and/or relevant 1951 Convention ground.

Next Steps

Participants encouraged UNHCR to develop international protection guidelines on these issues, including the regional refugee definitions and the EU Qualification Directive.

Expert Roundtable
Interpretation of the Extended Refugee Definition Contained in the
1984 Cartagena Declaration on Refugees,
Montevideo, Uruguay,
15–16 October 2013

APPENDIX II

Summary Conclusions on the Interpretation of the Extended Refugee Definition in the 1984 Cartagena Declaration

The Office of the United Nations High Commissioner for Refugees (UNHCR) convened an expert roundtable on the interpretation of the extended refugee definition contained in the 1984 Cartagena Declaration on Refugees ('Cartagena Declaration'), in Montevideo, Uruguay, 15–16 October 2013. The expert roundtable was organized as part of the 'Cartagena + 30' events to mark the thirtieth anniversary of the Cartagena Declaration in 2014 and a broader project to develop guidelines on international protection on the refugee status of persons fleeing armed conflict and other situations of violence.[1]

The background to the expert roundtable is that the Cartagena Declaration, in particular, the extended refugee definition contained in Conclusion III (Cartagena refugee definition), remains a solid protection tool for the Americas region, yet there is a need for further guidance on its interpretation in respect of the current protection challenges in the region. These 'Summary Conclusions' will contribute to guide the interpretation of the Cartagena refugee definition to persons fleeing, *inter alia*, the broader effects of armed

---

[1] For more on the broader project, see UNHCR, 'Summary Conclusions on International Protection of Persons Fleeing Armed Conflict and Other Situations of Violence, Roundtable 13 and 14 September 2012, Cape Town, South Africa', available at: www .refworld.org/docid/50d32e5e2.html.

conflict and other situations of violence. They also explain its relationship to the 1951 Convention and the 1967 Protocol (hereafter jointly referred to as the '1951 Convention').

Participants included experts from six countries in the region drawn from government, the judiciary, legal practitioners, international organizations, NGOs and academia. These 'Summary Conclusions' do not necessarily represent the individual views of participants or UNHCR but reflect broadly the themes and understandings emerging from the discussion.

Overarching Considerations to Guide Interpretation

Protection-Oriented, Purposeful Interpretation

1. The Cartagena Declaration is a regional protection instrument, adopted in 1984 by a group of experts from several Latin-American countries,[2] as the result of a Colloquium on International Protection for Refugees and Displaced Persons in Central America, Mexico and Panama held in Cartagena de Indias, Colombia. The colloquium focused on the legal and humanitarian problems affecting those displaced by conflict and violence in Central America and, because of this focus, serves as a common and neutral language for states and other stakeholders to develop a harmonized regional refugee protection framework in the context of humanitarian crises. The Cartagena Declaration reaffirms the centrality of the right to asylum and the principle of *non-refoulement*, the importance of searching actively for durable solutions and the necessity of co-ordination and harmonization of universal and regional systems and national efforts.

2. Although included in a non-binding regional instrument, the Cartagena refugee definition has attained a particular standing in the region, not least through its incorporation into fourteen national laws and state practice. The Cartagena Declaration, as a protection instrument, has at its foundation the commitment to grant the treatment provided by the 1951 Convention to individuals not covered by the classic refugee definition but who are nevertheless in need of international protection.[3] It drew inspiration from the 1969 OAU Convention Governing Specific Aspects

---

[2] Belize, Colombia, Costa Rica, El Salvador, Guatemala, Honduras, Mexico, Nicaragua, Panama and Venezuela.

[3] See Recommendation E of the Final Act of the 1951 United Nations Conference of Plenipotentiaries on the Status of Refugees and Stateless Persons, United Nations Conference of Plenipotentiaries on the Status of Refugees and Stateless Persons, 25 July 1951, A/CONF.2/108/Rev.1, available at: www.refworld.org/docid/40a8a7394 .html.

of Refugee Problems in Africa ('OAU Convention'), which incorporates a similarly worded extended refugee definition, as well as the doctrine of the Inter-American Commission on Human Rights.[4] As such, its interpretation is to be informed by international and regional human rights and humanitarian law, especially the norms and standards of the 1969 American Convention on Human Rights, and the evolving case law of the inter-American human rights bodies. Its adoption represented a humanitarian and pragmatic response by Latin American states to the movements of groups of persons from conflict and other forms of indiscriminate threats to life, security and freedom.

3. Furthermore, the humanitarian and protection orientation of the instrument calls for an inclusive, evolving and flexible interpretation.[5] Nonetheless, some guidance as to the scope of the definition's terms is needed to ensure consistency and predictability across the region and across cases, suggesting that where the ordinary meaning is not clear, the text should be given a purposive or teleological interpretation.

Interplay between the Universal and Regional Refugee Definitions

4. The 1951 Convention is the primary legal instrument for the protection of refugees, as recognized also by the Cartagena Declaration. The 1951 Convention's definition of a refugee is centred on persecution for reasons of race, religion, nationality, membership of a particular social group or political opinion. There is a perception that this definition does not easily map onto the size, scale and character of many modern conflicts or violent situations and refugee movements.[6] Yet, the 1951 Convention makes no distinction between refugees fleeing peacetime or conflict situations, and further, the impact of a conflict on an entire community can strengthen,

---

[4] Conclusion III (3), Cartagena Declaration on Refugees.

[5] There was consensus on the need to move beyond the overly legalistic approach presented in 'Principles and Criteria for the Protection and Assistance of Central American Refugees, Returnees and Internally Displaced in Latin America', CIREFCA, 89/9, April 1989, available at: www.refworld.org/docid/4370ca8b4.html), and rather focus on new developments in state practice and the value of the interpretation of the evolving case law of the inter-American human rights bodies.

[6] Such a view may be related to an interpretation out of context (or misinterpretation) of paragraphs 164 and 165 of the UNHCR 'Handbook on Procedures and Criteria for Determining Refugee Status under the 1951 Convention and the 1967 Protocol Relating to the Status of Refugees and Guidelines on Procedures and Criteria for Determining Refugee Status under the 1951 Convention and the 1967 Protocol Relating to the Status of Refugees', 1979, re-issued December 2011, HCR/1P/4/ENG/REV. 3, available at: www.refworld.org/docid/4f33c8d92.html.

rather than weaken, the risk to any particular individual. Moreover, methods of warfare are often used as forms of persecution.[7]

5. At the same time, it is recognized that persons fleeing from situations of indiscriminate violence without the necessary element of persecution linked to a 1951 Convention ground are not refugees within the meaning of the 1951 Convention.[8]

6. The wording of the Cartagena Declaration suggests the complementary nature of its extended regional refugee definition, to encompass a broader category of persons in need of international protection who may not meet the 1951 Convention definition. This approach reflects its principal purpose as a practical tool for extending protection in humanitarian situations beyond those foreseen by the 1951 Convention definition. There may, however, be situations that might trigger the application of both refugee definitions, cases of overlap or where it cannot be precluded that some persons might meet the criteria of both definitions.[9]

7. Given that there is no difference in the status or rights afforded to persons recognized as refugees under either the Cartagena refugee definition or the 1951 Convention definition at the national level, in terms of both legislation and state practice, dual recognition should not be of material consequence in most cases. For the purposes of legal certainty, however, a proper interpretation of each definition is to be encouraged, with a sequential procedural approach to adjudication being recommended.[10] Adjudicators need also bear in mind that the Cartagena protection system should be implemented in a manner that strengthens and complements, rather than undermines, the 1951 Convention regime.

Substantive Analysis of the Elements of the Cartagena Refugee Definition

Hence the definition or concept of a refugee to be recommended for use in the region is one which, in addition to containing the elements of the 1951

---

[7] UNHCR, 'Summary Conclusions on International Protection of Persons Fleeing Armed Conflict and Other Situations of Violence'.

[8] Caution should be exercised in applying the 1951 Convention definition as the source of the violence may seem on the surface to be generalized. Upon closer examination of the context, however, it may become evident that the situation in fact involves the targeting of particular individuals or groups of individuals for reasons recognized by the 1951 Convention. Violence is often not undertaken for its own sake but has a deeper underlying purpose or target.

[9] In some cases, for example, persons fleeing a situation of indiscriminate violence may also have a fear of persecution in terms of the 1951 Convention refugee definition.

[10] A 'sequential procedural approach' means that a claim for refugee status would be assessed, firstly, pursuant to the 1951 Convention definition and only if the claim fails in that assessment would the Cartagena extended definition be considered.

Convention and the 1967 Protocol, includes among refugees persons who have fled their country because their lives, security or freedom have been threatened by generalized violence, foreign aggression, internal conflicts, massive violation of human rights or other circumstances which have seriously disturbed public order.[11]

Scope of the Cartagena Refugee Definition

8. The extended refugee definition of the Cartagena Declaration aims to provide protection from situational or group-based risks. The five 'situational events' of the Cartagena refugee definition are characterized by the indiscriminate, unpredictable or collective nature of the risks they present to a person or group of persons, or even to the population at large.

9. As with any refugee claim, the Cartagena refugee definition requires an examination of the situation in the country of origin as well as the particular situation of the individual or group of persons who seek protection as refugees. The focus of the refugee assessment is, however, on the exposure of the individual or group of persons to the risks inherent in the five situations contained in the definition. An illustrative example of this would be civilians caught between confrontations between armed groups fighting for control over the territory, which endangers the lives and security of anyone living in the area. The risk for the individuals in this situation stems from being 'in the wrong place at the wrong time'. This example underlines the temporal and spatial/geographical dimensions of the risk, essential components of the Cartagena refugee definition. The Cartagena Declaration also covers the indirect effects of the five situational events – including poverty, economic decline, inflation, violence, disease, food insecurity and malnourishment and displacement.

10. At the same time, the Cartagena refugee definition is not intended to be an all-encompassing definition for every situation in which persons are compelled to leave their countries of origin and cross an international border. While states may choose to apply the Cartagena refugee definition to persons compelled to leave because of natural or ecological disasters, they are not, strictly speaking, protected pursuant to the Cartagena refugee definition.

11. As the Cartagena definition focuses on indiscriminate threats or risks, authorities are advised, where possible, to adopt a consistent approach to persons fleeing the same country (or area within a country) in similar

---

[11] Conclusion III (3), Cartagena Declaration on Refugees.

circumstances. This would contribute towards removing protection gaps in the region and inconsistency between cases.

Elements of the Cartagena Refugee Definition

12. The Cartagena refugee definition contains three criteria: (1) the person needs to be outside his or her country, (2) the country in question is experiencing at least one of the situational events and (3) the person's life, security or freedom is threatened (at risk) as a result of one or more of the situational events.

Outside Country of Origin

13. For the purposes of the extended definition, the concept 'out of the country' is to be interpreted in line with the 1951 Convention refugee definition's understanding of this term, to encompass not only the country of nationality/citizenship but also, in the case of stateless persons, the country of habitual residence.

Situational Events

14. Guided by the protection-purpose of the Cartagena Declaration, the situational events mentioned in the extended refugee definition are to be given their ordinary meaning, wherever possible, and interpreted in an evolutionary way so that they remain relevant to apply to new or unpredictable events or situations.

15. 'Generalized violence' is not a term of art, nor does it have a strict or closed definition. Adopting a case-by-case approach, the term would encompass situations characterized by violence that is indiscriminate and sufficiently widespread to the point of affecting large groups of persons or entire populations, compelling their flight.

16. As it is not a term found in international humanitarian law (IHL), participants strongly argued that it should not be circumscribed by the interpretation of the term in the CIREFCA document, which appears to restrict its application to situations of armed conflict as defined under IHL.[12] Drawing instead on international human rights law, the more appropriate approach was considered to be that of identifying indicators of the type and level of violence persisting in the country of origin.[13]

---

[12] CIREFCA.

[13] The Inter-American Commission on Human Rights (IACHR) has referred to similar indicators when describing situations of 'widespread violence' in some countries in the region. These include, but are not limited to, the following: (a) the number of violent

Situations of generalized violence would clearly include situations involving massive as well as serious violations of human rights. Notably, it is not always the intensity of the violence that would render it generalized but rather its geographical spread and density.

17. Situations of generalized violence would encompass violence carried out by state as well as non-state actors, in the latter in situations where the will or capacity of the state to provide protection to those under its jurisdiction is inadequate. That said, it is the situation on the ground, and the risk that such violence presents, that is at issue – rather than the question of state responsibility.

18. The effects of this type of violence would also be a relevant consideration, including whether the violence is sustained over time and/or space.

19. 'Foreign aggression' is related to the terms 'aggression', 'war of aggression' and 'act of aggression', as defined under international law. The CIREFCA document equates the concept to the definition provided by UNGA Resolution 3314 (XXIX) of 1974 as including 'the use of armed force by a State against the sovereignty, territorial integrity or political independence of another State, or in any manner inconsistent with the Charter of the United Nations, as set out in this definition.'[14] The same approach is

incidents as well as the number of victims of those incidents is very high; (b) the prevailing violence inflicts heavy suffering among the population; (c) violence manifests itself in most egregious forms, such as massacres, torture, mutilation, cruel, inhuman and degrading treatments, summary executions, kidnappings, disappearances of persons and gross breaches to IHL; (d) the perpetration of acts of violence is often aimed at causing terror and, eventually, creating a situation such that individuals are left with no option other than flee the area affected; (e) violence can emanate from state and non-state agents, and when it emanates from the first, or from others acting at the instigation or with the acquiescence of state's authorities, the authors enjoy impunity; (f) where violence emanates from non-state agents, authorities are unable to effectively control them; and (g) the level and extent of violence are such that the normal functioning of society is seriously impaired. For a more detailed analysis, see e.g. IACHR, 'Violence and Discrimination against Women in the Armed Conflict in Colombia', chap. II, OAS/Ser. L/V/II Doc. 67, 18 October 2006, 11; IACHR, 'Report on the Situation of Human Rights in Jamaica', chap. II, 'Citizen, Security and Human Rights', and chap. III, 'Administration of Justice', OAS/Ser. L/V/II.144 Doc. 12, 10 August 2012, 5 and 27; IACHR, 'Report on the Situation of Human Rights in the Republic of Guatemala: Introduction, Conclusions and Recommendations', OAS/Ser. L/V/II.53 Doc. 21, Rev. 2. 13 October 1981; and IACHR, 'Report on the Situation of Human Rights in the Republic of Guatemala: Conclusions and Recommendations', OAS/Ser. L/V/II.61 Doc. 47, Rev. 1. October 5 1983.

[14] UNGA res. 3314(XXIX), 14 December 1974, Annex, Art. 3, enumerates the following acts, regardless of a declaration of war, as qualifying as aggression: 'the invasion or attack by the armed forces of a State of the territory of another State, military occupation, however temporary, resulting from such invasion or attack, or any annexation by the use of force of the territory of another State or part thereof; bombardment by the armed forces of a State against the territory of another State or the use of any weapons by a State against

followed in Article 8bis of the Rome Statue of the International Criminal Court,[15] equating it to the crime leading to an international armed conflict as understood under IHL. The reference to international armed conflict was accepted by participants as the correct interpretation of 'foreign aggression' for the purposes of applying the Cartagena refugee definition, consistent with the object and purpose of the Cartagena Declaration and as widely understood both in its national and international senses.[16] Thus, persons fleeing the effects of an international armed conflict would be covered by the Cartagena refugee definition, applying the 'foreign aggression' component.

20. It was acknowledged that the term 'internal conflicts' in the Cartagena refugee definition has traditionally been interpreted by Latin American countries to reflect 'non-international armed conflict' (NIAC) provided by Article 1 of Protocol II to the Geneva Conventions of 1949 and under the conditions of application set in Article 3 common to the Geneva Conventions of 1949. While accepting that internal conflicts so characterized would be covered by the Cartagena refugee definition, it was stressed that this narrow approach does not match the protection purpose of the Cartagena Declaration, and keeping the approach in line with other regional protection instruments and the intention of the drafters of the Cartagena Declaration to respond to humanitarian crises, IHL was considered to be informative, though not determinative, of whether an internal conflict exists, as should the qualifications made by the parties

---

the territory of another State; the blockade of the ports or coasts of a State by the armed forces of another State; an attack by the armed forces of a State on the land, sea or air forces, or marine and air fleets of another State; the use of armed forces of one State which are within the territory of another State with the agreement of the receiving State, in contravention of the conditions provided for in the agreement or any extension of their presence in such territory beyond the termination of the agreement; the action of a State in allowing its territory, which it has placed at the disposal of another State, to be used by that other State for perpetrating an act of aggression against a third State; the sending by or on behalf of a State of armed bands, groups, irregular or mercenaries, which carry out acts of armed force against another State of such gravity as to amount to the acts listed above, or its substantial involvement therein.' See CIREFCA. See also *Case Concerning Military and Paramilitary Activities in and against Nicaragua (Nicaragua v. United States of America); Merits*, International Court of Justice (ICJ), 27 June 1986, available at: www.refworld.org/docid/4023a44d2.html.

[15] See, for summary, www.iccnow.org/?mod=aggression.

[16] See also ICRC, 'How Is the Term "Armed Conflict" Defined in International Humanitarian Law?', opinion paper, March 2008, available at: www.icrc.org/eng/resources/documents/article/other/armed-conflict-article-170308.htm: 'The armed confrontation must reach *a minimum level of intensity* and the parties involved in the conflict must show *a minimum of organization.*'

involved or affected by it.[17] There are situations of armed violence, for example, that may not meet the threshold of a NIAC for IHL purposes or where the status of the situation is unclear, yet the life, security or freedoms of civilians are at risk and they are in need of international protection. Likewise, the classification of a particular situation of armed violence as a NIAC is far from straightforward, involving at times political – rather than legal – considerations.[18]

21. Participants pointed to useful interpretative guidance on 'massive violations of human rights' in the jurisprudence of the Inter-American Court of Human Rights (the Court). The term 'massive' has been seen in relation to the scale or magnitude of the violations reported; for example, in contexts where the precise identification of victims is difficult due to the extent of the human rights violations perpetrated against groups of persons or entire communities.[19] Additionally, where the effects of the violations go beyond the actual/direct victims to reach other segments of the population or even the society as a whole, the Cartagena refugee definition would be activated. The elements of planning and organization on the side of the perpetrator, whether state or non-state, could also be indicia, although not a requirement. In cases of non-state actors, state responsibility is engaged where the authorities are either unwilling or unable to protect their citizens by failing to prevent, investigate, prosecute and sanction these violations. In this context, forced displacement

---

[17] For example, while a UN Security Council designation of a situation as a non-international armed conflict would be sufficient for the purposes of the Cartagena refugee definition, such a qualification cannot be a requirement. See also UNHCR, 'Expert Meeting on Complementarities between International Refugee Law, International Criminal Law and International Human Rights Law: Summary Conclusions', July 2011, para. 24, available at: www.refworld.org/docid/4e1729d52.html.

[18] By way of comparison, see also *Aboubacar Diakité* v. *Commissaire général aux réfugiés et aux apatrides*, C-285/12, European Union: Court of Justice of the European Union (CJEU), 30 January 2014, available at: www.refworld.org/docid/52ea51f54.html, in which the CJEU in interpreting the term 'internal armed conflict' as used in Article 15(c) of the European Union's *Council Directive 2004/83/EC of 29 April 2004*, 30 September 2004, OJL 304/12, stated that because the concept of 'internal armed conflict' is not the term used in IHL it should be given an autonomous interpretation to cover the situation in which a state's armed forces confront one or more armed groups or in which two or more armed groups confront each other within the territory of a state. No requirement of intensity or organization of the parties was required, according to the CJEU.

[19] The regulations of the court, approved in 2009, foresee in its Article 35 that in situations in which it is not possible to identify the victims of 'massive or collective' human rights violations, the petition or communication submitted by the Commission (Inter-American Commission on Human Rights) to the Court can nevertheless be exceptionally admitted for judgement.

may, in itself, amount to a massive violation of human rights[20] or lead to other serious human violations. The Cartagena Declaration makes no distinction between the types of rights that may be at issue for protection purposes, although protection would only be provided where such massive violations of human rights give rise to threats to life, security or freedoms.

22. It is important to note that such pronouncements of the Inter-American Commission or the Court are not required to qualify a situation as one of massive violations of human rights. That said, the existence of such pronouncements, or provisional[21] or precautionary measures,[22] in a given context would be a strong indication that such a situation exists. The statements of international human rights bodies or courts might also be used as reference material.

23. A similar approach is found in the CIREFCA document, which refers to situations where 'violations are carried out on a large scale and affect the human rights and fundamental freedoms as defined in the Universal Declaration of Human Rights and other relevant instruments'.[23] It further refers to, and has been followed in state practice, both 'qualitative' (serious, gross) and 'quantitative' (consistent) criteria, such as 'gross and consistent pattern' of human rights violations. Importantly, however, should the human rights violations, despite being massive, single out or target particular persons or groups of persons on account of their race, religion, nationality, membership of a particular social group or political opinion, the person or group would be a 1951 Convention refugee.

24. 'Other circumstances which have seriously disturbed public order', and its counterpart in the OAU Convention, is the less clearly understood phrase. In the regional context, it is the least applied when determining cases under the Cartagena refugee definition. The notion of 'public order', while not having a universally accepted definition, can be interpreted in the

---

[20] In most cases, force displacement comes as a consequence of grave and extended violations of human rights.

[21] Provisional measures are an instrument used by the court to prevent irreparable harm to the rights and freedoms ensured under the American Convention on Human Rights of persons who are in a situation of extreme gravity and urgency. The measures are ordered *ex officio* or at the request of a party and result in a protection request to the respondent state of the alleged victim(s).

[22] Article 25 of the Rules of Procedure of the Commission establishes that, in serious and urgent situations, the Commission may, on its own initiative or at the request of a party, request that a state adopt precautionary measures to prevent irreparable harm to persons or to the subject matter of the proceedings in connection with a pending petition or case, as well as to persons under the jurisdiction of the state concerned, independently of any pending petition or case.

[23] CIREFCA, para. 34.

context of the Cartagena refugee definition as referring to the peace and security/stability of the society and the normal functioning of the institutions of the state. This can take place in times of conflict and/or peace.

25. In the jurisprudence of the Inter-American Court of Human Rights, it has been defined by reference in part to the recourse of states to Article 27 of the American Convention on Human Rights (ACDH)[24] in cases of declaration of a state of emergency.[25] However, a declaration of a state of emergency should not be seen as a prerequisite for existence of a 'circumstance disturbing public order,' albeit it would ordinarily be indicative of such a situation.

26. The relationship between the 'public order' situation and the other situations in the Cartagena definition was discussed. It was considered by some that inclusion of the language of 'other' could reflect an intention to provide states with some flexibility to grant protection in circumstances that either do not meet the threshold of violence of the other four situations reflected in the Cartagena refugee definition or which do not match the character of the other situations. While it is open to states to adopt an interpretation that the Cartagena refugee definition can provide protection to persons fleeing natural disasters, for example, it was accepted that such an approach is not proscribed.[26]

---

[24] Article 27, 'Suspension of Guarantees': '1. In time of war, public danger, or other emergency that threatens the independence or security of a State Party, it may take measures derogating from its obligations under the present Convention to the extent and for the period of time strictly required by the exigencies of the situation, provided that such measures are not inconsistent with its other obligations under international law and do not involve discrimination on the ground of race, colour, sex, language, religion, or social origin.'

[25] Corte IDH. *Caso Bámaca Velásquez v. Guatemala, Fondo.* Sentencia de 25 de noviembre de 2000. Ser. C No. 70, paras. 143 and 174. Véase también Corte IDH. *Caso Juan Humberto Sánchez v. Honduras. Excepción Preliminar, Fondo, Reparaciones y Costas.* Sentencia de 7 de junio de 2003. Ser. C No. 99, paras. 86 and 111; Corte IDH. *Caso Baena Ricardo y otros v. Panamá. Fondo, Reparaciones y Costas.* Sentencia de 2 de febrero de 2001. Ser. C No. 72, paras. 126, 127, 168 and 172.; Corte IDH. *Caso Hilaire, Constantine y Benjamin y otros v. Trinidad y Tobago. Fondo, Reparaciones y Costas.* Sentencia de 21 de junio de 2002. Ser. C No. 94, para. 101; Corte IDH. *Caso Del Caracazo v. Venezuela. Reparaciones y Costas.* Sentencia de 29 de agosto de 2002. Ser. C No. 95, para. 127. Véase también Corte IDH. *Caso del Caracazo v. Venezuela. Fondo.* Sentencia de 11 de noviembre de 1999. Ser. C No. 58, para. 2(e); Corte IDH. *Caso Bulacio v. Argentina. Fondo, Reparaciones y Costas.* Sentencia de 18 de Septiembre de 2003. Ser. C No. 100, para. 124; Corte IDH. *Caso Zambrano Vélez y otros v. Ecuador. Fondo, Reparaciones y Costas.* Sentencia de 4 de julio de 2007. Ser. C No. 166, paras. 51–2. Ver también, *Caso Montero Aranguren y Otros (Retén de Catia).* Sentencia de 5 de julio de 2006. Ser. C No. 150, pára. 78.

[26] CIREFCA.

27. A novel suggestion was put forward by one participant that for the Cartagena refugee definition to be activated/triggered, it would only be necessary to meet the threshold set in the 'other circumstances which have seriously disturbed public order' element of the definition (taking into account that the other four situational events presuppose/imply the alteration of the public order).[27] Others cautioned against such an approach, however, as the ground is the least applied by state practice, and hence there seems to be the least common understanding regarding its interpretation. Further, such an interpretation could lead to rendering immaterial the other four situations of the definition, limiting in fact the scope of the Cartagena refugee definition and its object and purpose of extending refugee protection to persons fleeing different circumstances.

Risk to Life, Security or Freedom

28. The third element or criterion of the Cartagena refugee definition is the link between one of the 'situational events' and the risk this poses to the 'life, security or freedom' of the individual or group of individuals. The 'threat' or 'risk' element set out in the extended definition connotes the possibility of harm being inflicted on a person or group of persons; it does not imply that the harm has actually materialized. The link to 'life, security or freedom' likewise should not be interpreted in a manner as to curtail or restrict the scope of protection granted to persons fleeing these situations of violence unnecessarily, such as to import an individualized assessment as to risk equivalent to the 1951 Convention definition.[28] In fact, proximity of – temporal and/or spatial/geographical – or imminence of the threat would suffice to justify the need for international protection under the Cartagena refugee definition.[29] In most cases, the situational event will per se be such as to establish the link/risk automatically. State practice has also recognized *sur place* claims.

---

[27] See D. J. Cantor and D. Trimiño Mora, 'A Simple Solution to War Refugees? The Latin American Expanded Definition and Its Relationship to IHL', in D. J. Cantor and J. F. Durieux (eds.), *Refuge from Inhumanity? War Refugees and International Humanitarian Law* (Leiden, Netherlands: Martinus Nijhoff, 2014), 10: 'It is also, quite simply, beside the point, since the "other circumstances" element functions as a general minimum threshold that renders precise definition of the preceding elements largely irrelevant for the purposes of qualification for refugee status. A focus on "circumstances seriously disturbing public order" as the main referent for the objective situation element is therefore appropriate, as persons fleeing the situations described by other elements will also fall into this more general one.'

[28] Doing otherwise would make it largely redundant as a tool for extending the scope of international protection provided under the 1951 refugee definition.

[29] In generalized violence situations, the threat may be self-evident, and only the proximity, in terms of time and/or place, needs to be established for the risk element to be fulfilled.

29. The 'threat' element is distinct from the concept of 'well-founded fear' in the 1951 Convention definition, in that it should be understood as requiring a lower threshold of proof. The concept of persecution is also completely absent in the Cartagena refugee definition; therefore, there is no requirement under the Cartagena refugee definition of a discriminatory, intentional or individualized aspect of the harm feared. In fact, the Cartagena refugee definition was oriented towards group situations. The focus of this definition is not on the personal circumstances of the individual fleeing the harm/danger but on the objective circumstances in the country of origin. The personal circumstances of the individual will not therefore play a determining role.[30]

Procedural Approaches in Individual Procedures

30. State practice has generally followed a *sequential* or *phased* approach in relation to the application of the 1951 Convention definition and the Cartagena refugee definition. However, this practice is not consistent across the region.

31. States have resorted to other procedural approaches, in particular, circumstances, to deal with country-specific situations, for example.[31] This may be the case when an increase in the numbers of asylum applications from one country is being registered. In these cases, a 'nature of the flight' or 'pragmatic' approach may be preferred, where the Cartagena refugee definition is applied as the most efficient/expeditious way to provide protection to persons fleeing the country because of a Cartagena-related event.[32] Alternatively, some countries have followed a 'unified/single procedure' providing for a parallel analysis of both definitions without entailing a prioritization of one over the other, but determining the protected status under the one most suited to address the protection situation the applicant faces.[33]

---

[30] But it is certainly informative of the risk the individual may face.

[31] There may be circumstances, however, where authorities choose to apply the Cartagena refugee definition without a previous analysis of the classic refugee definition. The reasons for this may vary. Such circumstance may include, among others, trying to ensure consistency in the evaluation of claims from the same country or to achieve procedural efficiency. A possibility of overlap between the two refugee definitions may also arise in such situations.

[32] In Argentina, the recognition of refugee status under accelerated determination status procedures for Syrians fleeing the armed conflict in their country is one example of this practice.

[33] This is the practice of Mexico and was applied also under the 'Enhanced Registration' exercise by Ecuador.

32. Regardless of the procedural approach preferred, the 1951 Convention refugee definition and the Cartagena refugee definition are not cumulative, and the rejection of refugee status needs to be justified against both definitions.

33. A good practice identified in applying the Cartagena refugee definition is that national asylum authorities regularly assess and update information on specific country situations which could qualify as experiencing a Cartagena event, indicating which one of these applies and using it to determine refugee status.

34. Regardless of the procedural approach applied, in the fourteen countries where the Cartagena refugee definition is incorporated into domestic legislation, no differentiation is made in terms of status, documentation or associated rights and solutions for refugees.

Group Recognition (Prima Facie)

35. State practice makes no particular distinction between the application of the Cartagena refugee definition on a group basis (prima facie) or within individual procedures. Both cases have been practiced, although the most common is to maintain individual status-determination procedures irrespective of the refugee definition applied or the size of the caseload. In this vein, legislation in some countries[34] provides specifically for cases of mass influx of refugees, but the mechanisms[35] to be applied are the same if recognition is based on 1951 Convention refugee definition or on the Cartagena refugee definition. Further discussion on appropriate procedures – whether prima facie or individual procedures – is required.

Sur place Recognition

36. *Sur place* recognition of refugee status is applicable to the Cartagena refugee definition in the same terms as for the 1951 Convention refugee definition, according to state practice. This is so because the 'threat' element of the definition connotes the possibility of harm being inflicted on a person; it does not imply that the harm has actually materialized. A person who has not been at risk of harm at the time of departure from his or her country (e.g. because he or she moved for study or work

---

[34] Bolivia, Chile, El Salvador and Peru.

[35] These are procedural standards that do not distinguish if the person is recognized following one or the other of the applicable refugee definitions. In some cases, they refer to the provision of a 'temporal protection status' until individual determination can be carried out.

purposes) may nonetheless still qualify as refugee under the Cartagena refugee definition where there is a reasonable possibility that the harm will come to be if the person remains in the country or if he or she returns to it. This is in line with the purpose of the Cartagena refugee definition of extending protection to those who are at risk of the effects of conflict and violence but who do not meet the requirements of the 1951 Convention refugee definition. State practice has recognized this understanding by extending refugee protection under the Cartagena definition to refugees *sur place* and in situations where there is no other right to legally stay in the country and the person cannot be returned.[36]

Internal Flight Alternative (IFA)

37. State practice is mostly consistent in holding that IFA is not relevant, nor generally applicable, to the Cartagena refugee definition because of the nature of the situations causing flight. For state practice, it seems that the logic of applying the Cartagena refugee definition per se or on a situation or group basis precludes the possibility of analyzing internal relocation alternatives.

Cessation and Exclusion Considerations

38. Provisions contained under Articles 1(C), (E) and (F) apply to the Cartagena refugee definition in the same manner as under the 1951 Convention refugee definition, with the same due-process guarantees regardless of the size of the refugee population concerned and following UNHCR's guidelines.[37]

---

[36] Jurisprudence from Argentina, Brazil and Ecuador support this finding.

[37] See, on Article 1F, UNHCR, 'Guidelines on International Protection No. 5: Application of the Exclusion Clauses: Article 1F of the 1951 Convention Relating to the Status of Refugees', 4 September 2003, HCR/GIP/03/05, available at: www.refworld.org/docid/3f5857684.html; UNHCR, 'Guidelines on the Application in Mass Influx Situations of the Exclusion Clauses of Article 1F of the 1951 Convention relating to the Status of Refugees', 7 February 2006, available at: www.refworld.org/docid/43f48c0b4.html.

INDEX